Crime and Punishment in New Hampshire, 1812–1914

American University Studies

Series IX
History
Vol. 164

PETER LANG
New York • Washington, D.C./Baltimore • San Francisco
Bern • Frankfurt am Main • Berlin • Vienna • Paris

Timothy Dodge

Crime and Punishment in New Hampshire, 1812–1914

PETER LANG
New York • Washington, D.C./Baltimore • San Francisco
Bern • Frankfurt am Main • Berlin • Vienna • Paris

Library of Congress Cataloging-in-Publication Data

Dodge, Timothy.
    Crime and punishment in New Hampshire, 1812–1914 / Timothy Dodge.
        p.   cm. — (American university studies. Series IX, History;
    vol. 164)
    Includes bibliographical references and index.
    1. Crime—New Hampshire—History. 2. Punishment—
New Hampshire—History. I. Title. II. Series.
    HV6793.N3D63   364.9742′09′034—dc20   94-13603
    ISBN 0-8204-2516-8
    ISSN 0740-0462

Die Deutsche Bibliothek-CIP-Einheitsaufnahme

Dodge, Timothy:
Crime and punishment in New Hampshire, 1812–1914 / Timothy Dodge.
- New York; Washington, D.C./Baltimore; San Francisco; Bern; Frankfurt am
Main; Berlin; Vienna; Paris: Lang.
    (American university studies: Ser. 9, History; Vol. 164)
    ISBN 0-8204-2516-8
NE: American university studies / 09

The paper in this book meets the guidelines for permanence and durability of
the Committee on Production Guidelines for Book Longevity of the
Council on Library Resources.

© 1995 Peter Lang Publishing, Inc., New York

Printed in the United States of America.

Dedication

To my father, Peter Dodge, and the memory of my mother, Renata de Kanicky Dodge

Acknowledgments

This work was originally written as a doctoral dissertation in History at the University of New Hampshire. I would like to thank Peter Lang Publishing, Inc. for providing me with the opportunity to publish my dissertation as a book. Although the transformation of this work from dissertation to book has taken a lot of work, I feel honored and pleased that Lang has seen fit to publish *Crime and Punishment in New Hampshire, 1812-1914*.

Chapter Five, "Life in the New Hampshire State Prison, 1812-1914," was previously published in a much-modified form as "Hard Labor at the New Hampshire State Prison, 1812-1932" in *Historical New Hampshire* Vol. 47, Nos. 3 and 4 (Fall/Winter, 1992). Thanks are due the New Hampshire Historical Society for permission to publish this chapter here.

I am truly grateful to Robert M. Mennel for his guidance of my dissertation in all of its stages and for serving as chair of my qualifying examination committee. His comments and suggestions were crucial to the success of my academic career. This was also true a decade earlier when he directed my Master's thesis. I am especially thankful for his compassionate approach when I ran into the inevitable difficulties involved in a doctoral program.

Many thanks are due J. William Harris, Jr. for his assistance with quantitative analysis. Although I have never considered myself to be mathematically inclined nor a computer enthusiast, the application of quantitative techniques through the aid of computers proved essential for this project. I am very grateful for his bringing me fully into the computer age.

I would like to thank Laurel T. Ulrich, Lucy Salyer, and Stuart Palmer for serving as readers of my dissertation. Professor Ulrich provided a number of helpful suggestions which helped narrow my focus better. Professor Salyer's stylistic suggestions proved useful as did her references to recent literature on crime and punishment. Dean Palmer's criminological perspective was illuminating; he also helped me to focus more squarely on the meaning of crime in New Hampshire.

It is very likely I would not have chosen to pursue this degree if the opportunity for employment had not been made available to me by the late Donald E. Vincent, University Librarian at the University of New Hampshire. I am thankful to Ruth M. Katz who kept me on after Dr. Vincent's retirement and I am especially grateful to Bill Ross, head of Special Collections, who did his best to provide me with work in the face of state-mandated budget cuts. Thanks also go to Bill for providing me with much-needed storage space for my voluminous dissertation files during the course of this project. A real viii

source of energy and comfort during a rather difficult period of my life was the friendship of the members of the Special Collections Department at the U.N.H. Library: Bill Ross, Roland Goodbody, Nancy McCue, and Terri MacGregor. I wish there were space to name all of the very many true friends from other library departments whom I wish to acknowledge.

The assistance of several individuals was essential in gaining access to important original sources. Much of my research was done at the Division of Records-Management and Archives in Concord, N.H. Thanks are due Frank Mevers, State Archivist and Andrew Taylor, Records Manager, for their courteous assistance. I am grateful to Dr. Mevers for bringing the state prison records to my attention at the beginning of this project. I would like to thank Bill Copeley, Librarian of the New Hampshire Historical Society, for his aid in locating various sources, including original copies of nineteenth-century New Hampshire newspapers. Finally, I am very grateful to Don Goodnow and John McDaniels of the Strafford County Superior Court for allowing me to use original court records needed for this work. Their enthusiastic cooperation is much appreciated.

One of the benefits of employment at the Auburn University Library in Auburn, Alabama is the allocation of a weekly slot of research time. My thanks go to T. Harmon Straiton, Jr., head of the Microforms and Documents Department, for allocating me the maximum allowable weekly research time. The Library also provided me with the computer, printer, and other equipment necessary for revising my dissertation and the creation of a camera-ready copy.

Finally, the completion of my Ph.D. would have been very much in doubt without the aid of my father, Peter Dodge. On a practical level, my father was kind enough to allow me to use his Macintosh Plus computer for writing the original dissertation on which this work is based, sometimes at the cost of real inconvenience to himself. On top of this was his support when I lost my job to the recession of 1991-92. His provision of a home and financial aid at that time made all of the difference. Just as important was the moral support. His encouragement and sympathy were a source of real comfort. Much of my success is his.

CONTENTS

List of Tables

TABLE

List of Illustrations

FIGURE

Introduction

The changing economic circumstances of seacoast New Hampshire during the nineteenth century helped create new definitions and patterns of crime. The New Hampshire State Prison was established in 1812 as a means of coping with crime. Economic pressures helped to transform the prison into primarily a revenue-generating enterprise for the state from an institution designed for the reformation of offenders.

In 1810 less than 20% of the population of seacoast New Hampshire lived in towns or cities; by 1910 the proportion was over 60%. The economic base grew increasingly diverse and shifted away from agriculture to manufacturing and commerce. National developments helped foster these changes, for example, the opening up of vast farmlands to the West and the construction of railroad lines. Economic change was also accompanied by demographic change. Thousands of native-born New Hampshirites moved out of the state in the face of declining agricultural opportunities. Others chose to stay but moved to the growing milltowns and commercial centers in search of employment. Joining them was an increasing stream of immigrants from Canada, Ireland, Great Britain, and elsewhere. The foreign-born population of seacoast New Hampshire increased by fourfold between 1850 and 1910.

The social and economic changes unfolding in this region created tensions which were sometimes manifested in criminal behavior. Legislators perceived new threats to the social order and passed laws which defined criminal behavior. Definitions grew more complex as lawmakers grappled with the problems of an increasingly urban and industrial society. An analysis of the criminal statutes and felony cases in this work reveals a preoccupation with property offenses. There were alwo major changes in laws respecting violent, moral, and other types of crime.

Starting in 1812, lawmakers were guided by the establishment of the New Hampshire State Prison which represented a new direction in punishment. Instead of the age-old forms of corporal punishment, fines, or public humiliation, offenders were now sentenced to long terms of hard labor in an institution designed both to punish and rehabilitate the offender. The rise of imprisonment in nineteenth-century America marks a new stage in the history of crime and punishment. From the start, the state prison was conceived of as an institution designed to punish and rehabilitate *felons*. The prison was reserved for only the most serious offenders. The vast majority of crimes were punished by short terms (usually less than one year) in the county or town jail or house of correction, or by paying a fine. Because the state prison was designed for only felons and because court records for felony cases are much more complete and accessible than for cases involving less-serious offenses, I will analyze crime in New Hampshire only at the felony level. Admittedly, this is not a complete picture of crime but it is representative of what this society considered to be the most serious forms of crime.

The economic forces which helped create crime also played a major role in the failure of the prison as a reforming institution. Like most prisons of the time, the New Hampshire State Prison was expected to be a self-supporting concern. Hard labor thus had two main roles to play: in conjunction with moral instruction, it was supposed to reform an offender's character and it was also meant to generate funds to pay for the prison's maintenance via the contract labor system. The evidence found in the primary sources indicates that hard labor at the New Hampshire State Prison assumed a disproportionate role. The traditionally frugal state government provided only minimal financial support which meant that prison administrators had to extract the maximum amount of labor out of their charges to ensure the prison's functioning. However, there is also evidence that many prison administrators were only too glad to exploit the prison inmates in hopes of actually generating surplus revenues to be turned over to the state above and beyond the prison's operating expenses. When one considers that the inmates themselves received no payment for their labor until 1913, it is not hard to conclude that the primary focus of prison administration was on profits rather than reforming criminals.

The New Hampshire State Prison was established in 1812, which is a convenient starting point for an analysis of crime and punishment. It was the start of a new era characterized by new conceptions of crime and the role of punishment. This work will examine crime and punishment in the first century of the era of imprisonment. Imprisonment is still the dominant form of punishment in contemporary America. The period 1812-1914 is long enough to examine the rise, consolidation, and modification of the prison system in New Hampshire. This study ends in 1914 because that year marks the culmination of Progressive era reform in New Hampshire. The prison of the 1890's was at least outwardly a more oppresive place than that of the mid 1910's onward. Gone in 1914 were the parti-colored prison uniform, lockstep march, and downcast gaze. Progressive measures were introduced during the final decade such as a grading system of privileges and recreational team sports in 1914. Convict laborers were finally raised from their de facto status as state slaves by provision of pay for their labor in 1913.

Very little has been written on the history of crime and punishment in New Hampshire. Most of the literature consists of anecdotal, short pieces written by amateur historians or antiquarians.[1] The single most useful work on the early state prison is Henry Robinson's *Granite Monthly* article of 1897.[2] The author was the son of Nahum Robinson, warden of the state prison from 1894 through 1896, a circumstance which probably gave the younger Robinson special access to original sources. L.E. Richwagen wrote a follow-up article on the prison nearly 30 years later which provides an interesting commentary on how prison life had changed in the intervening years.[3] The prison is mentioned occasionally in more recent works but a comprehensive scholarly overview of the prison's history has never been published. Also lacking is such an overview of crime in nineteenth-century New Hampshire.

The purpose of this work is to analyze the changing definitions of crime and punishment in New Hampshire during a period of significant social and economic change. Research has focused on court and prison records to determine the types of crimes for which persons were convicted and to show relationships between changing patterns of convictions and social, economic, and demographic trends. Actual case histories derived from the primary sources and contemporary newspaper accounts will be used to provide more detailed examples.

The century getween 1812 and 1914 was a time of major social and economic change in New Hampshire. The economic base changed from agricultural to predominantly industrial. Much of the native-born population moved away either to other states or from the country to the growing urban centers. Joining them in the industrial towns and cities was a steadily growing number of foreign immigrants. All of these changes contributed to the nature of crime. As will be seen, crime was not a static phenomenon. Rates changed as did types of crime.

New Hampshire criminal law underwent a fundamental transformation from harsh Biblical prohibitions of the seventeenth century to an increasingly complex body of law that reflected a growing commercial and industrial society. The first major change occurred in the post-Revolutionary era when a number of capital crimes were dropped. Not only was imprisonment substituted for death or severe corporal punishment, but a more liberal attitude toward crimes of morality resulted in the decriminalization or abolition of certain offenses. Throughout the nineteenth century, criminal law became more complex as definitions of crime categories and subcategories emerged. Property crime was very important: new varieties were defined in response to the economic changes affecting the state. As will be seen, by far the most common type of conviction was for property crime. Some moral offenses were recriminalized in the post-Civil War era as a result of the imposition of middle class standards on the law.

Chapter One also illustrates the conflict between advocates of the old common law tradition and those who wanted to codify the law. New Hampshire's criminal statutes are a classic example of consolidation rather than true codification as described by Barry J. Stern.[4] New statutes were added but the old ones were not always removed. Until 1842 the criminal statutes of New Hampshire were relatively unstructured. The 1842 statutes in particular reflect the efforts of lawmakers to codify the law.

Chapter Two examines the law enforcement apparatus and court structure of New Hampshire during this period which were based largely on English antecedents. Police were introduced in only a few urban centers and represent a new professionalization of law enforcement. Also covered in Chapter Two is the role of jails and prisons before 1812. The establishment of the New Hampshire State Prison is a demarcation point in the history of crime and punishment in that state.

Chapter Three demonstrates the changing, complex social context for crime. As the seacoast region changed from a mainly agricultural to industrial economy, patterns of crime changed too. Property crime rates began to decrease after the Civil War while violent crime rates escalated between the 1840's and 1890's. Economic difficulties tied in to the national debate over dependency and forced labor and led to the passage of the Tramp Act in 1878 and the consequent conviction of many tramps in the following decade.[5]

The typical criminal in nineteenth-century New Hampshire was a white native-born male around 26 years of age, convicted of larceny. This description hides the fact that just as the nature of crime changed throughout this period so did the prototypical criminal. Chapter Four will use court records, prison registers, and published annual prison warden's reports to investigate such variables as age, ethnicity, and occupational status to define the prison population. The results indicate that the prison population became more diverse. An increasing number of Canadians (French and British), Irish, Germans, and Italians began appearing as the nineteenth century went on. British immigrants became fewer. In contrast to many other states, black participation in serious crime was virtually nonexistent and no black in the sample was convicted of a violent crime. However, the black population of New Hampshire was minuscule in 1812 and grew proportionately and numerically even smaller over the next century. Women made up a tiny fraction of the prison population (2%). Women were also distinct in that the female inmates in the sample were three times as likely as male inmates to have been convicted of a violent crime.

The New Hampshire State Prison between 1812 and 1914 was a classic example of the contract labor system in operation. If anything defined the prison experience in New Hampshire, it was hard labor. Profits definitely took precedence over all else as the inmates spent their time laboring for the state. The physician's annual report told of the horror of industrial accidents and harsh working conditions endured by the inmates. The warden's report was dominated by a concern for demonstrating the profitability of the prison to the state legislature. Aside from unremitting, unpaid labor the prison experience was characterized by poor living conditions, sometimes brutal discipline, and truly poor health conditions.

The rehabilitative mission of the prison was carried on almost single-handedly by the prison chaplain. Gradually, provision was made for secular education, but it was not until the Progressive era that rehabilitative methods were tried in a truly systematic way.

Even though the punitive aspects of the prison experience outweighed the rehabilitative aspects, the New Hampshire State Prison showed remarkably low rates of recidivism among the inmate population in Chapter Six. This is essentially the reverse of the present-day American state prison population. However, the picture becomes clouded when considering the ambiguous definitions of recidivism. More than half of those sentenced to hard labor in the state prison left before the expiration of their term. The two most common methods of early release were 1) pardons (which were granted on a large scale precisely when sentences handed down by the courts became longer) and 2) parole (which was in theory directly tied to the prisoner's potential for rehabilitation). On the surface, the raw numbers say that the New Hampshire State Prison was a success, but when interpreted more carefully the rehabilitative mission of the prison between 1812 and 1914 was of only dubious value.

The two most useful types of primary sources are court records and prison records. The court records used for this project include bills and indictments of the Rockingham County Superior and Supreme Courts for the period 1812-1914, located at the Division of Records-Management and Archives in Concord, New Hampshire, and those of the Strafford County Superior and Supreme Courts for the period 1870-1914, located at the Administration and Justice Building in Dover, N.H. The court records supply basic information such as the date and circumstances of a crime. Characteristically, they provide an itemized list and valuation of property affected or an exact description of the wounds sustained in the case of a violent crime.

Prison records consist of the manuscript "Register of Convicts 1812-1883," "[N.H. State] Prison Records [1874-1915]," and "New Hampshire State Prison. Record of Gain and Loss in Population [1905-36]." These sources are located at the Division of Records-Management and Archives in Concord, N.H. In a ledger-like form, these registers provide basic data such as age, birthplace, crime, and date of entry and exit from the state prison. Another very useful source is the published annual prison warden's report. In the early nineteenth century this was little more than an accounting excercise. From the 1830's on the report became much more narrative and grew to include sections by the prison physician and chaplain. Most of the information on health conditions and rehabilitative measures is found in these reports.

Most of the sources discussed above lend themselves easily to quantitative analysis which was performed using the SPSS computer program. Data were gathered for 820 cases originating in Rockingham and Strafford County. This number represents 19.5% of a total of 4154 cases listed in the prison and court records for the period 1812-1914.

A miscellany of other sources help to provide details on the quality of the prison experience during the nineteenth century. For example, the papers of Samuel Bell (a New Hampshire politician and governor), Rufus Dow (state prison warden from 1850 through 1853), and Charles Brewster (a New Hampshire newspaper proprietor and politician) all provide important details on prison life and the politics which often underlay prison management. Much of the information supplied in these papers is available nowhere else. They provide an eyewitness perspective on the state prison in the antebellum period. These papers are located at the New Hampshire Historical Society in Concord.

Published memoirs by persons who spent time in the prison as employees or inmates are extremely valuable for both the wealth of detail and the perspectives taken. Two prison chaplains published books recounting their experiences: Eleazer Smith in *Nine Years Among the Convicts: or Prison Reminiscences* (Boston, 1856) and Hosea Quinby, *The Prison Chaplaincy and Its Experiences* (Concord, N.H., 1873). The only published memoir from the inmate's perspective is *New-Hampshire State Prison Cruelty Exposed: or, The Sufferings of Joseph L. Shaw, In That Institution in 1837, while John M'Daniel Was Warden* by Joseph L. Shaw (Exeter, N.H., 1839). As one can see from the title, this work was prompted by the gross mistreatment suffered by the author while in prison (see Chapter Six for details).

The other primary sources consist of a miscellany including such items as state prison papers located at the Divison of Records-Management and Archives: everything from prison building plans to inmate work records to documents concerning the prison investigation of 1880. Newspapers on microfilm at the State Library in Concord or in the original at the New Hampshire Historical Society in Concord are a helpful source on the opening of the state prison in 1812 and for providing far more detail about crimes and their perpetrators than can be found in the court bills and indictments.

The published statutes of New Hampshire chronicle changing definitions of crime and new forms of punishment from colonial times through the present. Additional details are found in the published session laws from the early nineteenth century onward. The published New Hampshre House of Representatives and Senate journals provide amplification of details on the changes described in the statutes and session laws. Often, the minutes of the New Hampshire Legislature, chronicled in the journals of the late eighteenth century onward, provide the rationale behind legal reforms. These sources are located at the department of Special Collections at the University of New Hampshire Library in Durham and at the State Library in Concord.

8

Notes

1. For example, see Cal Cameron, "The Funny Bank Robbery," *Yankee*, 26 (August 1962), 36-37 and 74-76; Charles C. Wilbur, "David Wood's Speech from the Pillory," *Old Timer*, No. 71 (Jan. 1946), [1-2]; Allan Pospisil, "Henry Tufts: Lessons in Breaking Exeter Jail," *New Hampshire Profiles*, 19 (Sept. 1970), 20-21 and 51-53; or Renata Dodge, "The Ballad of Big Bill Worby," *New Hampshire Profiles*, 26 (July 1977), 44-45, 71-73, and 75.

An example of one of the rare scholarly articles on the history of crime in New Hampshire is David B. Davis, "Murder in New Hampshire," *New England Quarterly*, 28 (June 1955), 147-63.

2. Henry Robinson, "The New Hampshire State Prison," *Granite Monthly*, 23 (1897), 214-36.

3. L.E. Richwagen, "The New Hampshire State Prison," *Granite Monthly*, 56 (1924), 571-75.

4. Barry J. Stern, "Revising Vermont's Criminal Code," *Vermont Law Journal*, 12 (1987), 307.

5. Amy Dru Stanley, "Beggars Can't Be Choosers: Compulsion and Contract in Postbellum America," *Journal of American History*, 78 (1992), 1265-93.

Chapter I

Crime According to New Hampshire Law, 1641-1914

The economic and social transformation of New Hampshire from a rural, agricultural society to one increasingly urban and industrial and the strong Protestant cultural tradition of the region, led to an increasingly comprehensive and complex definition of crime, according to the statutes analyzed in this chapter. In 1812 legislators consciously set about defining felonies in an attempt to determine which offenses merited a term in the New Hampshire State Prison. The laws of 1812 onward were an official definition of what forms of behavior were considered to be most objectionable to this society. Property crime was defined more broadly, violent crime was defined more carefully than before, moral offenses were decriminalized and then reinstated but with milder penalties than previously, and a number of new crimes were defined to fit the circumstances of an evolving society.

The hardy English pioneers who set foot in New Hampshire in 1623 had a supernatural conception of crime. Criminal behavior was defined according to English common law and the Old Testament. Crime was sin inspired by Satan.[1] There was no elaborate theory informing the Puritan legislators who drew up the first criminal statutes of Massachusetts. Man was by nature sinful so the only way to solve the problem of crime was to enforce a righteous way of life based upon the Ten Commandments. Transgressors (i.e., criminals) would be punished severely. The most serious crimes were punishable by death while the rest merited a variety of corporal measures, public humiliations, or fines. The purpose of punishment was to exact vengeance and to instill compliance with the law.[2] Repentance was also the desired end.[3]

There were no published criminal statutes to guide New Hampshirites in the earliest days of settlement. In the 1620's and 1630's the pioneers struggled just to establish the four towns of Dover, Portsmouth, Exeter, and Hampton. However, the settlers had a long tradition of English common law on which to rely. Just a few years before, the jurist Sir Edward Coke had successfully defended the supremacy of the common law against the encroachments of King James I.[4] The common law had its origins in the Middle Ages. The theory behind it was that the law as administered by the King's superior courts was common to the whole kingdom and took precedence over laws of local jurisdictions.[5] Just as everyone else was subject to the common law, so too was the King. Coke's struggle with James I was over this very issue. James believed in the theory of the divine right of kings which led him to claim his authority from God. Coke proclaimed that even the King was subject to the common law.[6] The common law was not an orderly set of statutes but rather "an obscure system" according to Herbert Wechsler.[7]

The first real form of government in New Hampshire beyond the town level was established on July 4, 1639 when John Wheelwright and 34 other settlers formed a "combination."[8] The settlers agreed to be ruled by three elders who were to be elected by a legislature composed of all freemen. The legislature was to present laws to the elders for approval. The "combination" never really had the chance to create a criminal code or much else because the four towns of New Hampshire were incorporated into the colony of Massachusetts Bay. From 1641 until 1679 New Hampshire was controlled by Massachusetts and subject to its laws. These early laws will be examined briefly to see how this early New England society understood crime and the role of punishment.

In 1641 and 1642 the General Court of Massachusetts adopted the "Body of Liberties" which was based on ancient English common law, the Magna Carta, and the Mosaic Laws of the Old Testament.[9] Further refinement came in 1648 with the publication of *The Book of the General Laws and Libertys concerning the Inhabitants of the Massachusetts* [sic]. The *Book* is a curious document with its liberal enumeration of basic rights counteracted by the Jehovan wrath of Mosaic law expressed in the criminal statutes.

The Puritan legislators compiled a list of 15 capital crimes based directly on the teachings of the Old Testament. Death was automatically prescribed for idolatry, witchcraft, blasphemy, wilful murder or manslaughter, murder commited by a person "suddenly in his anger, or cruelty of passion," murder committed "through guile, either by poysonings or other devilish practice," bestiality, sodomy, adultery, sexual intercourse with "any Woman child under ten years old," rape of "any maid, or woman that is lawfully married or contracted," rape of any female above age 10, manstealing, bearing false witness to deprive another of life, or treason or conspiracy against Massachusetts of any "Town or Towns, Fort or Forts therein."[10] For every capital crime except the last listed there are one or more citations to the Bible included in the statute. Ten other crimes also might merit the death penalty. They included the cursing or hitting of parents by sons, burglary, robbery, and the defiance by Jesuits of the Puritan religious establishment.[11]

The most common punishment inflicted for non-capital crimes was whipping. Other punishments for serious crime consisted of branding with a hot iron, cropping of ears, or, rarely, piercing the tongue. Less serious crimes brought fines or public humiliations. Apparently, the famed ducking stool of

Puritan lore was hardly every employed. Finally, an offender could be placed "in durance vile" for a term in jail or prison.[12]

The modern reader might find the above catalog of punishments harsh but they were actually less severe than those in force in Britain at the time.[13] Further harsh penalties on the books does not necessarily mean that there were many convictions for serious crimes. Douglas Hay describes eighteenth century British criminal law as based on terror. The terror was mitigated by the fact that in reality there were relatively few executions; many death sentences ended up being commuted.[14] Most convictions were probably for fairly petty crimes such as theft, drunkenness, fornication, lying, or nonblasphemous swearing.

Religious strife, Indian warfare, and conflict over land grants led to dissolution of the political union between New Hampshire and Massachusetts in 1679 when King Charles II declared New Hampshire to be a royal province. In England as well as the colonies, political instability characterized the period 1679-92. There was the province of New Hampshire (1679-86), the Dominion (1686-89), the second union with Massachusetts (1690-92), and finally, the province of New Hampshire again from 1692 through 1775. What is important for our purposes is that the Provincial General Assembly met on March 16, 1679 and passed "The General Laws and Liberties of the Province of New Hampshire" in anticipation of King Charles's declaration later that year. This is the first appearance of statutes that applied strictly to New Hampshire.[15] Virtually the entire section on crime and punishment was taken from the Massachusetts laws just described. The "General Laws and Liberties" remained basically unchanged for the rest of the colonial period.[16]

It is worthwhile examining this document, as it had a definite influence on the laws in effect in 1812 when the State Prison was constructed. In New Hampshire crime was defined much in the same way as had been done while the colony was under the jurisdiction of Massachusetts. Though some of the wording was changed, there were fewer Biblical citations. Arson was added to the list of capital crimes. At the same time, the New Hampshire statutes were a shade more merciful than those of the Puritan founders. More provisions were made for criminals being "greevously punished" as an alternative to the "shall be" and "shall surely be put to death" of old.

New Hampshire law still depended upon original sin for an explanation of criminal behavior: witness the continuation of idolatry, blasphemy, and witchcraft as capital crimes. Corporal punishment was still prescribed for nearly all offenses yet it would be unfair to describe the criminal justice system of colonial New Hampshire as unduly oppressive. In 1927, Hobart

Pillsbury, author of the first comprehensive history of the state authorized by
the New Hampshire Legislature since Jeremy Belknap's work in the 1790's,
characterized the criminal law of the period 1679-1775 as one that was
"conspicuously and commendably free from those atrocious features which
have cast the darkest shadows upon the civilization of that age."[17] While
stern, the criminal statutes of colonial New Hampshire definitely sound more
merciful than the brutal laws in effect in Europe. No one in New Hampshire
was condemned to a stretch in the galleys as was frequently done in France.[18]
The number of capital offenses listed in the New Hampshire laws is relatively
puny compared to the "Bloody Code" that went into effect in eighteenth-
century Britain.[19] The actual application of the law may well have been
milder than not. Certainly the evidence for eighteenth-century Massachusetts
indicates that very few prosecutions for capital crimes actually resulted in
convictions.   In an investigation of 3000 prosecution records of the
Massachusetts Superior Court for the period 1750-96, Linda Kealey found
93.8% of the cases to enter the plea of not guilty.[20]

An examination of the New Hampshire Province Laws reveals a
preoccupation with maintaining a Christian social order. Biblical prohibitions
were employed liberally and there was a strong emphasis on moral behavior
as well as some concern for property. One property crime, arson, was listed
as a capital offense.[21] Under the regular criminal offenses, property crimes
included burglary, "ffelony" [larceny], the forgery of deeds, the burning and
breaking down of fences, defacing landmarks, and setting forest fires.[22] The
criminal laws outlined here manifest the same concern for property and
propriety discerned by Michael Hindus in his analysis of crime in
Massachusetts for the period 1767-1878.[23]

Along with a number of other states, New Hampshire set about rewriting
its laws during the post-Revolutionary War period.   Many American
lawmakers felt that the old laws were a relic of colonial times and did not
reflect American values. To many reformers, the common law tradition was
odious both because it was British and because it could be used as an
instrument of oppression.[24] This attitude tied in with the traditional Puritan
distrust of lawyers.[25] By the late eighteenth century the number of lawyers
had proliferated dramatically. More lawyers were needed because of the
increasing complexity of American life, which in turn resulted from increased
population and a dramatic growth in commerce.[26] For reformers,
codification of the law was a remedy. Codification would be one way to take
away unwarranted power of lawyers and judges over the people.[27] Legal
reformers were also influenced by ideas and social criticism stemming from

the Enlightenment in Europe.[28]

The most basic definition of codification is the reduction of the law to written form.[29] The intention of codification is to make the law permanent, organized, and comprehensive.[30] Legal scholars such as Jean L. Bergel would not consider the criminal code developed in post-Revolutionary New Hampshire to be a real code. Bergel characterizes most American legal codes as "mere compilations."[31] A true code is distinguished by the following characteristics according to Bergel. It is "a coherent body of new or renovated rules" within a whole aimed at "instituting or reviewing a legal order." A true code requires a restructuring of norms and it evolves as a society evolves. Principles of application are required.[32] This is a contrast to the more typical American compilation of statutes where judicial interpretation plays a much stronger role than principles of application.[33] Finally, a real code is constructed so that each individual article derives its meaning only from its relationship to the other articles surrounding it which in turn derive meaning only from their relationship to the whole legal system. A code is a unified whole, not a random collection of laws.[34]

Code law contrasted to the common law tradition found in New Hampshire and most of the English-speaking world. Common law consists of reported decisions that become part of the legal tradition. Judicial interpretation is of real importance. Common law is partly written statute and partly a matter of interpretation. Lawyers and judges have recourse to past decisions which they can use in fashioning their own interpretations.[35] This is referred to as the "doctrine of precedent" or "stare decisis." Lower courts are obliged to follow and apply decisions made by higher courts in all future cases. The highest court is thus bound by its own past decisions in similar cases.[36]

The law of common law countries exists in written form but this is not the same thing as codification. What pass for legal "codes" in countries that follow the English common law tradition are actually consolidations or restatements.[37] Such an approach is typical of many states up to the present day, including New Hampshire. Barry Stern concludes that this eclecticism usually results in duplication, an unorganized structure, occasional irrational penalties, and major areas of the law remaining undefined.[38]

The first compilation of state laws in New Hampshire was published in 1792. "An Act for the Punishment of Certain Crimes" is almost identical to the criminal statutes of 1679. Common law definitions of crime remained unchanged. Some moderation is evident in the reduction of capital crimes from fifteen to eight. Death by hanging was the automatic punishment for treason, murder, rape, sodomy, burglary, arson, robbery, or forgery of public

14

(State) securities.[39] The degree of these crimes was not treated but it is noteworthy that lengthy imprisonment is listed as an alternative punishment, thus taking some of the severity out of these harsh capital laws. In the neighboring state of Vermont, lawmakers believed that corporal punishment was unsuitable for advanced societies and that imprisonment at hard labor was the civilized alternative.[40] New Hampshire laws followed suit, prescribing imprisonment instead of death for those found guilty of "misprision of treason" (i.e., having knowledge of treason or intended treason and not turning the traitor in).[41] Also, the death penalty was no longer automatic for manslaughter. Now the State had the option of imprisoning the offender for up to 12 months, inflicting humiliation by setting him or her on the gallows "for the space of one hour with a rope about his neck, and one end thereof shall be cast over the gallows"; being bound to good behavior for up to three years, or fined up to L300.[42] For assault while trying to commit murder, rape, sodomy, or robbery, the penalty was a fine of up to L300, up to two years in prison, or to receive up to 100 "stripes" of the whip.[43] Several other crimes had punishments involving fines, imprisonment, humiliation, or whipping.

New Hampshire lawmakers, concerned with maintaining a stable social order, also passed "An Act for the Punishment of Certain Crimes Not Capital" in February 1791. These crimes included drunkenness, publishing a lie or libel, theft, receiving stolen goods, perjury, fornication, assault, maiming, obstructing state officers in their duties, riot or unlawful assembly, or blasphemy. Fines, imprisonment, or whipping were the usual punishments.[44] Finally, separate acts were passed for the punishment of "lewdness, adultery, and polygamy," "profane cursing and Swearing," and trespassing.

The Puritan influence of Massachusetts was by no means dead but several significant changes were apparent in the laws of 1791-92. First, there were no references to the Bible in the law with the exception of blasphemy. The basic catalog of offenses was unchanged but a significant number had been demoted to serious rather than capital crimes. The emphasis was still on property and propriety but crimes of violence were taken seriously too. A new category of crime was the concealment of the death of a bastard child no matter what the circumstances of death. The mother of such a child could be sentenced to an hour on the gallows, up to two years in prison, or to a fine of up to L300.[45] This provision reflects a concept of crime as originating in sin. However, punishment had become both slightly milder and different in method while the number of capital crimes was reduced. Some crimes such as witchcraft or sons's cursing of their parents were no longer listed and others, such as blasphemy, had been taken out of the capital category.

New Hampshire law also featured fewer corporal punishments. There were no more references to branding with a hot iron or the cropping of ears. There were fewer public humiliations. For example, the penalty for adultery no longer involved the wearing of the cloth capital letters "AD" on one's clothing.[46] Generally, the number of strokes or "stripes" in whipping had been reduced. The number of offenses punishable by fine had increased substantially and the amount of the fines had also increased. Frequent provisions for imprisonment showed the new direction of punishment. It is interesting to note that not all legal reforms under consideration in America during this era were so enlightened.[47]

Criminal law reveals that morality remained a serious concern for New Hampshire in 1792. The law was now more detailed in its definition of the crime of adultery with a separate act titled "An Act for the punishment of lewdness, adultery and polygamy." Those convicted of such misbehavior could still be publicly whipped (up to 39 stripes). They could also now be fined or imprisoned.[48] Morality was further defined in "An Act to Prevent Incestuous Marriages and to Regulate Divorces." Fourteen categories of prohibited marriage partners such as siblings or a person's siblings' offspring were systematically listed in one column each for men and for women. Penalties were serious. An offender could be "set on the gallows one hour with a rope about his or her neck and the other end thereof cast over the gallows," or fined up to L100, or imprisoned up to one year and bound to good behavior up to five years.[49] As of 1792, there was no state prison in New Hampshire so these statutes were enforced by local courts. Imprisonment at this stage meant confinement to the local or county jail.

The New Hampshire state laws were republished in 1797 with only a few changes. A concern for property was stronger than ever. The preamble to the new act on horse and livestock thieves noted "larcenies are frequent, and the guilty escape with little punishment, without making recompence; not withstanding the laws now in force." The new law now provided for physically marking persons convicted of stealing horses, mules, cattle, or sheep. "Every such person shall be marked with, a line of India-ink well and deeply inserted, above the eyebrows, from the hair of the temples on the one side, to the hair of the temples on the other side of the forehead, and by a line in the same manner inserted from the centre of the line aforesaid to the end of the nose, on the most prominent part thereof; on the first conviction, and for stealing any other personal property, shall be marked in like manner on the second conviction and every such person shall remain in custody not exceeding thirty days, till the said marks are well and effectually fixed, and shall be liable to be marked again, in case by any means he shall rub out or efface the same."[50] The marking was inflicted on top of any other punishment suffered by the convicted thief. This sounds like only a slightly more merciful punishment than branding with a hot iron. The intention was still the same: to humiliate and identify the transgressor and make his shame unavoidably and forever public. The law remained in effect until 1829.[51] A republication in 1805 added little to these changes.

The first truly new criminal statutes that appeared in the era were those published in 1815. The statutes of 1805 were still in effect when the state prison was constructed in 1812. More criminal statutes were passed (and older ones reaffirmed) in 1812 just before the prison went into operation. An analysis of the statutes of 1815 and those following up to 1914 should show changes and continuities in the definition of serious crime during the age of imprisonment. Such an analysis can also help us understand societal attitudes about crime and punishment and the meaning of legal changes such as codification.

The establishment of the State Prison did indeed herald a new approach to crime and punishment in New Hampshire. The June 1812 session of the New Hampshire Senate opened with a letter addressed to Governor William Plumer from a committee of three senators: Daniel Webster, Jeremiah Mason, and John Goddard. The committee presented Governor Plumer with two bills for his consideration: a revision of the criminal code and regulations for governing the unfinished State Prison.[52]

The letter is of interest due to the later prominence of the authors but also because it reflected the political culture and social and political alliances within the state. Daniel Webster had known Jeremiah Mason as a fellow lawyer in Portsmouth for several years when they had a friendly professional rivalry. Both men were strong Federalists in 1812 and opposed American entry into the war with Great Britain. Webster eventually supported the war.[53] William Plumer, on the other hand, started out as a Federalist but during his years as a United States Senator (1802-07) he became a friend of Thomas Jefferson and repudiated his old convictions. The campaign for the governorship of New Hampshire in 1812 was bitter and Plumer was out of office by 1813. He was reelected governor during the years 1816-19.[54]

The senators' motives were, in part, merciful perhaps in an attempt to demonstrate that, New Hampshire, like Vermont, was a modern, civilized state:

It has been the object of the committee to render the criminal code as mild as the safety of the public and individuals would permit, there are seven crimes, the punishment of which by the present laws of the State, is death. Although this list of capital offences is small, in comparison with the codes of most other countries, the committee, it will be perceived, have thought it would not endanger the well-being of society, to reduce the number to three. Treason, Murder and Rape are the only crimes which will be capital, if the Legislature should deem it expedient to pass the accompanying bill into laws of the State."[55]

There was, in addition, an increased concern with property crimes although here too the senators were anxious to call attention to what they regarded as New Hampshire's uniquely lenient approach.

Forgery and the counterfeiting of coins and bank bills, perjury and subornation of perjury, and the different species of larceny, are the offences which seem to call most loudly for further Legislative provisions. The penalties contemplated to be enacted for those offences by the enclosed bills, although considerably exceeding the provisions of existing laws, are yet far below the degree of severity with which neighboring States have thought it necessary to punish the like offences.[56]

Meanwhile the New Hampshire House of Representatives was stirring itself to action on the same proposed criminal acode, passing it on June 19, 1812.[57] Isaac W. Hill, publisher of *The New-Hampshire Patriot*, ran advertisements for his own publication of "this pamphlet [which] contains the new Criminal Law, which ought to be in the hands of every civil officer." A copy cost 37 1/2 cents.[58] Hill started out as a printer and publisher of *The New-Hampshire Patriot* in 1809. He is described as a "stalwart Jeffersonian" and unlike Webster and Mason, he strongly supported America's entry into the War of 1812 from the start. He vigorously denounced the Federalists through his newspaper editorials. Eventually, he became a state senator in the 1820's and was elected to the United States Senate in 1830. Hill was a strong supporter of Andrew Jackson and became Governor of New Hampshire in 1836.[59]

The new criminal code was passed but the laws of 1791-92 were not repealed. In other words, the new act was added to the old, the customary outcome despite enthusiasm for codification.[60] The New Hampshire criminal "code" of 1815 fits the common law model described by Bergel, Stern, and other scholars. Thus, the compiled statutes of 1815 provided for eight (not seven) capital crimes. For six capital crimes, rape, sodomy, burglary, arson, robbery, and the forgery of public securities, the convicted offender could suffer death by hanging or he could be sent to prison.[61] Death was the only option for treason and wilful murder.[62] There is a cross-reference next to each of the six offenses referring to the appropriate section of the act of June 19, 1812.

What exactly were the alternatives to death? For arson, rape, burglary, and robbery the punishment was solitary confinement up to six months and hard labor in prison for life. For sodomy it was up to six months of solitary confinement and hard labor in prison for one to ten years. For forgery of state securities and other legal documents the alternative to death was solitary confinement up to six months and hard labor in prison for five to twenty years.[63] The law of the land was indeed more merciful but it was hardly rendered as mild as the Senate committee seemed to imply in their letter to the governor. Of course, the actual punishment of convicted offenders may well have been milder than the stated penalties would suggest. This point will be examined in detail in Chapter Six. As of 1815, the two most serious crimes were murder and treason. The six remaining capital crimes reveal a concern for both persons and property.

Imprisonment for property crimes had been listed in the statutes since the 1790's. Now that there actually was a state prison, the terms of imprisonment were changed. Unlike previous provisions for prison sentences, the statutes now included the words "solitary imprisonment" in certain cases and "hard labour" in all cases. Prison sentences were made longer too. for example, someone convicted of theft in 1805 could be fined or whipped. Ten years later the term "theft" had been replaced by "larceny" which in turn was subdivided by type. All forms of larceny in 1815 were punishable by terms of from one to five or more years of "confinement to hard labour."[64]

The new criminal law was very specific as to which thieves should go to prison. Those persons convicted of stealing "any money, goods or chattels" worth $20 or more would be punished by a term of hard labor at the State Prison for between one and three years. For a theft worth less than $20 "such person shall be deemed and taken to be guilty of larceny, and shall be punished by imprisonment in the common gaol not exceeding one year nor less than three months and by fine not exceeding fifty dollars." The offender would also be sentenced to pay treble the value of the property stolen plus the costs of prosecution.[65] While it would appear from the statutes that $20 was the dividing point between felony and petty theft, my research reveals that a fair number of the cases sampled for this project were sentenced to a term at the state prison for larcenies involving sums under $20. The crucial distinction probably lay in the circumstances of the larceny. If a larceny occurred in a dwelling house, shop, warehouse, store, office, ship, or vessel, or from a person, the offender was liable to imprisonment at hard labor for at least one year. The actual value of the item(s) stolen did not matter.[66] The law is not clear if this was the case - perhaps the common law tradition of judicial discretion influenced sentencing. This point will be addressed in a later chapter.

Public humiliation was still an optional punishment in 1815. As in 1792, the mother convicted of concealing the death of a bastard child could be set upon the gallows for an hour, imprisoned for up to two years, or be fined up to L300.[67] Also unchanged was the punishment for manslaughter. The offender could be set upon the gallows for an hour with a rope around his or her neck, imprisoned for up to one year, bound to good behavior for up to three years, or be fined up to L300.[68]

The laws defined some crimes differently while others were unchanged in definition but were punished differently than before. For example, the crime of maiming was now referred to as "mayhem."[69] The penalty was changed from a prison sentence of up to seven years plus a fine of up to L300 to a prison sentence at hard labor of from one to twenty years plus up to six months of solitary confinement.[70] Perjury and subornation of perjury (incitement to commit perjury) were still classified as serious crimes. However, the punishment now consisted of confinement to hard labor and a term of solitary confinement rather than the relatively short prison term, fine, and humiliation in the pillory required in 1805.[71] Imprisonment was substituted for the older forms of punishment for the crime of assaulting another with the intention to commit murder, rape, sodomy, or robbery in the new criminal laws. Punishment was changed from fines, whipping and or short imprisonment to a lengthier term of hard labor in prison and solitary confinement.[72]

The appearance of an urban or commercial environment in larger population centers such as Portsmouth led to the creation of a new category of crime in 1812: entering a building "without breaking" with the intention of committing a felony. Punishment for this offense was a term in the prison at hard labor of one to five years.[73] This offense was not the same as burglary. Possibly, this new type of crime reflects a growing concern for the sanctity of property. An urban environment meant that there were now a significant number of uninhabited buildings which provided a new target for criminal behavior. Even though the intended crime may have been other than stealing or destroying property, the implication is that the violation of one's premises whether house, office, store, or even ship was the real offense.

A further illustration of the growing commercialization of the economy may be found in the changed law concerning livestock injury. The wilful destruction or injury of livestock was of concern to a society which was in the process of becoming part of a broader market economy.[74] Of course, this sort of crime had also been serious in an agricultural economy. For this crime, the most serious penalty was hard labor in the State Prison for one to three years. Otherwise, the offender could be fined up to $1000 or spend up to a year in the "common gaol."[75]

Although a market economy was being developed at this time, cash was not yet commonly used in rural America. The main use for cash was the purchase of imported goods and the payment of taxes.[76] Forgery of legal tender and documents and the counterfeiting of coins had been regarded as serious offenses before. Now the description of this type of offense was more detailed and the punishment consisted of terms of hard labor and solitary confinement in the state prison. Most serious, aside from the forgery of state securities, was the counterfeiting of gold or silver coins. The prison sentence was from five to twenty years.[77] Clearly, the propertied interests were concerned about this sort of crime. The power of the state government was asserted by the harshness of the punishment: passing counterfeit coins was also a serious offense against the state. The punishment in this case was from one to three years of hard labor at the prison plus up to two months of solitary confinement.[78]

New standards of morality reflected the changing priorities of New Hampshire society. As the state grew more commercial and urban, the old theocratic moral standards became less relevant. Several former felonies were now reduced to petty crimes and misdemeanors. Adultery, polygamy, and blasphemy along with gaming at billiards and cursing were now considered to be less-serious forms of crime. None of these offenses merited a term in the state prison as of 1815. Prior to that date some of these offenses had been punished by whipping, fines, or even death. A small number of offenders did end up in the prison for adultery and polygamy later on in the century; the apparent liberalization was not necessarily permanent. Finally, conviction of the crime of digging up corpses could bring a fine of up to $2000, public whipping of up to 39 stripes, and or up to two years in prison. This crime was an affront to community standards of decency and there was the likelihood that the grave robbers were after valuables that had been buried with the corpse. No mention is made of hard labor or solitary confinement, however.[79]

Fifteen years passed before the next compilation of New Hampshire statutes in 1830. It was an era of national expansion and well-being and an era of reform on several fronts. Institutions of various types were under construction in a number of states: insane asylums, orphanages, and prisons. The age of the penitentiary had arrived. Apparently, the official perception of crime in the state of New Hampshire was not very different in 1830 from what it had been in 1815. Many of the statutes in effect in 1815 had been passed in 1812 in response to the advent of the State Prison. Thus, it should not be surprising if the laws of 1830 were similar to those of 15 years before although the initial transformation had already taken place. In 1830 the New Hampshire legislature consolidated recent changes in the criminal laws. All of the acts of 1791-92, which had been the foundation of New Hampshire criminal law for nearly 40 years, were repealed and replaced with new laws restating old values in more modern terms.

An important change was the repeal of most capital crimes. Now the only capital crimes were treason and wilful murder.[80] The death penalty was no longer applicable to the crimes of rape, sodomy, burglary, arson, robbery, or the forgery of public securities. Now the punishment for these crimes was solitary confinement for up to six months plus hard labor in prison for life.[81] Forgery of state securities and other legal documents was punishable by up to six months of solitary confinement and hard labor in the prison for a term of five to twenty years.[82] Sodomy, which had been considered a capital crime or one meriting a serious prison sentence, was no longer mentioned in the statutes of 1830. It is unlikely the New Hampshire lawmakers approved of such behavior but the ommission is significant. Still, traditional moral standards remained important as is evident with the passage of "An Act for the punishment of lewdness [which covered a range of offenses], adultery, poligamy [sic], and fornication" on January 2, 1829. None of these offenses were serious enough for a term in the state prison. Instead, punishment for such moral lapses was a term in the "common jail" or a fine.[83] The community wanted to punish moral transgressors but not excessively.

By 1830 there was a growing concern for protecting property from burglary. The term "breaking and entering" made its appearance in "An Act for the punishment of certain crimes by solitary imprisonment and confinement to labor" passed on January 2, 1828. It was important not only whether an offender broke into a building but also whether the break occurred during the day or night. The indictments and court bills consulted for this project are almost formulaic in their invocation of the phrase "did break and enter" and of the time when an alleged crime took place. The distinction according the statutes was between breaking and entering during the day, or entering a building without breaking at night in order to commit a felony. Doing either of the preceding could bring the offender a sentence of between two and seven years in length.[84] No mention is made of entering a building without breaking at night or breaking and entering during the day. Presumably, the other aspects of the alleged crime would bring about punishment. This concern with day or night breaking or not was probably of some significance and not just a legal quibble. It is likely that the sanctity of one's own home, business, etc. was at stake. Similarly, too, with the distinction of time of day. A crime committed in the dark of night when the victim was probably asleep would be a greater violation of the standards of decency or a greater threat than a crime committed in daylight. Also, the growth of a market economy and urbanization would mean that more uninhabited buildings were present than before. They must have made a tempting target - especially if they contained material goods or cash necessary for conducting business.

A new refinement to the statutes on burglary was adopted in 1899, by which time more than half the population of seacoast New Hampshire resided in towns of 2500 inhabitants or more. Obviously, the intention was to nip burglary in the bud when a person could go to the state prison for up to 10 years or pay a fine of $1000 plus spend one year in jail for fitting into the following description:

> Whoever makes or mends, or begins to make or mend or knowingly has in his possession an engine, machine, tool, or implement adapted and designed for cutting through, forcing, or breaking open a building, room, vault, safe, or other depository, in order to steal therefrom money or other property, or to commit any other crime, knowing the same to be adapted and designed for the purpose aforesaid.[85]

Perjury and subornation of perjury were serious offenses in 1830. For either, the punishment consisted of solitary confinement for up to four months and hard labor for two to five years.[86] As in 1815 the sum of $20 was the dividing point between petty crime and felony. Of course, the circumstances of the crime could send a convicted offender to the state prison no matter what the actual value of the property in question. The theft of livestock was punishable by three to seven years of hard labor.[87]

Despite the increased reliance on prisons for punishment, already by 1830 the first signs of the failure of imprisonment as a method of reforming criminals were evident. As far back as 1797, New Hampshire lawmakers had addressed the problem of recidivism with the provision that recidivist thieves be tattooed in the face.

The problem of recidivism was again addressed in the statutes of 1830. The law stated that if any person who had already served a term in the state prison were convicted of another crime punishable by hard labor in the state prison, he or she would receive double the original sentence in his or her second conviction.[88] In 1829 the practice of marking the face of a livestock thief or recidivist thief with "a line of India-ink well and deeply inserted" was abolished. However, the new law provided that recidivists for any crime were to "be marked on the arm above the elbow with the letters N.H.S.P. and with figures denoting the year in which such convict shall have been so committed; which letters and figures shall be made with India ink well and deeply inserted...and in case the same shall be rubbed off or effaced during such confinement, it shall be repeated until it be indelibly fixed."[89] A third conviction brought a life sentence.[90] By 1893 the "habitual criminal" was defined and punished accordingly:

> Any person who has been twice convicted of crime, sentenced, and committed to prison for terms of not less than three years each, shall, upon conviction of a felony committed in this state, and upon proof of such former convictions, sentences, and concommittals, be deemed to be an habitual criminal, and shall be punished by imprisonment in the state prison for a term not exceeding fifteen years.[91]

An exception was made for the person "released from imprisonment upon any former sentence upon a pardon granted on the ground of innocence.[92]

To summarize: by 1830, the State Prison had become the preferred site of punishment. Hard labor and solitary confinement were the methods. Treason and wilful murder were still the two most serious crimes. Crimes of propriety were downgraded to petty crimes or even abolished. Whipping was now abolished. Punishment by humiliation was only vestigial and was applicable to very few offenses (i.e., being set on the gallows for the death of a bastard child). New Hampshire laws reveal a deepening concern with property offenses. The law was now very specific about monetary value and the circumstances of the crime. It is likely that commercial interests as well as private citizens felt increasingly worried over the possibility of robbery and burglary.

By the time the statutes were next compiled in 1842, the segregation of crimes of property from crimes of violence was made explicit. In appearance, the laws of 1842 were the closest thing to a proper legal code published up to that point. Closer inspection, however, reveals this document to be a "mere compilation" of statutes and thus not a true code according to the precepts of Jean Bergel.[93] These statutes distinguished among eight categories of crime: offenses against the state, against the "life or person," "against property, forgery and counterfeiting," against public justice, against "chastity, decency and morality," and offenses against public policy. Not all of these were punished by a sentence to the state prison.[94]

The changes of 1842 are important because they recognize the complexity in property law and in the definition of murder. In regard to offenses against the state, treason was no longer punishable by death. Nevertheless, punishment for this offense was severe: up to three years of solitary confinement and hard labor for life. Misprision of treason brought up to seven years at hard labor or a fine of of to $2000.[95]

Perhaps the inclusion of a new crime against the state (embezzlement) was a reaction against pork barrel politics. The Democratic party won every election in New Hampshire during the period 1829-46 largely because of the popularity of Andrew Jackson.[96] Offenders could be sentenced to up to two years of hard labor in the state prison, imprisonment in the common jail for one year, or a fine of up to $2000.[97] Perhaps the potential embezzlement of state funds was increasingly on the minds of lawmakers since the collection of state revenue was becoming more standardized. New forms of taxable property were added to the list as time went on: railroads, telegraph lines, telephone lines, etc.[98]

The new focus on crimes against the state may have been a result of increasingly obvious political corruption in some of the growing urban centers. Eric Monkkonen says that recent studies of urban political machines indicate that machines did better in small municipalities rather than the big cities with which they have been traditionally associated. The stability of smaller urban communities was often more conducive to machine politics than the fragmentation characteristic of truly large cities.[99] The late nineteenth and early twentieth century was a time when franchises were granted to entrepreneurs in the municipal services demanded by urban life. Reformers attacked the monopolies associated with urban utility franchises. There were, unfortunately, opportunities for corruption.[100]

Major changes in the statutes of 1891 took place in the areas of public justice and propriety. Under the chapter "Offenses against Public Justice" came a new heading: "Bribery and Corruption." For the first time, the laws directly confronted the problem of political corruption. Penalties were serious. A person convicted of bribing an executive or judicial officer or member of the general court "to influence his action, vote, or judgment" could receive up to five years in prison or be fined up to $3000.[101] Penalties were more severe for the official convicted of accepting a bribe. Such an offender could go to prison for up to 10 years or be fined up to $5000. They would also be disqualified from holding "any public office, trust, or appointment under the State."[102] Any public officer convicted of committing fraud while purchasing material in his official capacity could be fined up to $3000 and or be imprisoned for up to two years.[103] Even a rural state like New Hampshire may have felt the need to guard against the political corruption evident in American cities at the time. Anti-machine sentiment helped fuel the campaigns of Progressive Republicans of New Hampshire such as Winston Churchill at the turn of the century.[104] Political machines controlled votes and patronage - not a new phenomenon but increasingly obvious by this point.

By 1842 the law recognized the complexity of judging a person accused of killing another. Just as property crimes were defined in a more detailed way, so too was the killing of one person by another. For the first time in New Hampshire law, the degree of murder was specified beyond the old wilful or not wilful categories in Chapter 214, "Of Offences Against the Life or Person." This may be connected to a growing reluctance to impose the death penalty or it may be connected to the new philosophy of punishment by imprisonment rather than physical violence. Also, the growing influence of the positive school of criminology placed much of the blame for crime on the criminal's social environment or biological heritage. There was an active anti-gallows movement in New Hampshire in the 1840's that paralleled the ones found in other states.[105] "All murder committed by poison, starving, torture or other deliberate and premeditated killing, or committed in the perpetration of arson, rape, robbery or burglary, is murder of the first degree; and all murder not of the first degree is of the second degree."[106] If convicted of first degree murder, the sentence was death. If convicted of second degree murder, the sentence was solitary confinement of up to three years and hard labor for life

26

in the state prison.[107]   The difference between manslaughter and second degree murder was not made clear but options for punishing manslaughter were greater: a fine of up to $1000, a fine of up to $500 and a term in the common jail of up to one year, or solitary confinement of up to six months plus hard labor for life in the state prison.[108]

The remaining crimes against the person in 1842 consisted of robbery, rape, maiming, assault with intent to commit a violent crime, concealment of the death of a bastard child, and kidnapping. Robbery and rape brought a life sentence plus up to six months of solitary confinement. The other crimes brought lengthy prison sentences ranging from one to twenty years plus solitary confinement. A woman convicted of concealing the death of a bastard child could instead be sent to a common jail for up to two years or pay a fine of up to $2000.[109]   The old public humiliation of sitting on the gallows with a noose around the woman's neck was finally abolished.

Property crime (arson, burglary, breaking and entering, and larceny) was defined even more comprehensively than before. Other property crimes included the placing of obstructions on railroad tracks and maiming cattle. The three most serious property crimes were arson involving a house (seven years to life in prison plus six months of solitary confinement), burglary (five years to life plus up to six months of solitary confinement) and placing obstructions on railroad tracks (two years to life plus solitary confinement). The time and location of the offense remained important. Burglary was defined as breaking and entering a dwelling house at night for the purpose of committing a crime.[110]   The other property crimes were punishable by a term of anywhere from one to twenty years of hard labor in the state prison plus solitary confinement.

Some categories of property crime such as forgery and counterfeiting were treated separately in the 1842 statutes. The chapter devoted to this category laboriously lists every kind of forgeable document (public records, writs, insurance policies, to name a very few). Punishment ranged from three to twenty years at hard labor plus solitary confinement. Passing forged documents, counterfeit bank bills or counterfeit coins was also seriously punished: two to five years at hard labor plus solitary confinement.[111]

For the first time the statutes describe crimes related to the functioning of the State Prison itself. Any person convicted of helping a prisoner committed "before or after conviction, to any place of confinement, for any capital offence" to escape was to receive a sentence of up to life at hard labor. A person convicted of passing "any tool, weapon, or other thing" to a prisoner to help him or her escape would be punished by a prison sentence of up to ten years and solitary confinement, or a fine of up to $500.[112] Under the category of public justice offenses came the older crimes of perjury (two to five years plus solitary confinement) and subornation of perjury (same sentence). False swearing was now also considered to be perjury and was punished the same way.[113] Finally, a town clerk who "wilfully and corruptly" made a false record of any vote or legal proceeding could be punished with two to five years of hard labor in prison and solitary confinement.[114]

This brief survey of the criminal laws of 1842 reflects some of the social and demographic changes affecting New Hampshire. Twenty dollars was still the dividing point between grand and petty larceny. However, as in 1830, the circumstances of the larceny made this potentially a felony no matter what the value of the property. There was new concern over prison escapes - what does this say about the security of the State Prison? By suggesting the possibility of outside connivance, the laws reveal a broader current of distrust of the institution. This growing distrust influenced legislation concerning the institution established for juvenile offenders in 1855. The law of 1874 punished those who would "aid or abet any boy or girl held in the reform school." The reform school went into operation in 1858 and by 1874 the problem of escape was serious enough to warrant a statute. Such an offense was not a felony since a person so convicted would have to pay a fine of up to $100 or be sent to the common jail for up to 30 days. This is in contrast to the fine of up to $500 or imprisonment of up to 10 years for helping an adult prisoner to escape.[115]

The transportation revolution also had an effect on the law with the criminalization of the placement of obstructions on railroad tracks. Not only could such an action cause serious property damage but it could endanger life and limb. This was an age of railroad expansion throughout the United States and the railroad interests were well-represented in state governments.[116] A New Hampshire law was passed in 1883 forbidding anyone to "maliciously or wantonly stop, hinder, or delay...the running, management, or control of any railroad train car, or locomotive." Punishment was up to 10 years in prison and or up to a $1000 fine.[117] Again, the railroad interests showed up in the compilation of statutes in 1901. In the past, provisions had been made to punish severely anyone who damaged railroad property or interfered with railroad operations. As of 1899, an act was passed protecting railroad companies from any legal action brought against the railroads "unless the injuries are occasioned by the wilful or gross negligence of the railroad or its employees."[118] This act was also a form of self-protection for the railroads against frivolous lawsuits.

Also, murder was regarded as a more complex crime than previously. First degree murder was now the only remaining capital crime. Was the recognition of murder's complexity an attempt to avoid implementing the death penalty? A life sentence was certainly a grim alternative yet it was conceivably more merciful than death by hanging. Also, the issue of rehabilitation may have played a part in this possible reluctance to impose the death sentence.

Few changes were made in the 1853 compilation of New Hampshire criminal laws but one development listed under "Offences Against the Life or Person" merits discussion since it focuses on abortion. Ever since 1792 the concealment of the death of a bastard child had been listed as a serious crime. It had been considered a serious crime as far back as 1672, a time during which New Hampshire had been under the jurisdiction of Massachusetts. In 1848 the state legislature voted into law several detailed additions to the basic statute. Even though the term "abortion" does not appear, it is obvious that abortion was indeed defined as a crime. For the first time, accomplices to the death of a newborn child (bastard or otherwise) were liable to serious prison sentences. The law stated

> Every person who shall administer to any woman pregnant with a quick child, any medicine, drug or substance whatever, with intent thereby to destroy such child, unless the same shall have been necessary to preserve the life of such woman, or shall have been advised by two physicians to be necessary for such purpose, shall, upon conviction, be punished by fine not exceeding one thousand dollars, and by confinement to hard labor not less than one year nor more than ten years.[119]

The term "quick child" refers to the period in a pregnancy when a woman could feel movement of the fetus. This usually occurs between the fourth and six month of pregnancy.[120] A person causing the death of a woman in such a case "shall be taken and deemed guilty of murder in the second degree and punished accordingly" (i.e., three years to life in prison).[121] The inducement of a miscarriage in a pregnant woman did not rate a prison sentence. Instead, the offender was to be punished by up to one year in the county jail and or by a fine of up to $1000.[122]

Laws aimed at abortionists were often responding to the changing status of the medical profession in America. Joseph F. Kett describes the period 1820-

60 as the "Dark Ages" of the medical profession in the United States.[123] The period was characterized by the decline of medical societies and the rise of medical schools, the end result of which was a decline in the licensing of physicians. At the same time, a self-taught herbal doctor named Samuel Thomson inspired a movement to open the field of medicine up to amateur practitioners. This was partially an appeal to Jacksonian sentiments aimed against the existence of a privileged caste of medical professionals.[124]

Thomson's adherents did not necessarily promote abortion but the popularity of his ideas suggests that unqualified medical practitioners might have felt confident enough to perform such serious procedures. Eventually, the enthusiasm for Thomsonianism died out and medical schools did become, in effect, licensing bodies after 1860. They did so by raising the requirements for a medical degree, a process not completed until the twentieth century.[125] In the meantime, the only attempts made at regulating the medical profession were by medical societies and state laws, both of which failed.[126] The New Hampshire statute against abortion, like those passed in other states c. 1840-60, can be considered - in part - to be an attempt to protect the public from unlicensed quacks.[127]

A feminist interpretation of the abortion statute is suggested by Kathryn K. Sklar. Even while the licensing of professional physicians was in a state of chaos, professionals took over the function of midwives in childbirth. Doctors "emphatically denied that women had any right to control the birth of their children."[128] Kristin Luker sees the emergence of abortion as a social problem as a phenomenon of the period 1850-1900. Thus, the New Hampshire statute of 1848 was an early recognition of the issue. The increased involvement of professional physicians in childbirth helped create controversy over the issue of abortion.[129] Additionally, theories of fertility and embryology were changing, thanks to scientific discoveries. As American society grew more urban, it also grew more anonymous, a situation which allowed abortion to flourish.

The quickening pace of social and economic change in the late nineteenth century shaped definitions of crime. New technology entailed new forms of crime. The rise of railroads in New Hampshire affected property crime in 1842. By 1846 telegraph lines were also the object of lawmakers. Anyone convicted of wilfully damaging posts, wires, or any other component of a telegraph line was to be punished by a prison sentence of from two years to life.[130] Fifty years later, Frederick H. Wines observed, "The chief source of the additions to the code which have been made in the present century is found in the altered conditions of manufactures and trade, growing out of recent scientific discoveries and their application by inventors to the arts...There are accordingly, penalties pronounced against interference with the new modes of transportation by steam and electricity."[131] By 1880 there were 1146 railroad companies in operation in the United States and a total of 87,891 miles of tracks. In addition, there were 5139 steamships in operation and 2515 miles of canals.[132] In New England, there were 129 railroad companies and 5948 miles of track. There were 18 steamships in operation in New Hampshire in 1880 and only 5 miles of canals.[133]

The nature of work in New Hampshire was changing along with the population and technology. The percentage of those engaged in agricultural occupations declined from 38.8% of the workforce in 1870 to 19.1% by 1910, while those engaged in trade and transportation made up 7.2% of the workforce in 1870; by 1910 they had nearly doubled to 13.4%.[134] American economic life was now characterized by greater mobility and increased professionalism.

Changes in the economy provided a new opportunity for criminals. Obtaining someone's property by impersonating another was a completely new form of property crime. The penalty was a fine of up to $500, confinement in the common jail for up to one year, or hard labor in the state prison for up to seven years.[135] In effect, the crime defined here was another version of fraud. The fact that it was a fairly sophisticated crime might indicate the demographic changes affecting New Hampshire. Eric Monkkonen links the phenomenon of theft by trick to the growth of urban population centers.[136] At the time this law was passed in 1850, New Hampshire was mostly rural but some urban population growth was evident. For example, between 1800 and 1850 the population of such milltowns as Dover, Exeter, Concord, Somersworth, Manchester, and Rochester experienced dramatic if uneven growth. The seaport of Portsmouth grew from 5339 inhabitants in 1800 to 9738 by 1850.[137] Agricultural employment in New Hampshire began to decline as the fertile expanses of the West were settled. Persons employed in agriculture declined steadily between 1870 and 1910: 46,573 in 1870 to 36,591 in 1910. Growing networks of railroads and canals made the shipment of farm produce from the West to the East competitive with Eastern agriculture. The rise of Western agriculture and the success of industrial enterprise in Massachusetts helped spur the transformation of New Hampshire's economy to one based upon industry.[138]

Post-Civil War expansion and prosperity did not last very long. In 1873 the United States entered into a depression which lasted until 1877. One consequence was the widespread appearance of unemployed workers. For the first time, tramps became a common sight as thousands of jobless men caught rides on the railroads crisscrossing the country in a desperate search for work. New Hampshire had always had strict "settlement" laws which listed the requirements for becoming a local resident and thus eligible for assistance in case of impoverishment.[139] The old methods of dealing with the poor - warning out of town, "outdoor relief" in the pauper's own home, and more recently, sending the poor to the town or county poorfarm or workhouse - were inadequate to the task of controlling them now. In response to these conditions the New Hampshire legislature passed Chapter 270 of *The General Laws of the State of New Hampshire*, "Punishment of Tramps." A tamp was defined as "any person going about from place to place begging and asking or subsisting upon charity."[140] A person so convicted was sent to the state prison for up to 15 months. If a tramp were caught entering a person's house, he could receive up to two years of "hard labor," a phrase that had been part of the 1853 laws and was then dropped. J. Duane Squires describes this law as "rough surgery for the social sickness of unemployment." Supposedly, tramps did avoid New Hampshire thanks to this pitiless measure.[141] Women, minors under 17, and the blind were spared conviction as tramps.[142] Other states, mostly in the northeast, passed new legislation against the wandering poor, starting with Massachusetts which passed a law against "idle" paupers in 1866.[143] New Jersey passed the first explicitly anti-tramp law in 1876. A typical law was that passed in New York in 1880 which punished tramps with up to six months of hard labor at the nearest penitentiary.[144] The public lost interest in the subject of tramps until the depression of 1882-86 when these laws were put into practice.[145]

Thanks to economic and industrial developments, the concept of adolescence became important in late nineteenth century America. Traditionally, young people age 12 to 14 had left school to go to work. At age 18 youths could expect to be paid the same wages as an adult now that they were trained. However, by the late nineteenth century the rise of industrialism resulted in lower-class youths facing dead-end jobs at age 18. Factory work did not require much training. Middle-class youths were now being kept on in school longer to ensure their being able to find jobs with more potential than factory work. Consequently, middle-class youths age 14 to 18 were expected to exhibit more obedience and less independence. Becoming independent too early now meant economic failure, thanks to industrialization.[146] Thus, the concept of the adolescent as a distinct age group in American society became widespread.

Adolescents, especially females, were believed to require protection from vice. Social reformers of the 1880's agitated successfully in a number of states to raise the age of statutory rape. Between 1886 and 1895 the age of statutory rape was raised in 29 states. Such legislation was aimed at men since it was believed males were the "impure" element in society. By raising the age of sexual consent, the opportunity for men to "ruin" young girls and thereby lead them into a life of prostitution was supposedly diminished.[147]   Once again, in New Hampshire, the age of statutory rape was raised in 1897. Now a man convicted of "unlawfully and carnally knowing and abusing any woman child under the age of sixteen years" could go to prison for up to thirty years.[148]

A trend toward stricter public morality and growing concern over child welfare was also more noticeable. This seems to be confirmed by a couple of changes in the criminal laws of 1878 and 1891. In 1878 such concern led to the criminalization of enticing or abducting a female under the age of 18 for the purposes of prostitution. Anyone convicted of doing so could be imprisoned for up to three years or be fined up to $5000, an enormous sum at that time.[149]   In 1887 the age of statutory rape was raised from the appallingly young 10 years to 13 years. A man convicted of "abusing any woman child under the age of thirteen years" could be imprisoned for up to thirty years.[150]   The law of 1876 punishing a person for enticing or abducting a female under age 18 for prostitution was modified in 1889. Now anyone convicted of enticing or abducting a female under the age of 18 for "illicit sexual intercourse" was liable to a prison sentence of up to three years or a fine of up to $5000.[151]   In effect, the age of statutory rape was actually raised to 18, excluding the possibility of such behavior conducted with married females between ages 13 and 18, of course. The main goal appears to have been the elimination of teenage prostitution.

The growing concern over prostitution and other moral offenses led to increasingly strong criminal laws aimed at vice. A very detailed statute was passed in 1911. Basically, the new law said that anyone who was found guilty of "pandering" (i.e., causing a female to become a prostitute or keeping her as one) would be sent to the county jail or house of correction for six months to a year and be fined between $100 and $1000. A second conviction would bring one to ten years in the state prison.[152]

Public anxiety over prostitution was at a peak in the early 1900's. Reformers succeeded in getting strict laws against prostitution passed in a number of other states. Ruth Rosen characterizes the Progressive Era (c. 1900-18) as "one of Western society's most zealous and best-recorded campaigns against prostitution." Reasons for the campaign included pressure from feminists, fears of a growing "white slave trade" in Europe and the

United States, public fear of venereal disease, and a sense of moral self-righteousness which guided a number of reformers.[153]

Sensationalistic literature sounded the alarm in the 1900's. Best sellers included *Tragedies of the White Slaves* (1912) by H.M. Lytle, *The Shame of the Human Race* (1908) by Rev. F.G. Terrell, and *The White Slave Hell, or With Christ at Midnight in the Slums of Chicago* by Rev. F.M. Lehman.[154] Another influential book was *Maggie: A Girl of the Streets* by novelist Stephen Crane, originally published but not distributed in 1892 and then republished in 1896. It depicts the pathetic story of a girl in the New York slums who was driven to prostitution by a combination of bad luck and poverty. She suffered an early, tragic death. Crane's point was that the world was indifferent while the above literature was based on the belief that change and improvement was possible.

An important addition to the chapter "Offenses Against Chastity" in the 1901 laws was "unnatural and lascivious acts." This law, passed in 1899, does not specify the "acts" but the punishment was severe: three to five years in prison and or a fine of $100 to $1000.[155] Not since 1829 had deviant sexual behavior been so explicitly described as criminal behavior.

What does this overview of New Hampshire laws tell us about the official definition of crime? There were some significant changes over time. The major categories of crime against the person, agains property, and against propriety survived but the emphasis changed in some instances. Capital crimes were listed in all three categories from the Massachusetts laws of 1641-42 up through the New Hampshire statutes of 1815.

The greatest change came in the category of crimes against propriety. By the early to mid nineteenth century virtually all of these offenses had been either eliminated or downgraded to relatively petty crimes (i.e., they rated neither death nor a term in the state prison). After several decades, some offenses against propriety were placed back into the category of felonies. Adultery, once a capital crime, had been reduced to a fairly petty offense early in the nineteenth century but by 1867 it was considered serious enough to merit up to three years in the state prison. While prostitution itself was not a felony, procuring, pandering, or inducing a female under age 18 to become a prostitue definitely was so by the late nineteenth century. Deviant sexual behavior was recriminalized in 1899 with the catch-all phrase "unnatural and lascivious acts."

Social and demographic trends might explain the apparent liberalization which took place in New Hampshire between 1815 and 1867 regarding crimes of propriety. Quite possibly the effects of industrialization, immigration, and urbanization threatened the moral values of New Hampshire lawmakers by the late nineteenth century. D'Emilio and Freedman discern a changing pattern in American sexual behavior which they say was linked to the social and economic changes affecting the country in the nineteenth century. Love and intimacy became increasingly important and the close connection between sexuality and reproduction as such was loosened. At the same time, middle-class women were being put on a pedestal and were increasingly associated with "purity" (chastity).[156] Kathryn Sklar says, "Gender roles were an effective way to channel the explosive potential of nineteenth century social change and bring it at least partially under the control of a national elite."[157] Thus, prostitution and deviant sexual behavior came to be regarded as a threat to the emerging standards of the middle class. Such misbehavior threatened the moral foundation of the dominant social class which enshrined "purity" and motherhood as the American woman's defining virtue.[158] The earlier harshness of the criminal sanctions against moral lapses can be largely explained by Puritan values of seventeenth-century Massachusetts.

Crimes against the person or crimes of violence were never downgraded to the extent of crimes against propriety. The only crime to stay consistently capital was that of first degree murder. Second degree murder, manslaughter, rape, robbery, and burglary were all capital crimes at first. The appearance of the state prison was an important influence on the abolition of capital crimes from the statutes. Gradually these crimes were reduced from capital to life in prison at hard labor. From life in prison nearly all of these crimes were reduced to lengthy prison sentences and or fines - still serious but more lenient than before. The definition of murder changed too: it became more complex. For the first time, the law regarding murder reversed the longterm trend toward leniency in 1899. The legislature voted to make the punishment of second degree murder imprisonment up to life "or such term as the court having cognizance of the offense may order."[159] Until 1903 the punishment for first degree murder was death by hanging. In that year, for the first time, the jury was given the option of choosing life in prison instead of death. Even though the punishment for rape was gradually reduced in the nineteenth century, the statute was actually broadened by raising the age of statutory rape from 10 to 16 years. The change probably did not affect the incidence of forcible rape but it did serve to protect female minors.

There was now an alternative punishment for first degree murder. Death was still listed but now the law said, "If the jury shall find the respondent guilty of murder in the first degree the punishment shall be life imprisonment unless the jury add to their verdict the words, with capital punishment." For second degree murder the punishment was "life or for such term as the court having cognizance of the offense may order."[160]   As of 1994 the death penalty is still in place but the statute of 1903 seems to indicate a growing reluctance to put convicted criminals to death. The last execution in New Hampshire took place in 1939.[161]

One form of crime against the person particularly affected by changing definitions of social class and gender roles was abortion. Infanticide had been a crime for ages but it was not specifically addressed until 1791. Abortion was criminalized by 1848. One reason for this was the shift from the employment of midwives during childbirth to professional male physicians in the early nineteenth century. As childbirth became more of a professional (and male) concern, abortion became more of an issue, and, consequently, was criminalized.[162]

Crimes against property underwent a great deal of change during the period covered here. Most property crimes followed the longterm trend toward milder punishment. However, new and more inclusive definitions of property crime were enacted into law. The circumstances of the crime became crucial determinants of the level of punishment.

In sum, the official definition of crime in New Hampshire would seem to indicate a strong concern with property and propriety. But crimes of violence were also of great concern too - the only crime consistently punished by death was first degree murder. The only way to test these conclusions is to investigate the actual application of criminal law in New Hampshire.

Our examination of the New Hampshire criminal statutes also tends to confirm the differences between criminal justice in Massachusetts and South Carolina investigated by Michael J. Hindus. His ultimate conclusion is that both regions had the same goal in mind: race or class control.[163] Thanks to a differing court structure and social structure - black slaves in the South and foreign immigrants in the North - the prosecution patterns would seem to indicate a very different form of criminal justice. Hindus sees crimes of property and propriety as the main target of justice in South Carolina over the same period. He considers the frequent acquittal or downgrading of crime in South Carolina as a result of preferential class treatment and a disinclination to prosecute to the fullest extent. An equivalent measure was the frequent use of pardons in Massachusetts criminal cases.[164] As will be seen in Chapter Six, New Hampshire also used pardons extensively from the 1830's on. However, this seems to have been more for the purpose of preventing overcrowding rather than as an example of preferential class treatment.

Edward L. Ayers convincingly portrays the South as a region where criminal justice concerned itself with violence to a far greater degree than in the North. Ayers discerns a number of causes: the racial structure of the South, the ravaged economy of the post-Civil War period, and most important, a culture in which honor was the key to white male status. According to Ayers, the legacy of honor haunts the South to this day and explains the continued high rate of homicide and assault convictions.[165]

An analysis of crime and punishment in New Hampshire should help us to determine if New Hampshire followed the pattern of Massachusetts and how the situation in New Hampshire contrasted to that of the South described by Hindus and Ayers. In order more fully to understand how the state administered justice, a brief survey of the court system as it developed in New Hampshire is presented in the next chapter.

37

Notes

1. James P. Levine, Michael C. Musheno, and Dennis J. Palumbo, *Criminal Justice in America* (New York, 1986), p. 124 and Douglas Greenberg, "Crime, Law Enforcement, and Social Control in Colonial America," *American Journal of Legal History*, 26 (1982), 297.

2. Kathryn Preyer, "Penal Measures in the American Colonies: An Overview," *American Journal of Legal History*, 26 (1982), 333.

3. Kai T. Erikson, *Wayward Puritans: A Study in the Sociology of Deviance* (New York, 1966), p. 12.

4. "Edward Coke," *New Encyclopedia Britannica*, Vol. 3 *Micropedia* (Chicago, 1986), 439-40.

5. Roscoe Pound, "Common Law," *Encyclopedia of the Social Sciences*, Vol. 4 (New York, 1931), 50.

6. "Edward Coke," *New Encyclopedia Britannica*, Vol. 3 *Micropedia* (Chicago, 1986), 439-40.

7. Herbert Wechsler, "Revision and Codification of Penal Law in the United States," *Dalhousie Law Journal*, 7 (1983), 220.

8. Hobart Pillsbury, *New Hampshire: Resources, Attractions, and Its People: A History*, Vol. 1 (New York, 1927), p. 29.

9. Edwin Powers, *Crime and Punishment in Early Massachusetts 1620-1692: A Documentary History* (Boston, 1966), p. 82.

10. "By the Court: in the Years 1641. 1642. Capital Lawes, established within the Jurisdiction of Massachusetts," *Collections of the Massachusetts Historical Society*, Vol. 4 2nd. Series (Boston, 1846), 112-14.

11. Powers, *Crime and Punishment*, p. 223.

12. *Ibid.*, pp. 164, 180, 182-85, and 213.

13. Perry Miller and Thomas H. Johnson, *The Puritans* (Boston, 1938), p. 386.

14. Douglas Hay, "Property, Authority and the Criminal Law" in Douglas Hay et al., *Albion's Fatal Tree: Crime and Society in Eighteenth-Century England*, 1st. Am. ed. (New York, 1975), p. 22.

15. Pillsbury, *New Hampshire*, p. 151.

16. Elwin Page, *Judicial Beginnings in New Hampshire 1640-1700* (Concord, N.H., 1959), p. 42.

17. Pillsbury, *New Hampshire*, p. 151.

18. Gordon Wright, *Between the Guillotine and Liberty: Two Centuries of the Crime Problem in France* (New York, 1983), p. 6.

38

19. In 1718 Pennsylvania adopted the British code which listed 300 capital offenses. Greenberg, "Crime, Law Enforcement, and Social Control," 302.

20. Linda Kealey, "Patterns of Punishment: Massachusetts in the Eighteenth Century," *American Journal of Legal History*, 30 (1986), 163-86.

21. Albert S. Batchellor, ed., *Laws of New Hampshire*, Vol. 1 (1679-1702), (Manchester, N.H., 1904), p. 15.

22. *Ibid.*, pp. 15-17 and 19-22.

23. Michael S. Hindus, "The Contours of Crime and Justice in Massachusetts and South Carolina 1767-1878," *American Journal of Legal History*, 21 (1977), 235. Linda Kealey links the growing concern over property offenses in Massachusetts to socioeconomic problems during the period 1750-1800. This study, which focuses on the early statehood period, may also offer support to the studies of Hindus and others. See Kealey, "Patterns of Punishment," 167.

24. Lawrence M. Friedman, *A History of American Law*, 2nd. ed. (New York, 1985), p. 289 and Louis P. Masur, *Rites of Execution: Capital Punishment and the Transformation of American Culture* (New York, 1989), p. 65.

25. Pound, "Common Law," 52.

26. Richard E. Ellis, *The Jeffersonian Crisis: Courts and Politics in the Young Republic* (New York, 1971), p. 111.

27. Friedman, *History of American Law*, p. 290.

28. Harry E. Barnes, *The Story of Punishment: A Record of Man's Inhumanity to Man* (Montclair, N.J., 1972 reprint of 1930), p. 104.

29. Charles S. Lobingier, "Codification," *Encyclopedia of the Social Sciences*, Vol. 3 (New York, 1930), 606.

30. Edward McWhinney, "Legal Systems: III. Code Law Systems," *International Encyclopedia of the Social Sciences*, Vol. 9 (New York, 1968), 214.

31. Jean L. Bergel, "Principal Features and Methods of Codification," *Louisiana Law Review*, 48 (1988), 1091.

32. *Ibid.*, 1082.

33. Kent Greenawalt, "A Vice of Its Virtues: The Perils of Precision in Criminal Codification, as Illustrated by Retreat, General Justification, and Dangerous Utterances," *Rutgers Law Journal*, 19 (1988), 929.

34. Bergel, "Codification," 1083.

35. Edward McWhinney, "Legal Systems: II. Common Law Systems," *International Encyclopedia of the Social Sciences*, Vol. 9 (New York, 1968), 211-13.

36. *Ibid.*, 211-13.

37. Bergel, "Codification," 1076.

38. Barry J. Stern, "Revising Vermont's Criminal Code," *Vermont Law Review*, 12 (1987), 307.

39. *The Laws of New Hampshire* (Portsmouth, N.H., 1792), pp. 243-46.

40. William N. Hosley, Jr., "The Founding of the Vermont State Prison in Windsor, 1807-1810," *Vermont History*, 52 (1984), 243.

41. *Laws of New Hampshire (1792)*, p. 244.

42. *Ibid.*, p. 245.

43. *Ibid.*, p. 246.

44. *Ibid.*, pp. 252-57.

45. *Ibid.*, p. 244.

46. Compare Batchellor, ed., *Laws of New Hampshire (1679-1702)*, p. 16 to *Laws of New Hampshire (1792)*, pp. 257-58.

47. Among the punishments suggested by Thomas Jefferson for Virginia were castration for rape and maiming in kind for those convicted of maiming others. Kathryn Preyer theorizes that Jefferson may have contemplated such gruesome punishments as a method of deterring slaves from committing violent crimes. Preyer, "Crime in Virginia," 64.

48. *Laws of New Hampshire (1792)*, pp. 257-58.

49. *Ibid.*, pp. 265-66.

50. *Laws of the State of New-Hampshire...* (Portsmouth, N.H., 1797), pp. 281-82.

51. See "An Act for the Punishment of Certain Crimes by Solitary Imprisonment and Confinement to Hard Labour" in *The Laws of the State of New-Hampshire...* (Exeter, N.H., 1815), p. 324.

52. *Journal of the Honorable Senate of the State of New-Hampshire...June, Anno Domini, 1812*, 40.

53. "Daniel Webster," *Dictionary of American Biography*, Vol. 19 (New York, 1936), 585-92 and "Jeremiah Mason," *Ibid.*, Vol. 12 (New York, 1933), 365-66.

54. "William T. Plumer," *Dictionary of American Biography*, Vol. 15 (New York, 1935), 12-13.

55. *Journal of the Senate...June 1812*, 40.

56. *Ibid.*, 40-41.

57. *Journal of the Proceedings of the House of Representatives of the State of New-hampshire [sic]...June, Anno Domini, 1812*, 61-62 and 121-122 and *Journal of the House...June, 1812*, 116. Also passed was "An Act Providing for the regulation and government of the state prison," *Laws of New Hampshire (1815)*, pp. 143-48.

58. *New-Hampshire Patriot*, Aug. 11, 1812.

40

59. "Isaac Hill," *Dictionary of American Biography*, Vol. 9 (New York, 1932), 34-35.

60. For example, the Massachusetts criminal laws were amended in 1785 to include imprisonment at hard labor as an alternative but not a replacement for the old punishments. There was no immediate and total break with the colonial past. Adam J. Hirsch, "From Pillory to Penitentiary: The Rise of Criminal Incarceration in Early Massachusetts," in Kermit L. Hall, ed., *Police, Prison, and Punishment: Major Historical Interpretations* (New York, 1987), pp. 411-12.

61. See *Laws of New Hampshire (1815)*, pp. 310-12 and 317-18.

62. *Ibid.*, pp. 310-11.

63. *Ibid.*, pp. 317-18.

64. *Laws of New Hampshire (1805)*, p. 274 and *Laws of New Hampshire (1815)*, pp. 323-24.

65. *Laws of New Hampshire (1815)*, p. 327.

66. *Ibid.*, pp. 323-24.

67. *Ibid.*, p. 311.

68. *Ibid.*, p. 311.

69. "Maim," *The Oxford English Dictionary*, 2nd. ed., Vol. 9 (Oxford, 1989), 215 and "Mayhem," *Ibid.*, 514.

70. *Laws of New Hampshire (1805)*, pp. 275-76 and *Laws of New Hampshire (1815)*, 318.

71. *Laws of New Hampshire (1805)*, 275 and *Laws of New Hampshire (1815)*, p. 322.

72. *Laws of New Hampshire (1815)*, p. 318.

73. *Ibid.*, p. 317.

74. A number of historians recognize the period of the late eighteenth through early nineteenth century as an era of great economic change in the United States. See Stuart Bruchey, "Economy and Society in an Earlier America," *Journal of Economic History*, 47 (1987), 318; Allan Kulikoff, "The Transition to Capitalism in Rural America," *William and Mary Quarterly*, 46 (1989), 124-25; and Christopher Clark, "The Household Economy, Market Exchange and the Rise of Capitalism in the Connecticut Valley, 1800-1860," *Journal of Social History*, 13 (1979), 169.

On the other hand, Winifred B. Rothenberg found no significant change to a market for Massachusetts during the period 1750-1855. She posits the existence of a "commercial mentalite" from the very beginning of Massachusetts settlement by Europeans. Winifred B. Rothenberg, "The

Market and Massachusetts Farms, 1750-1855," *Journal of Economic History*, 41 (1981), 312-13.

75. *Laws of New Hampshire (1815)*, p. 319.

76. Clark, "Household Economy," 173.

77. *Laws of New Hampshire (1815)*, p. 321.

78. *Ibid.*, p. 321.

79. *Ibid.*, p. 340.

80. *The Laws of the State of New-Hampshire...* (Hopkinton, N.H., 1830), p. 148.

81. *Ibid.*, p. 137.

82. *Ibid.*, p. 139.

83. *Ibid.*, p. 147.

84. *Ibid.*, pp. 136-37.

85. William M. Chase and Arthur H. Chase, comp. and ed., *The Public Statutes of the State of New Hampshire, and General Laws in Force January 1, 1901* (Concord, N.H., 1900), p. 830.

86. *Laws of New Hampshire (1830)*, pp. 141-42.

87. See *Ibid.*, pp. 142-43.

88. *Ibid.*, p. 144.

89. *Ibid.*, pp. 144-45.

90. *Ibid.*, p. 144.

91. Chase and Chase, *Public Statutes (1901)*, p. 839.

92. *Ibid.*, p. 839.

93. Bergel, "Codification," 1074.

94. *The Revised Statutes of the State of New-Hampshire: Passed December 23, 1842...* (Concord, N.H., 1843), p. 432.

95. *Ibid.*, pp. 432-33.

96. J. Duane Squires, *The Granite State of the United States: A History of New Hampshire from 1623 to the Present* (New York, 1956), Vol. 1, p. 202.

97. *Revised Statutes (1842)*, p. 433.

98. Albert O. Brown, "An Outline of the History of Taxation in New Hampshire," *Granite Monthly*, 60 (1928), 6-7 and see "An Act to Establish Rates at Which Polls and Rateable Estate Shall Be Assessed in Making Direct Taxes," *Laws of the State of New-Hampshire: Passed November Session, 1832...* (Concord, N.H., 1833), 98-99. The statute of 1832 established a new principle of taxation in New Hampshire which was that the assessed valuation of property for taxation was to be the same as the valuation assessed of the property for sale.

99. Eric H. Monkkonen, *America Becomes Urban: The Development of U.S. Cities and Towns, 1780-1980* (Berkeley, Calif., 1988), pp. 209-10.

100. See, for example, Chapter 11 "Quasi-Public Corporations and Popular Sovereignty" in David P. Thelen, *The New Citizenship: Origins of Progressivism in Wisconsin, 1885-1900* ([Columbia, Mo.]. 1972).

101. *The Public Statutes of New Hampshire...* (Manchester, N.H., 1891), p. 744.

102. *Ibid.*, p. 744.

103. *Ibid.*, pp. 744-45.

104. James Wright, *The Progressive Yankees: Republican Reformers in New Hampshire, 1906-1916* (Hanover, N.H., 1987), p. 65.

105. Quentin Blaine, "Shall Surely Be Put to Death': Capital Punishment in New Hampshire, 1623-1985," *New Hampshire Bar Journal*, 27 (1986), 135 and David B. Davis, "Murder in New Hampshire," *New England Quarterly*, 28 (1955), 155, 161, and 163.

106. *Revised Statutes (1842)*, p. 433.

107. *Ibid.*, pp. 433-34.

108. *Ibid.*, p. 434.

109. *Ibid.*, pp. 434-35.

110. *Ibid.*, pp. 435-36.

111. *Ibid.*, pp. 439-40.

112. See Chapter 217 "Of Offences Against Public Justice," *Ibid.*, p. 442.

113. *Ibid.*, p. 441.

114. *Ibid.*, p. 443. The remaining categories of crime did not rate a term in the state prison and so will not be covered here.

115. *The General Laws of the State of New-Hampshire...* (Manchester, N.H., 1878), pp. 624-25.

116. Wright, *Progressive Yankees*, pp. 59-60.

117. *Public Statutes (1891)*, p. 714.

118. Chase and Chase, comp. and ed., *Public Statutes (1901)*, p. 807.

119. *The Compiled Statutes of the State of New-Hampshire...* 2nd. ed. (Concord, N.H., 1854), p. 44.

120. Kristin Luker, *Abortion and the Politics of Motherhood* (Los Angeles, 1984), p. 14.

121. *Compiled Statutes (1853)*, p. 544.

122. *Ibid.*, pp. 544-45.

123. Joseph F. Kett, *The Formation of the American Medical Profession: The Role of Institutions, 1780-1860* (New Haven, Conn., 1968), p. vii.

124. *Ibid.*, pp. 64-65, 101, and 110.

125. *Ibid.*, p. 180.

126. *Ibid.*, p. 180.

127. James C. Mohr, *Abortion in America: The Origins and Evolution of National Policy, 1800-1900* (New York, 1978), pp. 134-35.

128. Kathryn K. Sklar, *Catharine Beecher: A Study in American Domesticity* (New Haven, Conn., 1973), p. 208.

129. Luker, *Abortion*, p. 20.

130. *Compiled Statutes (1853)*, p. 45.

131. Frederick H. Wines, *Punishment and Reformation: An Historical Sketch of the Rise of the Penitentiary System* (Boston, 1895), p. 19.

132. *Compendium of the Tenth Census (June 1, 1880): Compiled Pursuant to an Act of Congress Approved August 7, 1882*, Rev. ed., Part II (Washington, D.C., 1883), microfilm (New Haven, Conn.: Research Publications, Inc.).

133. *Ibid.*

134. *Ibid.*

135. *Compiled Statutes (1853)*, p. 551.

136. Eric H. Monkkonen, *The Dangerous Class: Crime and Poverty in Columbus, Ohio, 1860-1885* (Cambridge, Mass., 1975), p. 70.

137. See *Return of the Whole Number of Persons within the Several Districts of the United States...February the twenty eighth, one thousand eight hundred* (Woodbridge, Conn.: Research Publications, Inc.), microfilm; *United States Census of Population 1810* (Woodbridge, Conn.: Research Publications, Inc.), microfilm; *Census for 1820* (Woodbridge, Conn.: Research Publications, Inc.), microfilm; *Fifth Census, or, Enumeration of the Inhabitants of the United States: 1830...* (Woodbridge, Conn.: Research Publications, Inc.), microfilm; *Sixth Census or Enumeration of the Inhabitants of the United States, as Corrected at the Department of State: In 1840* (Woodbridge, Conn.: Research Publications Inc.), microfilm; and *The Seventh Census of the United States: 1850* (Woodbridge, Conn.: Research Publications, Inc.), microfilm, p. 21.

138. Tamara Hareven and Randolph Langenbach, *Amoskeag: Life and Work in an American Factory-City* (New York, 1978), p. 13 and Paul G. Munyon, *A Reassessment of New England Agriculture in the Last Thirty Years of the Nineteenth Century: New Hampshire: A Case Study* (New York, 1978), p. 215.

139. Marcus W. Jernegan, *Laboring and Dependent Classes in Colonial America 1607-1783* (New York, 1965), p. 208 and Timothy Dodge, "Poor Relief in Durham, Lee, and Madbury, [N.H.], 1732-1891" (Unpublished M.A.

Thesis, U.N.H., History, 1982), 137. See also Title 10 "Of Paupers" Chapter 81 "Settlement of Paupers" in *General Laws (1878)*, pp. 196-97.

140. *General Laws (1878)*, p. 612.

141. Squires, *Granite State*, Vol. 1, p. 416.

142. *General Laws (1878)*, p. 613.

143. Amy Dru Stanley, "Beggars Can't Be Choosers: Compulsion and Contract in Postbellum America," *Journal of American History*, 78 (1992), 1273-74.

144. Paul T. Ringenbach, *Tramps and Reformers 1873-1916: The Discovery of Unemployment in New York* (Westport, Conn., 1973), pp. 22-24.

145. *Ibid.*, p. 24.

146. Jospeh F. Kett, *Rites of Passage: Adolescence in America 1790 to the Present* (New York, 1977), pp. 171-72.

147. John D'Emilio and Estelle B. Freedman, *Intimate Matters: A History of Sexuality in America* (New York, 1988), p. 153.

148. Chase and Chase, ed. and comp., *Public Statutes (1901)*, p. 832.

149. *General Laws (1878)*, pp. 619-20.

150. *Public Statutes (1891)*, p. 739.

151. *Ibid.*, p. 728.

152. William M. Chase, ed. and Arthur H. Chase, comp., *Supplement to the Public Statutes of New Hampshire (Chase Edition, 1901)...* (Concord, N.H., 1914), p. 521.

153. Ruth Rosen, *The Lost Sisterhood: Prostitution in America, 1900-1918* (Baltimore, 1982), pp. xi and 12-13.

154. D'Emilio and Freedman, *Intimate Matters*, pp. 209 and 389.

155. Chase and Chase, ed. and comp., *Public Statutes (1901)*, p. 822.

156. D'Emilio and Freedman, *Intimate Matters*, p. 56.

157. Sklar, *Catharine Beecher*, p. xii.

158. Ann Douglas, *The Feminization of American Culture* (New York, 1988), p. 75.

159. Chase and Chase, ed. and comp., *Public Statutes (1901)*, p. 831.

160. Chase and Chase, ed. and comp., *Supplement to Public Statutes (1914)*, p. 529.

161. Blaine, "Shall Surely Be Put to Death," 142.

162. Luker, *Abortion*, p. 16.

163. Michael S. Hindus, *Prison and Plantation: Crime, Justice and Authority in Massachusetts and South Carolina, 1767-1878* (Chapel Hill, N.C., 1980), pp. 250-51.

164. *Ibid.*, p. 252.

165. Edward L. Ayers, *Vengeance and Justice: Crime and Punishment in the Nineteenth Century American South* (New York, 1984), p. 276.

Chapter II

Structure of Criminal Justice in New Hampshire, 1641-1914
and the Establishment of the State Prison

Now that we have examined the evolution of criminal law in New Hampshire, we need to find out how the law was administered. Chapter Two will analyze the establishment of the formal mechanisms of criminal justice in New Hampshire for the period 1641-1914: the court structure, trial process, and law enforcement, and the establishment of the State Prison in the early nineteenth century.

There was no formal court structure in New Hampshire before 1641, however, starting in that year, the four towns that comprised New Hampshire were united with Massachusetts Bay and remained a part of Massachusetts until 1679. The administration of criminal justice in Massachusetts was located in judicial tribunals. The tribunals were based on the English judicial system and the Massachusetts Charter.[1] The Charter required the Assembly to meet four times a year and empowered the governor to summon the "Great and Generall Courtes."[2] The General Court, convening for the first time in 1630, had original and appellate jurisdiction in both civil and criminal matters.[3] The General Court was composed of the governor, his deputy, and 18 assistants chosen in annual elections. In 1631 the assistants were given magisterial powers. Although elected annually, magistrates could function as a standing council.[4]

To cope with an increasing workload, the Inferior Quarterly Courts were established in 1636. Edwin Powers describes them as the "workhorses of the judiciary" system. These courts had jurisdiction over civil cases and minor criminal cases. Serious criminal cases were tried at the General Court.[5] By 1634 Massachusetts law had provided for the summoning of a jury to any trial held in an inferior court when the potential punishment was death or banishment. The right to a jury trial in all criminal cases was formally adopted in the "Body of Libertys" in 1641.[6] This was the court system in existence when New Hampshire became part of Massachusetts in 1641.

Two years later, the court system was changed again with the establishment of counties. The county court consisted of a chief justice with an associate. The Norfolk County Court extended from the present-day Haverhill, Massachusetts north to Dover, New Hampshire. The county court was also known as the "Pasacataqua Court." A peculiarity of this system was the Court of Associates; it had common law jurisdiction which meant that it could fill-in when the county courts were not in session. The Court of Associates had the same authority as the county courts. It consisted of up to five prominent local officials who served as associate judges (they were also known as assistants or commissioners), plus a clerk of the court. Because the count courts only met on an annual basis, the Court of Associates, which met three times a year, was sometimes used to expedite matters.[7] Between 1641 and 1679 there was very little change in the court structure. Jurors were chosen from the local body of freemen after the clerk of the court issued warrants to the appropriate town constables.[8] The first recorded grand jury list in New Hampshire was issued in 1643.[9] Until 1686 professional attorneys were unknown in New Hampshire, and therefore the parties involved had to plead their own cases.[10] Those charged with a felony or treason could only receive advice from counsel but could not be represented by counsel before the bench. Several other colonies also prohibited lawyers in the seventeenth century.[11]

Who ran the criminal justice system beside the judges, jury, and clerks? Mostof the law officers were based on English antecedents. Constables, marshals, and sheriffs were the law enforcement officials. These officials were mainly involved in duties such as tax collecting and posting notices rather than law enforcement as we know it. For most of the seventeenth century the marshal, sometimes assisted by a constable or prison keeper, was the most important court officer. Sheriffs did not appear in the Massachusetts colony records until 1691 even though the office had been important in England since the Middle Ages.[12] The marshal collected and levied fines and court executions, and served warrants and attachments. Sheriffs eventually received more inclusive administrative duties and were in charge of jails and prisons.[13] Thus, in 1714, the provincial legislature of New Hampshire passed an act appointing the sheriff to have custody of the prisoners in the "common goal [jail]" in Portsmouth.[14] The English village constable had many duties: to prevent public disorder, apprehend criminals, administer tasks such as highway repair and poor relief, supervise local military affairs, and to collect taxes.[15] His duties were not much different in seventeenth-century New England.

The coroner's office was another important component of the legal structure. The coroner was authorized to take inquests of "Felonies, and other Violent and Casual Deaths committed, or happening within this Province." The coroner set the criminal justice system in motion when investigating a suspicious death. He made out a warrant for the local constable(s) who summoned a jury of 18 men to view the body. Fourteen or more of the jurors were then to make a declaration as to the nature of the death. In addition, the coroner was authorized to make out a warrant for witnesses. If the death appeared to be a criminal matter, the coroner then conveyed the findings to the nearest justices of the peace and the trial process was begun. In addition to serving warrants and apprehending suspects, constables were also required to attend the courts in session.[16]

In 1679 New Hampshire became a separate royal province from Massachusetts. Criminal justice in the newly-created province was administered on an annual basis. The General Assembly met at Portsmouth on the first Tuesday in March "to hear & determine all Actions of Appeal from inferior Courts, whether of a Civil or a Criminal nature."[17] The three inferior courts met at the following places and times: Dover on the first Tuesday in June, Hampton on the first Tuesday in September, and Portsmouth on the first Tuesday in December. All trials, "whether Capital, or Criminal" were to be tried by a jury of "Twelv good & lawful men according to the commendable custom of England: Except the Parties concerned do refer it to the Bench or some express Law doth refer it to their Judgment & Trial, or to the Trial of some other Court, where Jury is not..."[18] The defendant had the right to challenge the jury.

This structure served New Hampshire until the provincial reorganization of 1692. Probably the most significant change made at this time provided for more frequent holding of courts in order to accomplish a more expeditious resolution of criminal (and civil) cases.[19] Also, it was possible to appeal a case to the Supreme Court of Judicature meeting semiannually in Portsmouth in April and October.[20] The Supreme Court consisted of four justices "fully Impowred & authorized to have Cognizance of all please [sic] Civill, Criminall & mixt" and "twelve men of the Neighbourhood."[21] Justices of the peace heard petty crimes and misdemeanors. In 1699 "An Act for Establishing Courts of Publick Justice within This Province" elaborated this system which remained nearly unchanged until after the Revolutionary War.[22]

The Declaration of Independence animated the New Hampshire legislature to pass "An Act for Establishing Courts of Law for the Administration of Justice within This Colony" in 1776.[23] It is likely the establishment of counties in 1770 also prompted the passage of this act. Foremost, the new political reality meant removing the possibility of appeal to the Royal Governor and Council and King in Council. Lawyers participated in criminal trials but their professional influence was viewed with suspicion with "An Act relating to Attorneys." This law provided that any person appearing in court, whether as plaintiff or defendant, was entitled to plead for himself or to engage another to do so whether an attorney or not. Those attorneys who did appear were required to take an oath.[24] Anti-lawyer sentiment was not uncommon in the Early Republic. John E. O'Connor suggests that this was so partly because only lawyers could really interpret the mysteries of the common law.[25] By the late eighteenth century, however, lawyers were becoming a necessity because of the more complex demands of a growing population and commercial networks.[26] Maxwell Bloomfield links the unfavorable public opinion of lawyers during the Jacksonian era (the late 1820's through 1840's) to reformers who wanted to bring the law under the people's control rather than leave it in the hands of professionals. Several states, including New Hampshire, eliminated formal requirements for becoming a lawyer at this time. All that was now required for recognition as a lawyer was that one be a citizen of "good moral character."[27]

A major change in New Hampshire's court structure took place on February 21, 1794 when the legislature voted to abolish the courts of general sessions of the peace. All of the authority formerly vested in those courts was transferred to the courts of common pleas: "And it shall be the duty of said courts of common pleas, within their respective counties, to hear, try and determine all indictments, complaints, petitions, causes, matters and things of any name or nature whatsoever, except granting taxes..."[28] New Hampshire was following a national trend in substituting the courts of common pleas for the courts of general sessions. A number of states were growing in wealth and population and found the old court structure inadequate for the increasing volume of cases.[29] There was also a widening distinction between trial courts and courts of appeal. Courts of common pleas, an intermediate level of court, enjoyed a wide jurisdiction. Their presence resulted in uniting the state supreme courts to appellate jurisdiction.[30] In New Hampshire a related law of 1794 gave the justices of the superior court of judicature the power to grant one review or new trial after a judgment made in the same court or court of common pleas, or the just-abolished general sessions of the peace.[31]

The new Supreme Judicial Court, established in 1813, was intended for trying crimes rating a death sentence or life in prison.[32] "An Act Establishing a Supreme Judicial Court, and Circuit Court of Common Pleas" was passed on June 24, 1813. It was repealed on June 27, 1816 but is mentioned here because this arrangement was in effect during the earliest years of the state prison. The jurisdiction and authority held by the old Superior Court of Judicature was transferred to the new Supreme Judicial Court. The new court was composed of a chief justice and two associate justices appointed by the governor and council.[33]

State grants of legal autonomy to municipalities represents a major trend in American law. One manifestation of this was the establishment of professional police forces in American cities during the nineteenth century. It was a response to urbanization and Portsmouth may serve as an example for this change in New Hampshire. David R. Johnson links the appearance of police in America to urbanization after 1800. His thesis is that criminal behavior influenced the development of the modern police. In particular, Johnson discusses professional theft, street crime, and illegal enterprise (gambling and prostitution). These forms of behavior became increasingly problematic and the public took action with the creation of police forces in American cities starting in the 1830's.[34] As early as 1807 the New Hampshire legislature passed "An Act for the Regulation of the Police in the Town of Portsmouth" which created the state's first professional police force.[35]

Demographic changes helped lead the way to "An Act to establish a System of Police in the town of Portsmouth and for other purposes" passed June 28, 1823 by the New Hampshire legislature.[36] Instead of the old system of village constables, nightwatchmen, or private guards, the town of Portsmouth was to rely on seven "reputable freeholders" chosen by the selectmen for a one-year period.[37] Their main duty was to arrest persons engaged in "riotous, wanton or indecent conduct." The offenses described were not felonies but, like rural constables, the police were expected to apprehend anyone engaged in more serious offenses. These developments paralleled those in larger cities. Roger Lane sees the emergence of the police in Boston in 1822 as part of the urbanization process.[38] Linked to urbanization was the need to control behavior such as public drunkenness, vagabondage, assault, and lewdness.[39] In Philadelphia, the introduction of professional plice was a response to public disorders created by ethnic tensions and the presence of gangs.[40]

In New Hampshire an important component in the drive for local autonomy was the establishment of police courts in 1852. This gave local municipalities more power to determine which (nonfelonious) cases would be tried at the county level and which kept within town jurisdiction. Towns thus had more control over the judicial process than before. Every town was eligible to establish a police court made up of "one able, learned and discreet person, to be appointed and commissioned by the governor...to take cognizance of all crimes and offences and misdemeanors committed within said town, whereof justices of the peace now have or may hereafter have jurisdiction."[41]

The state increased the powers of the police. In 1842 "any police officer upon view of any offence committed against the provisions of this chapter [the law distinguished between offenders against the state and offenders against towns], may arrest the offender and forthwith carry him before a justice of the peace..."[42] Watchmen "shall be appointed and qualified in the same manner and shall have while on duty the same powers as police officers."[43] Watchmen remained a typical feature of most American cities until the 1850's.[44] By 1852 the police were becoming a more common part of the law enforcement apparatus in New Hampshire. They were still appointed on a temporary basis by town selectmen. The police were to be used "in the detection and conviction of criminals and the prevention of crime in their town..."[45]

The increasing professionalism of law enforcement methods is evident in the 1907 law permitting officers to measure and describe "prisoners, suspicious persons or lodgers" in their custody according to the Bertillon method. Officers were also authorized to photograph such persons and to take fingerprints.[46]

By 1911 the growth of urban centers in New Hampshire made it necessary to establish some sort of statewide level of coordination between municipalities to control crime. In that year sheriffs and deputies were given statewide power to "serve criminal or civil processes, investigate crime, and to pursue and apprehend criminals that they now have in their respective counties."[47] This arrangement was the forerunner of the state police system which did not emerge in New Hampshire until 1937. Some sort of statewide law enforcement was needed, especially with the advent of the automobile.

Jacksonian politics were very popular in New Hampshire during the years 1829-46 and thus some of the changes in the court structure found in the statutes compiled in 1842 reflect the Democratic character of the times.[48] No jurors were to be summoned to the Superior Court of Judicature. Instead, if it became necessary to ascertain any facts by a jury, "an issue shall be made up, under the direction of said court, and transmitted to the court of common pleas for trial, and the verdict of the jury thereon shall be certified to said superior court, and judgment rendered thereon as the case may require."[49]

Liberal reformers of the times were concerned about the potential danger of allowing unelected officials to excercise power over the general population. In theory, the jury could declare a defendant guilty only when the facts described in the trial fully matched the legal description of the crime in question. However, the jury was not obliged to defend or explain its verdict. By 1900 in New Hampshire the judge decided questions of law while the jury decided only questions of fact in most states.[50]

The Jacksonian impulse was not unlimited. A seat on the jury was not necessarily available to all citizens. Every December, the selectmen of each town in New Hampshire were required to draw up a list of potential jurors. The number of jurors was determined by the number of rateable polls (i.e., those white males who paid a minimum property tax). In practice, this meant a minimum of 15 potential jurors to a maximum of 45, per town. Persons of certain occupations such as ordained ministers, attorneys, and the Governor of New Hampshire were exempt.[51]

To summarize, the criminal justice system of New Hampshire was relatively stable after 1816. While some of the nomenclature changed, the essentials of a multilayered system created to deal with varying levels of crime stayed in place. At the lowest level, justices of the peace provided basic criminal justice. Police courts took over much of the burden in 1852 but did not fully replace justices of the peace. The greatest change in court structure took place at the middle level. The Court of Common Pleas and the Circuit Court periodically appeared and disappeared. Finally, in 1859, the Court of Common Pleas disappeared for good and the Supreme Court of Judicature took cognizance of all felony trials. Occasionally, the geographic boundaries and session dates changed at the highest level of appellate and trial court. The court also changed its name and was variously referred to as the supreme court or as the superior court.

Urbanization led to the introduction of police in Portsmouth in 1807 and thus paved the way for local legal autonomy for municipalities. Towns began to enjoy greater control over criminal justice as their law enforcement and judicial mechanisms became more professional. At the same time, the more traditional forms of law enforcement persisted. As late as 1914 nightwatchmen were still employed in some towns. While professional police officers did become more widespread as the state grew more urban, most of the law enforcement personnel found in New Hampshire were modified holdovers from medieval England: sheriffs and deputies, constables, and coroners.

We must now examine one final component of the criminal justice system: the trial process. Between 1641 and 1679, when New Hampshire was part of Massachusetts, a typical criminal cases might begin with the arrest of an alleged offender by the local constable, marshal, or sheriff. In serious cases the suspect was bound over by a justice of the peace to await trial. After a jury of 12 "good and lawful" men was summoned, the attorney general indicted the accused (i.e., formally charged him or her with an offense). If the jury found the indictment proper, they returned a presentment and the trial began.[52] If the accused was found guilty, he or she was detained in the local jail to await punishment. According to Douglas Greenberg, prosecutions were speedy in seventeenth-century Massachusetts.[53]

The trial process remained unchanged after New Hampshire was made a separate royal province in 1679. Law specified the number of jurors as 12 "good and lawful men according to the commendable custom of England." All serious criminal and capital trials were held before the Supreme Court of Judicature.[54] The basic process stayed unchanged with the provincial reorganization of 1692. Sheriffs and constables were given the right of requesting any person to help capture and arrest "any person or persons for violateing the same [peace], or for any other Criminal matter or cause." Those refusing such aid were liable to be fined up to twenty shillings, to be committed to forty-four hours in jail, or four hours in the stocks. This law stayed in effect until 1792.[55]

Antifederalism played a role in the development of the criminal justice system in New Hampshire just as it affected the judicial system of national government. Antifederalism had a long tradition in America. Antifederalists feared that the "consolidated government" outlined by the Constitution would result in the creation of a new aristocracy.[56] Conflict between the state and federal governments was a reality from the very beginning of American history. Some antifederalists were so worried about the power of the central government that several early state constitutions maintained the principle of the right to oppose the central government and the right to make their own constitutional changes.[57] Antifederalists such as Governor William Paterson of New Jersey in the 1790's considered the Federal Government of the United States to be a threat to the individual states and their citizens.[58] Antifederalists were concerned with the judicial system because they believed that under the common law tradition judges had the power to interpret the law so as to, within limits, create the law according to their own whim.[59] Thus, the selection and control of judges was crucial. Antifederalists feared the domination of the judicial system by an elite. Some of this sentiment found expression in New Hampshire laws dealing with the trial process. For example, safeguards protecting the rights of the accused were passed in 1791. No one accused of a capital crime was to be tried until the grand jury of the superior court of judicature found a bill of indictment against him or her. Such a trial was to be held in the county where the offense allegedly took place. The accused was also entitled to a copy of the indictment and a list of witnesses and jurors 48 hours before the trial. He or she was also entitled to have up to two lawyers assigned by the court.[60] This was consistent with antifederalist support for the original Bill of Rights.[61] Also, in a trial for a capital crime, the accused was permitted to challenge the jury.[62]

Early New Hampshire statutes also specified the oaths to be taken and procedures to be followed by grand jurors and petit jurors in criminal cases. Members of the grand jury had to swear that "The State's counsel, your fellows, and your own you shall keep secret; you shall present no man for envy, hatred or malice; neither shall you leave any unpresented for love, fear, favor, affection, or hope of reward; but you shall present things truly, as they come to your knowledge, according to the best of your understanding. So help you GOD."[63] A presentment was an accusation brought by the grand jury in the form of a bill of indictment. The indictment was now a written accusation found and presented by a grand jury to commit and charge the person with an act which was against the law and punishable. The indictment was the physical means for starting the trial. The main purpose was to identify formally the alleged offense.[64]

The laws on the trial process evolved over the first half of the century with antifederalism feeding into Jacksonian ideas. We can document this by looking at the laws as they existed in 1842 and as they continued to evolve in the remainder of the century. Briefly, the criminal trial process went as follows. A grand jury indictment was required for an offense punishable by a term in the state prison. No longer was this applicable just to capital cases. Every person indicted for a capital offense or a life term in the state prison was entitled to a copy of the indictment before arraignment. Again, this looks like an attempt by Jacksonian-era reformers to protect the rights of the people against undue oppression by the state. Arraignment was the process where the accused was brought before the court to plead to the charge as read. The choice of plea was guilty, not guilty, or nolo contendere (a plea subjecting the accused to conviction but not admitting guilt).[65] As before, the accused had the right to see a list of witnesses and jurors 48 hours before the trial and could request up to two lawyers to be assigned for his or her defense by the court. This was moved up to 24 hours before the trial by 1901. The defendant could peremptorily challenge up to 20 jurors and more if there was sufficient cause.[66]

From the early days, provisions had been made for bail. In 1901 the law stated, "All persons arrested for crime shall, before conviction, be bailable by sufficient securities, except for capital offenses where the proof is evident or the presumption great...Minors and married women, and their sureties shall be bound by their recognizances in the same manner as if the principals were of full age and unmarried." Even witnesses were required to pay a recognizance to ensure their appearance at court.[67]

Safeguards on behalf of the accused were also passed into law. "No minor under the age of sixteen years, or person supposed to be of unsound mind, shall be permitted to plead guilty or shall be put upon his trial until counsel have been appointed to advise him and conduct his defense. If such person is poor, witnesses may, on motion of his counsel, be summoned in his behalf at the expense of the county."[68]

Juvenile law sought to balance the rights of the accused with the public's right to be a parent, hence, these cases were often heard in equity or probate court. Ever since the 1850's juvenile offenders had been treated as a separate category in New Hampshire. Reform schools had been established in American cities as far back as the 1820's. By the late nineteenth century they were increasingly perceived as inadequate institutions.[69] Minors had been subject to the concept of *parens patriae* which authorized the state to intervene in family relationships whenever the child's welfare seemed to be at risk.[70] Beginning in Illinois in 1898, the concept of the juvenile court was eventually instituted in nearly all states by 1925.[71] The juvenile court was intended to provide a separate and more appropriate form of justice for juvenile offenders. Unfortunately, the juvenile court ended up as yet another form of social control that was not particularly beneficial for the subject.[72] The New Hampshire statute protecting minors under the age of 16 was part of the process of differentiating criminal justice by age group. Just as adolescence was regarded as a distinct phase in life in America by 1900, the institutionalization of a separate form of criminal justice was now considered to be appropriate for juvenile offenders.

While efforts were underway to ensure fair treatment of the accused in New Hampshire, there were also provisions for ensuring the public's right to produce enough evidence to convict a suspected criminal. In 1901 a justice of the peace or police court had the power to issue a search warrant for searching "any place therein described, in the daytime, upon complaint, under oath, that it was believed that a person liable to arrest for a crime was concealed therein, or that gambling was carried on therein."[73] A search warrant was also applicable in case it was believed that the following sorts of property were located inside the "place: property believed to have been stolen, embezzled, or fraudulently obtained; false, forged, or counterfeited bank bills and similar legal documents; gambling equipment; burglar's tools; spiritous or intoxicating liquors, gunpowder or explosives in a quantity or manner forbidden by law," and the catch-all "subject matter of any offense not here specially mentioned."[74] Unfortunately, the court records used for this project reveal nothing directly about the employment of this power. One can surmise that it was used by the extremely detailed descriptions of property affected in most property crimes. Not only is absolutely every item accounted for in most such records but the exact valuation is also provided. The ability to seize such crucial evidence must have been important for the prosecution of the accused. The only problem with this assumption is that detailed property inventories are available for the entire period, not just 1901-14.

So far we have reviewed the changing laws regarding crime and the evolution of the criminal justice system in New Hampshire. The changeover from corporal punishment and fines to imprisonment for serious crime was complete upon the opening of the State Prison in Concord in 1812. The construction of the prison marked a new stage in penal history. Some background information on the establishment of the institution is required in order to understand the prison's function in the criminal justice system of nineteenth-century New Hampshire.

Prisons were first described as distinct buildings in New Hampshire laws in "An Order Relative to Fort Loyal, the Compensation of the Commander and the Use of It as a Prison" on June 2-3, 1686. Captain Edward Ting or Tyng was made commander of Fort Loyal which was to be "made use of as a prison for the present."[75] At this time, prisons were rather impromptu structures with little resemblance to the imposing stone edifices to come.[76] Prior to Fort Loyal the only prisons mentioned in the laws were apparently private dwellings. In the 1679 laws, the "houses & yards of the said Keepers, shal be allowed & accounted the precincts of the said prisons."[77] The next mention of a prison in the New Hampshire province laws was "An Act for Providing for a Prison" (May 1695). The sole prison provided for all of New Hampshire was to be Samuel Cutts's windmill in Portsmouth which was "to be fitted for a Prison."[78] "An Act for Providing for a Prison in This Province" passed July 2, 1697 designated "the ffort on m'r Thomas Grafforts Hill at Portsmo'" as a prison.[79] On November 9, 1699 the Council and General Assembly voted, "That a strong logg house be built in the Province for a Prison, of thirty foot long, fourteen wide, one story of seven foot high, two brick chimneys in the mids, five foot each, to be don forthwith strong and substantial, the Treasurer, the Overseer, and the charge, to be paid out of the next Province Assessment, to be sett in Portsmouth, in or near the Great Fort."[80]

There was no concept yet of prison as an instrument for reforming criminals. Prison as a means of reforming criminals was an idea of the Enlightenment that did not fully emerge until late in the eighteenth century. Until then crime was viewed as sin which meant that punishment consisted of retribution and incapacitation. Even Cesare Beccaria focused on prisons more as a means of deterrence than reformation.[81] The first real prison legislation in New Hampshire was passed on May 15, 1714.[82] What were the purposes of and who were the inmates of such a prison? the only long-term inmates of a New Hampshire prison before the 1790's were debtors.[83] Imprisonment for debt was not so much a form of punishment as security for the creditor. A debtor in prison was much less likely to disappear from the scene - even if he couldn't very well manage to raise money to pay back his creditors. None of the criminal statutes before the 1790's specified imprisonment as a method of punishment for criminals. There was no concept yet of prison as an instrument for reforming criminals. Persons were committed to prison to await trial, to await the imposition of their punishment, for short-term detention as a public safety measure, or as prisoners of war. In fact, prison keepers who allowed a convicted prisoner to escape would be penalized by suffering the same punishment prescribed for the escapee. This applied to debtors too: "And if the prisoner soe Escaping were Imprisoned for Debt the prison Keeper whall be Answereable to the Creditor for the full debt."[84] Without a doubt, the law encouraged vigilance on the part of the prison keeper.

Until the laws were revised in the 1790's, the prison's function in New Hampshire cannot be accurately described as punitive. This began to change in the early nineteenth century. The first real proposal for a state prison was made in the New Hampshire House of Representatives on June 12, 1804. Governor John T. Gilman declared, "The frequent escapes of criminals and others from our common prisons seems to require the attention of the Legislature to the subject - when the hope of impunity is great, one mean [sic] of preventing crimes is wanting - If some plan could be devised and carried into execution for confining criminals to labour, it might have a tendency to reform them; or at least those who were able to labour might earn their living without expence to the public."[85] The idea of reforming criminals was a new concept; this is an early expression of an environmental explanation for crime. Rather than seeing criminals purely as sinners or purely as rational beings who made decisions to commit crimes, reformers began viewing criminals as a product of their environment. Reformers thought that it might be possible to undo the damage inflicted upon a criminal in his childhood and thus to "reform" him.[86]

Gilman's statement illustrates a major shift in regard to the purposes of punishment. Three purposes of imprisonment are evident in Gilman's statement: 1) preventing crime, 2) reforming the criminal, and 3) ensuring that the plan be economically self-supporting. The second and third points are very important. They represent a major intellectual shift in regard to the purposes of punishment. Instead of only deterrence, the purpose now included the reformation of the criminal which foreshadowed the change in criminology from the classical school to the positivist school. A committee of the House was formed to study the problem.[87] No further mention can be found in the New Hampshire House or Senate journals until December 26, 1805. At this date, the House merely agreed to postpone to the next session the committee's report. The report is probably the first link in the chain between Governor Gilman's proposal and the New Hampshire Senate committee headed by Daniel Webster which presented Governor Plumer with a proposal to revise the criminal code in 1812.

The report in question appears to exist only in manuscript form and is titled "Prison Commetee's [sic] Report of 1805." According to the committee, a location "near the Academy" in Concord was the most suitable site for a prison and that the total cost of the prison, the yard, overseer's buildings, and workshops was estimated to be $48,000.[88] The stone building material was to be supplied for free by "a number of Gentlemen belonging to said Town." Architectural plans were submitted along with the committee's report. The proposed stone was described as "in every respect Suitable for the importance of the work" by Stuart Park, superintendent of the Massachusetts State Prison. Park supervised the construction at Concord. Park had built several jails and prisons in New England including the Massachusetts State Prison in 1803-06 and the Vermont State Prison in 1809.[89]

Prison architecture was an essential component of reform ideology in the early nineteenth century. As early as 1768 in England the rebuilt Newgate Prison in London had been designed with reformation of the inmates in mind. John Bender says that the building "reminded all who would enter, or even pass by, of the power of confinement to alter the spirit through material representation."[90] David J. Rothman speaks of the "moral architecture" that characterized prisons and other institutions built in early nineteenth-century America. Architects designing prisons provided for the isolation of the prisoner and the establishment of a disciplined routine necessary for reform.[91] Museum curator William N. Hosley, Jr. points out that the workshop and individual cells housing each inmate at the Vermont State prison were "important features" of the reform program. He also states, "That a well-designed prison would resemble a university suggests the lofty aspirations of the prison reform movement."[92] The New Hampshire plans called for a three-story structure measuring eighty-five feet long by forty-two feet wide with sixteen rooms each on the first and second floor and eight rooms at the top. Cells measured seven and a half by ten feet except for the third floor where they were eleven and a half by eighteen feet. The first two floors had a "convict eating room" measuring approximately eighty-five feet long by ten feet wide. On the third floor this space was designated as the "Inspectors Walk." The walls were four feet thick except for the third floor where they were three feet thick.[93]

The New Hampshire State Prison plans cited above were similar to the Auburn, New York plan of 1816 in that inmates were isolated in their cells at night but mingled together in silence in the dining hall and while at work. These plans embodied some of the major objectives of the early prison reformers, including isolation and inspection of inmates. The initial plans for New Hampshire were not for a large prison; this would cause problems later on.

The prison plans languished in committees over the next three years. Finally, on December 17, 1808 the House authorized a committee of three to receive proposals for building the prison and to superintend its construction.[94]

Although a place of punishment, the prison was also a place of reformation and as such was a symbol of modernity. This ties in with the concept of the prison as a reforming institution. As Hosley points out, state prisons were looked upon as status symbols in the early nineteenth century. Prisons were regarded as progressive, humane institutions designed to create good citizens out of criminals.[95] Thus, one should not be surprised at the relative ease with which land and building materials for the New Hampshire State Prison were acquired: two acres of land were deeded to the State by Joshua Abbott and an initial 3000 tons of stone located in a Concord quarry a mile and a half away. However, the town fathers were taking no chances; the site chosen was so removed from the center of Concord that a special road had to be constructed just to reach the prison.[96]

The dimensions of the prison were enlarged from the original plan in 1810. Now the House of Representatives wanted two wings, each eighty feet long, thirty-six feet wide, three stories high, and containing thirty-six rooms each. Attached to the prison would be the superintendent's house, fifty feet long, twenty-two feet wide, and three stories high. In back of the prison would be a wooden workshop measuring one hundred feet long, twenty-five feet wide, and two stories high. The whole was to be enclosed by a fourteen-foot high stone wall. The cost was estimated at $35,000.[97] The deadline for completion was extended another four years.[98]

The era of imprisonment and belief in its reformative effect was about to begin. "As it is highly probable that the State Prison will, in the course of this season, be completed," observed Governor William Plumer on June 11, 1812, "it will be necessary that our code of criminal law should be revised, and also police laws enacted for the government of this new and important institution."[99] Two hundred copies of the proposed bill revising the criminal code were printed the next day and distributed to members of the New Hampshire House. Meanwhile, the House approved another installment of $10,300 for finishing the State Prison. On June 17 the House passed "An Act providing for the regulation and government of the State Prison" and "An Act to punish certain crimes by solitary imprisonment and confinement to hard labor" on June 19.[100] The Legislature also approved a $1200 appropriation as start-up costs for "stock and tools for labor, victuals and clothes for the prisoners &c."[101]

Once the new law mandating punishment at hard labor was passed on June 19, the directors of the prison took appropriate measures. On October 9 they voted to request the governor to place an order for $500 from the state treasurer "for the support maintenance and employment of the convicts" who would start arriving in the near future.[102]

Three weeks later the directors voted to use the money to purchase "sundry blacksmith's tools and apparatus now in the Smith's shop" and "also a quantity of Iron."[103] "An Act Providing for the Regulation and Government of the State Prison" was passed on June 19, 1812. It provided a legal framework for the powers of prison personnel and financial administration. On November 17 the directors drew up a six-article set of rules and bylaws regulating daily life within the prison.

As early as May 22, 1812 applications for the warden's position began to arrive in Concord. William Colston of Claremont, New Hampshire sent a letter addressed to "The Board of visitors or Derectors of the States Prison" expressing his interest in the job. His experience at the recently-constructed Vermont State Prison consisted of 21 months as an overseer and master weaver. Included with Colston's application was a "character" (letter of recommendation) signed by 12 of "the most respectable Gentlemen in Windsor [Vermont]" dated May 7, 1812.[104] Also included was a short "character" from William Leverett and Oliver Farnsworth, visitors of the Vermont State Prison. As it turned out, the governor of New Hampshire with the advice and consent of the council appointed the prison warden and Colston did not get the job.[105] Trueworthy G. Dearborn of Greenland, New Hampshire was appointed warden with a salary of $500 a year and Samuel Sparhawk and Samuel Green of Concord were appointed directors of the prison at a meeting of the governor and council held August 10.[106] It was impossible to find out whether Dearborn had been a political supporter of the governor but political loyalties definitely played a part in the appointment of some later wardens.[107]

The building which opened its doors in November, 1812 was made of granite quarried from Rattlesnake Hill near Concord, New Hampshire. Its final dimensions were one wing seventy feet long, thirty-six feet wide and walls three feet thick. There were thirty-six cells. Those on the first and second floor measured eight feet by nine feet while the six cells located on the third floor were a more generous ten feet by seventeen feet and were intended for sick prisoners. The structure was surrounded by a fourteen-foot granite wall. Initial costs came to $37,069.76.[108]

Warden Dearborn was not slow to advertise the fact that the prison was ready for business. In the *New-Hampshire Patriot* and *Concord Gazette* he ran the following notice: "The Sheriffs of the several Counties in the state of New-Hampshire, are hereby notified, that the STATE PRISON, at Concord, is now ready for the reception of any convicts sentenced to said Prison.[109] On November 23, 1812 the prison doors swung open to admit the State's first convict. He was a thirty-one year old horse thief from Meredith, New Hampshire named John Drew. His sentence was four years at hard labor.[110]

Chapter Three will be devoted to an analysis of the crimes committed by the inmates who served time in the State Prison during the period 1812-1914. We will attempt to make generalizations about the inmates themselves with the aid of a quantitative study in Chapter Four. Finally, we will examine punishment in action in a detailed analysis of prison practice over the period 1812-1914. Changes and their significance will be analyzed to understand how a society defined crime and coped with it.

Notes

1. Edwin Powers, *Crime and Punishment in Early Massachusetts: 1620-1692 A Documentary History* (Boston, 1966), p. 46.
2. *Ibid.*, p. 148.
3. *Ibid.*, p. 57.
4. *Ibid.*, p. 59.
5. *Ibid.*, p. 57
6. *Ibid.*, pp. 89-90.
7. Elwin Page, *Judicial Beginnings in New Hampshire 1640-1700* (Concord, N.H., 1959), pp. 16-17 and 20.
8. *Ibid.*, p. 50
9. Joseph M. Devine, "A Legal Study of Colonial New Hampshire, 1640-1692." Unpublished MS for Harvard Law School Class, (Oct. 1946), 17. New Hampshire Historical Society, Concord, N.H.
10. Page, *Judicial Beginnings in New Hampshire*, p. 55.
11. *Ibid.*, p. 58 and Lawrence M. Friedman, *A History of American Law*, 2nd. ed. (New York, 1985), p. 45.
12. Powers, *Crime and Punishment*, pp. 431-32.
13. *Ibid.*, pp. 432 and 599.
14. Albert S. Batchellor, ed., *Laws of New Hampshire*, Vol. 2 *1702-1745* (Concord, N.H., 1913), p. 144.
15. See Chapter Two of Joan R. Kent, *The English Village Constable 1580-1642: A Social and Administrative Study* (Oxford, 1986), pp. 24-56.
16. Batchellor, ed., *Laws of New Hampshire (1702-45)*, pp. 320-24.
17. Albert S. Batchellor, ed., *Laws of New Hampshire*, Vol. 1 *Province Period 1679-1702* (Manchester, N.H., 1904), p. 24.
18. *Ibid.*, p. 25.
19. *Ibid.*, p. 542.
20. *Ibid.*, p. 543.
21. *Ibid.*, pp. 543-44.
22. The Quarterly Court of Sessions was renamed the Court of Sessions of the Peace. The Supreme Court of Judicature was renamed the Superiour [sic] Court of Judicature. Further appeal was possible to the Governor and Council ("provided the value appealed for exceed the Sum of One Hundred Pounds Sterling"). Finally, one could appeal to the King in Council if the case involved over L300. *Ibid.*, p. 664.

23. The court structure was established as follows: a Superior Court of Judicature made up of four justices appointed by the Council and House of Representatives, an Inferior Court of Common Pleas for each county made up of four justices, and a Court of General Quarter Sessions of the Peace for each county. This act was in effect until repealed on June 20, 1792. Henry H. Metcalf, ed., *Laws of New Hampshire*, Vol. 4 *Revolutionary Period 1776-1784* (Bristol, N.H., 1916), p. 34.

24. *The Laws of the State of New-Hampshire...* (Portsmouth, N.H., 1792), p. 102.

25. John E. O'Connor, "Legal Reform in the Early Republic: The New Jersey Experience," *American Journal of Legal History*, 22 (1978), 113.

26. Richard E. Ellis, *The Jeffersonian Crisis: Courts and Politics in the Young Republic* (New York, 1971), p. 111.

27. Maxwell Bloomfield, *American Lawyers in a Changing Society, 1776-1876* (Cambridge, Mass., 1976), p. 85.

28. *Laws of the State of New-Hampshire...* (Portsmouth, N.H., 1797), pp. 64-65.

29. Friedman, *History of American Law*, p. 141.

30. *Ibid.*, p. 141.

31. *Ibid.*, pp. 75-76.

32. *Laws of New Hampshire*, Vol. 8 *Second Constitutional Period 1811-1820* (Concord, N.H., 1920), pp. 251-252.

33. *Ibid.*, pp. 251-252.

34. David R. Johnson, *Policing the Underworld: The Impact of Crime on the Development of the American Police, 1800-1887* (Philadelphia, 1979), pp. 3-11.

35. *A Journal of the Honorable Senate of the State of New-Hampshire...June, Anno Domini, 1807* (Amherst, N.H., 1808), 54.

36. *The Laws of the State of New-Hampshire, Enacted Since June 1, 1815...*, Vol. II (Concord, N.H., 1824), pp. 190-93.

37. *Ibid.*, p. 190.

38. Roger Lane, *Policing the City: Boston 1822-1885* (Cambridge, Mass., 1967), p. 3.

39. According to Lane, the old arrangement of sheriffs, constables, and watchmen was increasingly unable to cope with these problems in Boston, whose population had reached 43,298 by 1820. Portsmouth's population stood at 7327 in 1820 which was small compared to Boston but the largest urban center in New Hampshire at the time. *Ibid.*, pp. 6 and 238 and *Census for 1820* (Woodbridge, Conn.: Research Publications, Inc.), microfilm.

40. Allen Steinberg, *The Transformation of Criminal Justice: Philadelphia, 1800-1880* (Chapel Hill, N.C., 1989), pp. 119-20.

41. *The Compiled Statutes of the State of New-Hampshire...*, 2nd. ed. (Concord, N.H., 1854), p. 444.

42. *The Revised Statutes of the State of New-Hampshire, Passed December 23, 1842...* (Concord, N.H., 1843), p. 224.

43. *Ibid.*, p. 225.

44. Johnson, *Policing the Urban Underworld*, p. 15.

45. *The General Laws of the State of New-Hampshire...* (Manchester, N.H., 1878), p. 582.

46. William M. Chase, ed. and Arthur H. Chase, comp., *Supplement to the Public Statutes of New Hampshire (Chase Edition, 1901)* (Concord, N.H., 1914), p. 511. Alphonse Bertillon of France designed a method of identifying criminals through a system of bodily measurements and photographs in the late nineteenth century. Although the bodily measurement system is now outmoded, the photographic methods introduced by Bertillon are still employed by law enforcement agencies today. Jay R. Nash, *Encyclopedia of World Crime*, Vol. 1 (Wilmette, Ill., 1989), pp. 349-51.

47. Chase and Chase, ed. and comp., *Supplement to Public Statutes (1914)*, p. 502.

48. J. Duane Squires, *The Granite State of the United States: A History of New Hampshire from 1623 to the Present*, Vol. 1 (New York, 1956), p. 202.

49. Now New Hampshire was divided into five judicial districts. *Revised Statues (1842)*, pp. 340-41.

50. David J. Bodenhamer, "The Democratic Impulse and Legal Change in the Age of Jackson: The Example of Criminal Juries in Antebellum Indiana," *Historian*, 45 (1983), 206-19.

51. *Revised Statutes (1842)*, p. 348.

52. Page, *Judicial Beginnings in New Hampshire*, pp. 106-08.

53. Douglas Greenberg, "Crime, Law Enforcement, and Social Control in Colonial America," *American Journal of Legal History*, 26 (1982), 298-99.

54. Batchellor, ed., *Laws of New Hampshire (1679-1702)*, p. 25.

55. *Ibid.*, p. 685.

56. Alpheus T. Mason, *The States Rights Debate: Antifederalism and the Constitution* (Englewood Cliffs, N.J., 1964), p. 14 and John D. Lewis, ed. *Anti-Federalists Versus Federalists: Selected Documents* (San Francisco, 1967), p. 2.

57. J.R. Pole, "Preconditions of American Unity" in Rhodri Jeffreys-Jones and

Bruce Collins, eds., *The Growth of Federal Power in American History* (Dekalb, Ill., 1983), p. 1 and Willi Paul Adams, *The First American Constitutions: Republican Ideology and the Making of the State Constitutions in the Revolutionary Era* (Trans. by Rita and Robert Kimber) (Chapel Hill, N.C., 1980), p. 137.

58. Mason, *States Rights Debate*, pp. 67 and 77.

59. Friedman, *History of American Law*, pp. 124-25.

60. *Laws of New Hampshire (1797)*, p. 272.

61. Friedman, *History of American Law*, p. 150.

62. *Laws of New Hampshire (1797)*, p. 273.

63. *The Laws of the State of New-Hampshire* (Portsmouth, N.H., 1792), p. 97.

64. Henry C. Black, *Black's Law Dictionary*, 5th. ed. (St. Paul, 1979), pp. 695 and 1066.

65. *Ibid.*, p. 100.

66. *Revised Statutes (1842)*, pp. 457-58 and William M. Chase and Arthur H, Chase, comp. and ed., *The Public Statutes of the State of New Hampshire, and General Laws in Force January 1, 1901* (Concord, N.H., 1900), p. 783.

67. Chase and Chase, ed. and comp., *Public Statutes (1901)*, pp. 778-79.

68. *Ibid.*, p. 784. The minimum age was raised to 17 years in 1913. Chase, ed., *Supplement to Public Statutes (1914)*, p. 512.

69. Robert M. Mennel, *Thorns and Thistles: Juvenile Delinquents in the United States 1825-1940* (Hanover, N.H., 1973), pp. 124-25.

70. Steven L. Schlossman, *Love and the American Delinquent: The Theory and Practice of "Progressive" Juvenile Justice, 1825-1920* (Chicago, 1977), p. 8.

71. Mennel, *Thorns and Thistles*, p. 132.

72. Schlossman, *Love and American Delinquent*, p. 169.

73. Chase and Chase, ed., *Public Statutes (1901)*, p. 775.

74. *Ibid.*, p. 775.

75. Batchellor, ed., *Laws of New Hampshire (1679-1702)*, p. 114.

76. Negley K. Teeters, *The Cradle of the Penitentiary: The Walnut Street Jail at Philadelphia, 1773-1835* (Pennsylvania Prison Society, 1955), p. 8.

77. Batchellor, ed., *Laws of New Hampshire (1679-1702)*, p. 22.

78. *Ibid.*, p. 576.

79. *Ibid.*, p. 590.

80. Nathaniel Bouton, ed. and comp., *Provincial Papers: Documents and Records Relating to the Province of New-Hampshire from 1692 to 1722...*, Vol. 3 (Manchester, N.H., 1869), p. 88.

81. Marcello Maestro, *Cesare Beccaria and the Origins of Penal Reform*

(Philadelphia, 1973), pp. 24-27.

82. "An Act for the Regulation of Prisons and to Prevent Escapes" specified the duties and obligations of "Every Goaler [sic] or Keeper of the Queens [sic] Prison within This Her Majesties Province." See Batchellor, ed., *laws of New Hampshire*, Vol. 2 *(1702-1745)*, p. 22.

83. Batchellor, ed., *Laws of New Hampshire (1702-1745)*, p. 132.

84. *Ibid.*, p. 132.

85. *Journal of the House of Representatives...June, Anno Domini, 1804*, 24.

86. David J. Rothman, *The Discovery of the Asylum: Social Order and Disorder in the New Republic* (Boston, 1971), pp. 65-71.

87. On June 20 the committee reported, "That it is highly necessary to erect a State prison." The House agreed with the concept and decided to appoint another committee of three to investigate the idea further for purposes of writing a bill for the next session. *Journal of the House, June, 1804*, 56.

88. "Prison Commettee's [sic] Report of 1805," MS, State Prison Papers, Div. of Records-Management and Archives, Concord, N.H.

89. William N. Hosley, Jr., "The Founding of the Vermont State Prison in Windsor, 1807-1810," *Vermont History*, 52 (1984), 245.

90. John Bender, *Imagining the Penitentiary: Fiction and the Architecture of Mind in Eighteenth-Century England* (Chicago, 1987), p. 21.

91. Rothman, *Discovery of the Asylum*, pp. 82 and 84.

92. Hosley, "Vermont State Prison," 244-45.

93. Untitled State Prison Plans, MS, State Prison Papers, Div. of Records-Management and Archives, Concord, N.H.

94. *Journal of the House of Representatives...November, 1808*, 97-98.

95. Hosley, "Vermont State Prison," 245.

96. Henry Robinson, "The New Hampshire State Prison," *Granite Monthly*, 23 (1897), 217.

97. *Journal of the House of Representatives...June, 1810*, 108.

98. *Ibid.*, 108.

99. *Journal of the House of Representatives...June, 1812*, 28-29.

100. *Ibid.*, pp. 113-14, 116, and 121-22.

101. *New-Hampshire Patriot*, June 23, 1812.

102. Minute Book 1812-34, MS, State Prison Papers, Div. of Records-Management and Archives, Concord, N.H.

103. *Ibid.*

104. William Colston to The Board of visitors or Derectors of the States Prison, ALS, 22 May 1812, State Prison Papers, Div. of Records-Management and Archives, Concord, N.H.

68

105. *The Laws of the State of New-Hampshire...* (Exeter, N.H., 1815), p. 143.

106. Council Minutes Book 5, 10 August 1812, MS, Div. of Records-Management and Archives, Concord, N.H.

107. For example, Samuel Bell excoriated Governor Isaac Hill for appointing Abner Stinson warden of the state prison in 1834. Bell described Stinson as "at best a mere electioneering politician" and accused Hill of appointing Stinson in order to get back money he had loaned Stinson before his appointment as warden. Samuel Bell to Isaac Hill, ALS [c. June 1834], New Hampshire Historical Society, Concord, N.H. Bell was a member of the New Hampshire Legislature from 1804-08, a judge in the New Hampshire Supreme Court 1816-19, governor of the state 1819-23, and a U.S. senator 1823-35. He started his political career as a Jeffersonian Republican, then became a Federalist, and was swept out of office by the rise of Jacksonian Democrats (such as Hill). Allen Johnson, ed., *Dictionary of American Biography*, Vol. 2 (New York, 1929), pp. 162-163.

Warden Rufus Dow was blasted by the *New Hampshire Statesman* for alleged political corruption: "The Statesman has found a mare's nest in the State Prison - an institution which has furnished the federal party much electioneering capital in times past." *New Hampshire Statesman*, May 8, 1853. The paper retracted its accusation but not before ruining Dow's reputation. *New Hampshire Statesman*, May 14, 1853.

108. Robinson, "New Hampshire State Prison," 217.

109. *New-Hampshire Patriot*, Nov. 17 and Dec. 1, 1812; and *Concord Gazette*, Nov. 24 and Dec. 1, 1812.

110. Register of Convicts 1812-1883, MS, State Prison Papers, Div. of Records-Management and Archives, Concord, N.H.

Chapter III

Crime and Social Change in New Hampshire, 1812-1914

Upon opening the "Register of Convicts" located at the Division of Records-Management and Archives in Concord, one finds a brief entry for John Drew who was committed to the New Hampshire State Prison on November 23, 1812. He was a 31-year old horse thief from Meredith and he served a full sentence of four years at hard labor. His is the first of 4154 entries made in the State Prison registers in the next century.[1]

With the aid of a quantitative computer program, I will describe and analyze a large sample of these entries in order to draw some conclusions about crime in New Hampshire at the felony level. I will analyze and describe the offenses according to the original records and the New Hampshire laws, and provide a detailed portrait of serious crime in New Hampshire. We can learn, for example, the kind of property most commonly the object of crime in New Hampshire, its value, and how the nature of such crimes changed over time. I will ask similar questions applicable to violent and moral felonies and other crimes, and make comparisons to other regions of the United States.

Before we begin, however, we need to discuss the historiography of nineteenth century crime, and, in addition, to provide a description of the relevant New Hampshire records and the methods of analyzing the records. Even though my study is concerned only with felonies, it is possible to relate my findings in a general way to the findings of other scholars who have not limited themselves to analyzing felonies only. A brief discussion of their findings is necessary to provide a context to see how crime in New Hampshire compared to crime in other regions.

Since the 1960's, the history of crime has attracted significant interest. This is not surprising. Not only was the decade a period of civil unrest, but the discipline was focusing on the lives of ordinary people in order to give them a voice and a place in national history and to confront the emphasis on national politics and diplomacy that had dominated historical writing. In their study of crime, scholars focused on changes in the rates of various crimes and regional variations as well as differences between crime patterns in urban and rural Europe and America. Their findings have not always agreed but certain trends have been noted.

Theodore N. Ferdinand describes the overall pattern of crime in Boston as an "almost uninterrupted decline" from a peak in the late 1870's up to 1951.[2] Individual types of crime departed from this pattern, however. Murder, assault, and larceny most closely follow the general pattern of decline while manslaughter, rape, robbery, and burglary differ in varying degrees. Ultimately, Ferdinand says there are three explanations for Boston's pattern of crime: a) the attitude and effectiveness of the police, b) events like wars or economic depressions which temporarily disrupt community routines, and c) gradual structural changes such as the growth of a middle class.[3]

Roger Lane's study of Massachusetts between 1835 and 1900 agrees that serious crime decreased to a great extent.[4] At the same time, petty crime was on the increase. Lane suggests that the urbanization of Massachusetts had a "civilizing effect" on the population. Thus, the rate of serious crimes per 100,000 population declined but the rate of minor offenses increased. Lane derived his crime rates from lower court cases, jail commitments, grand jury cases, and imprisonments in Massachusetts for the years 1835-1900.[5] He concludes, "What had been tolerable in a casual, independent society was no longer acceptable" in an urban society which required close living quarters and a more regulated life and working conditions.[6]

Michael S. Hindus finds a significant difference in patterns of crime between Massachusetts and South Carolina for the period 1767-1878. The patterns for Massachusetts changed dramatically over time while South Carolina's did not.[7] In Massachusetts, the crime rate peaked in the 1850's, declined, then peaked again right after the Civil War, and then declined.[8] Massachusetts crime characteristically involved property offenses and a declining number of moral offenses. In contrast, crime in South Carolina stayed at a consistently high rate and was mostly a matter of violence.[9] Hindus says the patterns of crime are "distinctly correlated" to the economic, social, and cultural characteristics peculiar to each state.[10] The pattern of property and moral crimes in Massachusetts can be explained in part by the dislocation caused by urbanization and industrialization.[11] South Carolina's consistent pattern of violent crime can be explained by the presence of a strong cult of honor which required a violent response to perceived insult and by the absence of a "predatory class of whites."[12]

Edward L. Ayers confirms Hindus's general thesis that the American South exhibits a consistently higher level of violent crime than does the North. Property crime existed in the nineteenth-century South but it was mainly associated with the black population.[13] Ayers does not provide statistics on crime rates per population but his survey of incarceration rates in northern and southern penitentiaries reveals a "pattern strikingly similar to one another": a dramatic rise in the late 1850's.[14] Ultimately, Ayers links the incidence of crime in the South to economic changes. From the 1850's onward, the South's economy was linked to the national economy which made it more vulnerable to the business cycle experienced by the rest of the country.[15] The emancipation of the slaves was of great importance in relation to changes in patterns of crime. By the 1870's the most common form of crime had changed from white violence to black theft.[16] However, violent crime, even today, remains consistently higher in the South than in the rest of the United States.[17]

According to Ted Robert Gurr, the general pattern of serious crime in Europe and "perhaps also" the United States has been one of a long decline followed by a recent increase.[18] Violent crime in nineteenth-century America declined in the 1840's and then significantly increased in the 1850's.[19] Next came a decline which was followed by a surge upward right after the Civil War and then another decline in the 1890's.[20] Violent crime once again rose dramatically in the early twentieth century, declined from the 1930's through the 1950's, increased dramatically in the 1960's, and then slightly declined during the 1980's. This pattern was similar to that of Europe except for the fact that America's rate of violence was five times higher than that of Europe as a whole.[21] Rates of violent crime among black Americans have increased greatly while those among whites have decreased.[22] This pattern of violent crime in the United States over the past 150 years can be explained in part by the changing socioeconomic status of immigrants and blacks, and war, because American society is stratified along economic and ethnic lines.[23]

Eric H. Monkkonen supports Gurr's assertion that American and European rates of violent crime are very different. Monkkonen sees the years 1850-1875 as the crucial period when the United States "began its bloody divergence from the rest of the Western world."[24] The crucial difference lies in the magnitude and timing of American rates of violent crime.[25] Monkkonen based his study on a comparison of three cities: New York, London, and Liverpool. Liverpool more closely resembles New York than London because it had a high number of Irish immigrants and a higher level of violence than London.[26] After the Civil War the New York homicide rate declined but Britain's declined far more.[27] One reason for this phenomenon, Monkkonen argues, was the presence of guns in American society. Another was weak punishments in the United States. Many New York homicides were judged to be "reasonable" which was also typical of the American South.[28] The message received by American society was that punishment was likely to be slight or nonexistent as long as murder was kept within certain social bounds.[29] Monkkonen says the higher American homicide rate is mostly a result of high immigration, high population growth, modest punishment, and increased gun usage.[30]

Monkkonen also investigated crime rates in his study of crime and poverty in Columbus, Ohio for the period 1860-1885. His results present a different picture from the others cited so far. He found "considerable stability" between 1867 and 1891 for the whole state, which is in contrast to the decreasing crime rates more typical of other regions.[31] Monkkonen explains this by positing the existence of two different types of cities. Unlike eastern cities, which he describes as mature industrial cities, Columbus, Ohio was just making the transition from a pre-industrial economy. The significance of the difference lies in that, at some point during their development from pre-industrial to mature industrial stages, cities go through changes in crime patterns as well. There is a decrease in the incidence and prosecution of traditional, direct forms of criminal behavior like theft and murder.[32] Monkkonen also shows that violent crime rates were higher in the hinterland of Columbus and that a new form of crime - theft by trick - was emerging in the city.[33] On the other hand, Monkkonen finds a sharp increase in violent crime during and after the Civil War which he blames on changing values and looser social control caused by the war.[34]

Finally, Lawrence Friedman and Robert Percival corroborate the general consensus of a decline in serious crime after the Civil War in their study of Alameda County, California for the years 1870-1910. Their conclusion is based on arrest rates. They conclude that arrest rates for serious crimes such as murder, armed robbery, violent rape, and burglary "confirm the idea of a long, deep decline."[35] Alameda County had been a notoriously violent region in the 1850's which coincides partly with the period 1850-75 when, according to Monkkonen, homicide rates of Britain and the United States diverged. Friedman and Percival do not speculate on the reason for the decline in serious crime between 1870 and 1910. By point of comparison, they supply the arrest rates for serious crime in Alameda County in 1970 which "certainly do suggest a huge, real increase in crime."[36]

Before relating the New Hampshire records to the above findings, it is important to understand the scope and organization of these records. The criminal population examined here consists of all of those persons convicted of a felony in New Hampshire between 1812 and 1914 and sentenced to one year (the minimum term) or more in the state prison. Records on felons are far more complete and accessible than those for petty offenders. By focusing on felons we will be analyzing only the most serious forms of crime. Petty crimes and misdemeanors were more common phenomena but felonies were an indication of what forms of behavior were truly intolerable to society. The nature of a society's core values are expressed in part by the punishment given to transgressors.[37]

All felons who actually served time in the New Hampshire State Prison are recorded in the "Register of Convicts" for the period 1812-1883. The remainder are recorded in three other ledgers designated "[New Hampshire] State Prison Records [1874-1915]," "New Hampshire State Prison: Record of Gain and Loss in Population [1905-1936]," and an untitled ledger covering 1887-1907. These ledgers are located at the Division of Records-Management and Archives in Concord, New Hampshire. Characteristically, these manuscript ledgers supply extremely brief notations about the convicts: name, age, birthplace, date of conviction, crime, date of admittance to the prison, sentence, and date of discharge.[38]

At rare moments the ledgers provide brief notations on the prisoner's behavior, physical appearance, or status. For example, Edward J. Lynch, convicted of stealing a gold watch and sentenced to one to two years on May 3, 1905 in Portsmouth is described thus: "Left leg broken at knee. Foot turns in. Very lame."[39] Thomas Clark, convicted in September 1818 of stealing a pig and sentenced to two years in prison died on April 11, 1819 of the "French disease."[40] The notation "sixth time" by Sidney Nelson's entry for a burglary committed in Dover in 1875 would suggest a recidivist of major proportions.[41] Regrettably, such helpful annotations as these are few and far between. Slightly more detailed entries can be found in the "Description Registers" for 1881-98 and 1899-1906. The main value of these latter two sources is the listing of many prisoners' occupations before conviction.

After 1858 most of the published annual prison reports supply the information (except for the exact dates of admission and release) found in the ledgers. From the ledgers and publications one can construct a basic listing of inmates. Court records are the other major primary source of information. Because such records are often missing, restricted, or other wise unavailable, I decided to limit the scope of this analysis to 820 cases (19.5% of the total) from Rockingham County (1812-1914) and Strafford County (1870-1914).

Court records consist of written indictments (i.e., a formal charge made by the jury) or court bills (in form, very similar to indictments but clearly stating the jury's verdict and the court's sentence). Both the indictment and court bill were written on a standard form, employing legal phrasing that hardly varied throughout the period under consideration. Luckily for the researcher, most of the records consist of standard printed forms with blank spaces filled out by the clerk of the court. Court records frequently supply information missing from the prison registers and published reports: actual date and location of the crime, detailed description of the act, and residence of the offender and victim. In rare cases, the occupation of the offender is also listed. At times, pages were appended to the basic court record form. Sometimes one will find a piece of evidence such as counterfeit money, correspondence, or the coroner's inquest folded in with the court record. For example, enclosed with the court bill for the John Blaisdell manslaughter case is a 60-page trial transcription and a list of 22 witnesses.[42] Enclosed with the indictment accusing Isaac B. Sawtelle of murdering his brother Hiram F., are long detailed depositions, testimony transcriptions, a list of jurors, telegrams, and other documents.[43] Such finds are very rare, however.

Court bills and indictments are invaluable for providing a reasonably complete picture of crime in New Hampshire. The court records used for this project include 545 for Rockingham County covering the years 1812-1914 and 275 for Strafford County covering 1870-1914.[44] I chose these cases becaue they were accessible and nearly complete. I matched every prison ledger entry to an existing court record or reference in the published annual prison warden's reports. These court records represent every single felony conviction and incarceration for Rockingham County for the period 1812-1914 and Strafford County for the years 1870-1914.

It is important to note that the cases referred to here are of criminal *acts* not individuals. A recidivist (one convicted of a crime two or more times) would be counted as two or more cases. In an incident in which accomplices were sentenced to prison, each person's record was counted as a separate case. Most often each convict had his or her own separate court record, even if two or more of these persons were involved in the same crime. Thus, there were actually fewer than 4154 *people* who served time in the prison between 1812 and 1914 and there are fewer than 820 *people* in the sample to be analyzed here.[45] Recidivism is noted whenever possible in this study and will be discussed in relation to the efficacy of punishment.

Additional sources include newspaper accounts (suprisingly hard to find before 1840) and some miscellaneous documents such as trial accounts and inquests filed with the court records. Most newspaper coverage of crime before 1840 was of spectacular crimes committed in locations outside New Hampshire. Occasionally, newspapers would run a notice informing the public of a suspect-at-large or an escaped criminal. The miscellaneous documents are very few in number but very helpful. These sources were used to supplement the basic information found in the court records.

The data assembled from these sources were then coded and entered into a computer database (see Figure 1).[46] A basic list of crimes was drawn up based on the statutes outlined in Chapter One. Crimes were then divided into four major categories: property, violence, moral, and "other" including such disparate offenses as perjury and being a tramp.

Figure 1

CODING SCHEME

1) Case Number (ID): 01-03/Name:
2) Age: 06-07/
3) Sex: 08/
4) Race: 09/
5) Birthplace (BPLACE): 10-11/
6) Residence (RES): 12/Town, State, Etc.:
7) Year Committed (YRCOM): 14-17/
8) County Convicted (CTYCON): 18/
9) Crime: 19-20/
10 [Variable Deleted]:
11) Value of Property Crime ($) (VALPROP): 22-26/
12) Type of Property Affected (TYPPROP): 27-28/
13) Year Released (YRREL): 30-33/
14) Sentence (SENT): 34-35/
15) Sentence Served (SERV): 36-37/
16) How Discharged (EXIT): 38/
17) Known Recidivism (RECID): 39/
18) Occupation (OCCUP): 40/

NOTES:

Difficulties arose from the original sources.[47] In most cases, the entry for crime in the register matched up to the indictment or conviction described in the court record.

Court records are invaluable for the details they supply. Among the variables supplied by court records are the value of the property affected and the type of property involved. Value is given in dollar amounts which have been rounded off to the nearest whole number. Value was then converted to constant dollars to make a comparison possible.[48] Type of property has been categorized (see Tables 1-2). Whenever two or more types of property are involved they are classified as "Various." "Various" usually includes two or more the other types of property commonly listed: money, clothing, horse, etc. Sometimes less common sorts of property are present as well but single

Table 1

Type of Property Affected by Crime in New Hampshire, 1812-1914:

Frequencies

Property Type	Frequency	Valid Percent
Money	136	20.9%
Various	125	19.2%
Clothing	78	11.7%
Unknown	76	9.5%
Horse	42	6.5%
Other	37	5.7%
Watch	30	4.6%
Other Livestock	27	4.2%
Food	21	3.2%
Horse and Vehicle	16	2.5%
Liquor	13	2.0%
Jewelry	11	1.7%
Barn	11	1.7%
Vehicle	8	1.2%
Other Building	7	1.1%
Tools	5	0.8%
House	4	0.6%
Firearm	3	0.5%
TOTALS:	650*	100.0%

*Includes 11 cases from the "Other" crimes category that involved property but that were not classified as "Property" crimes.

Source: Court Bills and Indictments, 1812-1914, Rockingham County, MS, Div. of Records-Management and Archives, Concord, N.H. and Court Bills and Indictments, 1870-1914, Strafford County, MS, Justice and Administration Building, Dover, N.H.

examples of these are subsumed under the heading of "Other." We are concerned only with property most commonly affected by crime here. Naturally, this lowers the frequency for other categories of property whenever

Table 2

Type of Property Affected by Crime in New Hampshire, 1812-1914:

By Decade and Collapsed into Basic Categories

| Decade | Percentage of Cases | | | |
	Type 1	Type 2	Type 3	Type 4
1810's	30.9%	2.4%	2.4%	35.7%
1820's	44.4%		3.7%	14.8%
1830's	20.6%	3.0%	14.7%	23.5%
1840's	30.8%		3.8%	30.8%
1850's	25.0%	7.1%	10.7%	7.1%
1860's	29.7%	3.7%	5.5%	7.4%
1870's	16.1%	8.6%	5.4%	20.4%
1880's	36.1%	1.0%	2.1%	11.3%
1890's	13.6%	3.4%	9.1%	10.2%
1900's	28.9%	3.8%	9.6%	10.6%
1910's	38.6%			8.8%
TOTAL:	27.2%	3.4%	5.2%	14.3%

Decade	Percentage of Cases Type 5	Type 6	Total % and N
1810's	11.9%	11.9%	100% (42)
1820's	11.1%	26.0%	100% (27)
1830's	23.5%	38.2%	100% (34)
1840's	7.7%	26.9%	100% (26)
1850's	7.1%	43.0%	100% (28)
1860's	13.0%	40.7%	100% (54)
1870's	15.1%	34.4%	100% (93)
1880's	15.5%	34.0%	100% (97)
1890's	17.1%	46.6%	100% (88)
1900's	37.5%	37.5%	100% (104)
1910's	5.3%	47.3%	100% (57)
TOTAL:	13.2%	36.7%	100% (650)*

*Includes 11 cases from the "Other" crimes category that involved property but that were not classified as "Property" crimes.

BASIC PROPERTY CATEGORIES

Type 1 (Fungible): Money, Watch, and Jewelry

BASIC PROPERTY CATEGORIES

Type 2 (Structural): House, Barn, and Other Building
Type 3 (Edible): Food and Liquor
Type 4 (Agricultural): Horse, Horse and Vehicle, Vehicle, and Other

Livestock.
Type 5 (Dry Goods): Clothing, Firearms, and Tools
Type 6 (Miscellaneous): Other, Unknown, and Various

Source: Court Bills and Indictments, 1812-1914, Rockingham County, MS, Div. of Records-Management and Archives, Concord, N.H. and Court Bills and Indictments, 1870-1914, Strafford County, Justice and Administration Building.

one of them is present in the two or more "various" items listed in a single property crime.

Both the sentence given by the judge and the sentence actually served are analyzed since the two differ rather frequently.[49] How soon a convict was discharged from prison should also tell us something about the nature of punishment. For example, the introduction of parole might indicate a renewed faith in the rehabilitative powers of imprisonment. On the other hand, it might just serve as another method of preventing overcrowding.

In Chapter One we discussed the official definition of crime according to the New Hampshire Statutes, or the "law in the books." Here we will examine the law in action by examing how the courts implemented the statutes. The courts are presumably a reflection of society. Seacoast society was in a state of transition during the nineteenth century and this was reflected to an extent in the types of crimes prosecuted and punished.

Rockingham County and Strafford County are located in the southeastern corner of New Hampshire along the seacoast. This part of the state has been described as "typical coastal plain country" except for the Pawtuckaway Mountains in Nottingham, the Blue Hills in Strafford, and Hussey Mountain in Farmington.[50] Most of the country is gently rolling and becomes flatter as one approaches the sea. The major rivers of Rockingham County and Strafford County are the Piscataqua, Salmon, Cocheco, Lamprey, and Oyster. All 18 miles of New Hampshire's seacoast fall within Rockingham County and the state's only harbor is located there, at Portsmouth.[51]

The coast was the site of the earliest European settlement in New Hampshire (1623) and consequently was most extensively deforested and placed soonest under cultivation. A number of towns were established along the seacoast and rivers: Dover, Portsmouth, Exeter, Hampton, Rochester, Durham, Somersworth, Newmarket, and others. The economy was mainly agricultural except for the immediate seacoast in which fishing, shipbuilding, and trading dominated.

During the course of the nineteenth century Rockingham County and Strafford County underwent great changes in population and economic development. New Hampshire experienced an unstable rate of growth during the nineteenth century which was mirrored in the growth rates for Rockingham County and Strafford County (see Table 3). Several new counties were established and about half of the new county was created from towns that had belonged to Rockingham County.[52] This accounts for the loss of 19.6% of its population between 1820 and 1830. Between 1840 and 1850 Strafford County experienced a severe drop in population for the same reason: from 61,127 inhabitants to 29,374, a loss of 52.0%. Half of Strafford County was used in the creation of Belknap County and Carroll County in 1840.[53] Meanwhile, Rockingham County grew at a modest pace and experienced a slight loss of population during the 1860's. Between 1860 and 1910 the population of Rockingham County was nearly stagnant while Strafford County grew at approximately the same rate as the state except for a large spurt of growth in the 1880's (see Table 3).

John J. Cate described what the changing circumstances meant to local inhabitants on the occasion of the Northwood Centennial in 1873.

> I cannot undertake to show that farming is in a flourishing condition in Northwood...But, with regard to hard cash, it is like the heaps of hay in many of our fields, - small and far between...The great West, with its large heart and beckoning hands, has drawn largely from the young men in all our farming towns; and these sons of Northwood and the East have given character to that extensive tract of our country between the Ohio and the lakes and westward to the Rocky Mountains and the Pacific.[54]

He saw the solution to economic decline in manufacturing: "New England is, from her position, a manufacturing community, and a large portion of our own active men are engaged in the manufacture of shoes."[55]

Agriculture was not actually so much in decline as in transition. Between 1800 and 1860 wheat and beef production indeed declined because of Western competition, technological improvements in agriculture, and a revolution in transportation methods. On the other hand, hay production, dairying, wood production, apple and cider production, poultry production, and market gardening all increased during the course of the century.[56]

Meanwhile, the industrial development mentioned by Cate proceeded to

Table 3

Population Growth, 1810-1910:
New Hampshire, Rockingham County, and Strafford County

Year	Rockingham County Pop.	% Change	Strafford County Pop.	% Change	New Hampshire Pop.	% Change
1810	50,175		41,595		214,460	
1820	55,107	+9.0%	51,117	+18.6%	244,161	+12.2%
1830	44,325	-19.6%	58,910	+13.2%	269,533	+9.4%
1840	45,771	+2.9%	61,127	+3.6%	284,574	+5.3%
1850	49,194	+7.0%	29,374	-52.0%	317,976	+5.3%
1860	50,122	+1.9%	31,493	+6.7%	326,073	+2.5%
1870	47,297	-5.6%	30,243	-4.0%	318,300	-2.4%
1880	49,064	+8.3%	35,558	+14.9%	346,991	+8.3%
1890	49,560	+1.0%	38,442	+7.5%	376,530	+7.9%
1900	51,118	+3.0%	39,337	+2.3%	411,588	+8.5%
1910	52,188	+2.1%	38,951	-1.0%	430,572	+4.4%

Source: *U.S. Census Reports*, 1810-1910.

transform the seacoast economy. An examination of the statistics on occupations reveals something of the transition away from a rural economy between 1870 and 1910 (see Table 4). In 1870 nearly 40% of the New Hampshire workforce was engaged in agriculture. The same number were engaged in manufacturing jobs. Forty years later, the proportion of workers engaged in agriculture had fallen to less than 20% while manufacturing had picked up another 10%. Most of the rest of the jobs went to personal and

Table 4

Occupational Change in New Hampshire, 1870-1910

Occupation Category	Occupations as % of Total Working Population				
	1870	1880	1890	1900	1910
Agriculture	38.8%	31.3%	26.1%	21.7%	19.1%
Personal & Professional Services	15.2%	19.8%	18.5%	21.5%	17.8%
Mfg., Mech., & Mining Industries	38.8%	40.7%	43.4%	42.5%	49.7%
Trade & Transportation	7.2%	8.2%	12.0%	14.3%	13.4%
TOTAL %	100%	100%	100%	100%	100%
TOTAL WORKING POP. (N):	120,168	142,468	164,468	178,719	191,703

Note: Categories designated by U.S. Census Bureau

Source: *U.S. Census*, 1870-1910.

professional occupations or trade and transportation (see Appendix). As early as the 1820's large textile mills had been constructed in Dover, Somersworth, and Exeter.[57] Large shoe and leather factories were constructed in Rochester and Farmington.[58] Much of this economic growth was fueled by improvements in transportation and technology. The first state turnpike or toll road in New Hampshire was completed in 1797. It joined Durham to Concord and was the first in a series of turnpikes which linked the seacoast to the interior.[59] The first railroad chartered in New Hampshire was the Nashua & Lowell (Massachusetts) in 1835; it commenced operation in 1838.[60] As early as 1839 the state chartered the Dover & Winnipiseogee Railroad.[61] Railroads grew rapidly in the seacoast and the rest of the state from the 1840's on.[62] The greatest era of expansion took place between 1865 and 1920 when the state total of 700 miles of tracks jumped to 1252 miles. The seacoast's era of railroad expansion was at its height in the 1870's and 1880's.[63]

Economic development was connected also to the shipbuilding industry. Portsmouth was the center of shipbuilding in New Hampshire but the river towns of Exeter, Newmarket, Durham, and Dover produced hundreds of ocean craft too.[64] River and ocean craft transported both raw materials and finished products. The Portsmouth Naval Shipyard built many warships between 1812 and 1860. In addition, Portsmouth enjoyed an economic boom during the years 1843-1853 when the clipper ship industry was at its height. The arrival of ocean-going steamships cut the good times short.[65]

The population of Rockingham County and Strafford County changed in composition. Much of the rural population moved either to the American West or to the growing local mill towns. Seacoast New Hampshire became increasingly urban as the nineteenth century went on. The most noticeable urban growth took place in Strafford County in mill centers such as Dover, Rochester, and Somersworth. In Rockingham County too, Exeter and Newmarket experienced a large increase in population. It was not until 1890 that the majority of the population of both counties could be described as urban (see Table 5). In the 1820's most of the millworkers were young women from farming families and middle class homes.[66] By the 1850's this had changed with the arrival of poor Irish immigrants who, in turn, were followed by Swedes, Germans, Scots, French-Canadians, and eventually, Greeks and Poles.[67] The foreign-born population of New Hampshire grew from 4.49% of the whole in 1850 to 22.45% by 1910 (see Table 6). The seacoast - especially Strafford County - was the site of heavy foreign immigration during the second half of the nineteenth century. Starting in 1860, the proportion of foreign-born population of Rockingham County nearly tripled from 5.80% to 15.41% in 1900. This group grew from 8.45% in 1860 to 23.25% of the population in Strafford County (see Table 6). Thus, the depopulation of the countryside noted by Cate and others was offset by an increasing flow of European and Canadian immigrants to the milltowns. This was followed by a few decades of uneven decline and then there was a fast drop off to 60 per 100,000 population in seacoast New Hampshire (see Table 9).

Property crime was by far the most common category throughout the period. Nevertheless, some trends over time are evident when the data are broken down by decade. Property crime accounted for between 83.9% and 94.4% of the crimes punished between 1812 and 1839 (see Tables 7-8).

Table 5

Growth in Urban Population, 1800-1900: Seacoast New Hampshire

Rockingham County Alone, 1800-60; Strafford County Added, 1870-1910

Year	Urban Pop. & %		Rural Pop. & %		Total Pop.
1800	7989	7.6%	37,438	82.4%	45,427
1810	9700	19.3%	40,475	80.7%	50,175
1820	13,292	24.1%	41,815	75.9%	55,107
1830	10,861	24.5%	33,464	75.5%	44,325
1840	13,542	29.6%	32,229	70.4%	45,771
1850	13,112	26.7%	36,082	73.3%	49,194
1860	12,644	25.2%	37,478	74.8%	50,122
1870	30,549	39.4%	46,991	60.6%	77,540
1880	39,360	46.5%	45,262	53.5%	84,622
1890	48,914	55.6%	39,088	44.4%	88,002
1900	50,730	56.1%	39,725	43.9%	90,455
1910	56,077	61.5%	35,062	38.5%	91,139

Note: Urban is here defined as those residing in towns or cities having 2500 inhabitants or more. Strafford County figures have been added to those of Rockingham County for the period 1870-1900 because court records for Strafford County are available for the period 1870-1914.

Source: *U.S. Census Reports*, 1800-1910.

Table 6

Foreign-Born as Percentage of Population, 1850-1910:
New Hampshire, Rockingham County, and Strafford County

Year	New Hampshire % of Pop.	Rockingham County % of Pop.	Strafford % of Pop.
1850	4.49%	-----	-----
1860	6.43%	5.80%	8.45%
1870	9.30%	5.96%	10.86%
1880	13.34%	8.10%	17.57%
1890	19.21%	12.28%	23.45%
1900	21.41%	15.41%	23.25%
1910	22.45%	-----	-----

Source: *U.S. Census Reports*, 1850-1910.

The drop in property crime to 76.5% of the total in the 1840's is made more dramatic when contrasted to the high point of 94.4% in the previous decade. Property crime persisted at a relatively stable percentage over the next three decades, hovering at between 82.4% and 86.0%. Suddenly, property crime dropped to 68.1% of the total in the 1880's. It accounted for 72.0% of the total in the 1890's; 77.5% in the 1900's; and 70.5% of the total in the years 1910-14. Overall, property crime accounted for 77.9% of the total.

Expressed as a rate per 100,000 population, the pattern of property crime exhibits a slightly different pattern (see Table 9). Between the 1850's and 1870's property crime shot up from a rate of 57 to 120 per 100,000 population. This was followed by a few decades of uneven decline and then there was a fast drop off to 60 per 100,000 population in seacoast New Hampshire which was less than it had been a century before (see Table 9).

A changing percentage in property crime indicates also changes in

Table 7

Crime in New Hampshire, 1812-1914 According to Basic Type

Type of Crime	Frequency	Percentage of Total
Property	639	77.9%
Violence	120	14.6%
Moral	15	1.8%
Other	46	5.6%
TOTAL:	820	100%

Source: Court Bills and Indictments, 1812-1914, Rockingham Cty., MS, Div. of Records-Management and Archives, Concord, N.H. and Court Bills and Indictments, 1870-1914, Strafford Cty., MS, Justice and Administration Building, Dover, N.H.; "Register of Convicts 1812-1883," and "[N.H. State] Prison Records [1874-1915]," MS, Div. of Records-Management and Archives, Concord, N.H.; and *Prison Warden's Reports*, 1813-1914.

percentages and definitions of other types of crime. For all of the decades, except one, which show a relative decrease in property crime, the category of violent crime shows a relative increase. Thus, the 1840's exhibited an increase in violent crime from a low of 5.6% of the total in the 1830's to 20.6% of the total. "Other" crimes increased from nothing to a still rather insignificant 2.9% of the total. Violent crime continued at a relatively high rate over the next two decades at 17.6% and 15.4% of the total before dropping off to only 6.5% of the total in the 1870's. Violent crime as a percentage of the total exhibited a fluctuating percentage for the remainder of the period, ranging between 12.4% and 24.4% of the total. Overall, violent crimes accounted for 14.6% of the total (see Table 7). We can conclude that the most violent decades reported were the 1840's, 1890's, and the 1910's. Expressed as crime rates per 100,000 population, violent crime exhibits a steady increase from 15 per 100,000 population in the 1840's to a height of 32 per 100,000 in the 1890's. The only deviation from this pattern occurred in the 1870's when the rate dipped to 9 per 100,000 population (see Table 8).

Table 8

Crime in New Hampshire, 1812-1914 According to Basic Type:
By Decade and Percentage

Decade	Property % and (N)	Violence % and (N)	Moral % and (N)
1810's	89.3% (42)	8.6% (4)	
1820's	84.0% (26)	9.6% (3)	
1830's	94.5% (34)	5.6% (2)	
1840's	77.0% (26)	20.1% (7)	
1850's	82.4% (28)	17.6% (6)	
1860's	81.5% (53)	15.4% (10)	
1870's	86.9% (93)	6.6% (7)	3.7% (4)
1880's	68.0% (98)	12.8% (18)	2.1% (3)
1890's	71.9% (85)	23.9% (28)	2.5% (3)
1900's	78.3% (101)	12.3% (16)	3.2% (4)
1910's	70.4% (55)	24.4% (19)	2.6% (2)

Decade	Other % and (N)	Total % and (N)
1810's	2.1% (1)	100% (47)
1820's	6.4% (2)	100% (31)

Decade	Other % and (N)	Total % and (N)
1830's		100% (36)
1840's	2.9% (1)	100% (34)
1850's		100% (34)
1860's	3.1% (2)	100% (65)
1870's	2.8% (3)	100% (107)
1880's	15.6% (22)	100% (141)
1890's	1.7% (2)	100% (118)
1900's	6.2% (8)	100% (129)
1910's	2.6% (2)	100% (78)

Source: Court Bills and Indictments, 1812-1914, Rockingham Cty., MS, Div. of Records-Management and Archives, Concord, N.H.; Court Bills and Indictments, 1870-1914, Strafford Cty., MS, Justice and Administration Building, Dover, N.H.; "Register of Convicts 1812-1883" and "[N.H. State] Prison Records [1874-1915]," both MS, Div. of Records-Management and Archives, Concord, N.H., and *Prison Warden's Reports*, 1813-1914.

Table 9

New Hampshire Felony Conviction Rates, 1812-1914

Decade	Population	No. of Cases	Rate per 100,000 Pop.
1810's	50,175	47	94
1820's	55,107	31	56

Decade	Population	No. of Cases	Rate per 100,000 Pop.
1830's	44,325	36	81
1840's	45,771	34	74
1850's	49,194	34	69
1860's	50,122	65	130
1870's	77,540	107	138
1880's	84,622	141	167
1890's	88,092	118	134
1900's	90,455	129	143
1910's	91,139	78	85

```
----
820 cases
```

Crime Rates by Type of Crime
Showing Number of Cases and Rate per 100,000 Population

Property Crime and Violence

	Property Crime		Violence	
Decade	No. Cases	Rate	No. Cases	Rate
1810's	42	84	4	8
1820's	26	47	3	5
1830's	34	77	2	5
1840's	26	57	7	15

90

Decade	Property Crime No. Cases	Rate	Violence No. Cases	Rate
1850's	28	57	6	16
1860's	53	106	10	20
1870's	93	120	7	9
1880's	96	114	18	21
1890's	85	97	28	32
1900's	101	112	16	18
1910's	55	60	19	21
	----		----	
TOTAL:	639 cases		120 cases	

Crime Rates by Type of Crime
Showing Number of Cases and Rate per 100,000 Population

Moral Crime and Other Crime

Decade	Moral Crime No. Cases	Rate	Other Crime No. Cases	Rate
1810's			1	2
1820's			2	4
1830's				
1840's			1	2

Decade	Moral Crime No. Cases	Rate	Other Crime No. Cases	Rate
1850's				

	Moral Crime		Other Crime	
Decade	No. Cases	Rate	No. Cases	Rate
1860's			2	4
1870's	3	4	4	5
1880's	3	4	24	28
1890's	3	3	2	2
1900's	4	4	8	9
1910's	2	2	2	2
	---		---	
TOTAL:	15 cases		46 cases	

Source: Court Bills and Indictments, 1812-1914, Rockingham Cty., MS, Div. of Records-Management and Archives, Concord, N.H.; Court Bills and Indictments, 1870-1914, Strafford Cty., MS, Justice and Administration Building, Dover, N.H.; "Register of Convicts 1812-1883" and "[N.H. State] Prison Records [1874-1915]," both MS, Div. of Records-Management and Archives, Concord, N.H., and *Prison Warden's Reports*, 1813-1914.

Overall, the period from 1840 through 1899 was one of increasing violence, or they were times when criminal justice was applied most heavily to violent offenders. Moral offenses were a very small percentage of the total overall (1.8%). No person in our sample, male or female, was sent to the state prison for such an offense until the 1870's. Between the 1870's and 1914 moral offenses made up only between 1.7% and 3.7% of the total number of crimes. The high point of 3.7% was reached in the 1870's with two convictions for sodomy, one for bigamy, and one for adultery. The rate of moral crime was consistently low: typically around 4 per 100,000 population (see Table 9).

"Other" consist of the following: being a tramp, entering someone's home as a tramp, committing perjury, poisoning a cow, placing an obstruction on railroad tracks, robbing graves, cruelty to children, and violation of parole. These offenses are represented in every decade except for the 1830's and 1850's. "Other" crimes remained a very small percentage, ranging between

1.7% and 6.5%. The one major exception was the 1880's when "other" crimes made up 17.0% of the total (see Table 8). The rate for "other" crimes reached 28 per 100,000 population in the 1880's (see Table 9). Most of those convicted had committed the crime of being a tramp in New Hampshire. The sample contains 22 such convictions in the 1880's. In 1878 the New Hampshire legislature had tackled the problem of dealing with the transient unemployed by making the tramp's status a criminal offense. Other states resorted to similar measures.[68] In the mid 1870's the sheer number of wandering unemployed persons alarmed American social commentators. The term "tramp" made its first appearance then even though the phenomenon was not new. What was new was the number of tramps and the fear they inspired. Such fear was the result of increased labor militancy and the increasing visibility of the industrial proletariat. The new image of the tramp was sinister: tramps were associated with violence, they were considered to be labor agitators, and they were held up as a bad example to others because they were supposedly lazy and immoral. The very fact that tramps were homeless was threatening in an era when domesticity meant respectability. Finally, the presence of foreign immigrants among the tramps inflamed nativist prejudices.[69]

Statistics help in making generalizations but what does the preceding recitation of percentages actually mean? We will start with property crime which was by far the most common phenomenon.

First, we will consider the value of property affected. The mean value of 639 property cases sampled here was $182.58 (see Table 10). The four most common sorts of property were money, clothing, horses, and watches (see Table 1). The categories of "various," "other," and "unknown" were actually very common (in all, 36.6% of the types of property involved) but for obvious reasons cannot really be described in a distinct fashion. "Various," of course, overlaps frequently with commonly affected types of property such as money or horses but consists of two or more types of property involved in one crime.

The mean value of $182.58 was arrived at by averaging the values available for 639 cases. Included here were four unusually high values of $10,000; $13,165; $19,730; and $27,620. Such high values have skewed the property crime value upward. The overall median figure is only $14.50 which indicates that most property crime involved rather low values (see Table 10). In order to construct a meaningful picture of property crime, the mean and median values for property crimes have been recalculated in constant dollars by decade (see Table 11). The recalculations reinforce the notion that most property crime was on a modest scale. The lowest median value appears in

Table 10

Value of Property Affected by Crime in New Hampshire, 1812-1914

Decade	Mean	Median	No. of Cases
1810's	$94.96	$58.00	42
1820's	$1886.03	$27.00	26
1830's	$30.59	$23.00	34
1840's	$24.76	$8.00	26
1850's	$38.07	$9.00	28
1860's	$42.64	$11.00	53
1870's	$104.89	$43.00	93
1880's	$50.35	$7.50	96
1890's	$44.96	$5.00	85
1900's	$273.50	$10.00	101
1910's	$222.11	$4.00	55
TOTALS AND OVERALL FIGURES:	$182.58	$14.50	639 cases

Source: Court Bills and Indictments, 1812-1914, Rockingham Cty., MS, Div. of Records-Management and Archives, Concord, N.H. and Court Bills and Indictments, 1870-1914, Strafford Cty., MS, Justice and Administration Building, Dover, N.H.

the 1910's ($13.82). The highest values appear in the 1810's ($112.64) and 1870's ($129.90) (see Table 11). What is the significance of the type of property involved in property crime? We have collapsed the eighteen basic

Table 11

Value of Property Affected by Crime in New Hampshire, 1812-1914: Restated in Constant (1967) Dollars

Decade	Mean	Median	No. of Cases
1810's	$184.41	$112.64	42
1820's	$5312.95	$76.06	26
1830's	$97.31	$73.16	34
1840's	$70.74	$22.86	26
1850's	$117.37	$27.75	28
1860's	$116.83	$30.14	53
1870's	$316.87	$129.90	93
1880's	$181.87	$27.12	96
1890's	$173.82	$19.33	85
1900's	$1029.45	$37.64	101
1910's	$767.61	$13.82	55

TOTAL:			639 cases

Source: Court Bills and Indictments, 1812-1914, Rockingham Cty., MS, Div. of Records-Management and Archives, Concord, N.H. and Court Bills and Indictments, 1870-1914, Strafford Cty., MS, Justice and Administration Building, Dover, N.H.

Average Values per Decade in Constant (1967) Dollars

Base: 100 Cents (1967)

Decade	Value in 1967 Cents per Dollar
1810's	194.2
1820's	281.7
1830's	318.1
1840's	285.7
1850's	308.3
1860's	274.0
1870's	302.1
1880's	361.4
1890's	386.6
1900's	376.4
1910's	345.6

Source: Standard & Poor's Statistical Service, *Basic Statistics: Price Indexes...*

property types into six categories: fungible, structural, edible, agricultural, dry goods, and miscellaneous (see Table 2). Fungible property (money, watches, and jewelry) was the most common sort of distinguishable property as opposed to the miscellaneous category throughout this period. Of the fungible property, money, in the form of cash, promissory notes, bank bills, or checks was most often involved.

Fungible property was most commonly the object of crime in the 1820's when it accounted for 44.4% of the targets of property crime (see Table 2). The lowest point was during the 1890's when it accounted for only 13.6% of the types of property. Other high points were the 1810's, 1840's, 1880's, and 1910's when fungible property accounted for between 30.8% and 38.6% of the property affected.

We have included forged or counterfeit money in the category of money.

Forgery and the passing of counterfeit money and other bills of exchange dated back to the colonial era in New Hampshire, judging by the statutes. The incidence of forgery or counterfeiting was not very high according to the evidence of our sample (see Table 12). This crime was most common in the early years of the nineteenth century. The high point was reached between 1812 and 1819 when 8.5% of the inmates were convicted of this offense. Thereafter it gradually declined to become an extremely small proportion of the convictions found in our sample: none in some decades and no more than 4.6% in any decade following the 1830's.

Counterfeiting and forgery required a high degree of skill. A counterfeiter required good engraving and casting abilities to reproduce coins; he also required a supply of the appropriate metals. The secret of counterfeiting, according to Don Taxay, is to create a likeness of the currency but to leave out the one element that lends it value.[70] Skill was required when producing the stamping plates used for printing false bills and documents. At its most simple level, forgery might involve filling in the blanks and falsely signing a legitimate bill or promissory note. However, the latter variety could sometimes be confused with larceny. A case was listed here as "forgery or counterfeiting" only when explicitly described as such in the primary sources.

A typical example of forgery is the case of Noah Brown, age 47 and a resident of Hampton Falls, convicted of forgery in February 1816. The evidence consisted of "a certain false, forged and counterfeited bank bill or note, falsely made, forged and counterfeited in imitation and similitude of a true bank bill or note of the President Directors and Company of the Manufacturers and Mechanic's Bank." Brown attempted to pay Brackett Johnson with a counterfeit $3 note. For this crime, Noah Brown served a two-year sentence in the state prison.[71]

At first glance, it might seem odd that watches were a common object of property crime. Nearly all of the watches in the crimes surveyed here were made of silver or gold. Monetary value of a watch and chain could be surprisingly high. For example, 23-year old James Williams of Exeter stole a watch worth $100 from Niram [sic] Kayes on September 20, 1849 in the town of Kingston.[72] John F. Cochrane, age 25, also of Exeter, broke into the Peabody Hall dormitory of Phillips Exeter Academy on June 1, 1901 and stole a gold watch and chain worth $75 belonging to Albert Travis.[73] Like money, watches were easy to carry and hide and they may have been easy to convert into cash. Watches were most popular among thieves and burglars in the 1880's when watches made up 11.3% of the types of property affected by crime.

Table 12

Crime in New Hampshire, 1812-1914, by Category

Property Crime

Crime	Frequency (No. Cases)	Valid % of Total
Larceny	258	31.4%
Burglary	224	27.3%
Break and Enter	59	7.2%
Robbery	36	4.4%
Arson	22	2.6%
Forgery or Counterfeit	18	2.2%
Break and Enter Intent Steal	10	1.2%
Embezzlement	5	0.6%
False Pretence	5	0.6%
Att. Robbery	3	0.4%
TOTAL:	639 cases	77.9% of total crime

Violent Crime

Crime	Frequency (No. Cases)	Valid % of Total Crime
Murder	28	3.4%
Att. Murder	28	3.4%

Violent Crime

Crime	Frequency (No. Cases)	Valid % of Total Crime
Manslaughter	24	2.9%
Attempted Rape	18	2.2%
Rape	15	1.8%
Break and Enter and Assault	2	0.2%
Assault with Intent Steal	2	0.2%
Assault	2	0.2%
Maim	1	0.1%
	---	-----
TOTAL:	120 cases	14.6% of total crime

Moral Crime

Crime	Frequency (No. Cases)	Valid % of Total Crime
Adultery	5	0.6%
Bigamy	5	0.6%
Sodomy	2	0.2%
Unnatural and Lascivious Acts	1	0.1%
Entice Child for Prostitution	1	0.1%
Polygamy	1	0.1

Moral Crime

Crime	Frequency (No. Cases)	Valid % of Total Crime
Incest	1	0.1%
	---	-----
TOTAL:	15 cases	1.8% of total crime

Other Crime

Crime	Frequency (No. Cases)	Valid % of Total Crime
Tramp	28	3.4%
Perjury	7	0.9%
Parole Violation	4	0.5%
Place Obstruction on R.R. Tracks	2	0.2%
Enter Dwelling as Tramp	2	0.2%
Rob Grave	1	0.1%
Poison Cow	1	0.1%
	----	-----
TOTAL:	46 cases	5.6% of total crime

OVERALL TOTAL: 820 cases   100% of total crime

Source: Court Bills and Indictments, 1812-1914, Rockingham Cty., MS, Div. of Records-Management and Archives, Concord, N.H.; Court Bills and Indictments, 1870-1914, Strafford Cty., MS, Justice and Administration Building, Dover, N.H.; "Register of Convicts 1812-1883" and "[N.H. State] Prison Records [1874-1915]," both MS, Div. of Records-Management and Archives, Concord, N.H.; and *Prison Warden's Reports*, 1813-1914.

Most of the jewelry cases here involve values of under $100. William Mullen, 21, was convicted of armed robbery in 1885. The robbery netted him a gold ring worth only $3 from Freeman B. Dudley on April 11, 1885 in Exeter.[74]

In contrast, was the spectacular theft committed by Edgar R. Beach alias William Thomas on June 17, 1912. His crime was the theft of a very large quantity of jewelry with a value of $13,165 from Ada L. Studebaker's summer residence at North Hampton. The long list of items stolen includes a $5000 necklace, a $1000 diamond ring, a sapphire and gold ring worth $800, and numerous pieces of jewelry. Beach was born in England in 1872. Shortly before the crime Beach had been hired as the butler at Ada Studebaker's house. The theft was discovered late on the night of June 17 when Mrs. Studebaker checked on her safe before retiring for the night after spending the evening out with friends. A roll call of the servants indicated that the butler had left the house earlier that evening.[75]

Edgar Beach was tracked down and arrested in Philadelphia by the Pinkerton Detective Agency 12 days later. According to the *Portsmouth Herald*, "Beach has already served a term in prison for similar robberies at London, England and is wanted for a number of big jobs in other parts of America."[76] Beach was convicted in April 1913 and sentenced to four to five years in the State Prison. He was transferred to the State Hospital for the Insane shortly after his arrival.[77]

Next to money, clothing was the single most frequent type of property involved in a crime in our sample: 12% of the total (see Table 1). The theft of clothing reached its highest point in the early nineteenth century: 23.8% of the total in the 1810's and 23.5% in the 1830's. After that, clothing as the object of crime experienced a slow decline although it accounted for over 15% of the types of property involved in crime during the 1870's, 1880's, and 1890's. By the years 1910-14, clothing had declined to only 1.8% of the types of property involved in crime. Clothing was by far the most common component of property in the dry goods category. Dry goods were the third most common type of property involved in crime in our sample: 13.2% (see Table 2). This category was most numerous in the 1830's at 23.5% of the total. Dry goods were also popular objects of crime during the 1810's and from the 1860's through the 1890's.

John Davis was a 23-year old mariner from Providence, Rhode Island. On the night of July 13, 1816 he stole $286 worth of clothing from Leonard Lennat's [?] shop in Portsmouth. He served a five-year sentence in the state prison. Judging from the type and sheer quantity of clothing - among other things, Davis stole 18 woolen jackets, 25 shirts, and 25 waistcoats - Davis did not steal because he lacked adquate clothing of his own. Most likely, he hoped to market these items elsewhere and make a profit. Perhaps he had a buyer waiting at another port of call; the records do not say.[78]

On the other hand, the pitiful case of James D. Elliot of Exeter indicates a crime most likely inspired by need. Elliot stole one pair of pantaloons worth $6 from the house of Thomas Wentworth in Greenland in broad daylight on June 11, 1833. The 29-year old Elliot was caught, convicted, and sent to the state prison. He died on February 7, 1836, less than six months from completing his three-year sentence.[79]

One possible reason for the eventual decline in clothing thefts was the growth of textile manufacturing in New England throughout the nineteenth century. Clothing became more easily obtainable and cheaper in price, thus reducing its appeal as a target for criminals. Textile products in general for the United States experienced a decline in price of more than 50% between 1812 and 1860. After an increase in price of 100% during the Civil War, textile prices experienced a 50% drop and then remained fairly stable through 1914.[80]

In some ways horse theft was as serious a crime as automobile theft is in our era. Horses were essential for mobility, especially in rural areas. Even with the arrival of mechanized public transportation systems such as railroads and trolleylines, many people depended on horses for basic transportation. Henry Ford began production of the Model T in 1908. Mass production started in 1913. By the end of our study in 1914, automobiles were becoming widespread but horses still had a significant role to play in transportation, delivery of goods and services, and agriculture. From 1890 on the use of horses in urban areas began to decline due to public health concerns, rising real estate values (stabling horses in downtown areas became too expensive), and the development of mechanical substitutes. Nonetheless, three million horses were still employed in the United States for nonagricultural uses as late as 1910.[81] A very significant proportion of property crime involved agricultural animals. Under the category of agricultural property we have placed horses (even though many were no longer used purely for agricultural purposes), other livestock, horses plus vehicles, and vehicles alone. Our sample does not include any automobiles but there were several horsedrawn vehicles.

Thefts of horses and horsedrawn vehicles are found in every decade of the sample. As late as May 1914 James Carson, a 59-year old resident of Dover, stole a horse worth $200, harness worth $20, and wagon worth $30 from Walter H. Smith of Dover. Carson was given a sentence of five to seven years in prison in September 1914.[82] Theft of agricultural property and horses in particular reached a peak during the 1840's when this category made up 30.8% of the forms of property affected by crime (see Table 2). Livestock and horse thieves were marked by tattooing in the face between 1791 and 1829.[83] No other criminals of this era were so marked. Ironically, theft of livestock reached its peak while this cruel law was still in effect. During the 1810's livestock other than horses accounted for 14.3% of the property classifications and 11.1% in the 1820's. The tattooing law was abolished in 1830 and in the following decade this category of property dropped to only 2.9% of the sample. Nobody was convicted of other livestock theft in the 1850's and thereafter livestock theft represented only around 1-4% of the total.

Such a crime was taken very seriously in a rural economy. Livestock represented money on the hoof or wing at a time when most food could not be preserved for long. Asa Clay of Durham was apparently a sheeprustler. On September 9, 1816 the 25-year old Clay stole 11 sheep worth $5 each from Enoch Clark of Greenland. One week later Clay stole 37 sheep worth $6 each from John Wingate of Stratham. For these crimes, Clay served a full five-year sentence in the state prison and was also presumably marked with a line of India-ink in his face.[84]

Foodstuffs represents a small percentage of the types of property in our sample: 5.2% overall. Such property was not the object of crime in the 1830's or 1910's. The high points were 10.7% of the sample in the 1850's, 9.1% in the 1890's, and 9.6% in the 1900's (see Table 2).

As was true of other property crimes, those involving food or drink reflect both greed and actual need. An example of the former is the case of Samuel Caswell, 26, who broke into the house of Joseph Banks in Nottingham at 11 p.m. on November 22, 1852. Caswell and an accomplice removed 100 pounds of butter valued at $25 and 100 pounds of salt pork valued at $14. The court records indicate that Caswell and his accomplice broke into at least three other houses that night to steal large quantities of food and other items. However, he was convicted of only one crime and received a sentence of five years.[85] It is likely that Samuel Caswell planned to sell the food, judging by the nature and quantity. In contrast was the case of Harry Young, also 26, a resident of Dover. Young's larder was probably bare on January 21, 1896 when he stole a ham worth $1.50 from the J.M. Wilson and Company store in Dover. He was sentenced to three years.[86]

Arson was a rather uncommon form of property crime. Unlike most other property crimes, the main goal of arson was the destruction of property. The arsonist did not stand to gain anything material from his action unless it was to file a false insurance claim. None of the arsonists found in our sample were connected to any such scheme. Small wonder the punishment for arson was severe - destruction of someone's house, barn, or place of business was the likely equivalent of ruining him or her. Even if the arsonist's victim had the financial resources to rebuild, the sheer inconvenience was extreme in a time before power tools were widely available. Arson threated life and limb and farm animals faced potential destruction too. Arson was a more vicious crime than most others in the property category.

Arsonists preferred barns as their target. Eleven (50.0%) out of twenty-two arson cases involved barns. Seven (36.6%) involved other buildings such as stores and woodsheds. Only four (14.0%) involved houses (see Table 1). This would suggest that the arsonist's motive was the destruction of one's livelihood rather than physical harm to the victim. The loss of a barn filled with animals, supplies, equipment, or crops awaiting the market could be devastating.

Psychiatrist John M. Macdonald suggests the following as motives for arsonists in the present-day United States and Britain: revenge, jealousy, and hatred; financial gain; intimidation and extortion; a need for attention; social protest; a method of concealing other crimes or to facilitate other crimes; a form of vandalism; or accident.[87] None of the original sources provide information on the motives of the persons convicted of arson in seacoast New Hampshire between 1812 and 1914. However, we can probably eliminate financial gain and extortion. It is likely the court records would have mentioned a financial motive since these records typically provide detailed financial information for property crimes. For most of the decades between 1812 and 1914 arson accounted for 2 or 3% of the crimes surveyed here. Arson reached a peak in the 1870's when it made up 8.4% of the offenses. Arsonists were involved in all of the structural property crimes in our sample. Structural property reached 8.6% of the total in the 1870's (see Table 2).

There were only a scattering of other sorts of property crimes - robbery, embezzlement, and false pretenses. Some of the more interesting cases involve embezzlement and false pretenses. These crimes required both skill and planning and were not usually committed upon impulse. The following case would qualify as an example of "theft by trick," a phenomenon characteristic of urban locations according to Eric Monkkonen.[88] Forest N. Mace, 31, and Clyde F. McKenney, 32, both of Rochester, joined forces to defraud 80-year old Jacob Ford of his hard-earned money. The two men went to Dover on July 22, 1914 and perpetrated the following swindle on Ford. Mace told Ford that Clyde McKenney had agreed to help him purchase a horse from one Gilbert Boutine for $250. Mace then told Ford that McKenney had already paid Boutine $195 but that Boutine was demanding the remainder and threatening to remove the horse. Somehow Forest Mace convinced Jacob Ford to lend him the $55 needed to purchase Boutine's horse. In reality, Mace and McKenny obtained $55 from Ford under false pretences - the horse sale was fictitious. Mace was sentenced to four to five years in prison and McKenny for two to three years.[89]

Jacob Ford seems to have made the ideal victim. Mace and McKenny were convicted of only one count of obtaining money under false pretences but the court records imply that the pair had tricked Ford twice before. One one occasion Mace and McKenney pretended to be potato merchants. On April 15, 1914 they informed Ford that they purchase potatoes by the (train) carload, shipping the potatoes from Lewiston, Maine to Rochester, New Hampshire. They told Ford that they need $100 for purchasing potatoes; he evidently gave them the sum. On July 18, they committed another horse purchasing swindle involving the mysterious Gilbert Boutine. Apparently, Ford loaned the pair of scoundrels another $50.[90]

The Rochester Courier states that Mace and McKenney actually tricked the retired farmer out of $1796 "through a series of schemes realizing that he had the utmost confidence in their ability." Among other schemes, Mace told Ford that he needed money for legal help in retrieving $1500 from Prince Edward Island, Canada; that he needed money to start an automobile business; and that he needed funds to pay for an "alleged operation" of a family member.[91]

Embezzlement was a white collar crime that sometimes involved very large sums of money. One of the more interesting embezzlers was Albert O. Mathes of Dover. The first hint of trouble occurred on February 11, 1902. The Strafford County grand jury indictment dated September 1903 states that Mathes was accused of embezzling $1600 from the Strafford Savings Bank in Dover on that date. He was the treasurer of the bank and had worked there for 35 years. For some reason, the indictment ended up as *nolle prosequi*.[92]

Mathes was not so lucky with the indictment covering the events of May 1, 1903. The 61-year old treasurer was convicted of embezzling $10,000 in bank bills and silver certificates. He was sentenced to a term of two to three years in the state prison. Mathes was pardoned after two years but his future looked grim. Oddly enough, the day before Mathes's ruin, he made the news by falling under the wheels of a train at the Milton, New Hampshire train station. The accident (or attempted suicide?) resulted in the amputation of his left foot.[93] He was now a physically handicapped, disgraced convict in his sixties.

What can one conclude about property crime in nineteenth century New Hampshire? It was the most common form of crime. Property crime accounted anywhere from 68.1% to 94.4% of the crimes in our sample. The highest rate was reached in the 1870's (120 per 100,000 population) and the lowest in the 1820's (47 per 100,000 population) (see Table 9). The most common form of property crime was larceny which was closely followed by burglary and breaking and entering. Other forms of property crime represented smaller proportions of the whole.

The target of property crime was modest in most cases. Statistics on the type and value of property affected tell us something about New Hampshire society as well as about crime. Monetary value of the property involved in crime was fairly low: $182.58 is the mean value for the entire period and $14.50 the median.

A more accurate measurement would be to examine the median value of property values in constant dollars (see Table 11). This does not include the value of property destroyed by arsonists: court records of this period never list the valuation of buildings. The great majority of property crimes involved sums of less than $100. From the 1830's through the 1910's most property crimes involved sums of less than $20. In the 1870's the number of property crimes involving sums of $0-$19 and $20-$99 were nearly equal. Probably this reflects the $20 dividing point between petty and grand larceny. As of 1815 those convicted of stealing property worth $20 or more were automatically sent to the state prison.[94] Additional factors such as the time of day, location, use of force, etc., were taken into account by the court which could transform a petty crime into a felony and thus rate a prison term.

What can one conclude about crime in New Hampshire from the type of property involved? The typical thief, burglar, or robber was interested in money above all other forms of property. Money is portable, easy to hide, and it provides greater access to what one desires in material terms. Many of the "money" crimes involved promissory notes, certificates, and bank bills in addition to cash. In some ways it would seem to be a risky theft since a signature was usually involved. A transaction involving certificates could not be as anonymous as one involving cash only. Probably the main value of certificates, notes, etc. was the fact that they were often of large denomination, hence, worth taking the risk of detection. No doubt, counterfeiters and forgers felt the same way.

Some cases would indicate a need for clothing on the part of the criminal but most involve the theft of multiple items and sometimes the theft of clothing designed for the opposite sex. This was probably for resale to others. There may be a link between the gradual decline in popularity of clothing as an object of theft and the growing availability of manufactured clothing over time.

It is not surprising to learn that horses, livestock, and horsedrawn vehicles were a common object of property crime. Most crime seems to have occurred in large population centers but even here horses remained a very significant mode of transportation and motive power until at least 1914. Livestock and horses sound like a cumbersome form of property to steal but that did not deter 14.3% of the criminals convicted of property crime in the sample. Most crime took place in large towns and cities during the 1810's through 1860's (with the exception of the 1840's) than in the rural locations (see Table 13). It was not until the 1890's that seacoast New Hampshire was more urban than rural and the proportion of urban crimes to urban population was more or less equal (see Table 5).

Property crime rates in Rockingham County and Strafford County per 100,000 population increased dramatically between 1850 and 1870 when they rose from 57 to 120 (see Table 9). Thereafter they gradually declined until dropping steeply from 112 per 100,000 population in the 1900's to 60 in the 1910's. The general pattern of property crime rates in seacoast New Hampshire resembles that of other parts of the country at this time except that the decline in rates occurs several decades later.

Theodore N. Ferdinand's study of Boston confirms this impression (see Table 14). The arrest rates for larceny per 100,000 population in Boston jumped from 400 in 1850 to 1000 in 1860. They then dropped to 600 in 1870 and thereafter gradually declined to around 455 per 100,000 population in 1910.[95] Similarly, burglary arrest rates per 100,000 population jumped from approximately 60 in 1850 to just under 120 in 1860. They leveled off at approximately 85 per 100,000 population until a sudden rise to 120 in 1890, followed by a slight decline to 110 in 1910.[96] Arrest rates for robbery per 100,000 population in Boston rose dramatically from 20 in 1850 to about 33 in 1860. This peak was followed by a fall to 23 per 100,000 population in 1880 and the rates stayed steady through 1910 with the exception of 1900 when they rose to about 31.[97]

Michael Hindus found a dramatic increase in property crime prison commitments in Massachusetts between 1836 and 1873. Like Ferdinand, his rates were higher than those in New Hampshire but the pattern was similar (see Table 14). In Hindus's findings the sharpest increase took place between 1840 (approximately 125 per 100,000 population) and 1850 (approximately

Table 13

Urban Crime in New Hampshire, 1812-1914:
Comparing Percentage Urban Crime to Percentage Urban Population

Decade	Population % Urban	% Rural	Crime % Urban	% Rural	% Unknown
1810's	19.3%	82.4%	27.7%	63.8%	8.5%
1820's	24.1%	75.9%	25.8%	71.0%	3.2%
1830's	24.5%	75.5%	41.7%	44.4%	13.9%
1840's	29.6%	70.4%	47.1%	38.2%	14.7%
1850's	26.7%	73.3%	41.2%	55.9%	2.9%
1860's	25.2%	74.8%	53.8%	38.5%	7.7%
1870's	39.4%	60.6%	35.5%	48.6%	15.9%
1880's	46.5%	53.5%	49.7%	40.4%	9.9%
1890's	55.6%	44.4%	65.3%	30.5%	4.2%
1900's	56.1%	43.9%	78.4%	17.7%	3.9%
1910's	61.5%	38.5%	62.8%	28.2%	9.0%

Note: Urban is here defined as those towns or cities having 2500 or more inhabitants. Urban crime is defined as those crimes occurring in a town or city having 2500 or more inhabitants. Some crime is "unknown" because some of the court records do not specify the town, only the county. Also, some of the "unknown" crimes are listed as such because there are no surviving court records. These cases are listed in sources such as the "Register of Convicts 1812-1883" which list the county but not the town in which the crime occurred. See Table 5 for a more detailed description of urban versus rural population.

Source: *U.S. Census Reports*, 1810-1910; Court Bills and Indictments, 1812-1914, Rockingham County, N.H. Div. or Records-Management and Archives, Concord, N.H.; Court Bills and Indictments, 1870-1914, Strafford Cty., MS, Justice and Administration Building, Dover, N.H.; "Register of Convicts 1812-1883," "[N.H. State] Prison Records [1874-1915]," and "New Hampshire State Prison: Record of Gain and Loss in Population [1905-36]," all MS, Div. of Records-Management and Archives, Concord, N.H., and *Prison Warden's Reports*, 1859-1914.

175).[98] The commitments reached a peak in 1860 at approximately 210 and then declined to 160 per 100,000 population in 1870.[99] However, Hindus's rates include commitments for jails and houses of correction, as well as the state prison, so his base is broader than the one used in this project which is solely at the level of commitments to the New Hampshire state prison.

Monkkonen's Ohio study also shows a post-Civil War decline although the emergence of a new form of property is noted. Theft rates for Ohio fell from 60 per 10,000 population in 1867 to around 25 per 10,000 in 1870 and 1880.[100] Rates for theft by trick in Ohio gradually increased from about 5 per 10,000 population in 1867 to nearly 15 in 1975. The rates then exhibit a gradual, if uneven, levelling off at around 8 per 10,000 population through 1891.[101] The pattern for Franklin County, Ohio covers only the years 1865-85. Theft was nearly level at around 70 per 10,000 population. Theft by trick increased from approximately 2 to 25 per 10,000 population. Monkkonen theorizes that the increase in theft by trick was a sophisticated type of crime, well-suited for the growing and changing economic character of urban centers. Such an offender could exploit new commercial relationships and the anonymity of urban life.[102] Property crime was the dominant form of felony in New Hampshire. Reasons for this include the changing economic base of New Hampshire plus urbanization which may well have created economic insecurity for much of the population as well as new opportunities for crime such as burglary.

In Alameda County, California the rate of property felony arrest rates per 100,000 population noticeably declined from 439 in 1880 to 78 in 1910 according to the findings of Friedman and Percival.[103]

As one can see, comparisons of property crime rates between our sample and other studies is only partially possible. Different methods of measurement help explain why the rates for New Hampshire are so low in comparison to others at the time. Ferdinand measured arrest rates, Monkkonen measured prosecutions, and Hindus measured commitments to

Table 14

Property Crime Rates: New Hampshire, 1812-1914; Boston, 1850-1910; and Massachusetts, 1840-1870

	Rate per 100,000 Population				
Decade/Year	N.H. Prop.	Boston Larceny	Boston Burglary	Boston Robbery	Mass. Property
1810's	84				
1820's	47				
1830's	77				
1840's/1840	57				125
1850's/1850	57	400	60	20	175
1860's/1860	106	1000	118	33	210
1870's/1870	120	600	100	33	160
1880's/1880	114	625	80	23	
1890's/1890	97	410	120	23	
1900's/1910	112	475	110	27	
1910's/1910	60	455	92	31	

Note: New Hampshire rates were calculated by felony convictions per decade. Boston rates were calculated by arrest rates per year. Massachusetts rates were calculated by commitments to jails, houses of correction, and prisons per year. Boston and Massachusetts rates are approximate: the numbers are derived from charts.

Source: Court Bills and Indictments, 1812-1914, Rockingham Cty., MS, Div. of Records-Management and Archives, Concord, N.H. and Court Bills and

110

Indictments, 1870-1914, Strafford Cty., MS, Justice and Administration Building, Dover, N.H.; Theodore N. Ferdinand, "The Criminal Patterns of Boston Since 1849," *American Journal of Sociology*, 73 (July 1967) and Michael S. Hindus, *Prison and Plantation* (Chapel Hill, 1980).

prisons, jails, and houses of correction, and this study measured felony incarcerations. Another explanation for New Hampshire's lower rates lies in the fact that the other areas were urban. There were some cities in our sample (Portsmouth, Dover, Exeter, and Rochester) but compared to places like Columbus, Ohio or Boston, they were small cities indeed. Opportunities for crime were different thanks to a different social environment both in terms of actual numbers and concentrations of inhabitants and in settlement patterns. Even though crime rates derived from different sources and over different lengths of time make direct comparisons difficult, they all agree on one basic pattern. Somewhere between 1840 and 1870 property crime rates rose dramatically and then either leveled off or declined in the decades following the Civil War.

It is important to add that in this study arson and robbery have been placed under the category of property crime. Both of them share characteristics of violent crime. Arson is characterized by violence against property and it is potentially lethal to people inside the burning structure. Robbery is more of a violent assault than purely a property crime. Violent crimes represent the second most common sort of offense committed by those persons condemned to a stretch in the New Hampshire State Prison in the nineteenth and early twentieth century. We will now examine the incidence and nature of violent crime. Afterward, we will investigate moral felonies and other types of crime before making some broad conclusions about crime in general for New Hampshire 1812-1914.

Crimes of violence consisted of the following: murder, attempted murder, manslaughter, rape, attempted rape, assault with intent to commit a felony, assault, and maiming (see Table 12).

The pattern of violent crime that emerges here roughly parallels the findings of historians such as Ted Robert Gurr, Eric Monkkonen, and Roger Lane. Gurr says that the longterm trend in the Western world has been a gradual decline in the rate of serious crime.[104] Gurr correctly points out that the property crimes of burglary and larceny are actually of more "social importance" but that violent crimes are of more concern to the public.[105] In other words, burglary and larceny are more disruptive than violent crimes because they affect a far greater number of people more directly than crimes of violence. The spectacular nature of violent crimes results in more publicity.

Eric Monkkonen agrees that there was a longterm decline in violent crime but that the United States began to diverge from the rest of the Western world in the period 1850-1875. The decline of violent crime in the United States has been much less steep than in other countries and it has not been consistent.[106] One explanation for the persistence of violent crime in the United States is offered by historian Paul Gilje. Gilje argues that the Irish immigrant was a major contributor to the violence of New York City in the early nineteenth century. Gilje says that the Irish had a tradition of violent resistance which was further inflamed by nativism in the New York area.[107] Heavy Irish immigration to the United States began in the 1840's when the potato famine struck Ireland. Lower class Irish immigrants feature prominentaly in the police records of the 1840's onwards according to Gurr.[108] However, most of the cases documented by Gurr, Monkkonen, and others took place in New York, Philadelphia, and other urban centers. We will have to examine the ethnic composition of the violent criminals for Strafford and Rockingham counties in the next chapter to see if there is a link between violent crime and immigration in New Hampshire.

Roger Lane detects three "pronounced surges of interpersonal violence" starting in 1850, 1900, and 1960 in the United States.[109] There was a radical increase in the rate of attempted murder in the 1850's in two New Hampshire counties when this crime accounted for 11.8% of the incarcerations. There were no convictions for murder in the 1850's even though that was supposedly a very violent decade in other parts of the United States. Were the would-be murderers in New Hampshire inept? Since there was only one manslaughter conviction in our sample for this decade, the shortage of actual convictions for murder might also be explained by verdicts of justifiable homicide (such as self-defence) or accidental murder. Such killers would not have been sent to the state prison and thus do not show up in my sample.

Rates of violent crime per 100,000 population began rising in the 1840's when they reached 15 per 100,000 (see Table 9). Violent crime rates increased steadily except for a slight drop in the 1870's through the 1890's when they reached a peak of 32 per 100,000 population in Rockingham County and Strafford County. Thereafter, violent crime rates dropped to 18 per 100,000 population and then increased to 21 by the 1910's. Violent crime rates were much lower than those for property crime. After 1859 the patterns for violent and property crimes diverged: property crime declined while violent crime increased (see Table 9).

Violent crimes were relatively uncommon between 1812 and 1839. Violent crimes rates jumped from a low of 5 per 100,000 population in the previous decade to 15. What is most noticeable is the emergence of murder as a crime. Between 1812 and 1839 none of the felons in our sample were convicted of murder though a few were convicted of attempted murder. In the 1820's 3.2% of the prisoners were serving time for manslaughter and the figure was 2.8% in the 1830's. Violence reached new heights in the 1890's and 1910's but this was due more to conviction for violent crimes in general rather than just murder itself.

The violent crime rate derived from our sample does not reflect the national sharp upward trend in the decade following the Civil War detected by Gurr.[110] Violence comprised an unexceptional 9 per 100,000 population rate of the convictions in the 1870's in seacoast New Hampshire. However, violent crime in this region increased through the 1890's when it reached 32 per 100,000 population (see Table 9). The post-Civil War increase in homicide has been linked to the return of veterans, the availability of handguns, and immigration.[111] We will examine ethnic constitution in the next chapter and the use of weapons in violent crime in this chapter to determine how the persons in our sample fit into the broad picture. We also need to see if it is possible to determine the relationship between the attacker and his victim.

Murder, attempted murder, and manslaughter are legally distinct crimes. They became more distinct over time as illustrated by the growing complexity of the New Hampshire statutes. It would be incorrect to say that criminal intent was identical in all such convictions. The question of intent or *mens rea* was crucial for determining the degree of guilt. *Mens rea* means illegal intent but should not be confused with the motive for committing a crime. The law meant to punish purposeful attempts to do wrong while a motive is simply the reason discovered for committing a crime.[112]

First degree murder was defined as deliberate, premeditated action. The law eventually recognized the difference between such murder and "justifiable homicide" or murder committed in self-defense. Manslaughter and, up to a point, second degree murder imply that the offender did not actually intend to kill his or her victim. However, the intent was to harm the victim. Of course, the law recognized the accidental nature of many murders. A murder committed in the heat of passion or rage was still murder - but the lawmakers determined this to be less egregious than premeditated or deliberate murder. Very few court records are detailed enough to give us a clear picture of the circumstances surrounding a violent crime. Nevertheless, we will try to make some generalizations about murder, attempted murder, and manslaughter in

New Hampshire for the years 1812-1914.

Women were rarely the perpetrators of any serious crimes yet the statistics derived from the sample indicate that when a woman was the perpetrator, she was more likely than a man to commit crimes of violence. Out of all 820 cases surveyed here, 14.6% consisted of crimes of violence. Out of the 16 cases in which women were perpetrators of crime, 6 (37.6%) were crimes of violence. We will discuss the issue of female criminality in more detail in Chapter Four.

One disturbing factor is suggested by the presence of female victims in the cases of murder, attempted murder, and manslaughter. Of the 26 cases where it is known that the victim was female, 13 appear to be cases where the man killed or attempted to kill his own wife. A few records definitely indicate that the woman was the wife of the killer/attacker; the rest suggest it by virtue of the fact that the criminal and his victim share the same surname. The phenomenon of spousal and familial murder is by no means unknown to social scientists today.[113] In 1992, for example, 29% of all female murder victims in the United States had been murdered by husbands or boyfriends. In contrast, only 4% of male murder victims had been murdered by wives or girlfriends.[114]

Family violence was largely committed by males against females - but not always. Sometimes it was male against male as in the murder of Hiram F. Sawtelle by his brother Isaac B. on February 5, 1890. The case was widely covered in newspapers of the time.[115] There were three cases in which women killed either their daughters or nieces.[116]

The following cases of murder are cited because they were in some ways typical examples: the circumstances, persons involved, and weapons used provide a generalized picture of murder in seacoast New Hampshire. For example, on October 3, 1821 Edward Lee, a 44-year old resident of Epping, assaulted Dudley Norris, also of Epping, with a loaded gun held in both hands. The court records do not indicate if Lee actually fired the gun but he was convicted of attempted murder and sent to the state prison for four years.[117]

Eliza Ann Ferguson of Exeter died on October 2, 1840 from a "mortal wound" four inches deep and two inches wide located four and a half inches below her naval. The mortal wound was caused by her husband, Bradbury Ferguson, age 32, who shot his wife in the stomach with a "certain gun" valued at $5.[118] Ferguson had come home drunk on the evening of October 2 after attending a regimental muster in Epping. According to the *Exeter News-Letter and Rockingham Advertiser*, "He had been drinking, not to absolute drunkenness, but to the exciting of all his bad passions, and to the straining up of his muscles to an unnatural strength."[119] He quarreled with Eliza Ann and drove her out of the house. Later that evening he demanded her return from the neighbors who summoned the Exeter police. The domestic dispute was seemingly resolved when the police left. Later that night the Fergusons' six children were awakened by a blast from their father's gun which killed their mother. Bradbury Ferguson fled the scene after acknowledging his guilt to his children.[120] Ferguson was caught in Northfield, New Hampshire, about 50 miles northwest of Exeter. He had lived on apples for four days before being arrested. He was discovered in some nearby woods after begging for food.[121] Ferguson was convicted of second degree murder and sent to the state prison for life. He died there of "consumption" in 1853.[122]

One of the few female criminals found in the sample was 23-year old Lizzie Provinchia of Somersworth. She was convicted of second degree murder. On January 31, 1899 Provinchia was in Rochester where she fired a pistol three times at Annie Cox. Cox died from shots "in and upon the outer side of the left forearm, left of the body near the apex of the shoulder blade, and in and through the heart." Lizzie Provinchia was sentenced to 25 years in the state prison. Ten years later she was pardoned and released.[123]

This crime had its roots in an unfortunate marriage. Lizzie Hutchins married Henry Provencher, a 20 year old blacksmith, at age 15, probably because whe was pregnant as their child was born shortly after the marriage.[124] The marriage evidently was a happy one for the first two years. At that point Lizzie started drinking and Henry began spending nights away from home. The situation deteriorated so that eventually the unhappy couple separated and sent their young child to Manchester to live with relatives.

In the Spring of 1898, 27-year old Henry Provencher met Annie Cox, a girl of 17 from Calais, Maine. The newspaper says Annie Cox "appeared to be very much in love with the young blacksmith, and happy and contented."[125] She moved in with him in Rochester as his housekeeper. Although separated from Lizzie, Henry was not divorced. Lizzie lived in Somersworth. According to her mother, Lizzie Provinchia got drunk on January 31 and announced to her mother that she was going to kill Annie Cox with a revolver in her possession. She did, in fact, carry out her threat. Lizzie Provinchia then escaped via a freight train to Portland, Maine where she was arrested.[126]

James Palmer was one of the very few persons executed for first degree murder in New Hampshire. The 26-year old resident of Portsmouth was convicted of cutting Henry Whitehouse's throat with a knife on May 27, 1888 in Portsmouth. Whitehouse, 22, died instantly of a "mortal wound" five inches long and three inches deep. After two reprieves, Palmer was hanged in 1890.[127]

James Palmer had worked with Henry Whitehouse at the Electric Light Company in Portsmouth. Whitehouse had notified the authorities that Palmer was stealing tools and Palmer was fired. Thus, vengeance was probably the motive for the murder.[128]

At 11:30 p.m. on May 27, 1888 Whitehouse left the home of his fiancee, Cora Fernald, located in Kittery, Maine, for work at the Electric Light Company. Palmer was waiting for him in the darkness on the beach at Noble's Island. He struck Whitehouse on the head with a hammer and "the cowardly assassin then dragged the body down the bank to near the water's edge, and there cut the throat to the bone, apparently endeavoring to cut the head off, then pushing the body overboard. The face, the top and left side of the head, were shockingly cut and disfigured."[129] The next morning, two men found the corpse on the beach. Palmer's hammer was found sixty feet away and identified. He was arrested at work at a nearby shoe factory.[130] The next day, a search of Palmer's mother's house revealed wet, muddy, and bloodstained clothing belonging to Palmer. The clothing was recognized by witnesses who had seen him near the scene of the crime that night.[131]

Joseph E. Kelley of Somersworth was a 23-year old engineer. On April 16, 1897 he killed Joseph A. Stickney by beating him to death with a policeman's billy club. Stickney died of "divers severe, and mortal blows upon the head, thereby breaking the skull and causing mortal wounds." In addition, Kelley used a razor to cut Stickney's throat causing a wound five inches wide and four inches deep. Even though the court bill states this brutal crime was premeditated, Kelley was found of second degree rather than first degree murder. He served 23 years out of a 30-year sentence and was released in 1920.[132]

The most popular weapon was a firearm (see Table 15). Twenty-eight out of eighty cases involved the use of a firearm. Usually described as a gun, sometimes the weapon is more specifically described as a pistol, revolver, or shotgun. The second most common sort of weapon was a sharp metal object such as a knife or razor: 16 cases. Finally, a blunt, heavy object, usually described as a club or stick was the third most common: 12 cases. Included here were a few odd items such as an iron "pinch bar" or even an iron tea kettle which was used to smash in the skull of one victim.[133] Nearly as many cases involved the use of one's fists or other parts of the body. The remainder of the cases involved the use of an axe, poison, a cloth (for suffocation), kerosene (burning the victim to death), and even a boat which

116

Table 15

Violent Crime: Data on Murder, Attempted Murder, Manslaughter, Assault, and Maiming

I. 1812-1819 (3 Cases)
Percent and No. of Cases

Crime	Attacker	Weapon	Victim
Assault 33.3% (1)	Male 100% (3)	Chisel 33.3% (1)	Male 100% (3)
Att. Murder 66.7% (2)		Club 33.3% (1)	
		Knife 33.3% (1)	

II. 1820-1829 (3 Cases)
Percent and No. of Cases

Crime	Attacker	Weapon	Victim
Manslaughter 33.3% (1)	Male 100% (3)	Large Stick 33.3% (1)	Male 100% (3)
Att. Murder 33.3% (1)		Gun 33.3% (1)	
Maiming 33.3% (1)		Unknown 33.3% (1)	

III. 1830-1839 (2 Cases)
Percent and No. of Cases

Crime	Attacker	Weapon	Victim
Manslaughter 50.0% (1)	Male 100% (2)	"Waggon Stake" 50.0% (1)	Male 100% (2)
Assault 50.0% (1)		Unknown 50.5% (1)	

IV. 1840-1849 (4 Cases)
Percent and No. of Cases

Crime	Attacker	Weapon	Victim
Murder 75.0% (3)	Male 100% (4)	Gun 25.0% (1)	Male 25.0% (1)
Manslaughter 25.0% (1)		Unknown 25.0% (1)	Female 50.0% (2)
		Stick and Hands 25.0% (1)	Unknown 25.0% (1)
		Stick 25.0% (1)	

V. 1850-1859 (5 Cases)
Percent and No. of Cases

Percent and No. of Cases

Crime	Attacker	Weapon	Victim
Manslaughter 20.0% (1)	Male 100% (5)	Gun 40.0% (2)	Male 40.0% (2)
Att. Murder 80.0% (4)		Knife 40.0% (2)	Female 60.0% (3)
		Club 20.0% (1)	

VI. 1860-1869 (8 Cases)

Percent and No. of Cases

Crime	Attacker	Weapon	Victim
Murder 25.0% (2)	Male 100% (8)	Poison 12.5% (1)	Male 50.0% (4)
Manslaughter 12.5% (1)		Axe 25.0% (2)	Female 50.0% (4)
Att. Murder 62.5% (5)		Knife 25.0% (2)	
		Pistol 25.0% (2)	
		Unknown 12.5% (1)	

VII. 1870-1879 (7 Cases)

Percent and No. of Cases

Crime	Attacker	Weapon	Victim
Murder 42.9% (3)	Male 100% (7)	Pistol 28.4% (2)	Male 14.2% (1)
Manslaughter 14.2% (1)		Razor 14.2% (1)	Female 71.4% (5)
Att. Murder 42.9% (3)		Poison 14.2% (1)	Unknown 14.2% (1)
		Knife 14.2% (1)	
		Feet, Hands, and Knife 14.2% (1)	
		Unknown 14.2% (1)	

VIII. 1880-1889 (12 Cases)

Percent and No. of Cases

Crime	Attacker	Weapon	Victim
Murder 50.0% (6)	Male 83.3% (10)	Knife 25.0% (3)	Male 58.3% (7)
Manslaughter 50.0% (6)	Female 16.7% (2)	Club 8.3% (1)	Female 41.7% (5)
		Club & Revolver 8.3% (1)	
		Iron Tea Kettle 8.3% (1)	
		Body 25.0% (3)	
		Fire & Kerosene 8.3% (1)	
		Unknown 16.7% (2)	

118

IX. 1890-1899 (16 Cases)
Percent and No. of Cases

Crime	Attacker	Weapon	Victim
Murder 37.5% (6)	Male 87.5% (14)	Hands 31.3% (5)	Male 81.3% (13)
Manslaughter 50.0% (8)	Female 12.5%	Pistol 31.3% (5)	Female 18.7% (3)
Att. Murder 12.% (2)	(2)	Police Billy Club & Razor 6.3% (1)	
		Revolver 12.5% (2)	
		Shotgun 6.3% (1)	
		Knife 6.3% (1)	
		Body 6.3% (1)	

X. 1900-1909 (11 Cases)
Percent and No. of Cases

Crime	Attacker	Weapon	Victim
Murder 54.5% (6)	Male 90.9% (10)	Pistol 27.3% (3)	Male 81.8% (9)
Manslaughter 18.2% (2)	Female 9.1% (1)	Revolver 27.3% (3)	Female 18.2% (2)
Att. Murder 27.3% (3)		Iron "Pinch Bar" 9.1% (1)	
		Cloth (Suffocation) 9.1% (1)	
		"Iron Cuspidor" 9.1% (1)	
		Shotgun 9.1% (1)	
		Knife 9.1% (1)	

XI. 1910-1914 (10 Cases)
Percent and No. of Cases

Crime	Attacker	Weapon	Victim
Murder 20.0% (2)	Male 100% (10)	Pistol 30.0% (3)	Male 80.0% (8)
Manslaughter 20.0% (2)		Knife 30.0% (3)	Female 20.0% (2)
Att. Murder 60.0% (6)		Shotgun 10.0% (1)	
		Poison 10.0% (1)	
		Revolver 10.0% (1)	
		Boat (Overturned) 10.0% (1)	

Source: Court Bills and Indictments, 1812-1914, Rockingham Cty., MS, Div.

of Records-Management and Archives, Concord, N.H.; Court Bills and Indictments, 1870-1914, Strafford Cty., MS, Justice and Administration Building, Dover, N.H.; "Register of Convicts 1812-1883" and "[N.H. State] Prison Records [1874-1915]," both MS, Div. of Records-Management and Archives, Concord, N.H.; and *Prison Warden's Reports*, 1813-1914.

was deliberately tipped over in a pond.

Judging by the court records, most murders were impulsive affairs resulting from a quarrel or drunken brawl that got out of hand. A few court records reveal a sort of mad frenzy. For example, 49-year old Nelson N. Downing of Portsmouth killed Sarah Ann Spinney on March 28, 1858 by shooting her "in and about her head, face, eyes, neck, throat, and breast and other parts of the body." This brutal act was labeled manslaughter by the Supreme Judicial Court and Downing was given only one year in the state prison.[134]

A few court records reveal the other extreme - premeditated and coolly calculated murder. Richard Richardson, 38, and Sarah Ann Healey, both of Auburn, planned the demise of her husband, Stephen Healey. Richardson gave Stephen Healey "a large quantity of a certain deadly poison called strychnine" on March 6, 1860. Healey became "mortally distempered in his body" and "languished" one hour before dying. Richardson was sentenced to 30 years in the state prison for second degree murder. Healey's widow was not, probably because she did not actually administer the poison. Richardson died in prison four years later.[135]

Assault was classified as a misdemeanor which means that in nearly all cases the offender did not end up in the state prison. The four cases of assault in our sample were exceptional in that they went beyond the more common forms of simple assault. An examination of nonfelonious assault cases would help us to construct a more complete picture of violence but it is beyond the scope of this project.

Rape and attempted rape were the remaining forms of violent crime significantly represented in our sample. Rape and attempted rape comprised only 4.0% (33) of the total number of cases. If one breaks down the frequency of crime by decade the incidence of rape becomes more noticeable (see Table 16).

Rape is a crime of violence perpetrated through sexual means. According to criminologist Sue Bessmer, there are two elements to the crime: sexual penetration and non-consent.[136] Bessmer discerns five kinds of rape: 1) by force and violence; 2) by threat and fear; 3) statutory rape; 4) rape when the female is "imbecile, insane, drugged, intoxicated, asleep, or unconscious,"

Table 16

Rape and Attempted Rape as Percentage of Crime in New Hampshire, 1812-1914: Frequency by Decade

Decade	No. of Cases	Percentage of Total
1812-1819	Rape: 1	2.1%
1840-1849	Rape: 1	2.9%
	Att. Rape: 2	5.9%
1850-1859	Rape: 1	2.9%
1860-1869	Rape: 1	1.5%
	Att. Rape: 1	1.5%
1880-1889	Rape: 1	0.7%
	Att. Rape: 2	1.4%
1890-1899	Rape: 4	3.4%
	Att. Rape: 5	4.2%
1900-1909	Rape: 2	1.6%
	Att. Rape: 3	2.3%
1910-1914	Rape: 4	5.1%
	Att. Rape: 5	6.4%
TOTAL:	33 cases	100%

Source: Court Bills and Indictments, 1812-1914, Rockingham Cty., MS, Div. of Records-Management and Archives, Concord, N.H.; Court Bills and Indictments, 1870-1914, Strafford Cty., MS, Justice and Administration Building, Dover, N.H.; "Register of Convicts 1812-1883" and "[N.H. State] Prison Records [1874-1915]," both MS, Div. of Records-Management and Archives, Concord, N.H.; and *Prison Warden's Reports*, 1813-1914.

and 5) consent obtained by fraud.[137]

From the beginning of criminal law in New Hampshire, rape was an extremely serious offense; it was a capital crime until the early nineteenth century. All of the perpetrators in our sample were male and all of the victims were female. Criminologists acknowledge the existence of homosexual rape and even a few examples of females raping males, but it is overwhelmingly a crime of males against females.[138]

The social and demographic changes experienced in nineteenth century New Hampshire (such as urbanization, industrialization and the accompanying increase in numbers of female wage-earners, and changing definitions of adolescence) probably account for the increase in rape and attempted rape cases found in the sample from the 1890's on. By 1890, more than half of the seacoast's population resided in cities and towns of 2500 persons or more (see Table 5). The incidence of rape and attempted rape in New Hampshire was uneven during the nineteenth century. The high points were the 1840's at 8.8% (3) of the sample; the 1890's at 7.8% or 9 cases; and the 1910's at 11.5% or 9 cases. The rate of violent crime per 100,000 population peaked in these three decades, further reinforcing the concept of rape as violence (see Table 9). Rape and attempted rape were absent during the 1820's, 1830's, and 1870's and comprised only between 2.1% and 3.9% of crime during the other decades under consideration. In contrast, Barbara Lindemann found the rate of prosecution for rape and attempted rape in Masssachusetts to be low and fairly constant throughout the eighteenth century. She attributes this to the fact that that society was characterized by "small close-knit communities that discouraged free sexual expression by men outside of wedlock, and in which few women lived alone."[139]

It is unclear exactly how many of the 33 cases of rape and attempted rape were purely crimes of violence accomplished through sexual means or were the more ambiguous sort of crime with a sexual rather than violent motive. At least 14 out of 33 cases (42.1%) involved victims under the statutory age (see Table 17). Perhaps this indicates predatory violence with adult males assaulting the weakest members of society.[140] Some of the cases suggest that this was not always so. The age of consent was raised twice in the 1890's. Some of the rape cases involving teenage girls may have been the result of an unfortunate ignorance or disregard of the new laws. At least one rape case bears a resemblance to the modern phenomenon of "date rape" where a misunderstanding or alcoholic intoxication changed a romantic interlude into a case of rape.[141]

Most of the rape cases are unambiguously violent crimes committed against the will of the female concerned. Most of the court records employ the stock

Table 17

Rape and Attempted Rape in New Hampshire, 1812-1914:
Victim Characteristics: Age

Age of Victim	Number of Cases
Adult (Age Not Listed)	16
3 1/2	1
6	1
7	1
9	2
10	1
11	1
12	1
13	3
14	5
15	1

TOTALS: 16 Adults 17 Juveniles 33 Cases

Source: Court Bills and Indictments, 1812-1914, Rockingham Cty., MS, Div. of Records-Management and Archives, N.H. and Court Bills and Indictments, 1870-1914, MS, Justice and Administration Building, Dover, N.H.

phrases "to ravish and carnally know and other wrongs" or "carnal copulation" to describe the crime. The age of the victim is never listed if adult so it is impossible to generalize about the typical adult female victim. Most of the girls raped were in their early teens but there is one horrible example in which a three and a half year old toddler was the victim of an attempted rape.[142]

Generally, the rapist was a man between 20 and 40 years of age. A typical example was George F. Hartford of Epping, age 23. He was convicted of raping Sarah Currier in Epping on November 6, 1882. Hartford was sentenced to twenty years in prison but was pardoned after seven.[143] Michael Lorenzo alias Mike Lawrence, 26, was an unskilled laborer born in Italy. On June 28, 1892 Lorenzo attempted to rape Sarah A. McDuffee of Rochester. He served seven years in the state prison.[144] Joseph Nedeau was a 21-year old cook residing in Dover. He went on a rampage on July 14, 1900 when he raped three young girls, probably sisters: Dora Marcotte described as a 13-year old "spinster," 9-year old Mary L. Marcotte, and 6-year old Ida Marcotte.[145] Nedeau escaped conviction of raping the two older girls but he was found guilty of raping the six year old. He was sentenced to 30 years in prison and was pardoned 14 years later.[146] Rape contributed to the steadily increasing rates of violent crime which peaked in the 1890's.

Violent crime rates for Rockingham County and Strafford County are similar in pattern to those of other locations except for the fact that the peak came 20 or more years later in the sample. Instead of cresting shortly after the Civil War, violent crime rates in this sample reached their height in the 1890's and then only slightly tapered off during the following two decades (see Table 9). In addition, the sample rates per 100,000 population were lower than those for other regions. At their height, the rate for all violent crimes combined was 32 per 100,000 population in the 1890's (see Table 9).

Monkkonen found the period 1850-75 to be the point of departure when British and American homicide rates began their "bloody divergence."[147] Hindus's statistics for commitments in Massachusetts for crime against persons show a very great increase taking place in the 1840's. The rates leaped from 40 per 100,000 population in 1840 to 100 in 1850.[148] Thereafter the rate declined slightly to 80 per 100,000 population in 1860 and 1870.[149]

Ferdinand's arrest rates for Boston indicate a dramatic increase for murder, rape, and assault in the 1850's with a decline setting in for the rest of the nineteenth century. Only manslaughter deviated from this pattern.[150] Murder reached approximately 7.5 per 100,000 population in 1860. With the exception of 1880, the assault rate declined in Boston after reaching nearly 800 per 100,000 population in 1860 and 1870.[151] The murder rate per 100,000 population derived from the New Hampshire sample was at its height in the 1840's and 1880's through 1900's at 7 per 100,000 population (see Table 18). After declining to zero in the 1850's (although there were many *attempted*

Table 18

Seacoast New Hampshire Murder Rates, 1812-1914

Decade	Population	No. Cases	Rate/100,000 Pop.
1840's	45,771	3	7
1860's	50,122	2	4
1870's	77,533	3	4
1880's	84,622	6	7
1890's	88,002	6	7
1900's	90,455	6	7
1910's	91,139	2	2

Note: Rates before 1870 calculated with Rockingham County population only because Strafford County court records available only for 1870-1914.

Source: Court Bills and Indictments, 1812-1914, Rockingham Cty., MS, Div. of Records-Management and Archives, Concord, N.H.; Court Bills and Indictments, 1870-1914, Strafford Cty., MS, Justice and Administration Building, Dover, N.H.; "Register of Convicts 1812-1883" and "[N.H. State] Prison Records [1874-1915]," both MS, Div. of Records-Management and Archives, Concord, N.H.; *Prison Warden's Reports*, 1859-1914; and *U.S. Census Reports*, 1840-1910.

murders during that decade) and rising to 4 in the 1860's and 1870's, it reached a new peak of 7 per 100,000 population for the 1880's through 1900's before declining to 2 in the 1910's (see Table 18).

Monkkonen's violent crime rates for Ohio between 1867 and 1891 and Franklin County, Ohio for 1867-85 reveal a similar pattern.[152] Friedman and Percival's study of arrest rates for Alameda County, California between 1870 and 1910 reinforce their contention that serious crime in general was declining. Violent crime rates were at their height in 1880 at approximately

120 per 100,000 population and after that they declined steadily to 35 per 100,000 population by 1910.[153] In the 1880's New Hampshire showed a rate of violent felonies of 21 per 100,000 population which increased to 32 in the 1890's and then declined to 21 by 1910 (see Table 9).

Rates of violent crime differ among the studies cited here but their essential conclusions are similar: violent crime accelerated in the middle decades of the nineteenth century and then declined shortly after the Civil War. Unfortunately, neither Edward Ayers nor Michael Hindus supply rates of violent crime in the American South so it is not possible to directly compare our sample to their findings. The New Hampshire patterns resembles that for Boston, Massachusetts, and Ohio except for the fact that violent crime in New Hampshire reached its height around 20 years later.

Offenses against morality constitute the last distinct category of crime to be analyzed. These comprise a very small percentage of total convictions: 1.8% of all offenses. In the sample, out of a total 15 moral offense cases, 4 involved convictions for adultery, 5 bigamy, and 2 sodomy. The remaining four offenses were represented by one case each of polygamy, incest, enticing a female child for purposes of prostitution, and committing "unnatural and lascivious acts." The first conviction did not appear until the 1870's. Thereafter, moral offenses made up only between 2.1% and 3.7% of the total (see Table 8). Starting in the 1870's, moral crime rates hovered at around 4 per 100,000 population (see Table 9). In large part this can be explained by the fact that offenses against morality were progressively decriminalized between 1791 and 1830. At one time adultery and sodomy had been capital crimes.[154] In Chapter Two we traced the changing definitions of criminal law and saw that by 1830 virtually all moral offenses were either dropped from the books or relegated to the status of petty crimes and misdemeanors. Starting with the recriminalization of adultery in 1867, the law became increasingly strict in regard to moral offenses over the next half-century. Thus, it is not surprising that at least a few people were convicted of crimes against morality in the late nineteenth and early twentieth century.

In contrast to the statutes before 1830, the punishment for moral felonies was relatively light - usually on the order of one to three years in prison and or a heavy fine. The modern reader might find this to be excessive but one must remember that during the colonial era the same behavior was punishable by death, corporal punishment, and or extremely high fines.

It is difficult to generalize about adultery in New Hampshire since we have only four cases in our sample. All of the offenders were male; the female partner may have been punished but in one of the cases here did she go to prison. The law provided for more serious sanctions against the married partner. The four cases here involved married men and single women. For example, Charles W. Warren of Northwood was found guilty of adultery in April 1881. He and Annie M. Davis alias Warren were discovered practicing "lewd and lascivious cohabitation" in Northwood on October 1, 1880. The 24-year old laborer was married to Mary A. Warren at the time.[155]

Punishment was identical to that of adultery: one to three years in prison and or a fine of up to $500.[156] The law was careful to distinguish between intentional and unintentional bigamy. Three years was considered a sufficient waiting period to determine if a person's undivorced spouse were still alive even if the whereabouts were unknown. As with adultery, the punishment was aimed at the married partner rather than the single partner, and those convicted were primarily males. In some ways, bigamy was a greater crime than adultery because the commitment to marriage of the single partner was being violated. In the nineteenth century marriage was especially important to women due to their economic position in society. A woman who unknowingly entrusted her future to a bigamist was cruelly deceived when her "husband's" true status was discovered. She could probably expect to be left without economic support. She could probably also expect to suffer some sort of social disgrace even though she was a victim of the bigamist.

One bigamist was Thomas Morgan Jones of Rochester. Jones was born in Wales in 1865. He made his living as a salesman which probably entailed a mobile existence. He was one of the very few white collar criminals found in our sample. The court records show that Jones married Elizabeth Davies in Llandyssef, Wales on November 23, 1887.[157] He probably left his first wife behind in Wales when he next married Catherine M. Sullivan on October 1, 1893 in Boston. Certainly, Catherine was still alive when Jones went on to marry Marie Louise Marcotte on November 28, 1895 in Rochester, New Hampshire. The records indicate that Jones even had the nerve to steal $16 from Marie in 1896 though he was convicted only of bigamy.[158] This roguish character served the maximum three-year sentence for bigamy in the state prison.[159] Upon release from prison, Jones was only 35 years of age - still young enough for a smoothtalking unprincipled salesman to cause further mischief.

Only a handful of offenders went to the state prison for the remaining moral felonies. The two men convicted of sodomy and one man convicted of committing "unnatural and lascivious acts" appear to have been punished more for being homosexuals than for their specific sexual practices. One case, that of the "unnatural and lascivious acts," clearly describes the offending forms of behavior performed by one man upon the body of the other.[160] Twenty-five year old Arthur O. Preston of Dover was convicted of "committing and perpetrating that detestable and abominable crime of buggery (not to be named among christians [sic]" on August 2, 1877.[161] The law did not specify the sex of the participants in such behavior but the fact that only males were involved in the three cases found in the sample implies that homosexuality was what made the activity so offensive.

The one case of polygamy actually seems to be a case of bigamy, judging by the description in the court records.[162] The defendant went under three aliases. The term "polygamy" was no longer listed in the New Hampshire statutes by this point (1888).

The one case of incest sounds more like a doomed romance than an outright crime. Both parties involved were adults but there may have been a large enough age difference and the affair may have been begun early enough in the life of the female for this to have been considered an example of corrupting a minor. Possibly this may explain the different punishments meted out to the parties involved. Clifford Rand was convicted of committing incest with his niece Carrie Rand in Greenland in 1907. Carrie is described as a "singlewoman, she the said Carrie being then and there a daughter of a sister of Clifford and she the said Carrie being then and there also a daughter of a brother of Clifford's father." Clifford, a single adult male is described as "a brother of said Carrie's mother and he the said Clifford, being then and there also a son of a brother of said Carrie's father." Clifford Rand was punished with a sentence of two to two and a half years in the state prison plus a $20 fine; Carrie Rand was punished with a year in the Rockingham County House of Correction plus a $20 fine.[163]

Prostitution itself was not a felony, but procuring, pandering, or inducing a female under age 18 to become a prostitute definitely was so by the late nineteenth century. Ruth Rosen says that during the years 1911-15 the American public was in a panic about the issue of white slavery.[164] This coincided with the Progressive Era's campaign to eliminate prostitution. Portsmouth, New Hampshire had a thriving red-light district in the early twentieth century. A concerted effort was made to close down this area in 1912.[165] Constance Perry of Portsmouth, age 25, was convicted of "wilfully and deceitfully" enticing "one Ethel Duffy, a female child under the age of eighteen years, to wit of the age of fourteen years, for the purpose of prostitution" on August 12, 1912.[166] Probably other instances of such behavior were treated as petty crimes rather than felonies, and so do not show up in the sample.

The rates of moral crime in New Hampshire are much lower than those described by Michael Hindus for Massachusetts and Eric Monkkonen for Ohio (see Table 9). Most of the difference can probably be explained by the different ways of measuring this rate. In our sample, we included only those persons in Rockingham County and Strafford County who were actually convicted of a felony and sent to the state prison. Very few moral offenders were convicted as felons. Instead, most offenses against morality were considered petty crimes and misdemeanors and were punished by short terms in the local jail or house of correction, or by paying a fine.[167] Thus, the rates found by Michael Hindus for "crimes against morality, order, and chastity" are much higher than those found in our sample: more than 700 per 100,000 population in 1855 at their height in Massachusetts.[168] Much of this can be explained by Hindus's inclusion of liquor offenses under this category.[169] No one in our cample was sent to the New Hampshire State Prison for drunkenness or selling liquor illegally.

Eric Monkkonen treated liquor offenses as a separate category from what he calls "statutory crimes." Even so, he too finds a much higher rate for Franklin County, Ohio than is found in our sample: 36 per 10,000 population in 1870.[170]

It is possible that New Hampshire had a lower rate of moral offenses than more urban regions; prostitution was a common problem in large cities like Boston. Without more directly comparable rates the only firm conclusion we can make is that moral offenses constituted only a very small percentage of the total crime rate in seacoast New Hampshire and were considered worthy of a prison sentence only after the Civil War.

There were crimes found in our sample which do not neatly fit into any of the three major categories of property, violence, or morality. For the sake of convenience, they have been lumped together as a category called "other" and include: perjury, robbing graves, placing obstructions in railroad tracks, being a tramp, entering a dwelling as a tramp, poisoning a cow, cruelty to children, and violation of parole. Added together, "other" crimes made up 5.6% (46) of the total which is three times the number of offenses against morality but still quite small compared to violence (14.6%) and property (77.9%) (see Table 7).

The single most common sort of "other" crime was that of being a tramp. As we saw earlier, the New Hampshire legislature passed the "tramp law" in 1878 to help control the flood of unemployed persons who wandered about in a desperate search for work during the depression of the 1870's.[171] Many Americans were alarmed at the unprecedentedly large number of tramps that emerged during that decade. Possibly 20% of American workers at some point during the late nineteenth century found themselves unemployed and homeless.[172] The term "tramp" emerged in the 1870's when the middle and upper classes began to feel threatened by the presence of large numbers of the unemployed and homeless. For the first time in America, an industrial proletariat made its appearance. Labor militancy was on the rise in the 1870's as well.[173]

Few of the tramps in our sample appear to have been complete strangers to the community. All of the tramps were listed as having a residence in a town. Out of thirty tramps, only four were listed as out-of-state residents.[174] It is possible that the remaining 26 tramps were not actually residents of the New Hampshire towns listed but they were listed so for the sake of convenience. Such a person may have corresponded to the "homeless" of the present day who have no real residence. Ever since the early colonial period, New Hampshire laws had provided guidelines for determining a person's residence. This was important for the purpose of determining who was responsible for paying for poor relief.

As of 1878, the law was very explicit as to the "settlement of paupers." There were a total of 13 provisions for gaining the status of settlement in a town and thus obliging the town to support a person in case he or she became "poor and unable to support himself."[175] The main difference between a tramp and pauper was that the tramp "went about begging from place to place" instead of staying put and accepting the pittance doled out to him by the town. Able-bodied paupers were also sent to the town or county poor farm or workhouse to labor for their upkeep. Some of the persons convicted as tramps may have been resident paupers who had refused to submit to life in such an institution. The four tramps who were not residents of the town in which they were apprehended came from the neighboring states of Massachusetts and Maine. In practice, it looks as if the tramp law were being applied to local paupers rather than strangers.

Americans have always been a mobile people but the data on birthplace suggest that some of the tramps in our sample may actually have been outsiders after all and not really residents of the New Hampshire towns listed. Only two of these people were actually born in New Hampshire. Nine were born in Massachusetts, five in Ireland, four in Maine, two in Italy, two in New York, and one each in South Carolina, Pennsylvania, Illinois, England, Germany, and Canada. One third of the tramps in our sample were foreign-born. Being a tramp was a new crime in 1878 and the first convictions in the sample did not take place until 1880 which was at the start of the truly massive "new" European emigration to the United States. Generally speaking, immigrants to America started out at the bottom of the economic heirarchy so it should not be surprising that a large percentage of the men convicted as tramps were foreign-born. Michael Katz's study on tramps in New York State in the 1870's indicates that the proportion of foreign-born tramps (55.2%) was even larger there than in New Hampshire. The largest group of foreign-born tramps in New York was the Irish at 26.3% of the total.[176] The Irish also made up the largest group of foreign-born tramps in New Hampshire at 16.7% of the total. The tramp law was a harsh form of social control. Still, being a tramp was a rather minor sort of crime compared to most of the other "other" crimes and consequently, many, if not most tramps served a short sentence in the local jail or house of correction rather than the state prison.

A more serious form of crime was perjury which struck at the basic trust necessary for a functioning legal system. A total of seven persons in our sample were convicted of perjury. It is not easy to generalize about the type of case in which perjury might be committed. Two cases concerned perjured testimony in paternity disputes. Three involved larceny. One arose from a case of wilful and malicious destruction of property and one from a case of selling alcohol. Several of these cases originated in the lower courts, springing from trials for petty crimes and misdemeanors. Even though the initial trial was for something rather petty, such as improperly selling spiritous liquor, the discovery of perjury made it much more serious. The person found guilty of perjury ended up sentenced to a term in the state prison which was far more serious than the fairly short sentence to the county jail or house of correction or fine which was the punishment for the initial offense. Perjury was one of the few crimes in which women formed a significant proportion of the protagonists.

In September 1825 Lucinda Cilley of Exeter, age 21 and described as a "single woman and spinster" appeared before Justice of the Peace Peter Chadwick, Esq. of Exeter. She "falsely wickedly wilfully knowingly and corruptly" testified that as of April 12 she was "with child...to be chargeable to the town of Exeter." According to Cilley the child was "begotten" on July 4, 1824 in Portsmouth by a local tailor named Jeremiah Ross. The jury found that Ross was innocent and that in fact Lucinda Cilly had intended to injure Jeremiah Ross. Perhaps she had also hoped to swindle the town of Exeter out of money since the fictional child was "to be chargeable to the town."[177] Whatever the motive, Cilley served two years in the state prison for her crime.[178]

Nearly 20 years later William Kayes, age 28, of Danville, persuaded Almira Davis, a "singlewoman," to testify that she had been made pregnant with a bastard on September 15, 1843 by Amos Davis, a laborer who was apparently unrelated to Almira. Kayes was sentenced to two years in the state prison for perjury. The site of the alleged tryst was described as the pasture of Amos Davis "under some pine bushes by the path leading from the house of William Kayes..."[179] The records do not say what punishment, if any, was suffered by Almira Davis.

Fifty-two year old Mrs. Deborah Warren and Charles Hodgdon of Portsmouth entered the property of Thomas Roberts on April 25, 1866. They "did brake [sic] off, pull out and distroy [sic]" six pear tree grafts causing damage assessed at $6. As if this were not bad enough, Deborah Warren lied to the court and claimed that neither she nor Hodgdon committed the malicious destruction. The jury determined otherwise and Deborah Warren was sent to the state prison for two years.[180] There is an indictment for Deborah Warren dated October 1865 in which she was charged with destroying 18 seed cabbage heads worth $18 on the property of the same Thomas Roberts.[181] However, the jury did not find her guilty of this previous alleged offense.

Another offense related to the functioning of the legal system was that of violating parole. Parole violation was a new type of crime that made its appearance in 1901 when the system of punishment was modified by the introduction of parole. Parole will be discussed in more detail in a later chapter but, in essence, parole meant the early release of a prisoner contingent upon good behavior and other stipulations.[182] Violations of parole produced extensive case records such as that of Cleophas Valle or Valley, originally from Quebec, a resident of Somersworth. On March 17, 1903 Valle, together with two accomplices, broke into a Boston and Maine Railroad freight car during the day with the intention of stealing a keg of malt liquor worth $6.25. They were caught in the act and Cleophas Valle was given a sentence of two to three years in the state prison in September 1903.[183] Valle's accomplices did not go to prison. On October 3, 1905 Valle was paroled. The 20-year old former shoemaker was free to do as he pleased as long as he met three conditions. Valle was not to violate any New Hampshire law, he was not to "lead an idle or dissolute life," and he was to report in writing to the state prison warden once every three months.[184] Valle was to follow these conditions until October 1906. Unfortunately, Cleophas Valle could not resist temptation. At 3 a.m. on December 7, 1905 he broke into Philip Dumais's store in Somersworth and stole $9 worth of whiskey, brandy, and wine.[185] Valle went back to prison with a sentence of only one year. Amazingly, he was pardoned after serving only one month.[186] However, Cleophas Valle could not stay out of trouble. He was given a four to five year sentence for breaking and entering and stealing a clock worth $1 and a razor worth $0.50 from the house of Patrick J. Fitzgerald of Rollinsford on August 7, 1907. Shortly thereafter, Cleophas Valle was transferred to the State Hospital for the Insane and his trail vanishes.[187] There were only three convictions for violation of parole in our sample which seems to indicate that the example of Cleophas Valle was relatively uncommon.

What can one conclude about the nature of felony crime in New Hampshire during this period? By far, the most common sort of crime was that involving property. Larceny and burglary were the most common forms of property crime. Thus, the pattern of crime in nineteenth century New Hampshire resembles that of Massachusetts of the same period up to a point. Michael Hindus's survey ends in 1878 while this investigation goes up to 1914. The New Hampshire sample even more closely resembles the pattern of crime rates in Theodore Ferdinand's study of Boston except that the peak of New Hampshire crime rates took place about 10 years later. As we have seen, the proportion of violent, moral, and non-property crime in New Hampshire tended generally to increase after 1878. Still, the overwhelming majority of crimes continued to be those in which property was the main object.

Violent crime made up a much smaller proportion (14.6% or 120 out of 820 cases) than did property crime (77.9% or 639 out of 820 cases) (see Tables 7-8). At first glance, this statistic would seem to confirm Michael Hindus's contention that crime in nineteenth century Massachusetts was increasingly an affair of property and morality in contrast to the South where crime remained primarily a matter of violence.[188] The pattern of crime in New Hampshire suggests otherwise for the period after 1878 when Hindus's study ends. However, any conclusion is only on a general level since Hindus included lower court convictions in addition to felonies in his data while our sample used only felonies. Even though the actual number of violent crimes in New Hampshire was small, the trend discernible in the statistics from our sample indicates that violent crime increased steadily from 15 per 100,000 population in the 1840's to 32 per 100,000 in the 1890's (see Table 9). Murder, attempted murder, and manslaughter were the most common forms of violence.

Very few women were convicted of felonies in New Hampshire at this time, but the proportion of female felons convicted of violent crimes was greater than among the male felons in this sample. Women were also relatively common victims of murder, attempted murder, manslaughter, rape, and attempted rape. One does have to bear in mind the phenomenon of underreporting. According to recent studies, rape has been underreported which means that it is a more widespread crime than the reported convictions would indicate.[189] However, we are only covering convictions in this study.

Crimes against morality make up a miniscule proportion of the whole - only 1.8% (15 out of 820 cases). The significance lies not in actual numbers but in the fact that such behavior was reinstated as a criminal offense after the Civil War. All morals offenses had been demoted to petty crimes and misdemeanors or eliminated entirely from the statutes early in the nineteenth century. The statutes concerning crimes against morality or "chastity" were increasingly broadened during the late nineteenth and early twentieth century. One result was the conviction of those who violated the new (or revived) laws.

Finally, 5.6% (46 out of 820 cases) of the convictions fall into none of the three major categories discussed above. These crimes form a rather eclectic group with conviction for being a tramp being by far the most common. The tramp law was largely a response to the mass appearance of unemployed homeless men in the 1870's. The new law was most fully applied in New Hampshire in the 1880's when the national economy turned downward again. The tramp law was a blatant form of social control exercised over an undesirable group by those in power. Perjury was a crime that struck against the very basis of the legal structure. There were a handful of perjury cases; the apparent motives were greed, vengeance, and malice aimed at the injured party.

Changing patterns of crime in Rockingham County and Strafford County most likely were a result of unstable economic and social conditions during the nineteenth century. Both counties had near-stagnant population growth after the Civil War and most of the increase that did occur was due to foreign immigration. The presence of so many newcomers may have caused tensions that led to crime. Cultural differences plus economic disturbances may have encouraged some ethnic groups to participate disproportionately in certain types of crime. The economy endured a long period of transformation from an agricultural base to a mostly industrial base. Portsmouth, the largest city in the area, suffered instability thanks to the invention of steamships which helped to destroy the economic good times of the antebellum years.

Crime was partially a response to changing circumstances. Patterns of employment and settlement changed as more people moved into towns and cities. Economic status was insecure and new opportunities for crime arose. Burglaries may have become much more common because of the appearance of nonresidential structures in population centers. We do not mean to suggest that most poor people were thieves and burglars but it is likely that most such offenders were poor people.   An analysis of state prison inmates characteristics in Chapter Four will shed light on this possibility. Actually, the relationship between poverty and criminality is a complex phenomenon. In his study of crime and poverty in Columbus, Ohio for the period 1860-1885, Eric Monkkonen found that criminals were of a higher socioeconomic status than paupers.[190]

Chapter Four will be devoted to an analysis of the men and women who ended up serving time in the New Hampshire State Prison during the period 1812-1914.

Notes

1. Register of Convicts 1812-1883, MS, Div. of Records-Management and Archives, Concord, N.H.
2. Theodore N. Ferdinand, "The Criminal Patterns of Boston Since 1849," *American Journal of Sociology*, 73 (1967), 86.
3. *Ibid.*, 98-99.
4. Roger Lane, "Crime and Criminal Statistics in Nineteenth-Century Massachusetts," *Journal of Social History*, 2 (1968), 157.
5. *Ibid.*, 158.
6. *Ibid.*, 163.
7. Michael S. Hindus, *Prison and Population: Crime, Justice, and Authority in Massachusetts and South Carolina, 1767-1878* (Chapel Hill, N.C., 1980), p. 67.
8. *Ibid.*, p. 71.
9. *Ibid.*, p. 77.
10. Hindus, "The Contours of Crime and Justice in Massachusetts and South Carolina, 1767-1878," *American Journal of Legal History*, 21 (1977), 213.
11. Hindus, *Prison and Plantation*, p. 59 and "Contours of Crime and Justice," 213.
12. Hindus, "Contours of Crime and Justice," 213.
13. Edward L. Ayers, *Vengeance and Justice: Crime and Punishment in the Nineteenth-Century American South* (New York, 1984), p. 176.
14. *Ibid.*, p. 91.
15. *Ibid.*, p. 167
16. *Ibid.*, p. 169.
17. *Ibid.*, p. 276.
18. Ted Robert Gurr, "Historical Trends in Violent Crime: Europe and the United States" in Gurr, ed., *Violence in America*, Vol. 1 *The History of Crime* (Newbury Park, Calif., 1989), p. 21.
19. *Ibid.*, p. 35.
20. *Ibid.*, p. 35.
21. *Ibid.*, pp. 36-38.
22. *Ibid.*, pp. 38-39.
23. *Ibid.*, p. 41.
24. Eric H. Monkkonen, "Diverging Homicide Rates: England and the United States, 1850-1875" in Gurr, ed., *Ibid.*, p. 93.
25. *Ibid.*, p. 81.

26. *Ibid.*, p. 84.

27. *Ibid.*, p. 93.

28. *Ibid.*, p. 94.

29. *Ibid.*, p. 94.

30. *Ibid.*, p. 94.

31. Monkkonen, *The Dangerous Class: Crime and Poverty in Columbus, Ohio, 1860-1885* (Cambridge, Mass., 1975), p. 29.

32. *Ibid.*, p. 33.

33. *Ibid.*, p. 35.

34. *Ibid.*, pp. 53-54.

35. Lawrence M. Friedman and Robert V. Percival, *The Roots of Justice: Crime and Punishment in Alameda County, California 1870-1910* (Chapel Hill, N.C., 1981), pp. 27-28.

36. *Ibid.*, p. 31.

37. The form of punishment is of equal significance and will be the subject of later chapters.

38. Unfortunately, some of the entries were left blank for one or more of these variables. Most entries are easy to read but some, especially those for the 1840's, can be difficult to decipher due to poor handwriting on the part of the scribe.

39. Prison Register [1883-1915], MS, Div. of Records-Management and Archives, Concord, N.H. and State v. lynch, No. 5837, Rockingham Cty., N.H. (1905).

40. Register of Convicts 1812-1883, MS, Div. of Records-Management and Archives, Concord, N.H.

41. [N.H. State] Prison Records [1874-1915], MS, Div. of Records-Management and Archives. Concord, N.H.

42. State v. Blaisdell, No. 3938, Rockingham Cty., N.H. (1822).

43. State v. Sawtelle, No. [Unlisted], Strafford Cty., N.H. (1890).

44. It was found necessary to match up the prison register or report entry to the appropriate court record to get adequate information on each case. This was a fairly difficult process and involved locating register and index numbers of the Rockingham County cases. For Strafford County it meant examining all of the criminal court records for 1870-1914 since felony records are interfiled with those for more minor offenses. There were a small number of cases in which it proved impossible to locate a corresponding court record for an entry in the prison register or reports.

45. This method of counting cases was used by the following: Friedman and Percival, *Roots of Justice*, p. 15 and Monkkonen, *Dangerous Class*, p. 44.

46. Data were entered into the SP/SS quantitative computer program. Crime was one of the most important variables but it was also difficult to reduce to a single number which could be read by the computer. Each case was coded for 17 variables (see Figure 1).

47. It was decided to follow the original terminology as often as possible even though it sometimes was redundant or imprecise. For all intents and purposes "burglary" means the same thing as to "break and enter" or to "break and enter with intent to steal" even though these offenses are listed separately.

48. Constant dollars were obtained by locating each year's dollar value in 1967 dollars with the aid of a price index. The 1967 dollar values were averaged for each decade since mean and median values were needed for each decade. $1.00 (1967) = $0.31 (1986). Price index located in Standard & Poor's Statistical Service, *Basic Statistics: Price Indexes...* (New York, 1988), p.76.

49. A later chapter will cover this issue in an analysis of punishment.

50. Federal Writers' Project of the Works Progress Administration for the State of New Hampshire, *New Hampshire: A Guide to the Granite State* (Boston, 1938), p. 11.

51. *Ibid.*, p. 9.

52. D. Hamilton Hurd, ed., *History of Merrimack and Belknap Counties, New Hampshire* (Philadelphia, 1885), pp. 1-2. The towns transferred from Rockingham County to Merrimack County in 1823 were: Allenstown, Bow, Canterbury, Chichester, Concord, Epsom, Hooksett, Loudon, Northfield, Pembroke, and Pittsfield.

53. John Scales, *History of Strafford County, New Hampshire and Representative Citizens* (Chicago, 1914), p. 29. The towns transferred from Strafford County to Belknap County in 1840 were: Alton, Barnstead, Centre Harbor, Gilford, Gilmanton, Meredith, New Hampton, and Sanbornton. The towns transferred to Carroll County in 1840 were: Albany, Brookfield, Chatham, Conway, Eaton, Effingham, Freedom, Moultonborough, Sandwich, Tamworth, Tuftonborough, Ossipee, Wakefield, and Wolfeborough.

54. Elliot C. Cogswell, *History of Nottingham, Deerfield, and Northwood, New Hampshire* (Somersworth, N.H., 1972 facsimile of 1878), p. 22.

55. *Ibid.*, p. 23.

56. J. Duane Squires, *The Granite State of the United States: A History of New Hampshire from 1623 to the Present*, Vol. I (New York, 1956), p. 511; Charles B. Nelson, *History of Stratham, New Hampshire 1631-1900* (Somersworth, N.H., 1965), pp. 95-97; Howard S. Russell, *A Long Deep Furrow: Three Centuries of Farming in New England* (Hanover, N.H., 1982),

pp. 214-17; Paul G. Munyon, *A Reassessment of New England Agriculture in the Last Thirty Years of the Nineteenth Century: New Hampshire, A Case Study* (New York, 1978), p. 213; and Hobart Pillsbury, *New Hampshire: Resources, Attractions and Its People*, Vol. I (New York, 1927), p. 8.

57. Ronald and Grace Jager, *New Hampshire: An Illustrated History of the Granite State* (Woodland Hills, Calif., 1983), p. 96.

58. Squires, *The Story of New Hampshire* (Princeton, N.J., 1964), p. 64.

59. *Ibid.*, p. 58.

60. Squires, *Granite State*, Vol. I, pp. 270-71.

61. Pillsbury, *New Hampshire*, Vol. II, p. 477.

62. See *Ibid.*, pp. 466-69 and Charles A. Hazlett, *History of Rockingham County, New Hampshire and Representative Citizens* (Chicago, 1915), p. 88.

63. Squires, *Story of New Hampshire*, p. 111 and John P. Adams, *Drowned Valley: The Piscataqua River Basin* (Hanover, N.H., 1976), p. xii.

64. William G. Saltonstall, *Ports of Piscataqua* (Cambridge, Mass., 1941), p. 180.

65. *Ibid.*, pp. 201-03 and 225.

66. Jager, *New Hampshire*, p. 97.

67. *Ibid.*, p. 97.

68. Paul T. Ringenbach, *Tramps and Reforms 1873-1916: The Discovery of Unemployment in New York* (Westport, Conn., 1973), pp. 22-24.

69. Sidney L. Harrington, *Policing a Class Society: The Experiences of American Cities, 1865-1915* (New Brunswick, N.J., 1983), pp. 201 and 223; and Michael B. Katz, *Poverty and Policy in American History* (New York, 1983), pp. 157-58 and 162-63.

70. Don Taxay, *Counterfeit, Mis-Struck and Unofficial U.S. Coins* (New York, 1963), p. 23.

71. State v. Brown, No. 40791, Rockingham Cty., N.H. (1816).

72. State v. Williams, No. 289, Rockingham Cty., N.H. (1850).

73. State v. Cochrane, No. 3766, Rockingham Cty., N.H. (1901).

74. State v. Mullen, No. 2548, Rockingham Cty., N.H. (1885).

75. State v. Beach, No. 392, Rockingham Cty., N.H. (1914); [N.H. State] Prison Records [1874-1915], MS, Div. of Records-Management and Archives, Concord, N.H.; and *Portsmouth Herald* Microfilm (Cleveland, Ohio), June 18, 1912.

76. *Portsmouth Herald* Microfilm (Cleveland, Ohio), June 29, 1912.

77. [N.H. State] Prison Records [1874-1915], MS, Div. of Records-Management and Archives, Concord, N.H.

78. State v. Davis, No. 40790, Rockingham Cty., N.H. (1816).

79. State v. Elliot, No. 14406, Rockingham Cty., N.H. (1836) and Register of Convicts 1812-1883, MS, Dept. of Records and Archives, Concord, N.H.

80. U.S. Dept. of Commerce, Bureau of the Census, *Historical Statistics of the United States: Colonial Times to 1970*, Part 1 (Washington, D.C., 1975), pp. 200-01.

81. Francis Haines, *Horses in America* (New York, 1971), pp. 189-90.

82. State v. Carson, No. 884, Strafford Cty., N.H. (1914).

83. *Laws of the State of New-Hampshire...* (Portsmouth, N.H., 1797), pp. 281-82 and *The Laws of the State of New-Hampshire...* (Exeter, N.H., 1815), p. 324.

84. State v. Clay, No. 40795, Rockingham Cty., N.H. (1816).

85. State v. Caswell, N. 2071, Rockingham Cty., N.H. (1853).

86. State v. Young, No. 2, Strafford Cty., N.H. (1896).

87. John M. Macdonald, *Bombers and Firestarters* (Springfield, Ill., 1977), pp. 199-204.

88. Monkkonen, *Dangerous Class*, p. 125.

89. State v. Mace and McKenney, Nos. 886-87, Strafford Cty., N.H. (1914) and State v. McKenney, No. 887, Strafford Cty., N.H. (1914).

90. State v. Mace and McKenney, Nos. 888-89, Strafford Cty., N.H. (1914).

91. *Rochester Courier* Microfilm, July 31 and Oct. 23, 1914.

92. State v. Mathes, No. 221, Strafford Cty., N.H. (1903). *Nolle prosequi* is a formal entry on the legal record by the prosecuting officer declaring that he or she will prosecute the case no further. Henry C. Black, *Black's Law Dictionary*, 5th. ed. (St. Paul, Minn., 1979), p. 945.

93. *Foster's Weekly Democrat and Dover Enquirer* Microfilm (Waltham, Mass.), May 8, 1903.

94. *Laws of New Hampshire (1815)*, p. 327.

95. Ferdinand, "Criminal Patterns of Boston," 87.

96. *Ibid.,* 94.

97. *Ibid.,* 93.

98. Hindus, *Prison and Plantation*, p. 72.

99. *Ibid.*, p. 72.

100. Monkkonen, *Dangerous Class*, p. 31.

101. *Ibid.*, p. 31.

102. *Ibid.*, pp. 28, 47, and 97.

103. Friedman and Percival, *Roots of Justice*, pp. 30-31. The rates in their study are calculated per 1000 population, so the original figures were 4.39 per

1000 population in 1880 and 0.78 in 1910.

104. Gurr, "Historical Trends in Violent Crime" in Gurr, ed., *Violence in America*, Vol. 1, p. 21.

105. *Ibid.*, p. 23.

106. Monkkonen, "Diverging Homicide Rates" in Gurr, ed., *Violence in America*, Vol. 1, pp. 80-88.

107. Paul Gilje, *The Road to Mobocracy: Popular Disorder in New York City, 1763-1834* (Chapel Hill, N.C., 1987), p. 129.

108. Gurr, "Historical Trends in Violent Crime" in Gurr, ed., *Violence in America*, Vol. 1, p. 35.

109. Roger Lane, "On the Social Meaning of Homicide Trends in America" in Gurr, *Violence in America*, Vol. 1, p. 64.

110. Gurr, "Historical Trends in Violent Crime" in Gurr, ed., *Violence in America*, Vol. 1, p. 35.

111. *Ibid.*, pp. 35 and 37.

112. James P. Levine et al., *Criminal Justice in America: Law in Action* (New York, 1986), p. 55.

113. See, for example, Murray Straus et al., *Behind Closed Doors: Violence in the American Family* (New York, 1980).

114. Federal Bureau of Investigation, U.S. Dept. of Justice, *Uniform Crime Reports for the United States 1992* (Washington, D.C., 1992), p. 17.

115. It was described as "one of the greatest murder cases ever tried in New Hampshire" in the *Dover Enquirer*, Microfilm (Waltham, Mass.), Dec. 26, 1890. See also *Dover Enquirer*, Microfilm (Waltham, Mass.), Feb. 21; Mar. 14, Mar. 21; Sept. 5; Sept. 12; Oct. 3; and Dec. 19, 1890.

116. See State v. Jane and Mina Farnham, No. 3, Strafford Cty., N.H. (1886) and State v. Tracy, No. 386, Strafford Cty., N.H. (1906).

117. State v. Lee, No. 3937, Rockingham Cty., N.H. (1822) and Register of Convicts 1812-1883, MS, Div. of Records-Management and Archives, Concord, N.H.

118. State v. Ferguson, No. 19486, Rockingham Cty., N.H. (1841).

119. *Exeter News-Letter and Rockingham Advertiser*, Oct. 6, 1840.

120. *Ibid.*

121. *Ibid.*, Oct. 13, 1840.

122. Register of Convicts 1812-1883, MS, Div. of Records-Management and Archives, Concord, N.H.

123. State v. Provincia [sic], No. 8, Strafford Cty., N.H. (1899); and [N.H. State] Prison Records [1874-1915], MS, Div. of Records-Management and

Archives, Concord, N.H. According to the source, Lizzie Provinchia's last name was spelled three different ways: Provincia, Provinchia, and Provencher. Provinchia was the most common spelling.

124. *Foster's Weekly Democrat*, Microfilm, Feb. 10, 1899.

125. *Ibid.*, Feb. 3, 1899.

126. *Ibid.*, Feb. 3 and 10, 1899.

127. State v. Palmer, No. 4649, Rockingham Cty., N.H. (1888); and [N.H. State] Prison Records [1874-1915], MS, Div. of Records-Management and Archives, Concord, N.H.

128. *Portsmouth Daily Chronicle*, Microfilm (Cleveland, Ohio), May 29, 1888.

129. *Ibid.*

130. *Ibid.*

131. *Ibid.*, May 30, 1888.

132. State v. Kelley, No. 8, Strafford Cty., N.H. (1897); [N.H. State] Prison Records [1874-1915], MS and N.H. State Prison: Record of Gain and Loss in Population [1905-36], both MS, Div. of Records-Management and Archives, Concord, N.H.

133. See State v. Boudoir, No. 13 1/2, Strafford Cty., N.H. (1884).

134. State v. Downing, No. 5059, Rockingham Cty., N.H. (1858).

135. State v. Richardson, No. 6373, Rockingham Cty., N.H. (1860).

136. Sue Bessmer, *The Laws of Rape* (New York, 1984), pp. 58-59.

137. *Ibid.*, pp. 58-62.

138. *Ibid.*, p. 58. Homosexual rape is not actually defined as rape by the law. Instead it is termed "forcible sodomy." Charles W. Dean and Mary de Bruyn-Kops, *The Crime and Consequences of Rape* (Springfield, Ill., 1982), p. 38.

139. Barbara S. Lindemann, "To Ravish and Carnally Know': Rape in Eighteenth-Century Massachusetts," *Signs*, 10 (1984), 82.

140. Dean and de Bruyn-Kops, *Crime and Consequences of Rape*, p. 35.

141. State v. White, No. 1842, Strafford Cty., N.H. (1897).

142. State v. Wilkinson, No. 56, Strafford Cty., N.H. (1892).

143. State v. Hartford, No. 1991, Rockingham Cty., N.H. (1883); and Register of Convicts 1812-1883 and [N.H. State] Prison Records [1874-1915], both MS, Div. of Records-Management and Archives, Concord, N.H.

144. State v. Lorenzo, No. 54, Strafford Cty., N.H. (1892) and [N.H. State] Prison Records [1874-1915], MS, Div. of Records-Management and Archives, Concord, N.H.

145. State v. Nedeau, Nos. 90-91, Strafford Cty., N.H. (1900). Regarding Dora and Mary L. Marcotte, the indictments read "nole [sic] prosequi." *Nolle prosequi* is a formal entry made by the prosecuting attorney declaring that he

or she will prosecute the case no further. Black, *Black's Law Dictionary*, 5th. ed., p. 945.

146. State v. Nedeau, No. 89, Strafford Cty., N.H. (1900) and [N.H. State] Prison Records [1874-1915], MS, Div. of Records-Management and Archives, Concord, N.H.

147. See Monkkonen, "Diverging Homicide Rates" in Gurr, ed., *Violence in America*.

148. Hindus, *Prison and Plantation*, p. 72.

149. *Ibid.*, p. 72.

150. Ferdinand, "Criminal Patterns of Boston," 89-95.

151. *Ibid.*, 95.

152. Monkkonen, *Dangerous Class*, pp. 30 and 45-46.

153. Friedman and Percival, *Roots of Justice*, pp. 30-31.

154. "By the Court: in the Yeares 1641. 1642. Capital Lawes, established within the Jurisdiction of Massachusetts," *Collections of the Massachusetts Historical Society*, Vol. 4 2nd. Series (Boston, 1846), pp. 112-14.

155. State v. Warren, No. 943, Rockingham Cty., N.H. (1880 or 1881).

156. *The General Statutes of the State of New-Hampshire...* (Concord, N.H., 1867), p. 516.

157. State v. Jones, Nos. 4-5, Strafford Cty., N.H. (1897).

158. State v. Jones, No. 3, Strafford Cty., N.H. (1897).

159. [N.H. State] Prison Records [1874-1915], MS, Div. of Records-Management and Archives, Concord, N.H.

160. State v. Harrington, No. 3556, Rockingham Cty., N.H. (1901).

161. State v. Preston, No. 45, Strafford Cty., N.H. (1877).

162. State v. Richards, No. 4481, Rockingham Cty., N.H. (1888).

163. State v. Rand, No. 6667, Rockingham Cty., N.H. (1907).

164. Ruth Rosen, *The Lost Sisterhood: Prostitution in America, 1900-1918* (Baltimore, 1982), p. 112.

165. See Chapter 3 "The Red Lights Are Turned Off" in Raymond A. Brighton, *They Came to Fish*, Vol. 1 (Portsmouth, N.H., 1973), pp. 212-33.

166. State v. Perry, No. 9498, Rockingham Cty., N.H. (1912).

167. See, for example, Ch. 274 "Offenses Against Chastity" in *General Laws of the State of New Hampshire...* (Manchester, N.H., 1878), pp. 619-20.

168. Hindus, *Prison and Plantation*, p. 72.

169. *Ibid.*, p. 63.

170. Monkkonen, *Dangerous Class*, p. 32.

171. Squires, *Granite State*, Vol. 1, p. 416.

172. Michael Davis, "Forced to Tramp: The Perspective of the Labor Press,

1870-1900" in Eric H. Monkkonen, ed., *Walking to Work: Tramps in America, 1790-1935* (Lincoln, Neb., 1984), p. 33.

173. Katz, *Poverty and Policy*, pp. 157-58.

174. See State v. Kennedy, No. 2563, Rockingham Cty., N.H. (1884); State v. Hunt, No. 4001, Rockingham Cty., N.H. (1887); State v. Sullivan, No. 4022, Rockingham Cty., N.H. (1887); and State v. Collins, No. 5287, Rockingham Cty., N.H. (1904).

175. See Title 10 "Of Paupers" Chapter 81 "Settlement of Paupers" in *The General Laws of the State of New Hampshire...* (Manchester, N.H., 1878), pp. 196-97.

176. Katz, *Poverty and Policy*, p. 166.

177. State v. Cilley, No. 6712, Rockingham Cty., N.H. (1825).

178. Register of Convicts 1812-1883, MS, Dept. of Records-Management and Archives, Concord, N.H.

179. State v. Kayes, No. 21490, Rockingham Cty., N.H. (1844).

180. State v. Warren, No. 8990, Rockingham Cty., N.H. (1866).

181. State v. Warren, No. 8465, Rockingham Cty., N.H. (1865).

182. William M. Chase, ed. and Arthur H. Chase, comp., *The Public Statutes of the State of New Hampshire and General Laws in Force January 1, 1901* (Concord, N.H., 1900), pp. 850-51.

183. State v. Valle, No. 217, Strafford Cty., N.H. (1903).

184. State v. Valle, No. 370, Strafford Cty., N.H. (1906).

185. *Ibid.*

186. [N.H. State] Prison Records [1874-1915], MS, Div. of Records-Management and Archives, Concord, N.H. and *Statistics Relating to the New Hampshire State Prison...for the Two Years Ending November 30, 1906* (Bristol, N.H., 1906), p. 359.

187. State v. Valle, No. 43, Strafford Cty., N.H. (1907) and [N.H. State] Prison Records [1874-1915], MS, Div. of Records-Management and Archives, Concord, N.H.

188. Hindus, *Prison and Plantation*, pp. 250-51.

189. Vicki M. Rose and Susan C. Randall, "Where Have All the Rapists Gone? An Illustration of the Attrition-of-Justice Phenomenon" in James A. Inciardi and Anne E. Potteiger, eds., *Violent Crime: Historical and Contemporary Issues* (Beverly Hills, Calif., 1978), p. 86.

190. Monkkonen, *Dangerous Class*, p. 158.

Chapter 4

The Demography of Crime: An Analysis of the Inmates of the New Hampshire State Prison, 1812-1914

In Chapter Four we will attempt to describe the individuals behind the statistics in Chapter Three. An analysis of the criminal population should help us to construct a more meaningful picture of crime in New Hampshire. An analysis of the prison inmates should help to explain who committed what crimes and why. Were certain types of people more prone to crime than others? Is it possible to link certain types of people to certain types of crime? What distinguished the criminal population of New Hampshire from other states? These questions and others will be investigated here.

The original records provide us with a long list of names. Analysis of information available on these prisoners can allow generalizations about the hundreds of convicts surveyed in this project.[1] The amount of information pertaining to each individual is limited by the nature of the original records. It was necessary to consult several sources in order to piece together a reasonably complete picture of a single convict. Unfortunately, some inmates remain nothing more than a name connected to a crime which led to certain dates of admittance and discharge from the state prison. Even the date of discharge is not listed for a few cases. Despite limitations imposed by the original sources, it is possible to gather information about most of the convicts in our sample. The variables to be investigated here include: age, sex, race, birthplace, residence at time of conviction, and occupation (see Figure 1).

Information was extracted from several sources. The "Register of Convicts 1812-1883" is an extremely valuable document. It lists in reasonably consistent ledger-like form each inmate's name, age, and birthplace. The same data are found in the succeeding ledgers: "[N.H. State] Prison Records [1874-1915]," "Record of Population Gain and Loss [1905-36]," and an untitled ledger covering the years 1887-1907.[2] The Rockingham County and Strafford County court records provide information on the convict's sex and residence at time of conviction. Even though there is no listing of the convict's sex in the prison ledgers, virtually all of the names are identifiably masculine or feminine. In the few cases of ambiguity, the court records provide the answer with their standard reference to the accused/convicted as "yeoman" for males and either "spinster" or "singlewoman" for females for the antebellum period. By the time a married female showed up in our sample, the court records had stopped listing this form of reference. Evidently the practice died out in the

1860's. In rare instances, the court records mention the convict's occupation, such as that of John Davis, "a mariner," who stole $286 worth of clothing from a store in Portsmouth in 1816.[3] The best sources of information on occupation are the "Description Registers" for the years 1881-98 and 1899-1906, so conclusions about occupational status will have to be confined to this period.

At the end of every fiscal year the warden of the state prison was required to submit an annual report to the state legislature. The early reports are almost exclusively of a financial nature and are merely appended to the New Hampshire House or Senate journals. The first separate reports appeared in the 1830's and it was not until the late 1850's that truly detailed information on inmates was provided. Even so, the exact dates of admittance and departure are not provided in the annual reports. Most of the published information duplicates that found in the ledgers and had to be used in conjunction with the ledgers. Nevertheless, the published reports helped to fill in some gaps and to confirm the identity of some individuals.

More complete information on a few of the inmates is available in newspaper accounts. However, newspaper accounts of crime in New Hampshire are very hard to find before 1840. Even after that date, only the most spectacular crimes (usually murder) are covered in detail, so this source is only marginally useful.[4]

The Federal Census reports for 1860-1910 were used to identify the "population at risk." This phrase refers to the total number of people of a certain description in a given location. For instance, there were 15,623 males aged 15-19 in New Hampshire in 1880.[5] There were 17 males aged 15-19 in the New Hampshire State Prison in 1880. Males aged 15-19 in the state made up 4.5% of the total population while males aged 15-19 made up 11.3% of the total inmate population. From this, one can conclude that males age 15-19 were overrepresented in the prison population in 1880 because the population at risk - all males in New Hampshire age 15-19 - constituted only 4.3% of the entire population. From such analyses one can determine how the prison population was distinct from the general population. Unfortunately, it is not always possible to determine the population at risk since the census reports do not always list the population in groups directly comparable to the state prison population.

The original sources need to be used with care when compiling information on each convict. As mentioned in Chapter Three, we are analyzing 820 *cases*, not 820 *people*. Some of the crimes were committed by more than one person. These crimes were counted as two or more cases only if any accomplices were convicted and sent to the state prison. Conversely, in those cases involving recidivism, one or more cases actually represent the crimes of only one *person*.

Recidivism poses a challenge for the historian of crime.[6] The fact that a prisoner was a recidivist was often, but not always, noted in the "Register of Convicts 1812-1883." Similar names have been checked against each other for variables such as age and birthplace to confirm whether someone was or was not a recidivist. John Brown was convicted of breaking and entering and stealing in 1857. John Brown was convicted of the same crime in 1865. A quick check reveals that the first John Brown was born in Scotland in 1832. The second John Brown was born in New York in 1844.[7] Yet another entry for John Brown appears in the records for a conviction of bigamy in 1892. Further research reveals that this John Brown was a different person from the first two John Browns already mentioned: this individual was born in England in 1859.[8] A fair number of criminals used an alias but this fact is regularly noted in the sources. A person was counted as a recidivist if he or she was listed two times or more or if it was so noted in the records. This would apply even if he or she had entered the prison originally through a conviction in a county other than Rockingham or Strafford. Prisoners listed as having served time in a state prison outside of New Hampshire were also classified as recidivists. For example, Richard Burroughs was sent to the New Hampshire State Prison in 1832 for stealing $5.10 worth of food and stockings from Robert Calef's house in Kingston. Burroughs served a full seven-year sentence. Among the factors leading to such a lengthy sentence may have been the fact that Burroughs had served time in both the Massachusetts and Vermont state prisons previously.[9]

We will begin our analysis of the criminal population with a discussion of age. Most inmates of the New Hampshire State Prison for the period 1812-1914 were of a younger median age than present-day American state prison inmates: 26 years versus today's 30 years.[10] The overall statistic obscures the fact that the median age of the prisoners in our sample vacilated over time. The most extreme change took place between 1849 and 1880. The median age jumped from a low of 24.5 years in the 1850's to an all-time high of 30 years during the 1860's. It then fell back down to 24.5 years in the 1870's before rising to 26 years in the succeeding decade (see Table 19). Two factors may have contributed to the high median age of the 1860's: the opening of the State Reform (Industrial) School in 1858 and the Civil War.

The existence of youthful offenders prompted the concern of state prison officials and state legislators. The prison administration claimed in 1852 that

Table 19

New Hampshire State Prison Inmates, 1812-1914:
Age Distribution by Decade

Decade	Min. Age	Max. Age	Median Age	No. Cases
1810's	13	56	25.0	47
1820's	16	64	28.0	31
1830's	17	47	28.0	36
1840's	17	50	27.0	34
1850's	12	65	24.5	34
1860's	19	66	30.0	65
1870's	16	64	24.5	106
1880's	17	79	26.0	141
1890's	16	62	25.0	116
1900's	17	63	26.0	126
1910's	19	72	29.0	78

Note: Missing ages: 1 case 1870's; 2 cases 1890's; and 3 cases 1900's. 6 missing in all.

Source: "Register of Convicts 1812-1883," "[N.H. State] Prison Records [1874-1915]," "N.H. State Prison: Gain and Loss in Population [1905-36]," "Description Register [1881-98] and [1899-1906]," all MS, Div. of Records-Management and Archives, Concord, N.H.; and *Prison Warden's Reports*, 1859-1914.

"there has been for a few of the last years a great change in the character of criminals brought to our Prison. A large majority are *young* [sic] men, many of them mere youth [sic]."[11] Two years later, Warden Gideon Webster declared, "It is a startling fact, suggestive of mournful reflections that a very large proportion of those confined in this Prison are boys and young men."[12] He claimed that a nine-year old boy had been sent to the prison during the previous year. An intense scrutinization of the "Register of Convicts 1812-1883" reveals that no such person was formally admitted or discharged from the prison.[13] Still, some convicts *were* very young. The youngest in our sample was John Kehoe, a 12-year old boy from Portsmouth. Together with an accomplice, Kehoe stole 10 dimes from Barzilla Harding's store in Portsmouth in broad daylight on October 4, 1857. Kehoe served a year in the state prison. He was released in 1858, the year when juvenile offenders under the age of 16 were first sent to the State Reform School in Manchester.[14] Another youngster was 13-year old Parson Price. He stole promissory notes and coins worth $35.60 from Benjamin Emory, Jr. in Concord on September 5, 1816. Price served a full two-year sentence.[15] Such young convicts were uncommon in the New Hampshire State Prison. Convicts under the age of 18 account for only 3.4% of the total sample (see Table 20).

One solution to the problem of youthful criminals was the creation of an institution separate from the state prison. In 1855 the New Hampshire Legislature passed "An Act to Establish a House of Refuge for Juvenile and Female Offenders Against the Laws." It was designed to deal with males under 18 and females of any age.[16] Before the House of Refuge opened its doors as the State Reform School in Manchester in 1858, the inmate population was specifically restricted to offenders age 17 and under.[17] Female convicts age 18 and over were, in fact, sent to the State Prison in Concord as always. Convicted male felons as young as 16 were still occasionally sent to the State Prison after 1858.[18] Not until 1907 was the age dividing juvenile from adult offenders firmly placed at 17 years.[19] The implementation of separate treatment for juvenile offenders removed the youngest potential inmates from the state prison after 1857.

The Civil War may have contributed to a sharply higher median age for the prisoners in our sample by removing many of the most likely criminals - young men - from society. According to British historian John Styles, property crime indictments in eighteenth-century England fell whenever the country was at war because tens of thousands of young men were conscripted into the military forces.[20] Criminologist Samuel Walker says, "As criminologists have long known, criminal activity is highest among people 14 to 24."[21]

Few convicts in our sample were old. Most were under 45 years of age (see Table 20).

Table 20

New Hampshire State Prison Inmates, 1812-1914: Age Group Distributions by Decade

Decade	Percentage of Cases by Age Group			
	Under 18	18-24	25-34	35-44
1810's	4.3%	38.3%	29.8%	19.1%
1820's	6.5%	25.8%	35.5%	19.4%
1830's	5.6%	27.8%	47.2%	13.9%
1840's	11.8%	26.5%	44.1%	8.8%
1850's	11.8%	38.2%	17.6%	11.8%
1860's		27.7%	38.5%	20.0%
1870's	6.6%	43.3%	26.9%	16.0%
1880's	2.1%	41.1%	29.8%	16.3%
1890's	0.9%	44.0%	43.1%	5.2%
1900's	2.4%	34.9%	36.5%	17.5%
1910's		32.1%	34.6%	20.5%
AGGREGATE AGE GROUPS:	3.4%	36.9%	34.5%	15.2%
U.S.A. STATE PRISON AGE GROUPS (1991):	0.6%	21.3%	45.7%	22.7%

Decade	Percentage of Cases by Age Group			Total % and N	
	45-54	55-64	65+		
1810's	6.4%	2.1%		100%	(47)
1820's	3.2%	9.6%		100%	(31)
1830's	5.6%			100%	(36)
1840's	8.8%			100%	(34)
1850's	17.6%		2.9%	100%	(34)
1860's	7.7%	4.6%	1.5%	100%	(65)
1870's	3.8%			100%	(106)
1880's	6.4%	2.1%	2.1%	100%	(141)
1890's	5.2%	1.7%		100%	(116)
1900's	4.0%	4.8%		100%	(126)
1910's	6.4%	3.9%	2.6%	100%	(78)
AGGREGATE AGE GROUPS:	6.0%	3.1%	0.9%	100%	(814)
U.S.A. STATE PRISON AGE GROUPS (1991):	6.5%	2.4%	0.7%	100%	

Note: Missing cases: 1 in 1870's; 2 in 1880's; and 3 in 1900's. 6 missing in all.

Source: "Register of Convicts 1812-1883," "[N.H. State] Prison Records [1874-1915]," "N.H. State Prison: Record of Gain and Loss in Population [1905-36]," "Description Register [1881-98] and [1899-1906]," all MS, Div. of Records-Management and Archives, Concord, N.H.; *Prison Warden's Reports*, 1859-

1914 and U.S. Bureau of the Census, *Statistical Abstract of the United States: 1993* (Washington, D.C., 1993).

The oldest convict was Elisha Hoyt of Townsend, Massachusetts. The 79-year old Hoyt was convicted of "false pretenses" in October 1884. Hoyt had introduced himself to John W. Moses of Portsmouth on May 24 as the foreman of a large farm in Townsend, Massachusetts. He persuaded Moses to sell him $34 worth of clothing on credit. As it turned out, Hoyt the imposter was caught and given a sentence of four years in the state prison. The "[N.H. State] Prison Records [1874-1915]" do not record his exit, so it is unclear if he was pardoned, died in prison, or served his full sentence.[22] John Foster was a 72-year old resident of Dover in 1914. In September he was convicted of breaking, entering, and stealing from two houses in Dover during the day on July 30. First he stole a $50 diamond ring from Frank Christie's house. Later that same day he stole a $15 gold watch belonging to Marie Thornton from Thomas Thornton's house. The elderly burglar was given a sentence of three to four years in the state prison. He was paroled in 1917.[23]

Crime most often involved young adults and adults not very far advanced into middle age. The typical convict in our sample was between 18 and 45 years of age; 26 was the median, a figure which changed over time but basically stayed within narrow bounds. By age 45, most adults were probably established in or sufficiently resigned to their status to begin slowing down. Criminal-like impulsiveness, daring, and energy are more characteristic of youth than middle or old age.

Contrary to Eric Monkkonen's findings on criminals in Ohio, the actual distribution of our sample when divided by age groups was younger than in Ohio or today's American state prison population (see Table 20). The 18-24 year age group was the largest group in the sample while the largest in present-day state prisons is those in the 25-34 year age group. There were nearly six times as many inmates under the age of 18 in the New Hampshire State Prison than is typical for today. The 1840's and 1850's had the largest percentage of youthful felons, a fact which lends some support to the pessimistic observations of the annual prison reports of that era. Monkkonen's study of criminals in Columbus, Ohio for 1860-1885 showed a median age of 30. Two thirds of the offenders in his sample were between 15 and 39 years of age. He concludes that crime was more open to adults than is true today and that youths were more integrated into society than today, possibly because job opportunities were better for youths in America at that time.[24]

Men aged 20-44 were greatly overrepresented in the prison population when compared to the population at risk. Out of these men, those aged 25-34 were most disproportionately represented in the prison population. At times, they made up a proportion of the prison population that was four times greater than the male population aged 25-34 at risk (see Table 21). In contrast, men 55 and over were either the same or slightly under their proportion of the population at risk. Women were definitely underrepresented in the prison population. Thus, one can conclude that convicted felons were indeed disproportionately young and male.

Table 21

Age Group Distributions: Prison Population Compared to Population at Risk, 1880-1910: Males

Year	Age Group	PRISON N	(%)	Total	STATE N	(%)	Total
1880	15-19	17	(11.3%)	151	15,623	(4.5%)	346,991
	20-24	41	(27.2%)		17,267	(5.0%)	
	25-34	47	(31.1%)		25,974	(7.5%)	
	35-44	29	(19.2%)		20,398	(5.9%)	
	45-54	8	(5.3%)		17,724	(5.1%)	
	55-64	3	(2.0%)		13,657	(3.9%)	
	65-79	2	(1.3%)		11,712	(3.4%)	
TOTAL:		147	(97.4%)		122,355	(35.3%)	
1890	15-19	15	(14.0%)	107	17,683	(4.7%)	376,530

1890	20-24	19	(17.8%)	18,897	(5.0%)
	25-34	42	(39.3%)	29,710	(7.9%)
	35-44	17	(15.9%)	23,686	(6.3%)
	45-54	8	(7.5%)	19,052	(5.1%)
	55-64	3	(2.8%)	14,783	(3.9%)
	Unlisted	1	(0.9%)		
		---	------	-------	-------
TOTAL:		105	(98.1%)	123,811	(32.9%)
1900	15-19	16	(10.5%) 153	17,097	(4.2%) 411,588
	20-24	35	(22.9%)	19,038	(4.6%)
	25-34	52	(34.0%)	34,226	(8.3%)
	35-44	29	(19.0%)	27,922	(6.8%)
	45-54	15	(9.8%)	22,209	(5.4%)
	55-64	4	(2.6%)	15,601	(3.8%)
		---	------	-------	------
TOTAL:		151	(98.8%)	136,093	(33.1%)
1910	15-19	16	(11.8%) 136	19,262	(4.5%) 430,572
	20-24	30	(22.1%)	18,643	(4.3%)
	25-34	45	(33.1%)	33,033	(7.7%)
	35-44	24	(17.6%)	30,599	(7.1%)
	45-54	12	(8.8%)	24,824	(5.8%)
1910	55-64	6	(4.4%)	17,320	(4.0%)

1910	65-69	1	(0.7%)	6023	(1.4%)
		---	------	-------	------
TOTAL:		134	(98.5%)	149,706	(34.8%)

Source: *U.S. Census Reports*, 1880-1910 and *Prison Warden's Reports*, 1880, 1890, 1900, and 1910.

Table 22

New Hampshire State Prison Inmates, 1812-1914: Race and Sex

Race	No. of Cases	%	1991 U.S.A. State Prisons %
White	808	98.5%	49.0%
Black	7	0.9%	47.5%
Unknown	5	0.6%	3.5% (Other or Unknown)
TOTAL:	820	100%	100%
Sex	**No. of Cases**	**%**	**1991 U.S.A. State Prisons %**
Male	804	98.0%	94.5%
Female	16	2.0%	5.5%
TOTAL:	820	100%	100%

Source: "Register of Convicts 1812-1883," "[N.H. State] Prison Records [1874-1915]," "N.H. State Prison: Record of Gain and Loss in Population [1905-36]," all MS, Div. of Records-Management and Archives, Concord, N.H.; *Prison Warden's Reports*, 1859-1914; and U.S. Bureau of the Census, *Statistical Abstract of the United States: 1993*.

Virtually all of the convicts in the New Hampshire State Prison for this time period were white. Out of 820 cases, 808 (98.5%) were white, 7 (0.9%) were black, and 5 (0.6%) were of unknown race (see Table 22). These numbers

156

are accurate as far as is possible to determine but there is room for doubt. Nowhere in the original records is there a separate mention of the convict's race. Perhaps there were more black convicts than just the seven found in our sample but this is impossible to determine from the available sources. The only time a convict's race was definitely mentioned was by the inclusion of the terms "negro [sic]," "colored," or "mulatto" next to his or her name in the ledgers. However, this was always written in as an extra remark, much like the rare entry for other distinguishing characteristics such as scars, deformities, or tattooes. It is probably safe to assume that the designation of someone as black would be done every time a black convict was admitted to the prison if only for the reason that this was an unusual distinguishing physical characteristic in northern New England at this time. New Hampshire's small black population declined greatly both in numbers and as a percentage of the population between 1810 and 1860. Thereafter it grew very slowly. By 1910 the black population of New Hampshire was still smaller numerically and proportionately in 1910 than it had been in 1810 (see Table 23).[25]

Every black in the sample committed a property crime. The fact that the blacks in the sample were convicted only of property crimes is similar to findings of scholars in both the antebellum North and South (see Table 24).[26] Other ethnic groups occasionally participated in proportionately high numbers in property crime but not as high a proportion as the blacks in the sample. Not one of the black convicts was born in New Hampshire.[27]

There were apparently no convicts who could be classified as Asian and there is no indication that any of the convicts were of American Indian origin. By the nineteenth century it is likely that some of the surviving Indians would have adopted European names. It is impossible to determine if there were any such prisoners in our sample. The prison population for the period 1812-1914 was almost entirely white.[28]

Just because the prison population was at least 98.5% white does not mean that it was a homogeneous population. Convicts came from a number of ethnic groups. The concept of ethnicity is complex, but for our purposes, the most practical definition defines ethnicity by common geographic origin.[29]

Data on birthplace are available in 811 out of 820 cases (98.9%). Another definition is also helpful: an ethnic group defined as a group recognized as immigrants from a specific location. Data on birthplace is available for nearly every convict in the sample. Every convict in our sample was described as a resident of the United States which would imply that all foreign-born convicts in our sample were immigrants. Borrowing from Andrew M. Greeley's

Table 23

Black Population Growth in New Hampshire, 1810-1910

Year	Black Pop.	Total N.H. Pop.	Black Pop. as % of Total
1810	970	214,360	0.45%
1820	787	243,236	0.32%
1830	607	269,328	0.23%
1840	538	284,574	0.19%
1850	520	317,976	0.16%
1860	494	326,073	0.15%
1870	580	318,300	0.18%
1880	685	346,991	0.20%
1890	614	376,530	0.16%
1900	662	411,588	0.16%
1910	564	430,572	0.13%

Source: *U.S. Census Reports*, 1810-1910.

tabulation of religio-ethnic groups, the foreign-born New Hampshire prison inmates fall into the following categories: British, Germans, and Irish as Protestants, and Irish, Germans, and Italians as Catholics.[30] There were 42 Irish-born convicts in our sample (5.1% of the total or 25.6% of the foreign-born). It is not possible to compare percentages of crime to population size among ethnic groups before 1870 since the necessary figures are not reported by the census.

Having a common birthplace does not necessarily mean that other features such as race, language or dialect, religion, or even food preferences shared by

158

Table 24

Ethnicity and Crime in New Hampshire, 1812-1914

Type of Crime: Ethnic Group	Property N and %		Violence N and %		Moral N and %	
Canadians	44	74.6%	10	16.9%	3	5.1%
Irish	28	66.7%	8	19.0%		
British (Immig.)	26	76.4%	4	11.8%	2	5.9%
Italians	1	12.5%	5	62.5%		
Germans	6	75.0%	1	12.5%		
Blacks	7	100%				

Type of Crime: Ethnic Group	Other N and %		Total N and %	
Canadians	2	3.4%	59	100%
Irish	6	14.3%	42	100%
British (Immig.)	2	5.9%	34	100%
Italians	2	25.0%	8	100%
Germans	1	12.5%	8	100%
Blacks			7	100%

Source: Court Bills and Indictments, 1812-1914, Rockingham Cty., MS, Div. of Records-Management and Archives, Concord, N.H.; Court Bills and Indictments, 1870-1914, Strafford Cty., MS, Justice and Administration

Building, Dover, N.H.; "Register of Convicts 1812-1883," "[N.H. State] Prison Records [1874-1915]," and "N.H. State Prison: Record of Gain and Loss in Population [1905-36]," all MS, Div. of Records-Management and Archives, Concord, N.H.; and *Prison Warden's Reports*, 1859-1914.

an ethnic group are present.[31] For example, a large number of convicts were of Canadian birth. It is unlikely that Matthew Powers, imprisoned in 1883 for burglary, shared a common language or dialect with Albert Douville, imprisoned in 1898 for burglary. Yet both were born in Canada.[32] The Canadian example is most troublesome in this regard. Canadians were divided into French-Canadian and British-Canadian groups, not to mention those of American Indian origin. Thus, it would be inaccurate to assume that a Canadian birthplace always meant a French-Canadian (and, therefore, Catholic) background.[33] In fact, the majority of the Canadian-born convicts in the sample had British names. I have divided the Canadians by surname in an attempt to more precisely determine ethnicity. (This will be discussed in more detail shortly). Similar objections can be made in regard to the vast majority of convicts who were born in the United States. Language or dialect may not have been so different among this group but food preferences, folklore and music, and settlement and employment patterns may have varied considerably among native-born convicts. Birthplace as an indicator of ethnicity is imperfect but we should be able to draw a few conclusions about the relationships between ethnicity, immigration, and crime in New Hampshire. Another use for the data on birthplace is in drawing conclusions about the mobility of the criminal population of New Hampshire. Birthplace data will be used in conjunction with data on residence at the time of conviction. These will then be analyzed in relation to the demographic changes affecting New Hampshire and the United States during the nineteenth century.

The overwhelming majority of persons sent to the New Hampshire state prison during its first century of operation were white native-born Americans. The birthplace for 637 out of 820 cases (77.7%) was the United States (see Table 25). Of these, the largest percentage were born in New Hampshire: 312 out of 637 cases (49.0%). New Hampshire-born inmates thus represent 38.0% of the total number of cases. The next most common birthplace was Massachusetts with 145 cases represented (17.7% of the total or 22.8% of the American-born). The other New England states account for 116 cases or 14.2% of the total or 18.6% of those born in America. Most of the other New England-born convicts were born in Maine. Finally, the rest of the

Table 25

New Hampshire State Prison Inmates, 1812-1914: Birthplace

Birthplace	No. of Cases	% of Total	% of Subgroup
New Hampshire	312	38.1%	49.0% (U.S.A.)
Massachusetts	145	17.7%	22.8% (U.S.A.)
Other New England	116	14.2%	18.2% (U.S.A.)
Other U.S.A.	74	9.0%	11.4% (U.S.A.)
TOTAL:	647	78.9%	100%
Canada	59	7.2%	36.0% (Foreign)
Ireland	42	5.1%	25.6% (Foreign)
Britain (England, Wales, Scotland)	34	4.2%	20.7% (Foreign)
Italy	9	1.0%	5.5% (Foreign)
Germany	8	1.0%	4.9% (Foreign)
Other	12	1.5%	7.3% (Foreign)
TOTAL:	164	19.9%	100%
Unknown	9	1.2%	100% (Unknown)
TOTAL:	820	100%	100%

Source: "Register of Convicts 1812-1883," "[N.H. State] Prison Records [1874-1915]," "N.H. State Prison: Record of Gain and Loss in Population [1905-36],: all MS, Div. of Records-Management and Archives, Concord, N.H.

Finally, the rest of the native-born Americans came from 17 other states plus the District of Columbia. They accounted for 64 cases, 7.8% of the total or 10.0% of the American-born cases. Only New York and Pennsylvania are significantly represented in this sample. The other states and the District of Columbia supplied only one to five cases each. Overall, the proportion of foreign-born inhabitants in the state increased from 4.49% in 1850 to 22.45% in 1910 (see Table 6).

Foreign-born convicts accounted for 164 out of 820 cases or 20.0%. The largest single group of foreign-born convicts was born in Canada: 59 cases (7.2% of the total or 36.0% of the foreign-born). As we have seen, Canadians themselves were divided into French-Canadian and British-Canadian groups as well as those of American Indian origin. Thirty-five (59.3%) of the Canadians had British names while twenty-four (40.7%) had French names. The Canadian-born members of the sample were convicted of property crimes but, unlike blacks, nearly 17% were also convicted of violent crimes (see Table 24). It is interesting to note, however, that a decreasing number of Canadians were convicted of crime between 1870 and 1914, despite their growing population in the seacoast. Perhaps this phenomenon can be linked to a gradual improvement in the socioeconomic status of this group in New Hampshire.[34]

The Irish were a more homogeneous group than Canadians and like the French-Canadians, were mostly Catholic. However, there are problems with using birthplace as a guide to ethnicity. Many native-born American convicts had Irish-sounding names, as did some of those born in Canada. The religious differences between the Protestants and Catholics of Ireland were significant. Still, most of the Irish immigrants to America were Catholic, so it is reasonable to assume that most of the Irish-born convicts in our sample were Catholic. Mark E. Lender and James K. Martin describe the Irish immigrants of 1830-60 as "poor" and "almost invariably Roman Catholic."[35]

Paul Gilje and other historians have linked the Irish to the high rates of violent crime in America.[36] The percentage of Irish-born convicts in our sample participating in violent crime was higher proportionately than that of all other groups except the Italian-born (see Table 24). Irish violence came to an impressive height in the 1880's but then dropped in the 1890's. The 1890's were the most violent decade and it seems strange that the group most

162

commonly blamed for the violence was actually showing a decrease in violence precisely at the time when the rest of the society was becoming more violent (see Tables 9, 24, and 26). Of course, the actual numbers involved in this sample are rather small and violent offenses such as common assault were considered to be petty crimes, and so would not show up in the sample.

Also of interest is that the rates of property crime and other crime (mostly being a tramp) for the Irish also reached a peak in the 1880's. Irish participation in all types of crime except moral, were at their all-time height

Table 26

Immigrant Population Growth in Seacoast New Hampshire, 1870-1910

| | Ethnic Group and % of Total Population | | | | | |
| | Canadians | | Irish | | British | |
Year	N	%	N	%	N	%
1870	1628	2.1%	3136	4.0%	1117	1.4%
1880	4531	5.4%	3731	4.4%	2244	2.7%
1890	8177	9.3%	4201	4.8%	2036	2.3%
1900	10,160	11.2%	3692	4.1%	1872	2.1%
1910	9234	10.1%	2793	3.1%	1805	2.0%

| | Germans | | Italians | |
Year	N	%	N	%
1870	---	---	---	---
1880	178	0.2%	---	---
1890	142	0.2%	152	0.2%
1900	308	0.3%	205	0.2%
1910	325	0.4%	517	0.6%

Ethnic Group as % of Total Convict Population

Decade	Canadians N	%	Irish N	%	British N	%
1870's	4	3.7%	2	1.9%	5	4.7%
1880's	11	7.8%	12	8.5%	6	4.3%
1890's	16	13.6%	6	5.1%	7	5.9%
1900's	13	10.1%	3	2.3%	3	2.3%
1910's	3	3.8%	1	1.3%	2	2.6%

Decade	Germans N	%	Italians N	%
1870's	—	—	—	—
1880's	3	2.1%	---	---
1890's	1	0.8%	1	0.8%
1900's	1	0.8%	2	1.6%
1910's	1	1.3%	3	3.8%

Note: Population growth has not been calculated for ethnic groups before 1870 with the exception of blacks (see Table 22). The U.S. Census records do not supply detailed enough information on birthplace of immigrants at the county level before this date. Similarly, data revealing Italian origin of inhabitants at the county level are not available before 1890. Thus, the population figures listed here are for Rockingham and Strafford County ethnic groups (minus blacks) 1870-1910.

Source: Court Bills and Indictments, 1812-1914, Rockingham Cty., MS, Div. of Records-Management and Archives, Concord, N.H.; Court Bills and Indictments, 1870-1914, Strafford Cty., MS, Justice and Administration Building, Dover, N.H.; "Register of Convicts 1812-1883," "[N.H. State] Prison

164

Records [1874-1915]," "N.H. State Prison: Record of Gain and Loss in Population [1905-36]," all MS, Div. of Records-Management and Archives, Concord, N.H.; *Prison Warden's Reports*, 1870-1914; and *U.S. Census Records*, 1870-1910.

in the 1880's. Heavy Irish immigration to the United States began in the 1840's, but specific figures on the number of Irish immigrants in New Hampshire are not available before 1870. Thus, the crime percentages of the 1880's might not be as significant if they could be directly compared to those of the 1840's. Other immigrant groups may well have contributed to the overall crime rate. Those born in England, Scotland, and Wales accounted for 34 of 820 or 4.2% of the total or 20.7% of the foreign-born. Like the Canadians, this group showed a declining proportion of felony convictions between 1870 and 1914.

The remaining 28 foreign-born convicts were quite a diverse group. They accounted for only 3.5% of the total or 17.1% of the foreign-born. The Italians at 9 and the Germans at 8 were the best-represented here. The remainder, usually represented by one to three cases each, came from: France, "British Provinces," Portugal, Austria, Hungary, Puerto Rico, Greece, and Sweden.[37]

Three quarters of the German convicts in the sample committed property crimes and the number of Germans being sent to the state prison was declining at precisely the time when the number of German immigrants was increasing (see Tables 24 and 26). There are really too few Germans in the sample to say if for certain this group was adjusting easily to American life. Likewise, the number of Italian convicts is too small to confirm the apparent violence of this group. Proportionately, violence was higher among Italian convicts than any other group but one cannot make any firm conclusions regarding the true rate of Italian violence in New Hampshire.

In the aggregate, one can conclude that the prison population was a rather homogenous group. Almost all were white. Nearly 80% were born in the United States and nearly half of these were born in New Hampshire. Over a third of the foreign-born convicts were born in Canada. A quarter of the foreign-born convicts were of Irish origin and a fifth of British origin. The apparent uniformity of the prison population described thus far is somewhat deceptive. The prison population experienced demographic shifts along with New Hampshire and the rest of the country throughout the nineteenth century. Thanks to sweeping changes in agriculture brought about by the opening of the American West, new technology, and the transportation revolution, many native-born inhabitants either moved out of the state or into the growing milltowns. Replacing the departed and then going beyond replacement, foreign immigrants became a greater presence in New Hampshire. Strafford County in particular experienced a large increase of foreign immigrants during the late nineteenth and early twentieth century (see Table 6). Some of these changes are reflected in the changing composition of the inmates described here. It is possible to describe and analyze these shifts by examining the ethnic constitution of our sample by decade.

Even though the number of immigrants in seacoast New Hampshire increased in the late nineteenth and early twentieth century, the proportion of convicted felons of immigrant origin in the prison population did not show a similar increase when compared to the population at risk. The foreign-born inmates were overrepresented in the prison population in 1860 and 1870 when they were three to four times greater than their proportion of the population at risk. However, contrary to the assertion of nativists, the actual proportion of immigrant felons in the New Hampshire State Prison was not particularly high; in fact in 1880 and again in 1900, foreign-born prisoners were underrepresented (see Table 27). At various time between 1870 and 1900, the British, Canadians, Irish, and Germans were overrepresented in the prison population. None of these groups were consistently overrepresented and sometimes they were underrepresented or not even present.

The proportion of New Hampshire-born prisoners shrank greatly as time went by, probably due to increased mobility and the massive economic changes outlined in Chapter Three. New Hampshire-born inmates dominated the prison until the 1880's. Those born in New Hampshire made up 61.7% of the inmate population in the 1810's (see Table 28). New Hampshire-born inmates experienced a precipitous drop in the 1820's both in actual numbers and as a percentage of the total: from 29 to 13 and from 61.7% down to 41.9%. Thereafter they comprised between 47.1% and 58.3% of the total with the exception of the 1860's, when they dropped to 38.5%. From the 1880's on the percentage of inmates born in New Hampshire gradually declined to only 23.1% of the total in the 1910's, lower even than the 24.4% who were born in Massachusetts (see Table 28). A greater percentage of felony convictions over time involved outsiders. What does this say about geographic mobility and crime? We will now analyze residence patterns of the inmates by decade to see how the presence of outsiders was related to the patterns of felony convictions of seacoast New Hampshire. Inmates born in Massachusetts showed a very different pattern from those born in New Hampshire. With the exception of the 1830's, Massachusetts-born inmates remained the second-

Table 27

Ethnicity: Prison Population Compared to Population at Risk, 1860-1900

I. Prison Population

Year	Native-Born N	% N	Foreign-Born %	N	Total
1860	11	84.6%	2	15.4%	13
1870	15	71.4%	6	28.6%	21

Canadians (1) 4.8%
British (2) 9.5%
Irish (2) 9.5%
Germans (1) 4.8%
Other

1880	40	90.9%	4	9.1%	44

Canadians
British (4) 4.5%
Irish (1) 2.3%
Germans
Other (Italians) (1) 2.3%

1890	19	73.1%	7	26.9%	26

Canadians (1) 3.8%
British
Irish (3) 11.5%
Germans (3) 11.5%
Other

1900	19	82.6%	4	17.4%	23

Canadians (1) 4.3%
British (1) 4.3%

I. Prison Population (Continued)

	Native-Born		Foreign-Born		Total
	N	%	N	%	
			Irish (1) 4.3%		
			Germans (1) 4.3%		
			Other		

II. Population at Risk

	Native-Born		Foreign-Born			Total
	N	% N	%	N		
Year						
1860	47,213	94.2%	2909	5.8%		50,122
1870	71,436	92.1%	6104	7.8%		77,540

Canadians (1628) 2.1%
British (1117) 1.4%
Irish (3136) 4.0%
Germans (94) 0.1%
Other (129) 0.2%

| 1880 | 74,400 | 87.9% | 10,222 | 12.1% | | 84,622 |

Canadians (4531) 5.3%
British (1586) 1.9%
Irish (3731) 4.4%
Germans (178) 0.2%
Other (196) 0.2%

| 1890 | 74,992 | 82.9% | 15,100 | 17.1% | | 88,092 |

Canadians (8177) 9.3%
British (2051) 2.3%
Irish (4201) 4.8%
Germans (142) 0.2%
Other (524) 0.6%

| 1900 | 73,435 | 81.2% | 17,020 | 18.8% | | 90,455 |

II. Population at Risk (Continued)

Native-Born		Foreign-Born		Total
N	%	N	%	N

Canadians (10,160) 11.2%
British (1872) 2.1%
Irish (3692) 4.1%
Germans (308) 0.3%
Other (988) 1.1%

Note: In 1860 the Census listed foreign-born only in the aggregate, so specific groups are not listed here for that year. The population at risk consisted of persons from Rockingham and Strafford County for 1870-1900 but only Rockingham County for 1860 because the sample of prison inmates consists of convicted felons from both counties for the period 1870-1914 but only Rockingham County for the period 1812-69. Ethnicity in 1910 is not included here because the Census supplied information on ethnicity at the state level rather than the county level.

Source: *U.S. Census Reports*, 1860-1900 and *Prison Warden's Reports*, 1860, 1870, 1880, 1890, and 1900.

largest contingent in the state prison throughout this period. Unlike those born in New Hampshire, the Massachusetts-born inmates experienced an eventual doubling of their population from 10.6% in the 1810's to 24.4% a century later. The low point for Massachusetts-born inmates was reached in the 1830's when they accounted for only 8.3% of the total which was smaller than Maine's share and New Hampshire's 58.3% (see Table 28). In 1810 New Hampshire accounted for 14.5% of New England's population. Starting in 1830, New Hampshire's share of the region's population shrank steadily; in 1910 it was only 6.6%. Massachusetts, in contrast, steadily grew from 32.1% of the region's population in 1810, to 51.4% in 1910.[38] Other New Englanders made up a relatively large part of the total prison population throughout this period ranging from a low of 9.7% in the 1820's to a high of 17.0% in the 1890's. The remaining native-born Americans accounted for a low of 4.3% of the inmates in the 1810's to a high of 14.0% in the 1900's.

The start of large-scale European immigration had an effect on the composition of the New Hampshire state prison population. Foreign-born inmates were never a very large proportion of the total but their composition

Table 28

New Hampshire State Prison Inmates, 1812-1914: Birthplace Listed by Decade

% and No. of Cases (N)
Decade

Birthplace	1810's	1820's	1830's
N.H.	61.7% (29)	41.9% (13)	58.3% (21)
Mass.	10.6% (5)	16.1% (5)	8.3% (3)
Other New England	12.8% (6)	9.7% (3)	16.7% (6)
Other U.S.A.	4.3% (2)	12.9% (4)	8.3% (3)
Canada	2.1% (1)		
Ireland	4.3% (2)	6.5% (2)	2.8% (1)
Britain	4.3% (2)	9.7% (3)	2.8% (1)
Germany			
Italy		2.8% (1)	
Other			
Unknown		3.2% (1)	
TOTAL CASES (N)	47	31	36

Birthplace	% and No. of Cases (N) Decade		
	1840's	1850's	1860's
N.H.	55.9% (19)	47.1% (16)	38.5% (25)
Mass.	11.8% (4)	20.6% (7)	20.0% (13)
Other New England	11.8% (4)	11.8% (4)	16.9% (11)
Other U.S.A.	8.8% (3)	8.8% (3)	6.2% (4)
Canada			6.2% (4)
Ireland	8.8% (3)	5.9% (2)	7.7% (5)
Britain	2.9% (1)	5.9% (2)	1.5% 91)
Germany			1.5% (1)
Italy			
Other			1.5% (1)
Unknown			
TOTAL CASES (N)	34	34	65

Birthplace	% and No. of Cases (N) Decade		
	1870's	1880's	1890's
N.H.	48.6% (52)	31.9% (45)	33.1% (39)

% and No. of Cases (N)
Decade

Birthplace	1870's	1880's	1890's
Mass.	17.8% (19)	17.0% (24)	16.1% (19)
Other New England	12.2% (13)	16.3% (23)	17.0% (20)
Other U.S.A.	8.4% (9)	7.7% (11)	5.9% (7)
Canada	3.7% 94)	8.5% (12)	11.9% (14)
Ireland	1.9% 92)	8.5% (12)	5.1% (6)
Britain	5.6% (16)	4.2% 96)	5.9% 97)
Germany		2.1% (3)	0.8% (1)
Italy		1.4% (2)	0.8% (1)
Other	0.9% (1)	2.1% (3)	0.8% (1)
Unknown	0.9% (1)		2.5% (3)
TOTAL CASES (N)	107	141	118

% and No. of Cases (N)
Decade

Birthplace	1900's	1910's	Total No. of Cases
N.H.	27.1% (35)	23.1% (18)	312
Mass.	20.9% (27)	24.4% (19)	145
Other New			

% and No. of Cases (N)
Decade

Birthplace	1900's		1910's		Total No. of Cases
Other New England	12.4%	(16)	12.8%	(10)	116
Other U.S.A.	14.0%	(18)	12.8%	(10)	74
Canada	12.4%	(16)	10.3%	(8)	59
Ireland	3.1%	(4)	3.9%	(3)	42
Britain	2.3%	(3)	2.5%	(2)	34
Germany	0.8%	(1)	2.5%	(2)	8
Italy	1.6%	(2)	3.9%	(3)	9
Other	3.1%	(4)	2.5%	(2)	12
Unknown	2.3%	(3)	1.3%	(1)	9
TOTAL CASES (N)	129		78		820

Source: "Register of Convicts 1812-1883," "[N.H. State] Prison Records [1874-1915,]" and "N.H. State Prison: Record of Gain and Loss in Population [1905-36]," all MS, Div. of Records-Management and Archives, Concord, N.H. and *Prison Warden's Reports*, 1859-1910.

changed over time. The largest single group consisted of inmates born in Canada. With the exception of the 1810's when they made up 2.1% of the prison population, Canadian-born inmates did not make an appearance until the 1860's when they made up 6.2% of the inmate population (see Table 28). The percentage of Canadians varied over the next several decades and was at its height during the 1890's and 1900's, at 11.9% and 12.4%, respectively. Italians, Germans, and others began appearing in the prison register in the

1860's. Their presence becomes more noticeable from the 1880's onward (see Table 28). The presence of foreign-born convicts from a greater variety of countries indicates the growing mobility and heterogeneity of the American population as a whole.

The British and Irish were present from the beginning of the record. Also unlike the other immigrants, the British and Irish as a percentage of the total inmate population reached a peak before the Civil War. The Irish made up 8.8% in the 1840's and they reached 8.5% in the 1870's.[39] The British immigrants reached 10.0% of the inmate population in the 1820's (see Table 28).

With the exception of Italians and blacks, all ethnic groups showed a similar proportion of types of crime convictions (see Table 24). Overall, 77.9% of the crimes (639 out of 820) committed by the convicts in the sample were property crimes. Most ethnic groups showed a similar proportion but there were exceptions. Twenty-two point two or two out of nine Italian cases in the sample were involved in property crime. All seven black cases involved property crime. The modern day participation of blacks in violent crime is completely different from the pattern that shows up here. The numbers involved in this analysis of seacoast New Hampshire are so small that we must make this assertion only tentatively. The conviction of blacks for property rather than violent crime bears a strong resemblance to crime in the nineteenth-century South described by Edward L. Ayers. In the South of that era, property crime was most commonly associated with blacks.[40] The most common property crime among blacks was larceny; five out of seven cases or 71.4%, which was higher than the overall figure of 31.4%. Larceny was the most common property crime among all ethnic groups except Canadians, Germans, and Italians, who favored burglary (see Table 24).

The few Italian-born convicts showed a very high proportion of violent crime (see Table 24). The most common forms of violence among the Italians in our sample were manslaughter and attempted murder. In contrast, the second-most violent ethnic group was the Irish at a comparatively paltry 19.1% (8 out of 42 cases). The overall proportion of violent crime was 14.6% which makes the Irish convicts in our sample more violent than most groups, thus lending credence to Paul Gilje's assertion that the Irish were more violent than most.[41] Canadians too were slightly more likely to have been convicted of violent crime than the rest at 17.0% (10 out of 59 cases). The British-born at 11.8% (4 out of 34 cases) and German-born at 12.5% (1 out of 8 cases) were slightly less violent than the average convict in the sample. Blacks were the least violent group in our sample: none were convicted of violent crime.

Of course, ethnicity must be considered to be only one variable in the explanation of violent crime in seacoast New Hampshire. Other potential factors include social class, occupational group, sex, and ongoing social and economic transformation of the region.

Although moral offenses were only a small part of the picture, it is possible to speculate on what cultural factors inhibited most ethnic groups from engaging in such behavior - at least at the felony level. Canadian-born and British-born convicts were the only foreign-born convicts imprisoned for moral offenses in our sample. The Irish and Italians were predominantly Catholic as were some Germans too. Possibly, strict attitudes toward marriage were involved. Immoral behavior was not restricted to certain ethnic groups. Perhaps it was the public nature and seriousness of the offense such as adultery, which threatened social values, which led to arrest and conviction. There may have been some aspect about the Irish, Italian, and black American communities which controlled such behavior. However, with so few cases in the sample, this will have to remain only speculation.

The combination of religion, ethnic culture, and economic status played a role in sexual behavior. The Catholic Church and family structure of some groups had an influence on sexual relations. In the American Southwest, for example, Catholic families of Mexican descent insisted that marriage take place when premarital sex led to pregnancy.[42] On the other hand, despite teachings of the Catholic Church, a large number of Irish immigrant women became prostitutes in urban centers prior to the Civil War. They did so, largely because their economic opportunities were so limited.[43] Another Catholic ethnic group, immigrant Italians, exercised strict control over sexual behavior - at least for females. Unmarried females were carefully chaperoned because Italians placed a high value on the virginity of their unmarried daughters.[44] In 1911 a major study of foreign-born prostitutes was conducted in New York City and found that Jews, Irish, and Italians were underrepresented. According to Ruth Rosen, the women from these groups were unlikely to become prostitutes because their cultures placed a premium on family solidarity and female chastity.[45] Attitudes toward marriage and female sexuality and family values may well have helped to keep the participation of certain ethnic groups out of the New Hampshire State Prison as far as moral felonies were concerned.

Finally, Germans, Italians, Irish, and blacks all showed significantly different proportions of "other" crimes than the general prison population. Overall, "other" crimes represented only 5.6% (46 out of 820) of the total. One eighth of the Germans, a fifth of the Italians, 14.3% of the Irish, and none of the black prison population were convicted of "other" crimes.

Birthplace is one indication of a population's mobility; residence is another. Fortunately, the residence of the accused at the time of conviction is easy to determine as it was listed in virtually all of the court bills and indictments. This was true even of most of the tramps described in Chapter Three.[46]

Most crime in nineteenth-century New Hampshire was a local affair. Most convicted criminals were residents of the county where they were convicted. Out of 545 cases in Rockingham County. 433 or 79.4% of the convicted were residents of that county. The proportion is even higher for Strafford County: 234 out of 275 cases or 85.1% (see Table 29). A handful of people convicted in Rockingham County were residents of Strafford County but there were none vice-versa. Most of the convicts in our sample were residents of the same town in which they had committed their crime. Relatively few inmates were strangers in their county of conviction. Only 2.2% resided in New Hampshire but outside of Rockingham or Strafford County. The only large group of outsiders came from Massachusetts who made up 6.7% (55 out of 820 cases) of the sample. The other New England states made up only a handful: 17 out of 820 cases or 2.0% (see Table 29). Twelve persons (1.5% of the sample) were residents of Canada at time of conviction while for 37 (4.5%) the place of residence was impossible to determine. Gender was another variable in felony conviction.

Serious crime in New Hampshire was overwhelmingly a male phenomenon and female participation in serious crime in New Hampshire during the period 1812-1914 was of a different nature from male participation. Only 16 out of 820 cases or 2.0% were committed by females. This is a smaller percentage than is found in present-day state prisons.[47] Female convicts were present throughout the time period under consideration with the exception of the 1870's and 1880's. Women convicts were approximately the same age as males: 25 versus 26 years median age for the total (see Table 19).

With far fewer convicts, the age range for females was more restricted: three were as young as 19 while the oldest was 54 (see Table 30). The types of crime committed by the females in our sample were also distinct from the general pattern described in Chapter Three. Judging from our sample, women convicts were more likely than men convicts to commit crimes of violence. Overall, crimes involving violence accounted for 14.6% of all crime but 37.6% (6 out of 16 cases) of female crime (see Table 31). With so few women in the sample, a small number of cases represents a large percentage. Thus, the picture of female criminality may be distorted.

Table 29

New Hampshire State Prison Inmates, 1812-1914:
Residence at Time of Conviction

Residence	No. of Cases	Percentage
Rock. Cty.	433	52.8%
Strafford Cty.	248	30.2%
Other N.H.	18	2.2%
Massachusetts	55	6.7%
Vermont	1	0.1%
Maine	14	1.7%
Rhode Island	1	0.1%
Connecticut	1	0.1%
Canada	12	1.5%
Unknown	37	4.5%
TOTAL:	820	100%

Source: Court Bills and Indictments, 1812-1914, Rockingham Cty., MS, Div. of Records-Management and Archives, Concord, N.H.; and Court Bills and Indictments, 1870-1914, MS, Justice and Administration Building, Dover, N.H.

Female criminality was probably underrepresented in the sample. Women were certainly involved as partners in crimes of morality like adultery. They suffered less-serious punishment or none at all in the sample because in adultery the married partner was considered the more guilty. In the sample, adultery was committed only by married men with unmarried women. There also were female accomplices in property crimes and crimes of violence.

Table 30

Age Distribution of Female Convicts at the New Hampshire State Prison, 1812-1914

Convict	Age
Bertha G. Tracy	19
Mina Farnham	19
Etta Parker	19
Lucinda Cilley	21
Ann Brown	22
Lizzie Provinchia	23
Hattie Beckman	23
Constance Perry	25
Frances Chase	27
Hannah Farley	28
Maud Besse	31
Jane Farnham	32
Betsy Ferguson	44
Hepsey Cole	48
Deborah Warren	52
Lucy M. Reed	54
Minimum Age:	19 years

178

Maximum Age: 54 years

Mean Age: 30.4 years

Median Age: 25 years

Source: "Register of Convicts 1812-1883," "[N.H. State] Prison Records [1874-1915]," "N.H. State Prison: Record of Gain and Loss in Population [1905-36]," and "Description Register [1881-98 and 1899-1906]," all MS, Div. of Records-Management and Archives, Concord, N.H.; and *Prison Warden's Reports*, 1859-1914.

Again, most of them never served time in the state prison. This was probably because of their secondary role in the crime rather than because they were female. Many male accomplices also did not end up in prison. For example, John F. Hillsgrove of Farmington broke into a house in Strafford. Together with William H. Hillsgrove (their relationship is not indicated), he stole $51 in cash and bank bills on July 13, 1872. John died in 1878 in the state prison while service his sentence. William never went to prison at all.[48] In a few cases, the accomplice's fate is recorded in the court records. Sometimes the accomplice ended up serving a short term in the county jail or house of correction, or he or she paid a fine.

One contributing factor to the extremely low number of female criminals is the structure of American society at the time. As Kathryn Sklar, Ann Douglas, and others have pointed out, the nineteenth century was a time when American middle-class women were increasingly confined to the home. The cult of domesticity enshrined duty, submissiveness, and above all, sexual purity as virtues associated with middle-class women. Because of the social strictures in place, women had less of an opportunity to participate in public life than men.[49] Since they were relatively more passive than men, and dependent on men, women just were not able to commit more crimes, even if they were so inclined. Perhaps one reason for the high percentage of violent crimes among women is that this was one of the only types of crime possible in the domestic sphere. Tragically, half of the six violent crimes committed by the women in our sample involved the killing of a daughter or a niece.[50] The imposition of the cult of domesticity is only a partial explanation for low female participation in crime. Most likely, psychological factors, such as aggressiveness, played a larger role since female participation in serious crime has been very low in other eras as well.

Paradoxically, the cult of domesticity became popular just when women began working outside the home in unprecedented numbers. By the 1830's the phenomenon of women working outside the home was common. As early as 1816 more than half of those employed in the new cotton mills were female.[51] However, by the 1840's and 1850's the composition of the manufacturing workforce was changing from native-born to immigrant women.[52] Women usually left the workforce upon marriage both for social reasons (the cult of domesticity) and because most work available to women was low paid and monotonous. Most female workers were young and single.[53]

Table 31

Female Inmates of the New Hampshire State Prison, 1812-1914: Convictions

Crime	No. of Cases	Percentage of Total
A. Property Crime		
Larceny	6	37.5%
Burglary	1	6.3%
TOTAL:	7 cases	43.8%
B. Violent Crime		
Murder	3	18.8%
Manslaughter	3	18.8%
TOTAL:	6 cases	37.6%
C. Moral Crime		
Entice Child for Prostitution	1	6.3%
TOTAL:	1	6.3%
D. Other Crime		
Perjury	2	12.5%
TOTAL:	2 cases	12.5%

180

GRAND
TOTAL: 16 cases   100%

Source: Court Bills and Indictments, 1812-1914, Rockingham Cty., MS, Div. of Records-Management and Archives, Concord, N.H.; Court Bills and Indictments, 1870-1914, Strafford Cty., MS, Justice and Administration Building, Dover, N.H.; "Register of Convicts 1812-1883," "[N.H. State] Prison Records [1874-1915," "N.H. State Prison: Record of Gain and Loss in Population [1905-36]," all MS, Div. of Records-Management and Archives, Concord, N.H.; and *Prison Warden's Reports*, 1859-1914.

The increasing presence of working women probably had an influence on crime. This assertion will have to remain speculative since there is very little information in the data regarding this point. Occupation is listed for only one female convict. Despite the bonds of the domestic model, an increasing number of young, single women were part of a growing industrial labor force, thus, leaving them exposed to at least some of the same temptations and pressures of their male counterparts. The greatest increase in working women came from the lower classes and immigrants.

We have only very spotty information on occupational status before 1881 and none after 1909. Occupation at time of conviction was rarely listed in any of the sources. The most helpful sources are the two "Description Registers" kept by the State Prison for the years 1881-1898 and 1899-1906. Prior to the 1880's information on occupation was occasionally mentioned in the court records. Unfortunately, occupation was not listed in any of the court records for the years 1910-1914. Even for the years 1881-1906, occupational information is not listed very often. The "Description Registers" are an inconsistent, if valuable, source. There were a total of 54 different occupations listed in the original sources (see Appendix). For ease of calculation, they were subdivided into three subgroups: white collar, skilled manual, and unskilled manual.[54]

Most convicts came from an unskilled, manual occupational background. However, this assertion must be made with great caution because information on occupation is missing for fully 589 out of 820 or 71.8% of the cases. The available data reveal the following: 158 cases or 68.4% of the cases listing occupation can be described as unskilled manual laborers; 64 cases or 27.7% of the cases listing occupation were classified as skilled manual workers; and only 9 cases (3.9%) of the cases listing occupations were white collar workers (see Table 32).

The available data indicate that the overall occupational pattern of the convicts before conviction was rather consistent throughout this time period. The preponderance of unskilled manual laborers dropped during the 1880's through 1900's. The one major aberration from the general occupational pattern occurred in the 1880's when skilled manual workers were in the majority at 58.3% (see Table 32). White collar workers made their first appearance in the 1880's and constituted their largest percentage (8.3%) ever.

Was there any connection between occupational status and type of crime? In the case of white collar workers, yes. Any conclusion reached has to be tentative because there are only nine known white collar cases in our sample. Eight of these or 88.9% engaged in property crime; a higher proportion than the sample of 820 cases as a whole. The one case not involving property crime was bigamy, which falls into the classification of moral offenses.

The Federal Census reports were used to identify the population at risk for various occupational groups for the period 1880-1910. The conclusions reached about occupational group or social class are very tentative because of the following complications. First, the census provides a description on a statewide rather than county level. The sample of inmates is based only on those persons convicted in Rockingham and Strafford County, not the whole state. Second, the sample covers an entire decade at a time rather than just the single year of the census. Occupational information is available for only part of the sample. Third, the census reports of 1880-1910 divide the workforce by industry, rather than status such as white collar, etc. Thus, it is necessary to match up each listing in the sample with the contemporary census listing to ensure agreement between our definition and that of the census. The greatest problem was the changing definition of "laborer." According to the census, the designation of "laborer" without further specification was placed under the category of "domestic and personal service" for the years 1880, 1890, and 1900. In 1910 such laborers were listed under "manufacturing and mechanical industries."[55] A final complication is the fact that occupational information on specific inmates is available only through 1906. In 1908 the annual prison warden's report started supplying occupational statistics on the inmates - but only for the aggregate population. Even this is incomplete. Because names were unlisted in this tabulation, it was impossible to separate out those inmates belonging to the sample. The comparison for 1910 includes only the 45 out of 136 state prison inmates for whom an occupational status was listed. Finally, one should be careful not to confuse status with an industry. Manual workers were not necessarily lower class just as an ill-paid clerk (white collar) is not necessarily upper class. With all of

182

Table 32

New Hampshire State Prison Inmates, 1812-1914: Occupations by Decade

Decade	Occupational Category (Number of Cases and Valid Percent)		
	Unskilled Manual	Skilled Manual	White Collar
1810's	10 (100%)		
1820's	3 (75.0%)	1 (25.0%)	
1830's	4 (66.7%)	2 (33.3%)	
1840's	12 (100%)		
1850's	9 (100%)		
1860's	12 (100%)		
1870's	4 (100%)		
1880's	8 (33.3%)	14 (58.3%)	2 (8.3%)
1890's	39 (59.1%)	25 (37.9%)	2 (3.0%)
1900's	57 (67.9%)	22 (26.3%)	5 (5.8%)
1910's	-- ------	-- -------	- ------
TOTAL:	158 (68.4%)	65 (28.1%)	9 (3.5%)
231 cases			

Source: Court Bills and Indictments, 1812-1914, Rockingham Cty., MS, Div. of Records-Management and Archives, Concord, N.H.; Court Bills and Indictments, 1870-1914, Strafford Cty., MS, Justice and Administration Building, Dover, N.H.; and "Description Register [1881-98 and 1899-1906]," MS, Div. of Records-Management and Archives, Concord, N.H.

these caveats in mind, we can make the following conclusions.

Manual workers were overrepresented in the state prison population. Except for the 1880's, the "manufacturing, mechanical and mining" category was overrepresented: 87.5% in the prison population versus 36.2% of the state's population at risk (see Table 33). Many of these inmates were shoemakers, blacksmiths, and carpenters. The sample from the 1880's is unusual in that there is not a single listing for "laborer." Perhaps the prison keepers of that decade took more trouble to assign a specific occupational identity to the inmates than in later years. It is extremely difficult to compare these designations to white collar, skilled manual, etc. For example, the two inmates falling into the category of "trade and transportation" are what we would consider to be white collar workers: an agent for the Singer Sewing Machine Company and an agent for Pathe Brothers. "Trade and transportation" also covered teamsters who would not be described as white collar.[56]

In 1910 "professional services" were overrepresented in the prison. A journalist and a photographer accounted for 4.4% of the inmates whose occupations were listed. Those engaged in "professional services" were only 2.7% of the population at risk (see Table 33).

Possibly, the increasing urbanization of seacoast New Hampshire accounts for the fact that agricultural workers are consistently underrepresented in the inmate population. They were absent in the 1880's. Strangely enough, agricultural occupations were highest in 1910 but this may well have been due to the fact that the analysis of the 1910 prison population was based on a *statewide* sample unlike the previous decades which were based only on the *seacoast* population. The presence of many shoemakers and mill workers, as well as service workers such as barbers and waiters might also indicate that crime in New Hampshire was partly related to urbanization and industrialization. Certainly, conviction of crime was a class phenomenon. There are very few members of what we recognize as white collar workers found in the prison population.

Property crimes in our sample consisted of larceny, burglary, embezzlement, and arson. There were a total of five embezzlement cases in our sample; in four of them the convict was a member of the white collar group. White collar participation in embezzlement cases is far higher at 44.4% than any other group. The fifth case of embezzlement involved a convict of unknown occupational status. The known occupations of the embezzlers in our sample included a book keeper, two company agents, and a bank treasurer.[57] In contrast to the 88.9% of white collar workers convicted of property crime, the skilled workers stood at 75.0% and the unskilled at 77.5% (see Table 34).

Table 33

Occupational Groups: Prison Population Compared to Population
at Risk, 1880-1910

PART 1.

A. 1880-1900. Occupational Groups from Prison Sample (Rockingham and
Strafford County) by Decade

Decade Category
        N   (%)
1880's Professional and Personal Services
        1   (4.2%)

        Trade and Transportation
        2   (8.3%)

1880's Manufacturing, Mechanical Industries, and Mining
        21   (87.5%)

TOTAL: 24   (100%)

1890's Agriculture
        2   (3.0%)

        Professional Services
        1   (1.5%)

        Trade and Transportation
        4   (6.1%)

        Manufacturing and Mechanical Industries
        31   (47.0%)

        Domestic and Personal Service
        28   (42.4%)

TOTAL: 66   (100%)

Decade Category
N   (%)

1900's Agriculture
2   (2.4%)

Trade and Transportation
12   (14.3%)

Manufacturing and Mechanical Industries
32   (38.1%)

Domestic and Personal Service
38   (45.2%)

TOTAL: 84   (100%)

B. 1910 Occupational Groups from Whole Prison Population Listed for Year 1910

Year Category
N   (%)
1910 Agriculture
6   (13.3%)

Professional Service
2   (4.4%)

Transportation
6   (13.3%)

Manufacturing and Mechanical Industries
28   (62.2%)

Domestic and Personal Service
2   (4.4%)

Clerical Occupations
1   (2.2%)

186

Year	Category	
	N	(%)

TOTAL: 45 (100%)

PART 2. Occupational Groups in New Hampshire 1880-1910

Year	Category	
	N	**(%)**
1880	Agriculture	
	44,299	(39.4%)

Professional and Personal Services
16,158 (14.4%)

Trade and Transportation
11,208 (10.0%)

Manufacturing, Mechanical Industries, and Mining
40,675 (36.2)

TOTAL: 112,340 (100%)

1890 Agriculture
42,982 (26.1%)

Professional Service
6831 (4.1%)

Trade and Transportation
19,771 (12.0%)

Manufacturing and Mechanical Industries
71,408 (43.4%)

Domestic and Personal Service
23,711 (14.4%)

TOTAL: 164,703 (100%)

Year	Category	
	N	(%)

1900 Agriculture
38,782 (22.7%)

Professional Service
7765 (4.3%)

Trade and Transportation
25,651 (15.0%)

Manufacturing and Mechanical Pursuits
75,945 (44.4%)

Domestic and Personal Service
30,576 (17.9%)

TOTAL: 178,719 (100%)

1910 Agriculture and Forestry
35,195 (24.5%)

Professional Service
3855 (2.7%)

Transportation
10,777 (7.5%)

Manufacturing and Mechanical Industries
70,316 (49.0%)

Domestic and Personal Service
4745 (3.3%)

Public Service Not Elsewhere Classified
1910 (1.3%)

Clerical Occupations

Year	Category	
	N	(%)
1910	Clerical Occupations	
	3131	(2.2%)
	Extraction of Minerals	
	574	(0.4%)

TOTAL: 143,363 (Males Only) (100%)

Note: Occupational categories designated by U.S. Census.

Source: *U.S. Census Reports*, 1880-1910; Court Bills and Indictments, 1880-1910, Rockingham Cty., MS, Div. of Records-Management and Archives, Concord; Court Bills and Indictments, 1880-1910, Strafford Cty., MS, Justice and Administration Building, Dover, N.H.; "Description Register [1881-98 and 1899-1906]," and *Prison Warden's Report*, 1910.

In this sample, only manual workers had been convicted of violent crime (see Table 34). Violent crime was committed by 17.3% of the skilled workers and 17.7% of the unskilled. On the other hand, crimes of morality were proportionately higher among white collar workers (11.1%) than either skilled manual (3.2%) or unskilled workers (1.3%). Part of this might be due to economic and social circumstances. White collar workers probably had more money to spend and more comfortable surroundings and privacy to engage in such misbehavior. In some ways, it is paradoxical for white collar workers to be so well-represented in moral crime. During the nineteenth century, it was precisely the middle classes who were most concerned with the ideal of female sexual purity and restraint. At the same time as the doctrine of purity was used to confine women to the domestic sphere, it was also used to try to control male sexual excesses. John D'Emilio and Estelle B. Freedman say that thanks to the social and economic changes affecting America in the nineteenth century, attitudes toward sexual behavior changed: people were more conscious of personal choice in sexual behavior and the middle classes in particular began to combine sexual desire with a "romantic quest for intimacy." Despite the emergence of such ideals, adultery was common to all social classes.[58]

The limited data in our sample of New Hampshire state prison inmates

Table 34

New Hampshire State Prison Inmates, 1812-1914:
Occupational Status by Crime

I. White Collar
A. Property Crime

Crime	No. of Cases	Valid %
Larceny	1	11.1%
Burglary	2	22.2%

I. White Collar
A. Property Crime

Crime	No. of Cases	Valid %
Embezzlement	4	44.4%
Arson	1	11.1%
TOTAL:	8 cases	88.9%

C. Moral Crime

Crime	No. of Cases	Valid %
Bigamy	1	11.1%
TOTAL:	1 case	11.1%

GRAND TOTAL:	9 cases	100%

II. Skilled Manual
A. Property Crime

Crime	No. of Cases	Valid %
Larceny	13	20.3%
Break and Enter	6	9.4%

II. Skilled Manual (Continued)
A. Property Crime

Crime	No. of Cases	Valid %
Burglary	20	31.3%
Robbery	6	9.4%
Forgery/ Counterfeit	2	3.1%
Arson	1	1.6%
TOTAL:	48 cases	75.1%

B. Violent Crime

Crime	No. of Cases	Valid %
Murder	2	3.1%
Manslaughter	3	4.7%
Rape	1	1.6%
Att. Rape	2	3.1%
Break and Enter and Assault	1	1.6%
Assault with Intent to Steal	1	1.6%
Assault	1	1.6%
TOTAL:	11 cases	17.3%

C. Moral Crime

Crime	No. of Cases	Valid %
Unnatural and Lascivious Acts	1	1.6%

II. Skilled Manual (Continued)
C. Moral Crime

Crime	No. of Cases	Valid %
Bigamy	1	1.6%
TOTAL:	2 cases	3.2%

D. Other Crime

Crime	No. of Cases	Valid %
Tramp	1	1.6%
Violate Parole	2	3.1%
TOTAL:	3 cases	4.7%
GRAND TOTAL:	64 cases	100%

III. Unskilled Manual
A. Property Crime

Crime	No. of Cases	Valid %
Larceny	44	27.8%
Break and Enter	17	10.8%
Burglary	48	30.4%
Break and Enter with Intent Steal	1	0.6%
Robbery	5	3.2%
Forgery/ Counterfeit.	2	1.3%
Arson	5	3.2%

III. Unskilled Manual (Continued)
A. Property Crime

Crime	No. of Cases	Valid %
TOTAL:	122 cases	77.3%

B. Violent Crime

Crime	No. of Cases	Valid %
Murder	5	3.2%
Manslaughter	3	1.9%
Att. Murder	7	4.4%
Rape	5	3.2%
Att. Rape	7	4.4%
Assault with Intent to Steal	1	0.6%
TOTAL:	28 cases	17.7%

III. Unskilled Manual
C. Moral Crime

Crime	No. of Cases	Valid %
Adultery	2	1.3%
TOTAL:	2 cases	1.3%

D. Other Crime

Crime	No. of Cases	Valid %
Tramp	5	3.2%
Place Obstruction on R.R. Tracks	1	0.6%
TOTAL:	6 cases	3.8%

	No. of Cases	Valid %
GRAND TOTAL:	148 cases	100%

231 Cases Overall

Source: Court Bills and Indictments, 1812-1914, Rockingham Cty., MS, Div. of Records-Management and Archives, Concord, N.H.; Court Bills and Indictments, 1870-1914, Strafford Cty., MS, Justice and Administration Building, Dover, N.H.; and "Description Register [1881-98 and 1899-1906]," MS, Div. of Records-Management and Archives, Concord, N.H.

suggest that there is some correlation between occupational status and crime. White collar workers were convicted of few crimes. When they did transgress, it was more likely to involve property crime such as embezzlement. Moral offenses too were more likely to have been committed by white collar workers than others, or, perhaps, their social prominence made it more likely that such misbehavior would be noticed and punished. Violent crime was strongly associated with manual workers both skilled and unskilled in nearly the same proportions. Burglary was the most commonly convicted crime in the skilled and unskilled laboring classes. It was the most common property crime after embezzlement among white collar workers (see Table 34). Only a tenth of the white collar criminals committed larceny. One fifth of the skilled criminals committed larceny and a quarter of the unskilled did so.

The lower classes were convicted much more frequently than the middle and upper classes of serious crime in New Hampshire. Why? An answer can be found in the types of crime associated with each occupational group. Each social class faced a different set of temptations to commit crime. Certain aspects of an individual's social environment predisposed him or her to commit crime or placed him or her in a situation leading to criminal behavior. Property crime was dominant in each occupational group but there were differences - embezzlement was white collar crime while larceny was much more common among the lower classes.

By the nineteenth century violent crime in America was associated primarily with the lower classes. There were several factors contributing to this development. One of the major causes of violence in American society was and is the excessive consumption of alcohol. According to W.J. Rorabaugh, the United States experienced a "period of unprecedented heavy drinking" during the years 1790-1830. Rorabaugh links this phenomenon to the fact that

1790-1830 was an era of unprecedented change in American society.[59] Rorabaugh goes on to say that "among the lustiest consumers of alcohol" were stage drivers, lumberjacks, river boatmen, and canal builders. They were attracted to alcohol because they were mobile and rootless, and consequently lacked an adequate means of coping with change. Soldiers and sailors were heavy drinkers too.[60]

A disproportionate percentage of this group was composed of Irish immigrants. Rorabaugh characterizes them as heavy drinkers, aggressive, and violent.[61] Lender and Martin say that the Irish immigrants, justifiably feeling oppressed by the larger American society, "seized upon drinking as a major symbol of ethnic loyalty."[62] This reliance on alcohol had precedent in Ireland and was particularly indulged in by landless young men.[63] Paul Gilje discusses the growing popularity of street and tavern disorders in New York City in the early nineteenth century. In addition to linking part of the problem to the Irish, Gilje links street violence to occupational status: "not many rich New Yorkers or even affluent artisans participated. The vast majority of offenders were poorer mechanics, day laborers, sailors, and children."[64] All classes consumed alcohol but it seems likely that lower class consumption was more public and boisterous, thus providing a greater opportunity for violent confrontations. However, middle class consumption of alcohol was not only different in quality but was increasingly different in quantity.

The temperance movement helped drive a wedge between the middle and lower classes. The temperance movement which began spreading throughout the United States in the 1820's was largely a middle-class phenomenon and it was connected to religious revivalism. Paul E. Johnson explains that with the spread of religious revivalism, members of the middle class began to look upon alcohol as the cause of all evil and crime.[65] A decade earlier, social reformers had blamed alcohol as the major cause of pauperism.[66] Thanks in part to the growing middle class fear of alcohol, the old patterns of sociability between masters and workers were disrupted. Work patterns and mobility meant that masters and workers were driven farther apart, especially with new demands made by masters for discipline and regular work habits.[67] While respectable members of the middle class endorsed temperance, alcohol became the "angry badge of working-class status" according to Johnson. Alcohol was now associated with "new, perhaps looser cultural controls."[68]

It is not surprising to find the crime of being a tramp to be a phenomenon exclusively associated with manual workers, especially the unskilled. In times of economic distress, unskilled workers are usually more likely to suffer unemployment than white collar workers. Also, alternative sources of support may be inferior or lacking among unskilled workers. The social stigma associated with tramps might also have been too much for members of the white collar labor force to bear, thus eliminating them from consideration as tramps.

Rates of recidivism in nineteenth century New Hampshire were very different from modern day rates. Only 12.3% (101 cases out of 820) were identifiable as recidivists (see Table 35). Recidivism is here defined as habitual antisocial behavior or criminal activity and imprisonment.[69] A word of caution is in order. The exact meaning and measurement of recidivism is disputed among criminologists. For example, is a person considered to be a recidivist if he or she is reimprisoned for a serious crime but not the person who is reimprisoned for a less-serious (and different) offense? Other problems associated with the definition of recidivism include changing definitions of criminal behavior. It is impossible to label someone a recidivist if there is no record of previous imprisonment even though the person may have been previously imprisoned after all. Would one consider someone to be a recidivist if he or she were acquitted or pardoned for the first offense but not subsequent offenses? Would merely technical violations of parole make one a recidivist? How long a period between imprisonments is enough before someone is considered a recidivist? The question of recidivism has been a continuing point of controversy among criminologists.[70]

For our purposes, a recidivist will be defined as a convict who has previously been convicted of a felony and who has served a prison sentence. this definition will be employed here due to limitations of the original sources. Recidivism was noted in the "Register of Convicts 1812-1883." Next to a few names, the prison record kepper inscribed helpful notations such as "Once in Mass. and Vermont Prison" or "2d time this Prison."[71] Unfortunately, such direct and helpful indications of recidivism are rare. They are absent in the "[N.H. State] Prison Records [1874-1915]" and "N.H. State prison: Record of Gain and Loss in Population [1905-36]." Another method of determining recidivism is to check for the reoccurance of names. This required careful checking to see if the the entries referred to the same or a different person. The example of the three John Browns discussed at the start of this chapter is a useful illustration of how this was done. Because the sample is limited only to those persons convicted of a crime in Rockingham and Strafford Counties, we did not count as recidivists those persons convicted of a crime in another county if it occurred after the Rockingham or Strafford County conviction. We did, however, count a person as a recidivist if he or she had been convicted of a felony (and served time in a state prison) in a different county or or even a different state before their appearance in the Rockingham and Strafford County records. The reason for counting recidivists in this manner was practical. To analyze a recidivist's actions in another county or state would have meant going beyond the defined population of criminals. In addition, records for criminal cases outside the two counties under discussion are either nonexistent or extremely difficult to locate.

Recidivism rates for inmates of the New Hampshire state prison were consistently low throughout the period 1812-1914. The rates were uneven and fluctuating (see Table 35). The lowest point reached was 6.4% in the 1880's while the highest was the 1820's at 25.8% with the average being 12.3% of the cases. This is a real contrast to present-day figures. According to Carl Sifakis, 85% of the male felons in California prisons in 1969 and 85% of the male felons in Massachusetts prisons in 1971 were recidivists - a mirror image of our statistics.[72] As of 1991 80.8% of American state prison inmates were recidivists.[73] Some of the enormous disparity between our recidivism statistics and those of the present day may be due to different ways of measuring or defining recidivism, but perhaps also, punishment was more effective in the past. We will examine this issue in more detail in Chapters Five and Six.

Federal prisoners were a special category of inmate at the New Hampshire State Prison. We will not cover them in great detail since none of them were convicted by a New Hampshire court. They do deserve mention since they were a significant proportion of the prison population in 1865 and 1911.

The presence of federal prisoners in New Hampshire was the result of the fact that the federal government made no provision for the incarceration of persons convicted of a federal offense. Until 1894 federal prisoners were housed in various state prisons and county jails across the country. General R.B. Brinkerhoff of the National Prison Association made the first survey of federal prisoners and discovered that as of 1885 there were 1027 federal prisoners in state prisons and 10,000 more in county jails.[74] The National Prison Association pressured Congress into dealing with the problem in 1891. The first federal prison, a military prison, opened at Fort Leavenworth, Kansas in 1894. Within a decade two more federal prisons were constructed at Atlanta, Georgia and McNeil Island, Washington.[75]

The federal government was slow to use the New Hampshire State Prison. In 1842 the state legislature passed an act that required the warden "to receive all convicts sentenced to hard labor by any United States court."[76] However, no federal prisoners were sent to New Hampshire until 1865 which was

Table 35

Known Recidivism among New Hampshire State Prison Inmates, 1812-1914

Decade	% and No. of Cases (N) Yes	No	Total % and No. (N) of Cases
1810's	14.9% (7)	85.1% (40)	100% (47)
1820's	25.8% (8)	74.2% (23)	100% (31)
1830's	19.4% (7)	80.6% (29)	100% (36)
1840's	8.8% (3)	91.2% (31)	100% (34)
1850's	8.8% (3)	91.2% (31)	100% (34)
1860's	10.8% (7)	89.2% (58)	100% (65)
1870's	17.8% (19)	82.2% (88)	100% (107)
1880's	6.4% (9)	93.6% (132)	100% (141)
1890's	7.5% (9)	92.4% (109)	100% (118)
1900's	17.1% (22)	82.9% (107)	100% (129)
1910's	9.0% (7)	91.0% (71)	100% (78)

SUMMARY:
12.3% (101) 87.7% (719) 100% (820 cases)

Source: "Register of Convicts 1812-1883," "[N.H. State] Prison Records [1874-1915]," "N.H. State Prison: Record of Gain and Loss in Population [1905-36]," all MS, Div. of Records-Management and Archives, Concord, N.H.

undoubtedly a disappointment since the state received payment from the federal government for boarding these prisoners and was able to earn even more money by employing the prisoners at contract labor.[77] In June 1865 the state prison was designated a military prison.[78] In that year 47 men were listed as "U.S. Convicts" in the "Register of Convicts 1812-1883." Most were convicted of strictly military offenses: twelve desertions, three bounty jumpers, one "sleeping at post," and another "disobedience of orders." Most of these men were sentenced to two to five years in prison. The shortest term was four months given to Bazil [sic] Bowchard, a 21-year old Canadian immigrant, for desertion. Life in prison was given to Thomas Brown, age 16 and Alfred Brown, age 21, for murder.[79] Most of these inmates were pardoned in 1865-66. In 1866 only four federal prisoners were sent to New Hampshire: a rapist, a murderer, and two men convicted of breaking and stealing.[80] For the next 45 years federal prisoners were sent to New Hampshire rarely and sporadically: a total of 43. Most of these offenders were convicted of crimes against the Post Office, counterfeiting currency, or obtaining funds, such as pensions, under false pretenses.[81]

Between 1911 and 1914 the New Hampshire State Prison functioned as an auxiliary naval prison. Seventy-four court-martialed naval prisoners were sent to the prison in 1911. In 1912 47 court-martialed naval prisoners were sent, in 1913 the number was 45, and in 1914 only 13.[82] As early as 1891 the Secretary of the Navy had recommended that the naval prison located at Boston be transferred to the Portsmouth Naval Shipyard. Twelve hundred Spanish prisoners of war were housed in a stockade on Seavey Island at the Portsmouth Naval Shipyard in 1898.[83] In 1903 the U.S.S. Southerly was transferred from Boston to Portsmouth and anchored in a back channel pier to serve as an auxiliary naval prison until being transferred back to Boston in 1922.[84] Meanwhile, construction on the Portsmouth Naval Prison began in 1903 and the prison was opened in 1908. There were 320 cells in this structure yet the Navy saw fit to transfer 179 court-martialed sailors to the New Hampshire State Prison between 1911 and 1914.[85]

Most of these prisoners were young men in their twenties. The vast majority of them were imprisoned for moral and disciplinary offenses. The largest single category of offense was "scandalous conduct tending to the destruction of good morals": 57 inmates or 31.8%. Related convictions included sodomy and drunkenness. Disciplinary offenses included assault and refusing to obey an officer, sleeping at one's post, desertion, and fraudulent enlistment. Some of the naval prisoners were convicted of crimes similar to inmates in the sample of Rockingham and Strafford County inmates: 42 or 23.5% were convicted of theft. There were a few robbers and murderers too.[86] Most of these men were sentenced to two to five years and had begun their sentences elsewhere (presumably Portsmouth Naval Prison).[87] Federal prisoners were a special group of convicts and did not exhibit all of the attributes suggested by my data. Characteristics of the more standard inmates of the New Hampshire State Prison are summarized below.

In conclusion, ethnicity had a connection to criminal behavior in New Hampshire during the period 1812-1914. Some ethnic groups were present in such small numbers as to be possibly misleading. We lack sufficient data to be able to make more definite conclusions. Why were the blacks in our sample involved only in property crime? Why were the Italians in our sample so very violent? What inhibited the Irish from engaging in moral crime? It is impossible to provide firm answers to these questions without more information.

Ethnicity was an important component in crime although we can make definite conclusions only for the years 1870-1914 (except in the case of blacks). First of all, most non-British-American ethnic groups participated at disproportionately high rates in comparison to the total sample. One possible reason for this was the difficulty of adjustment to a new society. Possibly, immigrants may have presented easier targets for law enforcement officials than did native-born offenders. The law may have been selectively enforced at times. Tensions caused by poor living conditions and possibly religious and social discrimination helped propel members of certain ethnic groups into crime. Cultural factors such as heavy drinking and pugnacity may have played into the frustrations felt by some members of immigrant groups. Ethnicity is not the deciding factor - although some nineteenth-century criminologists thought otherwise - in criminal behavior. It is an important factor, but one of several which helps to describe the typical criminal of nineteenth-century New Hampshire. Most of the convicts in our sample, after all, were native-born Americans and not immigrants.

Female participation in serious crime was different from male participation. There were very few women in the state prison and those who were, exhibited a different pattern of crime from the male majority. The proportion of violent offenders among women was greater than that found among males. A similar phenomenon has been noted by Nicole H. Rafter in her analysis of the New York State Prison for Women at Auburn for the years 1893-1933.[88] The presence of violent female offenders runs counter to the emerging middle-class ideal of the American woman as domestic, submissive, and pure. Unfortunately, it is possible to determine the occupational status of only one female convict out of the sixteen. She is described as a "table girl" which implies that she came from a low social class.[89]

The sample of state prison inmates analyzed here exhibits certain characteristics that help to explain the phenomenon of crime in New Hampshire during the years 1812-1914. No single characteristic discussed here explains criminality but each contributed to the overall incidence of serious crime. First, most of the convicts were young. Most were between 18 and 45 years of age which is similar to the age groups found in today's state prisons. There were times in the past (the 1840's and 1850's) when the proportion of youthful offenders confined in prison was far larger than today. The opening of the state reform school in 1858 may have helped to reduce this statistic in later decades. The overall median age came to 26 years, younger than today's 30 years. This is somewhat of a surprise since criminals of the present are generally recognized to be younger than those of the nineteenth century.[90] Some of this may be attributable to the fact that very few juvenile offenders are confined to state prisons today.

The state prison population reflected the racial and ethnic composition of New Hampshire society at the time: nearly all-white with a tiny minority of blacks. Most prison inmates were native-born Americans and nearly all were male. Native-born inmates outnumbered the foreign-born by five to one. Most foreign-born inmates came from Canada, Ireland, and Great Britain. Some association seems to exist between ethnic group and type of crime but the connections between ethnicity and crime has to be tempered with the knowledge that other factors such as occupation and living conditions have an effect on criminality as well. Overall, 77.9% of the cases involved property crime, 14.6% violent crime, 1.8% moral crime, and 5.6% other crime. The most marked differences from this pattern were as follows. Every black in our sample committed property crimes while only 22.2% of Italians did so. The small Italian cadre of criminals showed a violent crime rate of between 49 and 66 per 100,000 population. The Irish rate of violence was between 48 and 107 per 100,000 population and the Canadian ranged from 33 to 61 per 100,000 population. Blacks were least violent. Those in our sample committed no violent crimes. Only the Canadians and British showed higher overall percentages for moral crimes. Finally, the Italians, Germans, and Irish were more likely to commit "other" crimes which usually meant being a tramp (see Table 24).

Although the convict population showed an increasing diversity in birthplace, most serious crimes were committed by local residents. Most of the convicts in our sample were born in New Hampshire. A large proportion were born in Massachusetts and the other New England states. Over 85% of the inmates in our sample were New Hampshire residents at the time of conviction. Crime was rarely committed by outsiders. Most crime was committed by members of the local community. This was especially true of Strafford County in which 234 out of 275 cases or 85.1% listed a location in Strafford County as residence of the convict. The remaining criminals were residents of other New England states with the exception of 12 cases listing a residence in Canada. Even these were in relatively close proximity to New Hampshire: Quebec, Prince Edward Island, or Nova Scotia were the most common locations. The population of New Hampshire became more mobile as technological, demographic, and economic changes took place which may explain the increasing number of outsiders committing crimes in New Hampshire.

Judging from the available data, crime was overwhelmingly associated with members of the lower classes. Fully 68.4% (158 out of 231) convicts were employed in unskilled manual occupations. Another 28.1% (65 out of 231) were skilled manual workers and only 3.5% (8 out of 231) were white collar workers. Certain aspects of lower class life such as a low income, uncomfortable living conditions, and a boisterous social existence with alcoholic drinking an important pastime combined with other factors, helped create opportunities for crime. Rorabaugh and others have described the nineteenth century as a time of change. Adding in the social stresses of such change, criminal behavior is not a surprising response. One component to consider is the use of the criminal laws as a method of controlling an unruly, changing population. Indeed, David J. Rothman says the emergence of penitentiaries and other institutions in the 1820's and 1830's was partly an attempt by the established elites to control American society.[91]

Rates of recidivism among the convicts in our sample are the obverse of rates found in American state prisons today.[92] Part of the explanation may lie in differing definitions of recidivism. Additionally, there may be peculiarities about our sample which would create such a different picture of recidivism. On the other hand, perhaps recidivism among inmates at the New Hampshire state prison in the nineteenth century was genuinely different from today. Part of the answer may lie with the concept and function of punishment.

The next chapter will analyze punishment in operation in the context of the New Hampshire state prison during its first century of existence. What was life like in the New Hampshire state prison? We will examine aspects of the prison experience such as the routine of hard labor, living conditions, improvement or deterioration in conditions, and disciplinary measures to make an assessment of the prison experience. We will investigate the punitive and rehabilitative aspects of the prison in practice. After this, we will analyze such variables as sentence passed, sentence served, method of discharge from the prison, and recidivism. Our findings will then be synthesized with those about crime and criminals for an overall assessment of crime and punishment in New Hampshire between 1812 and 1914.

Notes

1. The SP/SS computer program was used to provide statistics.

2. These sources are located at the Divison of Records-Management and Archives in Concord, N.H.

3. State v. Davis, No. 40790, Rockingham Cty., N.H. (1816).

4. Newspapers were consulted for only a few cases and proved more useful in discussing crime in Chapter Three than in discussing the convicts themselves.

5. Dept. of the Interior, Census Office, *Statistics of the Population of the United States at the Tenth Census (June 1, 1880)* (Washington, D.C., 1883), p. 608, Microfilm (Woodbridge, Conn.: Research Publications, Inc.).

6. Recidivism has been counted whenever possible and will be more fully addressed in the chapters on punishment.

7. "Register of Convicts 1812-1883," MS, Div. of Records-Management and Archives, Concord, N.H.

8. *Ibid.*

9. State v. Burroughs, No. 13258, Rockingham Cty., N.H. (1832) and "Register of Convicts 1812-1883," MS, Div. of Records-Management and Archives, Concord, N.H.

10. U.S. Bureau of the Census, *Statistical Abstract of the United State: 1993*, 113th. Ed. (Washington, D.C., 1990), p. 211.

11. *Reports of the Warden, Physician and Chaplain of the N.H. State Prison, June Session, 1852* (Concord, N.H., 1852), 22.

12. *Report of the Warden of the N.H. State Prison...June Session, 1854* (Concord, N.H., 1854), 21.

13. *Ibid.*, 21 and "Register of Convicts 1812-1883," MS, Div. of Records-Management and Archives, Concord, N.H.

14. State v. Kehoe, No. [Not Listed], Rockingham Cty., N.H. (1857).

15. State v. Price, Np. 40788, Rockingham Cty, N.H. (1816) and "Register of Convicts 1812-1883," MS, Div. of Records-Management and Archives, Concord, N.H..

16. *Laws of the State of New Hampshire, Passed June Session...1855* (Concord, N.H., 1855), 1553-58.

17. *Laws of the State of New Hampshire, Passed June Session...1857* (Concord, N.H., 1857), 1881.

18. See State v. Thompson, No. 15322, Rockingham Cty., N.H. (1878) and State v. Miller, No. 79, Rockingham Cty., N.H. (1895).

19. See Chapter 125 "An Act to Regulate the Treatment and Control of Dependent, Neglected and Delinquent Children and to Provide for the Appointment of Probation Officers," *Laws of the State of New Hampshire, Passed January Session, 1907* (Concord, N.H., 1907), 120.

20. John Styles, "Crime in 18th.-Century England," *History Today*, 38 (1988), 38.

21. Samuel Walker, *Sense and Nonsense about Crime: A Policy Guide*, 2nd. Ed. (Pacific Grove, Calif., 1989), p. 59.

22. State v. Hoyt, Nos. 2748-49, Rockingham Cty., N.H. (1884).

23. State v. Foster, No. 870, Strafford Cty., N.H. (1914) and "N.H. State Prison: Record of Gain and Loss in Population [1905-36]," MS, Div. of Records-Management and Archives, Concord, N.H.

24. Eric H. Monkkonen, *The Dangerous Class: Crime and Poverty in Columbus, Ohio, 1860-1885* (Cambridge, Mass., 1975), pp. 83-84.

25. The black population of New Hampshire declined from 970 persons (0.45%) out of a total population of 214,360 in 1810 down to only 494 (0.15%) out of 326,073 in 1860. In 1910 the black population jumbered only 564 (0.13%) out of a total population of 430,572. *U.S. Census Reports 1810-1910* (Title Varies) Microfilm (Woodbridge, Conn.: Research Publications, Inc.). It is also possible that a few persons who might be classified as black were not listed because they appeared to be white. The definition of blackness has been an ambiguous concept in American history. It is probably safest to conclude that only those convicts exhibiting obvious African features and dark complexions were listed as black in the prison records.

26. Edward L. Ayers, *Vengeance and Justice: Crime and Punishment in the 19th.-Century American South* (New York, 1984), pp. 125-31 and Michael S. Hindus, *Prison and Plantation: Crime, Justice, and Authority in Massachusetts and South Carolina, 1767-1878* (Chapel Hill, N.C., 1980), pp. 140-42.

27. See a) entry for Royal Allen in "Register of Convicts 1812-1883," MS, Div. of Records-Management and Archives, Concord, N.H.; b) State v. Allen, No. 46735, Rockingham Cty., N.H. (1819); State v. Gray, No. 37781, Rockingham Cty., N.H. (1814); c) State v. Jackson, No. [Not Listed], Rockingham Cty., N.H. (1823); d) State v. Addison, No. 6986, Rockingham Cty., N.H. (1861); e) State v. Miles, No. 8951, Rockingham Cty., N.H. (1911); and State v. Williams, No. 395, Rockingham Cty., N.H. (1914). They were born in the following locations: Connecticut, the District of Columbia, Georgia, Maine, Ohio, and Mississippi.

28. The five convicts for whom race could not be determined are: a) Luther Collins alias Luther Sherburne. See State v. Collins, No. 38, Strafford Cty.,

N.H. (1892), "[N.H. State] Prison Records [1874-1915]" and "Description Register [1881-98]," both MS, Div. of Records-Management and Archives, Concord, N.H.; b) Edwin A. Emery. See State v. Emery, No. 5, Strafford Cty., N.H. (1897); c) William H. Hagar. See State v. Hagar, No. 5, Strafford Cty., N.H. (1898), "[N.H. State] Prison Records [1874-1915]," and "Description Register [1881-98]," both MS, Div. of Records-Management and Archives, Concord, N.H.; d) Albert M. Glass. See State v. Glass, No. 127, Strafford Cty., N.H. (1902); and e) George E. Moore. See State v. Moore, No. 5831, Rockingham Cty., N.H. (1905), "[N.H. State] Prison Records [1874-1915]" and "Description Register [1899-1906]," both MS, Div. of Records-Management and Archives, Concord, N.H.

The presence of five persons of unknown race in this sample is easily explained. The five convicts of unknown race have been listed as such only because their records are fragmentary. Some are listed in the registers but not the published prison warden's report while for others the opposite situation obtains. The court records are extant for the five but, as usual, provide no stated information on the convict's race. Most likely these individuals were white but in the absence of complete records the convicts have been classified as "unknown" rather than white, black, or Asian.

29. Fourteen characteristics associated with an ethnic group include: a) common geographic origin, b) migratory status, c) race, d) language or dialect, e) religious faith, f) ties that transcend kinship, neighborhood, and community boundaries, g) shared traditions, values, and symbols, h) literature, folklore, and music, i) food preferences, j) settlement and employment patterns, k) special interests in regard to politics in the homeland and the United States, l) institutions that specifically serve and maintain the group, m) internal sense of distinctiveness, and n) external perception of distinctiveness. See Stephan Thernstrom, ed., *Harvard Encyclopedia of American Ethnic Groups* (Cambridge, Mass., 1980), p. vi.

30. Andrew Greeley, *Ethnicity in the United States: A Preliminary Reconnaissance* (New York, 1974), p. 39.

31. Thernstrom, ed., *Harvard Encylopedia of American Ethnic Groups*, p. vi.

32. "Register of Convicts 1812-1883" and "[N.H. State] Prison Records [1874-1915]," both MS, Div. of Records-Management and Archives, Concord, N.H.

33. Both language and religion distinguished French-Canadians. Catholicism was closely linked with language and culture in the identity of French-Canadians in New Hampshire. Ashley W. Doane, Jr., "The Franco-Americans of New Hampshire: A Case Study of Ethnicity and Social Stratification," Unpublished M.A. Thesis, Sociology, U.N.H., 1983, p. 58.

34. According to Gerard J. Brault, French-Canadians in the United States have not done as well as other ethnic groups in attaining high educational and occupational status, yet they "have made enormous strides in this century." See Gerard J. Brault, *The French-Canadian Heritage in New England* (Hanover, N.H., 1986), pp. 155-57.

35. Mark E. Lender and James K. Martin, *Drinking in America: A History* (New York, 1982), p. 58. David Ward concurs. See David Ward, *Ethnicity and the American City, 1840-1925: Changing Conceptions of the Slum and the Ghetto* (New York, 1989), pp. 16 and 204.

36. Paul Gilje, *The Road to Mobocracy: Popular Disorder in New York City, 1763-1834* (Chapel Hill, N.C., 1987), p. 129 and Ted Robert Gurr, "Historical Trends in Violent Crime: Europe and the United States" in Gurr, ed., *Violence in America*, Vol. 1 *The History of Crime* (Newbury Park, Calif., 1989), p. 21.

37. State v. Richardson, No. 5635, Rockingham Cty., N.H. (1905) and "Description Register [1899-1905]" and "[N.H. State] Prison Records [1874-1915]," both MS, Div. of Records-Management and Archives, Concord, N.H.

38. U.S. Dept. of Commerce, Bureau of the Census, *Historical Abstracts of the United States: Colonial Times to 1970*, Bicentennial Ed., Part 1 (Washington, D.C., 1975), pp. 25-35.

39. On the local level, Irish immigration had a more noticeable impact. By 1880 nearly 30% of the population of Dover in Strafford County was of Irish origin. Three quarters of these people were employed in the lower levels of the textile industry. Paul F. Bergen, "Occupation, Household and Family among the Irish of Nineteenth Century Dover, New Hampshire," Unpublished M.A. Thesis, History, U.N.H., 1989, pp. 1-2.

40. "Blacks and property crime were virtually synonymous in Southern courts from Reconstruction on," Ayers, *Vengeance and Justice*, p. 176. In South Carolina "local theft was viewed as almost exclusively as the work of blacks," Hindus, *Prison and Plantation*, p. 78.

41. Gilje, *Road to Mobocracy*, p. 129.

42. John D'Emilio and Estelle Freedman, *Intimate Matters: A History of Sexuality in America* (New York, 1988), p. 88.

43. *Ibid.*, p. 136.

44. *Ibid.*, p. 184.

45. Ruth Rosen, *The Lost Sisterhood: Prostitution in America, 1900-1918* (Baltimore, 1982), pp. 140-41.

46. How the town of residence was determined is not explained in the sources so residence cannot be considered to be an absolutely reliable guide to determining the mobility of New Hampshire's criminal population.

47. Today the proportions are 94.5% male and 5.5% female. U.S. Bureau of the Census, *Statistical Abstract 1993*, p. 211.

48. State v. Hillsgrove, No. 65/87, Strafford Cty., N.H. (1872) and "Register of Convicts 1812-1883," MS, Div. of Records-Management and Archives, Concord, N.H.

49. Kathryn K. Sklar, *Catharine Beecher: A Study in American Domesticity* (New Haven, Conn., 1973), pp. 83, 156, and 158 and Ann Douglas, *The Feminization of American Culture* (New York, 1988), pp. 51 and 75.

50. See State v. Jane and Mina Farnham, No. 13, Strafford Cty., N.H. (1886) and State v. Tracy, No. 386, Strafford Cty., N.H. (1906).

51. Carl N. Degler, *At Odds: Women and the Family in America from the Revolution to the Present* (New York, 1980), p. 367.

52. *Ibid.*, p. 371.

53. *Ibid.*, pp. 371 and 376.

54. Many occupations were easily assigned to a subgroup but there were some ambiguities in deciding if a certain occupation would be best described as skilled or unskilled (i.e., sashmaker, currier, or baker).

55. See *Thirteenth Census of the United States Taken in the Year 1910*, Vol. IV *Population 1910: Occupational Statistics* (Washington, D.C., 1915), pp. 124-36, Microfilm (Woodbridge, Conn.: Research Publications, Inc.).

56. *Ibid.*, pp. 124-36.

57. See State v. Mendum, No. 5247, Rockingham Cty., N.H. (1904); State v. Bignell, No. 19, Strafford Cty., N.H. (1881); State v. Millett, No. 16, Strafford Cty., N.H. (1886); State v. Hagar, No. 5, Strafford Cty., N.H. (1898); and State v. Mathes, Nos. 221-22, Strafford Cty., N.H. (1903).

58. D'Emilio and Freedman, *Intimate Matters*, pp. 57, 77, and 82-84.

59. W.J. Rorabaugh, *The Alcoholic Republic: An American Tradition* (New York, 1979), pp. 145-46.

60. *Ibid.*, pp. 140 and 144.

61. *Ibid.*, p. 144.

62. Lender and Martin, *Drinking in America*, p. 60.

63. *Ibid.*, p. 59.

64. Gilje, *Road to Mobocracy*, p. 242.

65. Paul E. Johnson, *A Shopkeeper's Millenium: Society and Revivals in Rochester, New York 1815-1837* (New York, 1978), p. 55.

66. Alice F. Tyler, *Freedom's Ferment: Phases of American Social History to 1860* (Freeport, N.Y., 1970), p. 317.

67. Johnson, *Shopkeeper's Millenium*, p. 57.

68. *Ibid.*, pp. 59-60.

69. Jay R. Nash, *Encyclopedia of World Crime*, Vol. 5 *Dictionary* (Wilmette, Ill., 1989), p. 307.

70. Richard Hawkins and Geoffrey P. Alpert, *American Prison Systems: Punishment and Justice* (Englewood Cliffs, N.J., 1989), pp. 198-99.

71. See entries for Richard Burroughs, committed to the prison in 1832 and St. Patrick [sic] Purry, committed to the prison in 1828 and 1832, "Register of Convicts 1812-1883," MS, Div. of Records-Management and Archives, Concord, N.H.

72. Carl Sifakis, "Recidivism," *Encyclopedia of American Crime* (New York, 1982), p. 605.

73. U.S. Bureau of the Census, *Statistical Abstract 1993*, p. 211.

74. Blake McKelvey, *American Prisons: A Study in American Social History Prior to 1915* (Montclair, N.J., 1968 reprint of 1936 ed.), p. 169.

75. *Ibid.*, p. 169.

76. *The Revised Statutes of the State of New Hampshire, Passed December 23, 1842...* (Concord, N.H., 1843), pp. 465-66.

77. In 1865 the state prison was paid $286.39 by the United States "for board of deserters." *Report of the Warden of the New-Hampshire State Prison, Accompanied by the Reports of the Chaplain and Physician...* (Concord, N.H., 1865), 12.

In 1912 the warden stated, "Assuming charge of enough of these cases to utilize a normal capacity of the prison is a financial advantage to the state and a convenience to the Government." *Report of the Officers of the New Hampshire State Prison to the Governor and Council for the Two Years Ending Aug. 31, 1912* (Penacook, N.H., n.d.), 10. In 1911 the U.S. Government paid the state $1750.80 and in 1912 $10,425 to board naval prisoners. *Ibid.*, 11.

78. *Report of the Warden of the New-Hampshire State Prison: Accompanied by Reports of the Chaplain and Physician...June Session, 1866* (Concord, N.H., 1866), 10.

79. "Register of Convicts 1812-1883," MS, Div. of Records-Management and Archives, Concord, N.H.

80. *Ibid.*

81. *Ibid.* and "[N.H. State] Prison Records [1874-1915]," both MS, Div. of Records-Management and Archives, Concord, N.H.

82. "[N.H. State] Prison Records [1874-1915]," MS, Div. of Records-Management and Archives, Concord, N.H.

83. *Cradle of American Shipbuilding: Portsmouth Naval Shipyard, Portsmouth, New Hampshire* (Portsmouth, N.H.,1978), p. 32.

84. *Ibid.*, p. 35.

85. *Ibid.*, p. 35 and "[N.H. State] Prison Records [1874-1915]," MS, Div. of Records-Management and Archives, Concord, N.H.

86. "[N.H. State Prison Records [1874-1915]," MS, Div. of Records-Management and Archives, Concord, N.H.

87. *Ibid.*

88. Nicole H. Rafter, "Hard Times: Custodial Prisons for Women and the Example of the New York State Prison for Women at Auburn, 1893-1933" in Rafter and Elizabeth A. Stanko, *Judge, Lawyer, Victim, Thief: Women, Gender Roles, and Criminal Justice* (Boston, 1982), p. 246.

89. State v. Besse, No. 3568, Rockingham Cty., N.H. (1901).

90. In his study of Columbus, Ohio, Eric H. Monkkonen found that 22% of the criminals in the 1870 census for Ohio were under 21 years of age. Monkkonen says that today, 50% of all property crime is commited by persons under age 21 and between 30% and 37% of violent crime is committed by persons under age 21. Monkkonen, *Dangerous Class*, p. 82.

91. David J. Rothman, *The Discovery of the Asylum: Social Order and Disorder in the New Republic* (Boston, 1971), p. xviii.

92. According to one source, 80.5% of the nation's state prison inmates in 1991 were recidivists. U.S. Bureau of the Census, *Statistical Abstract 1993*, p. 211.

Chapter V

Life in the New Hampshire State Prison, 1812-1914

On December 1, 1812 *The New-Hampshire Patriot* reported that

> The Prison in this town, we hope 'a terror to evil doers,' is
> now completed, and its respective officers have entered upon
> their several duties. On Tuesday last [November 23], the
> massy gates creaked on their hinges to receive the first
> unhappy man who is doomed by the rude hand of justice to
> expiate his crimes by confinement to hard labor. *John Drew*,
> of Meredith, Strafford County, for horse-stealing, is the first
> person who has been committed to the State Prison, and will
> have to wear out five years of a life, which might have been
> serviceable to himself and to mankind, in seclusion from the
> world, & the remainder of that life in the disgrace which is
> always attached to a State convict. May the fate of this first
> tenant of the state prison operate as a striking lesson to
> those who are disposed to be knaves, and who have no other
> inducement to do well than the fear of punishment in this
> world. Those who appreciate the enjoyments or torments of
> an uncertain hereafter, need not the terrors of a prison to
> induce them to walk upright before God and man.[1]

The above editorial is an example of the philosophy of deterrence which was inspired by the classical school of criminology of half a century before. By the early nineteenth century reformation of the criminal was becoming just as important a consideration as deterrence.[2] In this chapter we will examine the experience of punishment in the New Hampshire State Prison. Which was emphasized more, punishment or reformation? Did the emphasis change over time? Was there yet another objective? There is evidence that the state prison quickly became a money-making operation; a concern for profits seems to have taken priority over either the punishment or reformation of the convicts. Hard labor was also viewed as an integral part of the reformation process in that it would help instill discipline, regular habits, teach a skill to the inmates, etc. This will be discussed later. Much can be discovered through the careful use of original sources - even if most sources originated from the prison administration itself.

On November 17, 1812 the directors of the New Hampshire State Prison drew up a six-article set of rules and by-laws designed to maintain an institution of silent efficiency. The document covered every aspect of prison life and was replete with instructions. On the humanitarian side, the warden was specifically enjoined to

> guard himself against every impulse of passion or personal resentment: with the powers entrusted to him it cannot be necessary to strike his prisoners (unless in self-defense) much less can it answer any good purpose to give his orders in a violent tone or attended with oaths. He should give his commands with kindness and dignity and enforce them with promptitude and firmness.[3]

At the same time, there was no mistaking the central role of discipline in prison life. Prisoners were expected to exhibit "a quiet and ready obedience to the rules and regulations...and a decent submission to the officers."[4] If not, they would be "inevitably subject...to condign punishment."[5] Condign punishment was mostly solitary confinement: "The warden shall commit to the cell any prisoner who may be guilty of disobedience, ill language or misbehaviour, or any other conduct contrary to the rules and regulations of this institution." However, the potential for more severe punishment was opened by the inclusion of "to be further dealt with and punished in such manner as the board of Directors...may order and determine."[6] The inmates were under constant surveillance while working. The rule of silence was in place from the very beginning as well as the infamous prisoners' lockstep march: "In going to and returning from their cells or meals the prisoners shall walk in such order as the Warden may direct."[7]

Discipline was maintained by force. Every prison officer was to have a gun, bayonet, and "at least twelve cartridges and balls" kept in a "safe and convenient place." While supervising the inmates at work, officers were to wear "a strong and suitable cutlass or hanger, to be used as a side arm."[8] Every prisoner was to be searched every evening and the officers were to inspect every cell lock too.[9]

Hard labor was instrinsic to early prison regimes and New Hampshire was no exception. The new laws of June 1812 specified the centrality of work in the prison regime.[10] We will begin our analysis of the prison experience with an examination of the role and changing nature of work.

Prison labor in America took three main forms. The contract system involved the selling of inmate labor to a private contractor who supplied the necessary tools and raw materials; at times the contractor assumed direct supervision of the laboring inmates within the prison itself. In the convict-lease system the state leased prisoners to a private business for a fixed annual fee. Finally, in the state-account or state-use system, prisoners produced items on the premises for the use of other state institutions or for sale by the state.[11]

Naturally, such arrangements could result in the abuse of prisoners. Profits came before reformation in many prisons, leading to overwork and poor conditions.[12] In effect, prisoners became slaves of the state since the money earned by their labor rarely went to the prisoners themselves. In some ways this was a more obvious attempt to make prisoners pay for their accommodations than had been the practice before. In the eighteenth century and earlier, prisoners or their families had had to pay jailers for room and board. However, these earlier regimes had provided few opportunities for prisoners to systematically "earn" their keep. In the nineteenth century the worst abuses occurred under the convict-lease system in the post-Civil War South. Prisoners on the chain gangs were totally at the mercy of brutal overseers whose main concern was getting the most labor out of them.[13] Gross abuse does not seem to have taken place in the New Hampshire state prison but concern with profits remained central throughout the nineteenth century.

Prison labor fulfilled two vital missions in American prisons. It was an instrinsic component of the reform program and it could make prisons financially self-supporting. As far back as the Raspuis in sixteenth-century Amsterdam labor had played an important part in prison administration.[14] Cesare Beccaria had called for imprisonment at hard labor as a substitute for the bloody and capricious punishments in use in Europe in his *Of Crimes and Punishments* in 1764. From the beginning of prison reform in America in the 1790's, the role of hard labor was both punitive and reformative.[15] By the 1830's most reformers agreed that the reformative aspects of hard labor included the following: it instilled a sense of discipline and order, it taught inmates economic skills, and it taught "lifelong habits of industriousness."[16] Thomas L. Dumm sees the role of prison labor as a means of creating citizens appropriate for a new country. In effect prisons can be viewed as inculcators of "the desire to work" - a necessary attribute of citizens in a capitalist democracy.[17]

To make prisons self-supporting was fully as important as the reformation of prisoners. Governor John T. Gilman was careful to point out the self-supporting nature of prison labor when he first floated the concept of a state prison before the legislature in 1804.[18] A number of historians maintain that the top priority of most American prison wardens was the development of prosperous prison industries.[19]

Labor also made prison life bearable for the inmates. Alexis de Tocqueville surveyed American prisons in 1831-32 for possible application in France. On the role of labor, he commented, "Labor gives to the solitary cell an interest; it fatigues the body and relieves the soul." In any case, de Tocqueville claimed, idleness was the "primary cause of [the prisoners'] misfortune."[20]

Prison labor was viewed as rehabilitative, vital to the financial health of the institution, and as a humane necessity to make the solitary conditions of American prison life bearable. We will trace these three threads through an analysis of contract labor in the New Hampshire State Prison.

The very first prison industry in New Hampshire was a blacksmith shop. A month before the first prisoner was admitted, the board of directors voted to buy "sundry blacksmith's tools and apparatus now in the Smith's shop" and "also a quantity of Iron."[21] Every prisoner was expected to work unless "Excepted by order of the Directors, or [who] are confined to the cells."[22] One week after John Drew's admittance as the first inmate, the directors hired Jonathan Shaw, a blacksmith from Chichester, to run the smith's shop.[23] By January 5, 1813 the first prison products were ready for sale: axes at 10 shillings or $1.50 each by the dozen.[24] On February 2 a wheelwright named Josiah Rogers proposed delivering 10 wagons to the prison for fitting with iron components.[25] Evidently, this arrangement was satisfactory and on July 16 the board of directors and Rogers agreed that the prison would do "certain wood-work of the waggons" and that Rogers "be allowed seventy-five cents each for the chairs or seats."[26] This was the first prison labor contract.

After 1813 the variety of prison industries proliferated beyond work at the forge. In 1814-15 the prison entered into contracts for screw-cutting and latch-making. The prison received at first $0.40 and then $0.35 per man per day for these contracts.[27] By 1816 Warden Trueworthy Dearborn reported that inmates were employed in the smith's shop and at weaving, tailoring, making shoes, and making barrels.[28]

Prison industries developed prior to the Civil War were typically labor-intensive. This was partly due to the fact that mechanization was not widely introduced into prisons until after the War.[29] One very labor-intensive and lucrative prison industry was hammering and cutting stone. Between 1816 and 1819 inmates of the state prison prepared granite for the new statehouse under construction in Concord. Twenty-two men were engaged in this project at $0.50 per day per man. Warden Dearborn proudly observed that the prison's stonework "exhibits a specimen of workmanship, not deficient in beauty and in strength not exceeded by any work of the kind, it is believed in the United States."[30] Frugal state legislators must have rejoiced at the employment of state prison inmates in such an undertaking. Even after the statehouse was finished, stone hammering and cutting remained the prison's main industry until it was eclipsed by the prison's cabinet shop in the 1840's.[31] In the 1820's finished stone was shipped to New Orleans and New York City.[32]

Profits, not reformation, was the real purpose of prison labor according to the testimony of the annual prison warden's reports. Over and over again, earnings of the prison labor force were the main focus. Many of the early reports made no mention at all of any connection between hard labor and rehabilitation. Many reports were little more than accounting exercices demonstrating to legislators the profitability of the prison. Whenever possible, wardens brought attention to the fact that the prison was a self-supporting concern.[33] Prison records indicate that profits above and beyond the costs of covering expenses were considered essential. Wardens expressed dismay whenever poor economic conditions impinged on prison industries. For example, Warden John W. Foss blamed the Civil War for the "complete stagnation of business owing to the financial crisis caused by the unholy rebellion existing in our beloved country." The prison was saved from financial disaster only by a contract for shoes and 3000 canteens for the Union Army.[34] In 1875 the prison was stuck with unsold goods thanks to the depression and in 1894 another depression meant that the prison had to settle for a reduction in contract wages.[35]

Different kinds of prison industry were tried out in an attempt to maintain profits. Stone hammering and cutting was replaced by cabinet and chair-making in the 1840's. The revived cabinet shop was a modern enterprise powered by a steam engine.[36] In 1853 the smith and cooper shops were discontinued while the shoe and cabinet shops remained. A short-lived machine shop was added.[37] The prison's mainstay from the 1850's through the 1890's was bedstead production in the cabinet shop.[38] In 1879 the prison produced 68,000 bedsteads which were sold all over the United States. Some were even exported to South America and Africa.[39] By the 1890's strong midwestern competition undercut bedstead production so the prison cabinet shop switched to chair production and made a new contract with Converse & Whitney of Ashburnham, Massachusetts in 1896.[40] The state prison kept most of its inmates employed at making chairs via the contract labor system until May 31, 1932.[41] At that point the prison turned to what Samuel Walker describes as the state-account or state-use system, making items for the use of other state institutions.[42]

Working conditions at the New Hampshire State Prison were rather poor. First, all work was conducted in silence and under constant surveillance of prison guards or contractors.[43] This was standard procedure in most American prisons of the time. Typically, the inmates worked six days a week. According to Orlando F. Lewis, the work schedule at the New Hampshire State Prison was as follows: rise at 4:30 a.m., work until 7 a.m., breakfast, work from 8 a.m. to noon; lunch (length of time not specified); and work until 7 p.m.[44] A May 1825 report on stone-cutting indicates that 52 men worked 26 days that month, cutting a total of 2421 feet 9 inches of stone. Most men cut around 50 to 60 feet but one heroic worker managed to cut 158 feet six inches.[45] Most of the evidence of poor working conditions comes from the physician's reports from 1832 on.

The first official acknowledgment of trouble in the workplace was when an inmate mutilated himself to avoid work. In 1852 he cut his arm to the bone with a razor; the year before he had cut off a thumb with a hatchet. His reason for such desperate actions were described as "for the purpose of getting rid of labor...that 'he had done enough."[46] Beside potential overwork, inmates also faced dust, smoke, and gases in improperly ventilated workshops. Inmates suffered from "intense heat" from a defective furnace. Noise from a trip hammer was "very troublesome to the officers, and almost destructive to the discipline of the shop."[47] Efforts were made to rectify the situation but in the 1850's the prison buildings were described as "deplorably wretched" and the cabinet shop as "in a ruinous condition...The building is actually unsafe."[48] Timothy Haynes, prison physician, was alarmed at the "cloud of dust" emitted by the cabinet shop.[49] Other physicians commented on the "vitiated atmosphere" caused by poor ventilation.[50] In his memoirs, former Prison Chaplain Eleazer Smith described the pre-1855 workshops as "miserably poor, choked with dust and smoke, ill-constructed, and badly ventilated."[51] The situation was greatly improved in 1868 with the installation of Robinson's Patent United States Ventilators.[52]

Post-Civil War mechanization of prison labor exacted a terrible price in industrial accidents. Dr. A. Crosby reported, "We have been, however, especially unfortunate in the way of accidents from machinery, several having lost fingers, or had them so injured that amputation was necessary." In 1868 alone, Dr. Crosby treated 13 accident victims including one inmate who suffered a fractured rib and contusions when he was carried over a mainshaft.[53] Another cause of accidents was the prison's new circular saw.[54] Industrial accidents became so common that prison physicians found it appropriate to mention the absence of accidents as an unusual phenomenon.[55]

The grim toll exacted by industrial accidents did not end with the move to a modern new prison in 1880. In that year, the prison physicians reported three accidents as "the result of carelessness while working upon the irregular planer."[56] Things were even worse in 1881. One inmate was killed when the circular saw threw a stick of green timber at him, cracking his skull. Another inmate lost a finger to the saw and a third suffered "permanent deformity of the hand" from the same machine.[57] Industrial accidents occurred throughout the 1880's and 1890's.[58]

Until 1913 prisoners were literally slaves of the state in New Hampshire. None of the money earned through the contract labor system was ever paid to the prisoners until new legislation was enacted during an era of reform. Progressive Republican Governor Robert P. Bass took some interest in prison affairs. Virtually his last act in office was to recommend to the General Court the passage of legislation in which a percentage of a prisoner's earning would go to his dependents, or if he had none, to be set aside and made available upon his release.[59]

The prison contract labor system came increasingly under fire from free labor and business interests. They saw the system as taking away jobs and as a threat to their markets. For example, in the 1920's local industries in Oklahoma used their political and economic power to force the state prison to abandon production of certain items.[60] In the New Hampshire biennial prison report of 1912, Warden Henry K.W. Scott reported, "The labor interests that oppose the sale of prison made goods suggest that prisoners be employed simply in the manufacture of such articles as may be used in the various state institutions."[61] In other words, they were suggesting the prison turn to the state-account or state-use system described by Samuel Walker. Twenty years later the state prison did just that because of new federal regulations, private business and labor pressure, and the Great Depression.

Hard labor had several roles to play in prison management. In practical terms, it paid for most, if not all of the costs associated with running the state prison. In a state as frugal as New Hampshire this was a real virtue. Prison wardens took great pains to report on the profitability of prison labor. Hard labor was also a way of promoting discipline by keeping the prison population under control.[62] Prison labor can further be viewed as a form of indoctrination. Reformers stressed the rehabilitative aspects of hard labor which ranged from instilling discipline and respect for hard work to practical training for life after prison. Some scholars see a more sinister purpose - Foucault the development of a "carceral" society and Ignatieff the creation of an orderly, disciplined lower class that could be exploited by emerging capitalist interests.[63] For Thomas L. Dumm, prison discipline applied through a regime of hard labor created "a diligent, literate laborer. A moderate self-interested citizen. In short, the released inmate was to be a member of the great middle class that was, at point, emerging as a dominating force of public life in the United States."[64] Thus, prison labor was both a supplement to and a component of rehabilitation. We will now examine methods employed by the New Hampshire State Prison in the reformation of convicts.

Religion played a vital role in reform efforts throughout the period 1812-1914 at the New Hampshire State Prison. The earliest records reveal an ongoing concern with the religious welfare of the inmates. The original prison rules and by-laws of 1812 state that each prisoner was to be given a Bible.[65] Self-directed guidance was too much to expect from convicted felons, so on June 21, 1814 Governor John T. Gilman approved the engagement of the Reverend Asa McFarland to "attend prayer with the convicts" on Sundays. In addition, the prison was to supply each cell with a Bible and hymn book, and to distribute religious tracts.[66] The warden himself took part in religious instruction in the absence of a minister.[67] The first paid prison chaplain was not hired until the early 1830's.[68]

The prison chaplain had a central role to play in all measures designed to reform the prisoners throughout this period. The first chaplain's report appeared in 1832 and it was included in all subsequent annual warden's reports. The chaplain's reports are invaluable for the information they provide on rehabilitative measures introduced at the prison.

The religious component of prison rehabilitation expanded steadily in the antebellum period. By 1831 the prison had a functioning Sabbath school held in the chapel. Warden Abner Stinson declared, "It is confidently believed that the convicts were never more peaceable, industrious and happy and have never evinced a better state of morals since the organization of the institution."[69] In 1855 Sabbath school teaching reached a new level of professionalism with the utilization of teachers from a local biblical institute.[70]

The public was invited to attend services held for the prisoners.[71] In a letter to his sons, Charles W. Brewster describes such a service he attended in June, 1843. The service was held at 8 a.m. at the prison chapel. All inmates attended while the minister preached an appropriate sermon on guarding against evil thoughts. The convicts maintained "a downcast look, scarcely one of them seemed disposed to look up."[72] Brewster warns his sons to heed the minister's advice in this object lesson.

The focus on religion as a reformative agent was constant during this period of the prison's history. Time after time, religion was cited as the key to success. In 1835 the Reverend Moses G. Thomas cited the case of a pardoned inmate who "visited his teacher, and with tears of gratitude expressed his thanks for the interest taken in his religious welfare."[73] Similar examples abound in the published memoirs of former chaplain Eleazer Smith.[74] In 1865 Reverend Samuel Cooke directed, "Furnish these men with means of knowing their duty to God, and their fellow man, and if they do not become reformed, the blame will entirely rest on themselves."[75] It is possible than an inmate's demonstration of religious fervor was considered in his eligibility for pardon. The records provide no information as to whether this really was the case but it probably helped at a time when evangelical Protestantism flourished.

Some chaplains developed a more sophisticated understanding of the inmate's situation. Shortly after his arrival as prison chaplain in 1884, the Reverend Elijah R. Wilkins expressed great concern over "the exceeding weakness of moral and intellectual power possessed by the majority of the prisoners." He described them as "but children in conscience and thought."[76] However, he did not give up hope - Wilkins stayed on as prison chaplain for another 20 years. Two notebooks survive sketching out his prison sermons for the years 1884-96 and 1899-1905. Unfortunately, they do not reveal much about the reforming mission of religion in prison. Most of his sermons appear to have been exhortatory, telling his audience to obey God rather than Satan, and so forth.[77] Wilkins did show his sympathy and growing insight in a sermon about the plight of the discharged prisoner:

That is a moment full of peril to himself when the Prison doors open and he is discharged. Of a weak, moral nature, with a predisposition to crime, branded as an unfit associate for honorable men; without money and friends; his condition is pitiable in the extreme. Then who can measure the fascination of fresh [sic] plunge into pleasures of depraved [?]"[78]

As late as 1910 the chaplain was convinced that Christianity was the key to reform.[79] In 1914 each inmate continued to be supplied with a Bible plus psalm, prayer, and hymn books for their moral inspiration.[80]

The ethnic changes in the prison population analyzed in Chapter Four were reflected in the provisions made for Catholics. By 1885 there were enough Catholics (mostly Irish and French-Canadians) to warrant visits from the local priest. As early as the 1850's one eighth of the prison population was Catholic.[81] The growing presence of Irish Catholics in Manchester had sparked a nativist reaction in the 1850's. Thanks to a local election pitting nativist Republicans against increasingly Irish Democrats, alarmist articles in Manchester newspapers, and the opening of a Catholic school, a fireman's muster in 1859 flared into an anti-Irish riot.[82] Catholics became an increasingly large proportion of the general population and the prison population as well. In 1887 the prison population consisted of 71 Protestants and 50 Catholics.[83] The prison continued to rely on Father Barry's "gratuitous work" with Catholic inmates.[84] The chaplain played a crucial role in prison affairs.

Secular education became an increasingly important component of prison life. Most of the information on the subject is found in the prison chaplain's reports from the 1830's on. In addition to purely religious work, the chaplain acted as a counselor to the prison, and was responsible for educational programs. There is no mention of secular education in the rules and by-laws of 1812 but the connection to religious education is natural. Literacy was required before the Bible, hymn book, and tracts given to each inmate could be useful. Secular education mainly consisted of teaching the inmates basic literacy. In 1837 a class of six inmates was learning how to read and within 10 years arithmetic was part of the curriculum.[85]

Educational opportunities widened considerably after the Civil War, reflecting both more ambitious goals of the budding reformatory movement and possibly the higher level of literacy of post-war inmates.[86] A night school was established in 1868 along with a series of lectures described as a "lycaeum course."[87] The first reference to education for female prisoners is found in the 1869 report where it was noted that females were given classes (subject not listed) by the warden's wife.[88] Education "may awaken the throbbing impulses for good," hoped Rev. Sullivan Holman in 1880.[89] In the 1900's the educational opportunities ranged from "a school for illiterates" to courses in arithmetic, geography, grammar, "other branches," and lectures given by visiting speakers.[90] In 1914 the prison enrolled 10 inmates into courses offered by the International Correspondence Schools.[91]

The growing emphasis on literacy as a component of the rehabilitation program created the need for a prison library. In August 1844 Warden Samuel G. Berry and Chaplain John Atwood presented State Representative Charles W. Brewster with a signed petition asking for a donation of books for the prison library. Berry and Atwood argued that books would "serve to improve his [the convict's] mind, abate the rigor and gloom of his confinement, and prepare him thereafter to go forth into community [sic] a better man."[92] In 1847 Reverend Eleazer Smith mentioned the creation of a library through the donation of 300 volumes. "Without expense to the State," he hastened to add.[93] By 1853 the library had grown to 700 volumes and covered the subjects of religion, history, biography, and natural and "moral" sciences.[94] Unfortunately, the library became a target of vandals who marked and mutilated books.[95]

Prisoners had access to the library through the chaplain. Presumably, inmates had time to read at night and on Sundays. On Saturday mornings, prisoners could request three to ten books per week by writing their titles down on a tablet left outside each cell window. Titles were listed in a printed catalog. In 1881 the library catalog listed 1936 titles in no discernible order. Subjects were mainly religion, history, travel, and even some fiction.[96] Inmates had a far greater choice of literature in 1881 than in the past. In 1912 inmates could borrow books twice a week from a selection of 2112 volumes. Religion was still the largest category; other subjects included history, biography, travel, and "miscellaneous."[97]

The library received a great deal of use. The prison reports frequently mention the existence of books damaged through overuse. Reverend Hosea Quinby saw fit to put condemned murderer Josiah Pike to work regluing the backs of 200 books to help distract him from his impending execution in 1869.[98] The prison administration sometimes boasted of library success stories. In 1862 one inmate read 40,000 pages "not of a superficial character."[99] Nevertheless, the benefits of secular education, religious instruction, and hard labor were not always evident to the inmates. Disciplinary measures were required to ensure compliance with the prison regime and to maintain order. The warden was given authority to enforce discipline as needed for the proper functioning of the prison. The most common form of punishment in the New Hampshire State Prison was solitary confinement. The rules and by-laws adopted in 1812 empowered the warden to place "any prisoner who may be guilty of disobedience, ill language or misbehaviour, or any conduct contrary to the rules and regulations of this institution" into "the cell."[100] Solitary confinement was also an integral mandatory component of the inmate's sentence in the antebellum era. Typically, it lasted anywhere from two to ten days depending on the length of the total prison sentence. In this capacity, solitary confinement was used to intimidate new inmates and make them amenable to their new life. When used specifically as a punitive measure, solitary confinement meant the complete isolation of the prisoner with no work to keep him occupied, a diet of bread and water, and often no light.

Despite the professed humanitarian goals of imprisonment, punishments were retained to enforce discipline. In New Hampshire the door was opened to potential abuse with the open-ended discretion granted the administration in the rules and by-laws concerning behavior. The miscreant prisoner was to be immediately placed in solitary confinement "to be dealt with and punished in such manner as the board of Directors...may order and determine."[101] The purpose was to punish; it seems as though the term in solitary confinement was determined by the prisoner's breaking point. For example, in April 1814 three prisoners were found guilty of "riotous and disorderly conduct." Each was put into solitary confinement with one rug and a "small quantity of straw" for bedding. Each was allotted twelve ounces of bread and one pint of water per day.[102] After an indefinite period each of the three was chained to a block of stone and "put to labour." A few years later seven prisoners attempted to escape. Their punishment consisted of a reduced diet (one pint of boiled potatoes for breakfast and the same for lunch, and one pint of porridge for supper) and at the same time they were set to "strict labor." Within a month the seven "had discovered a great degree of penitence and humility" and so were restored to their previous status.[103] In 1862 Warden John Foss claimed that solitary confinement was rarely used and never for more than 24 hours at a time - a contrast to the 12 to 20 days at a time he had witnessed while deputy warden.[104] Actually, the legal limit throughout the period 1812-1914 was 30 days.[105] Solitary confinement on a diet of bread and water remained the favorite punishment for refractory inmates; occasionally, they were shackled to a ball and chain.[106]

Solitary confinement as a punishment could be abused, as the tragic case of Joseph L. Shaw makes clear. It was used here as a method of torture but led to unintended consequences. In February 1837 Shaw, an inmate, was accused of stealing the valve to the boiler in one of the workshops. In his published account of the story, Shaw claimed total innocence, on which basis he refused to confess to the act. Warden John McDaniels put Shaw into solitary confinement on February 28. The unheated cell had a solid rock floor covered with one inch of ice. There was no furniture, bedding, or even straw.[107]

Shaw complained of the bitter cold to which McDaniels answered, "I must dance hornpipes, if I thought I was freezing, and I should be well enough."[108] Despite repeated entreaties for release, Shaw was kept in the freezing cell for one week on account of his refusal to confess to a crime he did not commit. The warden finally relented after a week but by this time Shaw was suffering from extreme frostbite to his feet. He was placed in the prison infirmary for 10 to 12 days before the doctors summoned decided to "experiment."[109] Shaw then describes in excrutiating detail the attempts made to operate on his feet and failing in this, the amputation of both legs midway between ankle and knee on March 29 and April 3 - a harrowing experience in a time before anesthesia.[110] Warden McDaniels was present during the first operation and during the height of Shaw's agony sadistically observed, "I think Shaw has got the worst temper of any person I ever saw; he wont [sic] as much groan when his leg is being amputated."[111] Shaw was pardoned in July and "set at liberty mutilated: and weak, and poor. They had taken from me my means of supporting myself, when it is remembered, that I was by trade a wheelwright." Upon his release, Shaw was given the standard release sum of $3.[112] On the grounds that the town rather than the state should bear the cost, the governor vetoed attempts by State Senator Burleigh of Hampton (Shaw's home town) to provide Shaw with at least $200 compensation.[113]

Harsh discipline was the rule rather than the exception. In 1870 Warden Joseph Mayo proudly declared, "Brutal and degrading punishments have been discountenanced" but the next year Warden John C. Pilsbury (son of Moses Pilsbury who was warden 1818-26 and 1837-40) instituted a 10-year reign of terror over the hapless inmates.[114] A decade later, Pilsbury commented, "The discipline of our prison is indeed strict, without it reformation is out of the question in an institute of this kind...I am satisfied that it is none too severe for the good of the convicts."[115] Pilsbury justified his position by pointing out that in the past decade their had been no escapes and that no officer had been killed or seriously injured by the inmates. In fairness, it must be acknowledged that he had inherited a disorderly institution.[116] Among other things, Pilsbury found a number of tools and weapons in inmates' cells. He also found correspondence and a photograph from a local woman addressed to one of the inmates; this was contrary to prison regulations.[117]

Pilsbury's administration ended in a scandal with a widely publicized investigation into alleged abuses and brutality.[118] The investigation was launched in the Fall of 1879 by Burnham Wardell, a prison investigator from Virginia and by Marilla Ricker of Dover, N.H., a social activist and the state's

first female lawyer. Wardwell filed 45 written charges with the Governor and
Council. A hearing was begun in March 1880 and adjourned until June 10.
The hearings involved 84 witnesses and 10 lawyers and were held in 18
sessions.[119] The 78-year old warden was exonerated in July and retired soon
afterward. Public sentiment was stirred up against Wardwell by local
newspapers who described the Virginian as a "foreigner."[120] One letter to
the editor of the *Concord Daily Monitor* excoriated "those of sickly
sentimentality who forget the crime in a mawkish sympathy for the criminal;
or else, being half criminal themselves, have no good opinion of the law, from
personal considerations."[121]

The opening of the new prison in 1880 and the hiring of a new warden
resulted in no abatement of rigor. Warden Frank Dodge (the former sheriff
of Merrimack County and who had appeared as a witness for Pilsbury during
the investigation) declared that he would follow Pilsbury's guidelines for
prison discipline.[122] Some inmates found the strain too much. One inmate
simulated tuberculosis to escape from prison life by sticking a broom wire
down his throat and "with a little violence could induce a free hemorrhage at
any time." Another pretended to have a severe spinal disorder which
prevented him from working - until discovered walking about by the
warden.[123] In 1886 Warden Dodge introduced a new mode of punishment
known as "the slide." He claimed this reduced the number of disciplinary
actions by 75 percent. The prison physicians thought the slide was "a more
humane mode of punishment [than solitary confinement]...which does not
leave a permanent disability but inflicts a temporary discomfort."[124] The
slide consisted of suspending a prisoner by his wrists manacled together; it was
abolished in 1906.[125]

Every aspect of prison life was designed to make the inmate malleable.
The lockstep march, downcast eye, and rule of silence were three disciplinary
measures incorporated into the daily routine. All three were integral
components of prison life from the very beginning.[126] In a letter to his sons
written in 1843, Charles W. Brewster describes the pernicious effects of such
a life. He wrote, "The discipline of the prison is very strict during the whole
week, while at work, they are not allowed to raise their eyes to look upon a
single [illegible]...The prisoners are in so much fear, that if you pass in front
of them some of them close their eyes that they may escape the lash."[127]
The Reverend Eleazer Smith praised the enforcement of silence. He
regarded unrestrained communication among inmates as a "school for
crime."[128]

The lockstep march probably had its origins in military discipline. Several early American prison wardens had a military background.[129] After the Civil War, military discipline was deliberately incorporated into prison discipline. In 1869 all of the guards and officers at the New Hampshire State Prison save one were Civil War veterans.[130] Warden John C. Pilsbury enforced the lockstep march with "military precision."[131] Post-war reformers argued if soldiers and the population at large could learn self-control and obedience through the experience of the Civil War, so too could prisoners.[132] The Reformatory at Elmira, New York actually incorporated military training directly into the reformatory program via military organization, drilling, military uniforms, and dress parades with fake weapons.[133] The prison uniform was another component of prison discipline. The New Hampshire State Prison uniform consisted of a cotton shirt, woolen vest, short jacket, and woolen trousers all "of strong and cheap materials" in alternating sections of blue and red. Prisoners also were furnished with shoes, socks, and a wool hat or cap.[134] As early as 1869 there was official opposition to the uniform on the grounds of its "tending to degrade and destroy the self respect of the prisoners."[135] However, the uniform continued unchanged for another 40 years, along with the lockstep march, downcast eye, and rule of silence.

Most of these measures were abandoned with the introduction of a more liberal conception of prison discipline in the early twentieth century.[136] Henry K.W. Scott made several changes upon his appointment as warden in 1906.   He called for the abolition of the downcast eye because "it superimposed the sloping shoulder...Moreover, when a man is released from prison he will carry with him as a result of this rule a furtive and hangdog expression."[137] Scott demanded and got the abolition of the parti-colored uniform in January 1907. Now prisoners were to be furnished with grey suits of their own construction.[138] He also succeeded in eliminating the lockstep march by order of the Governor and Council.[139]

Prison discipline entailed the use of the carrot as well as the stick. The laws of 1812 allowed the warden and board of directors "to offer such encouragement and indulgencies as may be deemed consistent" to obedient and well-behaved prisoners.[140] In an unusually compassionate move, the board of directors voted to provide the state's first prisoner with "a small quantity of the cheapest spirit - never exceeding a gill in any twenty-four hours" while engaged in "the most laborious exercises at the forge."[141] In 1856 Prison Physician William Prescott fulminated against the daily use of tobacco: "Every week, a ration of this sedative poison is regularly dealt out."[142] The "sedative poison" may well have helped maintain order in the prison.

Warden Joseph Mayo listed the three annual "festivities" that had become customary by 1869: the Dorsey dinner on January 31 (described shortly), July 4, and Thanksgiving.[143] In 1900 the warden reported that holiday entertainments "have been growing in interest." The governor had supplied "elaborate entertainments" on the previous two Thanksgivings.[144]

The reformatory movement was a major influence on post-Civil War prison discipline. It was inspired by a new interest in prison reform and entailed a new emphasis on professional prison administration. The model followed by many was the Reformatory at Elmira, New York, established in 1876 by Zebulon Brockway. Although it was designed for males age 16-30 who were first-time offenders, the methods used by Brockway were adopted by a number of other penal institutions.[145] However, Elmira's image as the ideal reformatory became tarnished as revelations surfaced of the cruelty inflicted on inmates by Brockway to gain their compliance. It also turned out that Elmira's success in reforming offenders was just as dubious as that of other insitutions.[146]

The reformatory influence is evident in the prisoner grading system and organized sports introduced to the state prison in 1911 and 1914. The grading system was clearly based on the highly regarded system employed at Elmira.[147] The system consisted of three grades of prisoner. The first grade were permitted to write a letter once every two weeks, receive visits from relatives once every two weeks, receive letters and periodicals approved of by the warden, to borrow prison library books, and they were given additional privileges for good behavior.[148] New prisoners were assigned to the second grade which enjoyed fewer privileges. The third grade was reserved for poorly- behaved prisoners. Thus, inmates were given positive incentives for good behavior from the start. Warden Henry K.W. Scott claimed this new measure "is working out splendidly in its results, raising the standard of good behavior beyond our expectations."[149]

Sports were introduced at Elmira in the 1890's on the principle that discipline, self-control, and cooperation taught by such activity were part of the process of rehabilitation.[150] Organized sports were introduced to the state prison in July 1914. Every Saturday afternoon after work, the first grade prisoners were allowed to play baseball and "mingle undisturbed" with one another. The usual rule of silence was suspended during the games and the privilege of attendance was granted to well-behaved inmates.[151]

Sufficient food was an absolute requirement for prisoners engaged in hard labor six days a week. Former prison chaplain Eleazer Smith describes the food as "coarse, but nutritive" in his 1856 memoirs.[152] The prison diet is first mentioned in the rules and by-laws of 1812. The daily allowance consisted of

> three gills of indian [sic] or rye-meal one gill of molasses or
> six gills of milk - three quarters of a pound of coarse meat
> with one pint of potatoes, or instead of coarse meat and
> potatoes, six ounces of salted pork with half a pint of peas or
> beans - one pound of bread; and in lieu of coffee a
> decoction from rye or peas for breakfast. The whole of their
> food which requires it, to be properly seasoned with salt.[153]

Such a diet would quickly grow monotonous and the modern reader would probably notice the absence of fresh vegetables or fruit. On the other hand, the list reflects the fact that the prison needed to acquire cheap supplies that could be stored in bulk over long periods. The food was probably not much worse than that enjoyed by lower class New Englanders in an era without refrigeration or processed foods. The meat ration was greater than the standard half pound of pork per day allotted to slaves in the nineteenth-century South. However, slaves were able to supplement their diets by hunting and fishing. Other components of the typical slave diet included corn meal, sweet potatoes, hominy, and vegetables in season.[154] Fresh vegetables and fruit were seasonal phenomena even for the wealthy. A strict diet of bread and water was reserved for those inmates undergoing punishment in solitary confinement.

Within a year the standard fare was modified. Beef and potatoes were served three times a day ("hash'd or minc'd" for breakfast and supper) with soup or pork and beans occasionally served to vary the noonday meal. The inmates were served "a reasonable proportion of rye Indian bread" with each meal and were allocated up to one pint of cider a day in place of rye or peas coffee.[155] Judging by the lists of supplies and financial reports in the annual prison warden's reports, prison fare of the pre-Civil War era remained largely unchanged. Unfortunately, the quality of prison food sometimes fell below Reverend Smith's standard of "coarse, but nutritive."

The first prison physician's report (1832) referred to "bowel complaints" which the physician blamed on the "use of crude, indigestible vegetables" and "atmospheric influence." He suggested substituting salted fish for salted beef and rice porridge for "coarse Indian meal" at night.[156] On the other hand, Dr. Thomas Chadbourne lauded the "wholesome plain food" served at the prison in 1847.[157]

The variety if not the quality of food improved in the late 1860's. For the

228

first time a "bill of fare" for the entire week was listed in the prison reports. In 1866 the weekly menu consisted of the following:

Monday:
        Morning - flour bread, molasses, and coffee.
        Noon - corned beef, potatoes, and brown bread.
        Night - corn meal mush and molasses.

Tuesday:
        Morning - meat hash, brown bread, and coffee.
        Noon - salt fish, potatoes, butter gravy, and brown bread.
        Night - corn meal mush and molasses.

Wednesday:
        Morning - fish hash, brown bread, and coffee.
        Noon - beef soup and brown bread.
        Night - corn meal mush and molasses.

Thursday:
        Morning - meat hash, molasses, and coffee.
        Noon - corned beef, potatoes, and brown bread.
        Night - corn meal mush and molasses.

Friday:
        Morning - white bread, molasses, and coffee.
        Noon - fish chowder and brown bread.
        Night - corn meal mush and molasses.

Saturday:
        Morning - fish hash and coffee.
        Noon - stewed peas, pork, and brown bread.
        Night - corn meal mush and molasses.

Sunday:
        Morning - baked beans, pork, brown bread, and coffee.
        Afternoon - boiled rice, molasses, and brown bread.[158]

In 1868 vegetables and soup with vegetables were added to the bill of fare.[159]
Things got even better in 1869 with the advent of the annual Dorsey Dinner

on January 31. H.C. Dorsey, a resident of Pawtucket, Rhode Island, initiated an annual donation of $60 to the warden "for your unhappy little community." The money was to go for an annual feast for the prisoners which in 1869 was a "turkey and mince-pie dinner."[160] On July 4, prison contractor George F. Comings supplied a "bountiful supply of strawberrries and cream."[161] Unfortunately, the Committee of Council expressed opposition to the Dorsey Dinner in 1871: "It is very questionable whether it is any advantage to the prisoners or to the discipline of the prison, as it throws them off their regular diet and often brings on sickness from which it takes them some time to recover."[162]

The abolition of the Dorsey Dinner was part of the imposition of a harsh new regime under Warden John C. Pilsbury. Chaplain Hosea Quinby provides a discouraging account of how the quality of food deteriorated under Pilsbury's administration. Quinby had had a serious quarrel with Pilsbury; thus his testimony is likely to be negatively biased. Quinby describes Pilsbury's philosophy as "money-making and punishing." Quinby claimed the prisoners were now fed on watery potatoes, boiled cracked wheat, "a little meat chopped" served without any sauce, and fish so rotten it was covered with red mold.[163] He claimed the food was so bad that inmates were actually starving.[164] In 1880 Pilsbury's administration ended in any investigation conducted by the New Hampshire Council Chamber into alleged abuses. The food was alleged to be of insufficient quantity, fish and meat were rotten, and the soup was full of maggot skins, and the inmates were fed a monotonous diet of "beans and pease constantly."[165] In 1874 Pilsbury had described the food as "coarse, but sweet, wholesome, and an abundant quantity."[166] He was exonerated by the Chamber.

Presumably, the quality of prison food improved after Pilsbury's retirement and there is no mention of it in the prison records until 1902. In that year Prison Physician Ralph E. Gallinger attributed the improvement in health of the inmates after their arrival to "the quality of the food" among other factors.[167] However, one clue that the prison diet did not improve much after Pilsbury's resignation is found in the 1906 prison report. Warden Scott referred to a bill of prison fare dated 1899 as "in our opinion, coarse and monotonous, not only to the verge of severity but to the point of hardship."[168] Scott abolished the list and as a health measure issued a pint of milk per inmate per day.[169]

On the whole, state prisoners in New Hampshire appear to have had a typical institutional diet: "coarse, but nutritive" in the words of Reverend Smith. There were times when excessive frugality led to a serious deterioration in quality. However, the unappetizing conditions of the 1850's and 1870's were probably exceptional. Even slaves of the state required good enough food for the daily performance of hard labor. Decent food was also intimately connected to the condition of the prisoners' health.

Life in the prison was unhealthy as a result of the combination of hard labor, overcrowding, poor physical surroundings, and at times, a poor quality diet. We can get some insight into health conditions at the prison through the physician's reports which began listing cause of death in the 1850's. Additional clues are provided in the memoirs of Eleazer Smith and Hosea Quinby, former prison chaplains, an affidavit of the 1850's, and documents concerning the prison investigation of 1880.

Reasonably healthy workers were needed if the prison contract labor system was to function effectively. The original rules and by-laws of 1812 prescribed standards of hygiene: "suitable cribs, straw beds and pillows and woollen blankets or rugs" were furnished in each cell. Inmates were supposed to air the beds and bedding once a day. Inmates were supposed to wash daily, be shaved twice a week, get their hair cut once a month, and change their shirts once a week. In addition, they were supposed to sweep the cell floor every day and wash the floor "as often as found necessary...All foul straws and filth shall be immediately burnt."[170] Apparently, the standards of cleanliness were not always maintained. A visitor to the Vermont State Prison in 1819 contrasted the "beautiful garden" he found there to the "yard filled with filth and rubbish" he saw at the New Hampshire State Prison.[171]

Another health hazard was overcrowding. The courts sent a steady stream of convicted felons to prison. By 1831 82 inmates jammed a prison designed to hold 36. Beds were placed in the hallways and infirmary. Even so, some of the cells housed up to eight men.[172] Such conditions were good for neither the inmates' health nor discipline. The prison of this era was described as filthy, and stifling in summer and freezing in winter.[173] A large new addition containing 127 cells was finished in 1833.[174]

Once again, in the late 1860's, overcrowding became a problem and beds were placed in the infirmary and hallways. The prison contained only 120 cells but there were 130 inmates.[175] Most cells measured only seven feet by three and a half feet by six feet three inches in height.[176] Warden John C. Pilsbury harped on the need for a new prison throughout the 1870's.[177] By 1878 it was so crowded that 40 men were sleeping in the chapel. The wash-room was now used for religious services.[178] At last, in 1877, the state legislature approved the funding for a new prison.[179] The new structure, completed in 1880, was located one and a half miles northwest of the state house in Concord on a 21-acre site near the railroad tracks. It was chosen with regard to production and marketing opportunities because prison industries were so important.[180]

The new prison was much larger than the old one. The North Wing measured 46 feet by 277 feet, was 4 stories high, and contained 248 cells. Cell dimensions were more generous than before: eight feet long, six feet wide, and seven and a half feet high. The South Wing, 80 feet by 46 feet and 3 stories high, included 10 cells for female convicts. Other buildings were storerooms, a chapel, a guard room, and the new two-story warden's house, designed for two families.[181]

The old prison, on three and three quarter acres of land, was put up for auction on April 12, 1881. According to a promotional broadside, it was "well adapted to manufacturing purposes, and presents an unusually fine opportunity for investment. The attention of capitalists and manufacturers is especially invited to this sale."[182] The site was auctioned off for $16,050 to Nahum Robinson and Oscar V. Pitman. The old prison was torn down around 1890 and replaced by "handsome dwellings." Only some of the brick workshops survived.[183]

Even after the problem of overcrowding was solved, the inmates' health was imperiled by the hazardous, poorly-ventilated conditions described earlier. When combined with a miserable diet of rotten food, it is no wonder the inmates' health suffered. Conditions became so bad in the 1850's that one inmate claimed to have known occasions when 16 inmates were sick at one time in the shoe shop.[184]

Deaths were reported in the physician's report from 1852 on. These reports provide some insight into the nature of health at the state prison. Death rates per 1000 population were sometimes very high. Death rates for specific causes of death have not been calculated because the numbers are so small. We have, however, listed causes of death as percentages of causes of death. The worst period was the 1870's and 1880's when prison death rates were nearly three times higher than those of New Hampshire males aged 10-69 years (see Table 36).[185] Between 1852 and 1900 prison death rates were consistently higher than those of the general population of New Hampshire. Not until the 1890's was the prison death rate lowered to a level approaching that of the general population. In 1910 the prison death rate for males was actually slightly lower than that for New Hampshire males age 15-69 (10.4 per 1000 versus 11.3 per 1000 population; see Tables 36-37). One can conclude that from 1890 on, life in prison became much healthier than before. It is surprising that the big improvement did not start in 1880 when the new prison

Table 36

New Hampshire State Prison Mortality Rates, 1812-1914

POP. Rate Decade	TOTAL PRISON POPULATION Deaths (N)	Pop. at Risk	Rate/1000
1810's			
1820's			
1830's			
1840's			
1850's	20	372 (x 2.8)	19.2
1860's	22	486 (x 2.7)	16.8
1870's	52	573 (x 2.6)	34.9
1880's	35	512 (x 2.6)	26.3
1890's	22	642 (x 2.9)	11.8
1900's	22	707 (x 2.6)	12.0
1910's	13	598 (x 2.1)	10.4

POP. Rate Decade	SEACOAST SAMPLE Deaths (N) Pop. at Risk		Rate/1000
1810's	1	46 (x 2.8)	7.8
1820's	1	49 (x 3.2)	6.4

POP. Rate Decade	SEACOAST SAMPLE Deaths (N) Pop. at Risk		Rate/1000
1830's	2	39 (x 3.8)	13.5
1840's	4	41 (x 4.0)	24.4
1850's	2	42 (x 2.8)	17.0
1860's	4	71 (x 2.7)	20.9
1870's	11	126 (x 2.6)	33.6
1880's	6	179 (x 2.6)	12.9
1890's	7	132 (x 2.9)	18.3
1900's	0	138 (x 2.6)	0
1910's	1	93 (x 2.1)	5.1

Note: Population at risk was derived by counting the number of males in prison during each decade. The population at risk for the 1890's includes females because the single female inmate who died while in the New Hampshire State Prison died in 1892 (she was not from either Rockingham or Strafford County).

Population at risk was multiplied by the mean sentence served for that decade in order to make mortality rates comparable to those derived from the U.S. Census (see Chapter Four). This served to convert prison decadal rates to man-years making them more comparable to census rates which were calculated for only a given year, not a whole decade.

Source: "Register of Convicts 1812-1883," "[N.H. State] Prison Records [1874-1915]," and "N.H. State Prison: Record of Gain and Loss in Population [1905-36]," all MS, Div. of Records-Management and Archives, Concord, N.H.; and *Prison Warden's Reports*, 1852-1914 (missing: 1858, 1860, and 1872-73).

was opened. Apparently, overcrowding was not the only factor which made good health in the old prison so very precarious. Tuberculosis and respiratory diseases were the most common causes of death at the state prison. A total of 64 different causes of death were listed in the prison reports between 1852 and 1914. For purposes of analysis, they were grouped into nine basic categories (see Table 38). Tuberculosis accounted for fully 40% of the deaths. The dusty, choking conditions of the workshops did not help. Living conditions encouraged the spread of tuberculosis: a "vitiated atmosphere" caused by deficient ventilation and inadequate heating. Over the decades, prison physicians blamed the poor health of the inmates on deficient ventilation and overcrowding.

Table 37

New Hampshire Population at Risk Mortality Rates, 1850-1910

A. Males and Females, All Ages

Year	No. of Deaths	Pop. at Risk	Rate/1000
1850	4231	317,976	13.3

B. Males, Age 15-69

Year	No. of Deaths	Pop. at Risk	Rate/1000
1860	989	102,795	9.6

C. Males, Age 15-69

Year	No. of Deaths	Pop. at Risk	Rate/1000
1870	970	109,039	8.9

D. Males, Age 10-69

Year	No. of Deaths	Pop. at Risk	Rate/1000
1880	1129	146,157	7.7

E. Males, Age 10-69

Year	No. of Deaths	Pop. at Risk	Rate/1000
1890	1634	145,716	11.2

F. Females, Age 10-59

Year	No. of Deaths	Pop. at Risk	Rate/1000
1890	1353	135,235	10.0

G. Males, Age 10-69

Year	No. of Deaths	Pop. at Risk	Rate/1000
1900	1611	158,298	10.1

H. Males, Age 15-69

Year	No. of Deaths	Pop. at Risk	Rate/1000
1910	1692	149,706	11.3

Note: U.S. Census, N.H. Secretary of State, and N.H. Board of Health provide an inconsistent listing of populations at risk and death, thus the divisions in A-H.

Source: *U.S. Census Reports*, 1850-1910; *Registration and Return of Births, Marriages, Divorces, and Deaths in N.H.* (Secretary of State), 1883-1911; and *Annual Reports of N.H. Board of Health*, 1882-1902.

Prison conditions were an ideal breeding ground for tuberculosis. The treatment of tuberculosis includes a well-balanced diet, cleanliness, and good ventilation, none of which characterized prison life.[186] Tuberculosis was a scourge throughout the period 1860-1914.

At its worst, the disease accounted for 61.5% (32 out of 52) deaths in the 1870's (see Table 38). This disease was a major problem in other penal institutions of the time too. Blake McKelvey reports that in the 1880's tuberculosis accounted for 45% of the deaths at "a dozen major prisons" in the United States.[187] Doubtless, the terribly overcrowded conditions of the 1870's in the New Hampshire State Prison contributed to the spread of tuberculosis. The inadequate diet allegedly characteristic of the John C. Pilsbury years probably contributed to the inmates' susceptibility. Poor ventilation and inadequate heating no doubt contributed to the frequency of lung diseases other than tuberculosis too. Prison physicians often mentioned the high incidence of coughs and lung problems in general.[188]

Tuberculosis was the leading cause of death in New Hampshire from 1860

Table 38

New Hampshire State Prison Mortality: Major Causes of Death, 1852-1914

Decade	Cause of Death (Percentage of Total Deaths)						
	1	2	3	4	5	6	7
1850's	5.0%	10.0%	10.0%	20.0%	10.0%	10.0%	
1860's	4.6%	31.8%	4.6%	13.6%	4.6%	13.6%	4.6%
1870's	3.9%	61.5%	1.9%	1.9%	7.7%	1.9%	9.6%
1880's		40.0%	2.9%	2.9%	2.9%	5.7%	5.7%
1890's	19.0%	38.1%	4.8%			4.8%	10.5%
1900's	13.6%	27.3%	22.7%		4.6%	18.2%	
1910's	15.4%	38.4%				23.1%	
TOTAL:	7.0%	40.0%	5.9%	4.9%	4.9%	8.6%	5.4%

Decade	Cause of Death (Percentage of Total Deaths)		
	8	9	Total % and (N)
1850's		35.0%	100% (20)
1860's		22.7%	100% (22)
1870's		11.5%	100% (52)
1880's	2.9%	37.1%	100% (35)
1890's	4.8%	19.0%	100% (21)
1900's		13.6%	100% (22)

Decade	Cause of Death (Percentage of Total Deaths)		
	8	9	Total % and (N)
1910's	7.7%	15.4%	100% (13)

Causes of Death:

1. Heart Disease

2. Tuberculosis

3. Non-Tubercular Lung Disease

4. Dysentery, Etc.

5. Fever and Infectious Disease

6. Suicide

7. Execution

8. Industrial Accident

9. All Other

Source: *Prison Warden's Reports*, 1852-1914 (missing: 1858, 1860, and 1872-73).

through 1880. In 1890 tuberculosis was still the leading cause of death for females. It was the third leading cause of death in 1890 for the entire population and the second leading cause in 1900 (see Table 39). Tuberculosis as a percentage of causes of death in the prison was consistently much higher than that found in the general population from 1860 through 1890 (see Table 37).

Non-tubercular lung diseases such as pneumonia actually became a smaller proportion of causes of death in prison than among the general population in 1880 and 1890 (see Tables 40-41). The percentage of those inmates dying from non-tubercular lung disease roared back up in the 1900's when it was more than double the percentage of deaths in the general population (see

Table 39

New Hampshire Mortality, 1860-1900:
Causes of Death for Population at Risk

Cause of Death	Percentage of Deaths for Population at Risk		
	1860	1870	1880
	Males 1	Males 2	M and F 3
Tuberculosis	25.5%	34.3%	15.5%
Heart Disease	5.6%	8.2%	
"Heart and Dropsy"			
Non-T.B. Lung Dis.	7.5%	9.3%	11.3%
Influenza			
Dysentery, Etc.	5.2%	3.2%	5.6%
Digestive Diseases			4.3%
Fever and Infect.	16.7%	13.0%	5.3%
Diphtheria & Croup			
Whooping Cough			
Nervous System Dis.			13.4%
Violent Death	5.8%		
Accident		6.5%	
Suicide		1.6%	
Homicide		0.1%	

Cause of Death	Percentage of Deaths for Population at Risk		
	1860 Males 1	1870 Males 2	1880 M and F 3
Execution		0.1%	
All Other	33.7%	23.7%	38.1%
TOTAL:	100%	100%	100%

Cause of Death	Percentage of Deaths for Population at Risk		
	1890 Males 4	1890 Females 5	1900 M and F 6
Tuberculosis	9.0%	13.2%	8.5%
Heart Disease			
"Heart and Dropsy"	9.2%	10.5%	
Non-T.B. Lung Disease	9.4%	10.5%	11.8%
Influenza			2.5%
Dysentery, Etc.	8.4%	8.6%	6.8%
Digestive Diseases			
Fever and Infect.	6.5%	4.7%	2.1%
Diphtheria and Croup			1.4%
Whooping Cough			1.1%
Nervous System Dis.	12.6%	15.1%	
Violent Death			
Accident			

Cause of Death	Percentage of Deaths for Population at Risk		
	1890 Males 4	1890 Females 5	1900 M and F 6
Suicide			
Homicide			
Execution			
All Other	44.9%	37.4%	65.7%
TOTAL:	100%	100%	100%

POPULATION AT RISK:

Males 1: Males, All Ages

Males 2: Males, Age 15-69

M and F 3: Males and Females, All Ages

Males 4: Males, All Ages

Females 5: Females, All Ages

M and F 6: Males and Females, All Ages

Note: U.S. Census provides and inconsistent listing of populations at risk and causes of death. Causes of death listed were not always the leading cause of death in New Hampshire but were listed as measures of comparison with other states. The New Hampshire Secretary of State and Board of Health annual reports do not match causes of death to specific age and sex groups for this period.

Source: *U.S. Census Reports*, 1860-1900.

Tables 38-39).
    The spread of dysentery was also encouraged by overcrowding. The disease

is characterized by an inflammation of the large intestine. The result is a sometimes fatal diarrhoea in which large quantities of blood and fluids are

Table 40

New Hampshire Mortality Rates, 1860-1900:
Major Causes of Death

A. Males, All Ages

Year	Cause	N	Rate/100,000	Pop. at Risk
1860	Heart Disease	116	72.6	159,816
	Tuberculosis	526	329.1	
	Non-T.B. Lung Disease	154	96.4	
	Dysentery, Etc.	107	67.0	
	Fever and Infect.	344	215.2	
	Violent Death	120	75.1	
	All Other	694	434.2	

B. Males, Age 10-80

Year	Cause	N	Rate/100,000	Pop. at Risk
1870	Heart Disease	134	102.1	131,266
	Tuberculosis	386	294.1	
	Non-T.B. Lung Disease	121	92.2	
	Dysentery, Etc.	52	39.8	
	Fever and Infect.	160	121.9	
	Suicide	18	13.7	

B. Males, Age 10-80

Year	Cause	N	Rate/100,000	Pop. at Risk
1870	Accident	78	59.4	131,266
	Homicide	1	0.8	
	Execution	1	0.8	
	All Other	339	258.3	

C. Males and Females, All Ages

Year	Cause	N	Rate/100,000	Pop. at Risk
1880	Tuberculosis	866	249.6	346,991
	Respiratory Disease	633	182.4	
	Whooping Cough	15	4.3	
	Diarrhoeal Disease	314	90.5	
	Digestive Disease	241	69.5	
	Scarlet Fever	138	39.8	
	Enteric Fever	117	33.7	
	Measles	37	10.7	
	Nervous System	751	216.4	
	All Other	2128	613.3	

D. Males, All Ages

Year	Cause	N	Rate/100,000	Pop. at Risk
1890	"Heart and Dropsy"	329	176.3	186,566

D. Males, All Ages

Year	Cause	N	Rate/100,000	Pop. at Risk
1890	Tuberculosis	320	171.5	186,566
	Non-T.B. Lung Disease	336	180.1	
	Diarrhoeal Disease	300	160.8	
	Fever and Infect.	230	123.3	
	Nervous System	447	239.6	
	All Other	1598	856.5	

E. Males and Females, All Ages

Year	Cause	N	Rate/100,000	Pop. at Risk
1900	Measles	45	10.9	411,588
	Scarlet Fever	29	7.0	
	Diphtheria and Croup	107	26.0	
	Whooping Cough	78	19.0	
	Diarrhoeal Disease	505	122.7	
	Typhoid Fever	69	16.8	
	Malarial Fever	18	4.4	
	Influenza	185	44.9	
	Pneumonia	873	212.1	
	Tuberculosis	627	152.3	
	All Other	4864	1181.8	

244

Note: U.S. Census provides an inconsistent listing of populations at risk and causes of death. Causes of death listed were not always the leading cause of death in New Hampshire but were listed as measures of comparison with other states.

Source: *U.S. Census Reports*, 1860-1900.

expelled from the body. The causes of dysentery include chemical irritants, bacteria, protozoa, viruses, or parasitic worms.[189] One of the inmates who died of bilious diarrhoea "was in the habit of eating lime, old plaster, &c."[190] The generally filthy conditions of the prison contributed to the presence of bacteria, viruses, etc. Spoiled food may well have played a part too.

Dysentery in prison shows a very different pattern from that of tuberculosis. In 1860, for example, the percentage of prison deaths caused by dysentery were nearly three times higher than that for the general population. However, by the 1880's the proportion of the general population dying from dysentery and "diarrhoeal diseases" was 5.6% while the prison's was only 2.9% (see Tables 38-39). From 1890 on, this scourge seems to have been defeated at the prison. Dysentery and diarrhoeal diseases continued at a fairly high proportion in New Hampshire in 1890 and 1900 (see Table 39).

Infectious fevers of various kinds carried off some of the inmates. Again, overcrowded and unsanitary conditions of prison life helped spread cholera, typhoid fever, and influenza.

Heart disease became a major cause of death from 1890 on. It is unclear why this was so. Certainly, the prison population was not increasing in age. In fact, in the 1890's, when heart disease claimed the greatest number of victims, the median age was 25.0 years, slightly lower than the 26.0 years of the total sample from 1812-1914. Perhaps the increase in heart disease was due to changes in the prison diet, more accurate diagnoses, or perhaps a decrease in the other forms of death.

Heart disease death percentages in prison in the 1890's were over two times higher than those for all males and females in New Hampshire. Except for the 1880's, the heart disease death percentage in the New Hampshire State Prison between 1852 and 1914 was consistently much higher than that of the New Hampshire population of the present (see Tables 38-39). This is a surprising phenomenon since heart disease is the leading cause of death at present in New Hampshire (see Table 42). Heart disease was never the leading cause of death in New Hampshire during the period 1852-1914 (see Tables 38-40).

Table 41

**New Hampshire State Prison Mortality, 1852-1914:
Causes of Death for Population at Risk**

Cause of Death	% of Deaths for Population at Risk				
	1850's	1860's	1870's	1880's	1890's
Heart Disease	5.0%	4.5%	3.8%		17.4%
Tuberculosis	10.0%	31.8%	61.5%	40.0%	34.8%
Non-T.B. Lung Disease	10.0%	4.5%	1.9%	2.9%	4.3%
Dysentery	20.0%	13.6%	1.9%	1.9%	
Fever & Infect.	10.0%	4.5%	7.7%	2.9%	
Suicide	10.0%	13.6%	1.9%	5.7%	4.3%
Execution		4.5%	1.9%	5.7%	17.4%
Industrial Accident				2.9%	4.3%
All Other	35.0%	22.7%	11.5%	37.1%	17.4%
TOTAL:	100%	100%	100%	100%	100%

Cause of Death	% of Deaths for Population at Risk	
	1900's	1910's
Heart Disease	13.6%	15.4%
Tuberculosis	27.3%	38.5%
Non-T.B. Lung Disease	22.7%	
Dysentery		

Cause of Death	% of Deaths for Population at Risk 1900's 1910's	
	1900's	1910's
Fever & Infect.	4.5%	
Suicide	18.2%	23.1%
Execution		
Industrial Accident		7.7%
All Other	13.6%	15.4%
TOTAL:	100%	100%

Note: Population at risk is number of male convicts in prison each decade except the 1890's when female convicts were added. The only recorded death of a female convict occurred in 1892. Population at risk was derived from prison records by counting those males present in the prison during each decade and those males and females present during the 1890's.

Source: *Prison Warden's Reports*, 1852-1914 (missing: 1858, 1860, and 1872-73), "Register of Convicts 1812-1883," and "[N.H. State] Prison Records [1874-1915]," both MS, Div. of Records-Management and Archives, Concord, N.H.

The third most common cause of death in the prison was suicide. Suicide was at its height in the 1900's and 1910's. Surely living conditions circa 1900-1914 were far more bearable than in the 1850's or 1870's when overcrowding and harsh discipline were at their worst. The only time prison officials ventured to speculate on a suicide's motives was in 1908 when the physician blamed a suicide on the fact that an inmate "was a chronic alcoholic without home or friends, and in a fit of depression hanged himself to a cell door."[191]

By the time the prison reports began listing cause of death in the 1850's, suicide was considered to be the result of mental illness.[192] Until the mid-eighteenth century, suicide had been considered to be a sin and nothing more. Starting then, suicide was linked to insanity and melancholy. Later, in the nineteenth century, medical doctors thought suicide was the result of an imbalance in a person's body. This imbalance created a debilitated nervous system which led to melancholy which led to insanity, which might lead to

Table 42

New Hampshire Mortality Rates, 1989:
Major Causes of Death

Males and Females, All Ages

Cause of Death	No. Deaths	% Deaths	Rate/100,000
Heart Disease	2806	33.2%	141.6
Malignant Neoplasms	2160	25.6%	137.5
Cerebrovascular Dis.	568	6.7%	25.3
Chron. Obst. Pulmonary	383	4.5%	20.8
All Accidents	366	4.3%	20.5
Pneumonia & Influenza	277	3.3%	11.1
Diabetes Mellitus	202	2.4%	10.3
Suicide	126	1.5%	9.9
Chron. Liver Disease	116	1.4%	8.7
Atherosclerosis	100	1.2%	3.5
TOTAL:	8451	100%	478.4

Source: *New Hampshire Vital Statistics: 1989 Annual Report* (pub. 1991).

suicide. Such an imbalance was thought to be the result of such disparate causes as masturbation and the stresses of modern life.[193] By 1900, psychiatrists traced the root of suicide to individual behavior arising from specific organic disorders while sociologists, influenced by the French scholar, Emile Durkheim, blamed social conditions. They thought suicide was a result of the pressures and alienation characteristic of modern urban life.[194]

Prison inmates had only a few methods available for committing suicide. The single most common method was hanging. "Successful" suicides in the general population typically choose methods such as firearms, hanging, and jumping.[195] Firearms, obviously, were not an option in the state prison, and not every inmate hanged himself. One inmate swallowed lime and pulverized glass which he had smuggled into his cell in his shoes and clothing.[196] One even drowned himself in his night bucket.[197] The sheer desperation of some of these suicides is suggested by the case of one inmate who made three attempts before finally taking his life. First, he cut his arm. Next, he cut his throat with a "rude instrument made of a piece of sawplate, two inches long and one quarter inch wide, fixed into a bit of wood for a handle." When this didn't work, the unhappy man leapt eight feet from the gallery, striking his head on the granite floor. At last, he cut his throat and died.[198] Apparently, there were enough suicide attempts for the administration to demand the construction of an iron grille along the outside cell corridors in 1904 to prevent desperate inmates from hurling themselves to the prison floor.[199]

Executions and industrial accidents comprise the remaining forms of unnatural death. We have already covered accidents in the section on working conditions in this chapter and we will discuss executions in Chapter Six.

The remaining 21.6% of causes of death in prison covered a very wide variety. They included everything from old age to "nostalgia of homesickness" to tetanus to Bright's disease (an affliction of the kidneys). Perhaps the most bizarre cause of death listed, in the modern reader's eyes, is masturbation.

From the 1850's through the 1880's, the prison administration expressed great alarm at the practice of masturbation among the inmates. According to the physician's reports, it was the cause of four deaths and a direct contributor to another four. For example, a 20-year old inmate died of "general dropsy" in 1855. Dr. William Prescott's diagnosis claimed, "There remains scarcely a doubt that the above case was produced, and the increase in the disease first brought about the first of October, by excessive and obstinate perseverance in the practice of the secret vice of masturbation."[200] Some of the accounts of masturbation-induced death appear ludicrous today. In 1874 a "young colored man...fell victim to that degrading habit so common among prisoners. He was first attacked with paralysis in the lower limbs, but finally became completely and entirely helpless. After enduring a living death for many weeks, he finally passed away. His confession to the warden as to the extent to which he practised [sic] masturbation was without parallel in prison history."[201]

Beginning in the eighteenth century, American medical doctors regarded masturbation as a disease. At its mildest, masturbation depleted a male's energy while at its worst it led to insanity and death. It was even linked to suicide in the nineteenth century.[202] By the early twentieth century such extreme views, derived from theories about somatic causes of behavior, were discredited by the medical establishment although it still thought masturbation could weaken the nervous system and at least indirectly affect one's health.[203]

Nineteenth-century prison reports were frank in discussing masturbation yet not once was the problem of homosexuality mentioned. As we saw in Chapters Two and Three, sodomy and "unnatural and lascivious acts" were recriminalized in the post-Civil War era. A few inmates in the sample were sent to prison for just such behavior so it is likely the prison administration would have been seriously concerned with homosexuality among the inmates. Perhaps the stigma associated with homosexuality was so strong that prison officials could not bring themselves to mention it in the annual reports for fear of public outrage.

Penologists recognize that the prison environment is conducive to homosexual behavior. With one major exception (discussed shortly), the basic prison experience of the nineteenth century is similar enough to that of the present day. Thus, it is very likely that some homosexual activity took place even though it is not reported in any of the original sources.

Richard Hawkins and Geoffrey P. Alpert discern three main settings for homosexuality in men's prisons: a) affection and sexual release, b) sex for hire, and c) domination and sexual gratification through forced sex (rape).[204] The nature of prisons helps to create the situation: enforced mingling in an all-male society, overcrowding, no escape for unwilling participants, and prison staff unable or unwilling to intervene.[205] Consensual homosexual behavior is facilitated by the prison environment: no accessible females for heterosexual inmates needing sexual release. An underground economy based on accumulated favors and partly on goods smuggled in from outside is characteristic of penal institutions. Some inmates participate in this economy by bartering homosexual favors to acquire money, goods, or protection from stronger inmates.[206]

The main cause of homosexual behavior in prison is the violent culture of prison life. Sex in prison is most commonly an expression of dominance by the most aggressive inmates. Because a masculine identity is very important to an inmate, the only way in which a heterosexual inmate can continue to view himself as a male while participating in homosexual behavior is by using violence. Thus, homosexual rape by an aggressive male of a weaker male is, paradoxically, regarded as a validation of one's masculinity in prison.[207] The weaker male who is forced to submit is considered to be the equivalent of a woman. New inmates are subjected to baiting and threats of homosexual rape. The only defense for a new inmate is protective custody, which automatically arouses the wrath of the other inmates. Seeking protective custody is viewed as siding with the authorities. A violent response establishes the new inmate as aggressive, thus diminishing the likelihood of homosexual advances. A vicious cycle of homosexual rape and violent response is thus established.[208]

An aggravating factor not characteristic of the nineteenth century is racial antagonism. Since the 1960's there has been a tremendous growth in the number of black and Hispanic inmates. This has been accompanied by an attitude of extreme militancy on the part of many of these inmates. This situation feeds into the problem of homosexual rape in prison. Most prison rapists today are black. According to Anthony M. Scacco, Jr., black prison rapists seek to humiliate white inmates in an attempt to demonstrate power over them and to get revenge for the racism prevalent in American society.[209] Scacco and Daniel Lockwood blame much of this also on the prevalence of violence in ghetto culture. Blacks and Hispanics from such a culture are less averse than whites to use violence. Whites are also at a disadvantage in that black and Hispanic inmates are much more likely to form gangs in prison.[210] Ultimately, Scacco and Lockwood blame sexual violence in prisons on the glorification of violence in American society.[211]

Homosexual behavior among female prison inmates is much different from males. The constant quest for dominance is absent. In its place, female inmates seek to fulfill themselves by creating a family structure. Thus female inmates will play the role of husband, father, brother, etc. as well as the more traditional wife, mother, sister, etc.[212] Women in prison will frequently switch roles. However, Hawkins and Alpert point out that many of these "family" relationships are motivated by a desire for companionship or prestige. Female inmates in such relationships do not necessarily engage in homosexual activity.[213]

The number of female inmates at the New Hampshire State Prison between 1812 and 1914 was very small. Until 1880, female inmates lived in the prison warden's house and had meals with his family. The opportunity for female inmates forming homosexual liaisons was limited.

The experience of female inmates at the state prison was significantly different from that of male inmates in several ways. The difference was a result of two factors: women were a much smaller proportion than males of the inmate population and they were accorded different treatment than men. There is evidence that the New Hampshire State Prison female inmates had more comfortable living conditions than males and were subject to milder discipline. However, women were neglected and they missed some of the reformative programs offered to men in the prison. It is also possible that gender roles restricted their options.

Women were present in the New Hampshire State Prison from the very beginning. Right away, they received different treatment from men. On October 21, 1813 the board of prison directors voted that Abigail Sweatt "should be employed in making clothing for the prisoners and that until more suitable provision can be made she be suffered to remain carefully watched and secured, in that part of the prison occupied by the warden and his family."[214] With some modifications, this was to be the lot of female inmates at the New Hampshire State Prison over the next 67 years.

Such treatment was typical practice in early nineteenth century America but it contradicted some of the goals of prison discipline. Females typically encountered lower levels of surveillance, discipline, and care than males.[215] Abigail Sweatt and the women who followed her never participated in the contract labor system for obvious reasons, yet it would be inaccurate to say they escaped hard labor. Half a century later, women inmates were still employed at making and mending prison clothing.[216] No doubt, this could be extremely tedious work since the female inmates, greatly outnumbered by males, had to provide uniforms for all.

Female inmates in New Hampshire enjoyed a milder regime of prison discipline than their male counterparts. Women were not housed in any of the prison cells before 1880. Instead, they resided in the warden's home and even had meals with his family. Warden Rufus Dow complained of "the anxiety and annoyance of being compelled to receive [female inmates] into the family and at the table" in 1852.[217] Warden Gideon Webster complained of the same thing in 1853.[218]

American prison officials of the antebellum period were unsure of what to do with female prisoners. "Fallen women" were considered to be more reprehensible than male criminals so there was little disagreement that they deserved a prison sentence. At first, women were housed in the same buildings with men but problems soon became evident: they distracted men and were in danger of sexual exploitation. Discipline became impossible to maintain under such circumstances. By 1820 most female prisoners were separated from the males and put into a separate women's section of the main prison, an annex, or a separate building located near to the main prison.[219]

In New Hampshire female prisoners were removed to the warden's house and apparently kept there all of the time. The problem with such an arrangement was that women prisoners suffered from neglect. Perhaps they had a less regimented and less brutal existence than male prisoners, but by the same token they missed out on religious and educational programs. In 1871 Warden Pilsbury was scandalized to learn that female convicts had attended religious services and sabbath school together with male convicts. This was quickly "corrected" by sending the women to the sewing room where they were taught by "Mrs. Jerould, a very worthy lady."[220]

Because women were such a small group they tended to receive only limited attention. This reinforced sexual stereotyping such as having the prison sewing and washing delegated to them.[221] Warden Rufus Dow hoped to install the four female prisoners in his care into the newly remodeled South Wing in 1852.[222] Aside from being a nuisance at the dinner table, female convicts sometimes found it easy to escape from the warden's house. In 1852 one female inmate escaped from her bedroom in the attic with the aid of a "common pocket knife." She was recaptured. A similar incident occurred in 1853.[223]

Women as well as men suffered under the strict administration of John C. Pilsbury in the 1870's. Pilsbury was charged with punishing females who disobeyed the downcast eye regulation and he was charged with denying them proper clothing and supplies. It was alleged that he "cuffed" one female inmate before placing her in solitary confinement.[224] A more serious allegation was made by State Representative Edward O. Rand during the same investigation: that "in a space of not much over three years he has caused eleven men and three women to be flogged on their bare backs."[225] Pilsbury was exonerated again. These charges are significant in that they suggest that women were in fact, subject to as harsh a discipline as that experienced by men at the state prison under Pilsbury's administration.

There is some evidence that the female prisoners in New Hampshire suffered from neglect. In 1869 Warden Joseph Mayo admitted, "The crowded conditions of the department allotted to them is unhealthy, and at times renders their management most difficult."[226] Efforts were made on their behalf. In 1870 Warden Mayo remodeled their quarters. The women now spent their days in a "large, airy, well ventilated and warmed sewing or workroom" and their nights in improved rooms of a similar description.[227] Steam heating was installed in the new prison in 1878-79. However, radiators were installed in only certain locations, including three cells for women and the women's work-room. No radiators were installed in the cells occupied by men or in their workshops.[228] In 1906 the women's cells were described as "large and well ventilated, the work pleasant and not overhard." The warden recommended walling off part of the prison yard so that the women could get some outdoor exercise.[229]

New Hampshire never participated in the women's reformatory movement of the post-Civil War era. The movement was based on three principles: women should be kept in separate penal institutions from men; women required specialized, feminine care; and female staff and management were necessary to administer women's reformatories.[230] The reformatory ideal for both men and women was aimed at young, first-time offenders. Reformers strongly believed in the classification of inmates by sex, age, and offender type.[231] The only women who were sent to the state prison were convicted felons. Petty female offenders went to the local jail or house of correction or paid a fine.

In one way, it was a blessing in disguise that the women's reformatory movement never resulted in the construction of a separate institution for female offenders in New Hampshire. At least New Hampshire women were spared the injustice of going to prison for petty offenses such as vagrancy, drunkenness, and nonfelonious sexual misbehavior as happened in states where women's reformatories were constructed.[232] There were too few female inmates in New Hampshire during the period 1812-1914 to justify the construction of a women's reformatory. Most female convicts in the United States were incarcerated in custodial prisons rather than reformatories, thus, enduring the usual stress on security and order rather than rehabilitation.[233] Thus, New Hampshire female convicts never enjoyed the benefits of reformatory discipline. They also never suffered the brutality and sexual abuse visited upon women inmates in some other state prisons. For instance, the forced prostitution of female inmates at the Indiana State Prison became a national scandal when discovered.[234] Similarly, they never had to endure the horrors of labor on the chain gangs in the South. Sometimes women were chained together with men and this could lead to sexual abuse. Female chain gang prisoners had to endure the same hard labor and discipline as the males.[235]

Because they were women and because they were so few, their experience was different from that of men at the New Hampshire State Prison for the period 1812-1914. Females usually had more comfortable quarters. They led a life closer to normal family life than did the male inmates but the warden and his family were not necessarily pleased with the arrangement. Female inmates probably enjoyed a higher quality of food than males. They had

254

better working conditions than male inmates who were faced with noisy, dusty, and physically dangerous work under the contract labor system. On the other hand, the burden of sewing and repairing prison uniforms for the entire institution must have been very tiring, especially when the number of female inmates dwindled to only one or two. Women were usually barred from attending religious services and classes with male inmates. In 1869 the warden's wife taught classes to the female inmates.[236] While conditions for women were never as terrible as they became for men in the late 1820's, 1850's, and 1870's, they did occasionally suffer neglect. In New Hampshire female convicts experienced only the custodial approach typical of the state prison. They never had the chance to enjoy the mixed blessings of the reformatory approach. Thankfully, New Hampshire female convicts never endured the appalling conditions some women found in other custodial prisons or chain gangs. In sum, the female experience of the New Hampshire State Prison was unpleasant but it was easier than that of the male majority.

Life was hard in the New Hampshire State Prison during the years 1812-1914. At times it was unbearable - gross overcrowding, abominable food, and harsh working conditions. Prison life was unhealthy compared to life in the rest of the state. Many inmates suffered from tuberculosis and various other lung and infectious diseases. At least 16 inmates committed suicide.

The prison environment was not conducive to good health. Infectious and lung diseases flourished. The overcrowded, dirty, and either stifling or freezing conditions of the prison seriously undermined the inmates' health. Improvements were made from time to time - a large new prison was constructed over the years 1878-80 - but things did not get much better. Although steam heating had been installed, the new prison was still too cold for some inmates in 1880.[237] Suicide remained the third most common cause of death through the 1910's, a circumstance suggesting that the inmates' emotional health was as poor as their physical health.

The prison administration gradually became more active in the rehabilitation of inmates. At first reformative efforts were minimal: each cell was furnished with a Bible and religious services were conducted once a week. Gradually, basic education in reading and writing was introduced. After the Civil War secular education was slowly expanded to include other subjects. The prison library was an important component of prison life.

The prison experience was ameliorated somewhat in the early twentieth century. Between 1906 and 1914 the hated parti-colored prison uniform was abolished, as were the oppressive lockstep march and downcast eye regulation. One major improvement was paying the inmates for their labor.

The experience of women at the New Hampshire State Prison was hard but not necessarily for the same reasons as for men. Overall, women experienced less brutality. Their work was less dangerous than what the men endured in the workshops under the contract labor system but it was probably just as tedious and long. Women were shunted aside and largely neglected. They were an awkward presence in an institution designed for male offenders.[238]

There is no doubt that the New Hampshire State Prison was a custodial, rather than reformatory institution. In this regard, it fully resembled the prisons described by David J. Rothman and other revisionists. It was not particularly bad compared to other prisons but it is unlikely that very many inmates left as improved human beings. The prison was a self-financing operation most of the time. Probably, State Representative Edward D. Rand's characterization of the prison sums up the experience best. With few exceptions, it was "a false, wretched, miserly, miserable economy, on behalf of the state, whereby the souls and bodies of men were sacrificed to the love of gain."[239] This assessment could be applied to other American prisons of the era as well.[240]

The single most valuable primary source of information on life in the New Hampshire State Prison is the annual prison warden's report. At first, the reports were brief financial documents appended to the journals of the New Hampshire House of Representatives and Senate. By the 1840's they were published separately. The reports became longer and more detailed over time. From the 1830's on the prison reports included separate sections by the prison physician and chaplain. The prison warden's reports provide a wealth of statistical information and much insight into the policies of prison administration. Of course, they are biased in favor of the administration's perspective but they do not hesitate to describe - sometimes graphically - the serious problems encountered in the state prison. Sometimes it was in the administration's interest to describe prison affairs in a negative fashion in order to get money from a reluctant legislature. Prison physicians forthrightly describe awful working and living conditions of the institution when they report on deaths and illnesses.

Another valuable source is the manuscript "Minute Book 1812-34: Records" and the "Ledger [1834-55]" located in the State Prison Papers kept at the Division of Records-Management and Archives in Concord, N.H. These ledgers contain minutes of meetings of the board of prison directors. Some of the information listed in these ledgers is found nowhere else. Especially valuable are the original rules and by-laws of the state prison which are far more detailed than the statutory regulations on the administration of the state prison. One can trace the ad hoc measures taken by the board as they faced new problems, such as how to occupay the first inmate at hard labor or what to do with the first female inmate.

As always, legal documents such as statute and session laws and the journals of the New Hampshire House of Representatives and Senate provide useful information on official policy. They provide an initial framework by describing the prison as it *should* function. Thus, they are helpful in analyzing how much or how little the prison lived up to the ideals described in Chapters Two and Three.

The published memoirs of two former prison chaplains provide much information available only to a prison insider. Particularly helpful in this regard is Eleazer Smith's *Nine Years among the Convicts: or Prison Reminiscences* (1856). Although a good portion of the book is filled with sentimental recollections and exemplary tales of reformed inmates, this source is useful for its specific descriptions of everyday life in the institution. Almost as useful is Hosea Quinby's *The Prison Chaplaincy, and Its Experiences* (1873). Quinby's account of prison life is definitely a biased appraisal of the contrast between the benign "reformatory system" run by Warden Joseph Mayo and the "punitive and money-making system" of his successor, Warden John C. Pilsbury. At least Quinby is honest in acknowledging the fact that he and Pilsbury had a serious quarrel. *The Prison Chaplaincy* is still a useful source which provides an insider's view of prison life just after the Civil War.

Joseph L. Shaw's *New-Hampshire State Prison Cruelty Exposed* (1839) is an aptly-titled first person account of the incredible brutality suffered by the author as an inmate. This small book is a personal horror story but it provides some more general information on the nature of life and working conditions at the prison and the role of solitary confinement.

In the summer of 1880 Warden John C. Pilsbury's administration came crashing down in allegations of cruelty and mismanagement. Located in the State Prison Papers at the State Archives is a manuscript copy of the charges made against Pilsbury by Burnham Wardwell (a roving prison investigator from Virginia). The investigation was held in the New Hampshire Council Chamber and attracted much publicity. Although Pilsbury was acquitted of all 45 charges, the document is valuable for the insight it gives into life in prison in the 1870's. State Representative Edward D. Rand published the closing remarks he gave at the prison investigation and they too provide an impassioned indictment of Pilsbury's administration.

The Rufus Dow papers, located at the New Hampshire Historical Society in Concord, provide a glimpse into prison management. Dow was warden of the prison from 1850 through 1853. The most valuable part of the collection is correspondence concerning prison affairs. Regrettably, most of the collection concerns Dow's political activities and post-prison experiences.

Construction specifications, plans, contracts, and related documents from c. 1877-80 found in the State Prison Papers at the State Archives provide much information on the physical environment of the new prison which opened in 1880. From these sources, one can create an authentic picture of everyday life. Very little of this information is found in the prison warden's reports.

The remaining primary sources are a miscellany: a few newspaper articles, the Reverend Elijah R. Wilkins's sermon notebooks (Wilkins was prison chaplain during the years 1884-96 and 1899-1905), and correspondence of Charles Brewster (a New Hampshire politician and newspaper publisher in the 1840's).

258

Notes

1. *New-Hampshire Patriot*, Dec. 1, 1812. Drew's sentence was incorrectly stated. It was four years, not five. See "Register of Convicts 1812-1883," MS, Div. of Records-Management and Archives, Concord, N.H.
2. See Gov. John T. Gilman's message to the New Hampshire House of Representatives on June 12, 1804. *Journal of the House of Representatives of the State of New Hampshire...June, Anno Domini, 1804* (Concord, N.H., 1804), 24.
3. "Minute Book 1812-34: Records," MS, [4-5], Secretary of State. State Prison Papers, Div. of Records-Management and Archives, Concord, N.H.
4. *Ibid.*, [10].
5. *Ibid.*, [10].
6. *Ibid.*, [5 and 11-12].
7. *Ibid.*, [3 and 10-11].
8. *Ibid.*, [15-16].
9. *Ibid.*, [16].
10. See "An Act Providing for the Regulation and Government of the State Prison" passed June 19, 1812 in *The Laws of the State of New-Hampshire...* (Exeter, N.H., 1815), pp. 143-48.
11. Samuel Walker, *Popular Justice: A History of American Criminal Justice* (New York, 1980), p. 71.
12. *Ibid.*, p. 73.
13. Edward L. Ayers, *Vengeance and Justice: Crime and Punishment in the 19th.-Century American South* (New York, 1984), p. 177. Thorsten Sellin says that southern elites reintroduced penal servitude after the Civil War to make public slaves out of black, poor, and friendless white convicts. Financial profit was the main goal. J. Thorsten Sellin, *Slavery and the Penal System* (New York, 1976), pp. 145-47 and 163-70. In Louisiana, for example, leasing prisoners was implemented after the Civil War in an attempt to solve the problem of a labor shortage caused by the freeing of slaves and because financial profits could be realized by the state. Mark T. Carleton, *Politics and Punishment: The History of the Louisiana State Penal System* (Baton Rouge, La., 1971), p. 13.
14. Pieter Spierenburg, "From Amsterdam to Auburn: An Explanation for the Rise of the Prison in Seventeenth-Century Holland and Nineteenth-Century America," *Journal of Social History*, 20 (1987), 445.
15. Richard Hawkins and Geoffrey P. Alpert, *American Prison System:*

Punishment and Justice (Englewood Cliffs, N.J., 1989), p. 39 and David J. Rothman, *The Discovery of the Asylum: Social Order and Disorder in the New Republic* (Boston, 1971), p. 92.

16. Alexis M. Durham, "Rehabilitation and Correctional Privatization: Observations on the Nineteenth Century Experience and Implications for Modern Corrections," *Federal Probation*, 53 (1989), 45-46.

17. Thomas L. Dumm, *Democracy and Punishment: Disciplinary Origins in the United States* (Madison, Wis., 1987), p. 109.

18. *N.H. House Journal (1804)*, 24.

19. See, for example, Blake McKelvey, *American Prisons: A Study in American Social History Prior to 1915* (Montclair, N.J., 1968, reprint of 1922), p.30; Rothman, *Discovery of the Asylum*, p. 104; and John A. Conley, "Prisons, Production, and Profit: Reconsidering the Importance of Prison Industries," *Journal of Social History*, 14 (1980), 257.

20. Alexis de Tocqueville and Gustave de Beaumont, *On the Penitentiary System in the United States and Its Application in France*, (Carbondale, Ill., 1964), p. 57.

21. "Minute Book 1812-34," [1].

22. *Ibid.*, [10-11].

23. *Ibid.*, [19].

24. *Ibid.*, [22].

25. *Ibid.*, [23].

26. *Ibid.*, [27].

27. *Ibid.*, [32 and 39].

28. *Journal of the Honorable Senate of the State of New Hampshire...November, Anno Domini, 1816* (Concord, N.H., 1817), 138.

29. Walker, *Popular Justice*, p. 73.

30. *N.H. Senate Journal (1816)*, 38.

31. Donna-Belle Garvin, "Concord: A Furniture-Making Capital," *Historical New Hampshire*, 45 (1990), 28.

32. "Minute Book 1812-34," [87].

33. Typical examples include the following. In 1842 Warden Lawson Cooledge declared, "The N.H. State Prison will not again very soon be obliged to ask legislative aid for its support," *Report of the Warden, Physician and Chaplain of the New-Hampshire State Prison, June Session, 1842* (Concord, N.H., 1842), 10. In 1867 Warden Joseph Mayo cheerfully predicted the prison would become "a source of large and increasing revenue" rather than a burden on the state. *Report of the Warden of the New-Hampshire State Prison...June*

Session, 1867 (Concord, N.H., 1867), 5-7.

34. *Report of the Warden of the New-Hampshire State Prison...June Session, 1862* (Concord, N.H., 1862), 5-6.

35. *Reports of the Warden and Inspectors of the New Hampshire State Prison...June Session, 1875* (Concord, N.H., 1875), 8 and *Reports of the Warden and Inspectors of the State Prison at Concord, N.H....December 1, 1894* (Concord, N.H., 1894), 5.

36. Garvin, "Concord," 40.

37. *Reports of the Warden, Physician, Chaplain, and Ex-Warden of the N.H. State Prison, June Session, 1853* (Concord, N.H., 1853), 4.

38. Garvin, "Concord," 41 and 47.

39. *Reports of the Warden and Inspectors of the New Hampshire State Prison...June Session, 1879* (Manchester, N.H., 1879), 8 and Garvin, "Concord," 47.

40. Garvin, "Concord," 50-52 and *Statistics Relating to the New Hampshire State Prison...for the Two Years Ending November 30, 1896* (Concord, N.H., 1897), 20.

41. The Schoonmaker Chair Company went out of business in 1932, thus terminating the contract for prison labor. The prison's decision to end its participation in the contract labor system was also in response to federal legislation passed in 1929 and due to go into effect on January 1, 1934 (the Hawes-Cooper Act). *Report of the Officers of the New Hampshire State Prison...for the Two Years Ending June 30, 1932* (Concord, N.H., 1932), 6 and "An Act to Divest Goods, Wares, and Merchandise Manufactured, Produced, or Mined by Convicts or Prisoners of Their Interstate Character in Certain Cases," Ch. 79, *The Statutes at Large of the United States of America from December, 1927 to March, 1929*, Vol. 45, Pt. 1 (Washington, D.C., 1929), p. 1084.

42. Walker, *Popular Justice*, p. 71 and *Prison Warden's Report (1932)*, 6.

43. "Minute Book 1812-34," [10-11] and "State's Prison Records [1834-55]," MS, Secretary of State. State Prison Papers, Div. of Records-Management and Archives, Concord, N.H.

44. Orlando Lewis, *The Development of American Prisons and Prison Customs, 1776-1845* (Montclair, N.J., 1967), p. 150.

45. "Report of Stone Cut May 1825. May 31st. to M L [sic] Pilsbury Warden N H State Prison," MS, Secretary of State. State Prison Papers, Box 1, f. 2, Div. of Records-Management and Archives, Concord, N.H. Note: the warden's name was Amos C. Pilsbury.

46. *Reports of the Warden, Physician and Chaplain of the N.H. State*

Prison...June Session, 1852 (Concord, N.H., 1852), 15-17.

47. *Report of the Warden of the N.H. State Prison...June Session, 1854* (Concord, N.H., 1854), 18 and 27-28 and *Report of the Warden of the N.H. State Prison...June Session, 1855* (Concord, N.H., 1855), 18.

48. *Report of the Warden of the N.H. State Prison...June Session, 1857* (Concord, N.H., 1857), 8 and *Report of the Warden of the N.H. State Prison...June Session, 1859* (Concord, N.H., 1859), 1.

49. *Prison Warden's Report (1859)*, 14.

50. *Prison Warden's Report (1867)*, 18.

51. Eleazer Smith, *Nine Years among the Convicts: or Prison Reminiscences* (Boston, 1856), p. 248.

52. *Annual Report of the Warden and Inspectors of the New-Hampshire State Prison...June Session, 1868* (Manchester, N.H., 1868), 16.

53. *Ibid.*, 53.

54. *Reports of the Warden and Inspectors of the New Hampshire State Prison...June Session, 1871* (Concord, N.H., 1871), 30 and *Reports of the Warden and Inspectors of the New Hampshire State Prison...June Session, 1874* (Concord, N.H., 1874), 20.

55. *Reports of the Warden and Inspectors of the New Hampshire State Prison...June Session, 1876* (Concord, N.H., 1876), 34; *Reports of the Warden and Inspectors of the New Hampshire State Prison...June Session, 1877* (Concord, N.H., 1877), 36; and *Prison Warden's Report (1896)*, 16.

56. *Reports of the Warden and Inspectors of the New Hampshire State-Prison...June, 1880* (Manchester, N.H., 1880), 37.

57. *Reports of the Warden and Inspectors of the New Hampshire State-Prison...June, 1881* (Manchester, N.H., 1881), 36.

58. See *Reports of the Warden and Inspectors of the New Hampshire State Prison...June, 1882* (Concord, N.H., 1882), 30; *Reports of the Warden and Inspectors of the New Hampshire State Prison...June, 1883* (Concord, N.H., 1883), 30; *Reports of the Warden and Inspectors of the New Hampshire State Prison...June, 1885* (Concord, N.H., 1885), 29; *Reports of the Warden and Inspectors of the New Hampshire State Prison...June, 1886* (Manchester, N.H., 1886), 25; *Reports of the Warden and Inspectors of the New Hampshire State Prison...June, 1888* (Manchester, N.H., 1888), 24; and *Prison Warden's Report (1896)*, 16.

59. Typed Speech, "Retiring Message to the General Court," Jan. 2, 1913, 6-7. Box 59, Robert Perkins Bass Papers, Dartmouth College Library, Hanover, N.H. See also William M. chase and Arthur H. Chase, ed. and comp.,

Supplement to the Public Statutes of New Hampshire (Chase Edition, 1901) (Concord, N.H., 1914), pp. 535-36.

60. Conley, "Prisons, Production, and Profit," 263-64.

61. *Report of the Officers of the New Hampshire State Prison...for the Two Years Ending Aug. 31, 1912* (Penacook, N.H., n.d.), 6.

62. Michael S. Hindus, *Prison and Plantation: Crime, Justice, and Authority in Massachusetts and South Carolina, 1767-1878* (Chapel Hill, N.C., 1980), p. 166.

63. See Michel Foucault, *Discipline and Punish: The Birth of the Prison*, trans. by Alan Sheridan (New York, 1977) and Michael Ignatieff, *A Just Measure of Pain: The Penitentiary in the Industrial Revolution, 1750-1850* (New York, 1978).

64. Dumm, *Democracy and Punishment*, p. 120.

65. "Minute Book 1812-34," [13].

66. *Journal of the House of Representatives...of the State of New-Hampshire...June, 1814* (Concord, N.H., 1814), 131-32.

67. "Minute Book 1812-34," [69].

68. The first paid prison chaplain was the Reverend Samuel Kelly c. 1830-32. E. Smith, *Nine Years among the Convicts*, p. 13.

69. *Journal of the House of Representatives...June...1831* (Concord, N.H., 1831), 90.

70. *Prison Warden's Report (1855)*, 35.

71. O. Lewis, *Development of American Prisons*, p. 152 and Dorothea L. Dix, *Remarks on Prisons and Prison Discipline in the United States* (Montclair, N.J., 1967 reprint of 1845 ed.), p. 50.

72. ALS, Charles W. Brewster to Lewis N. and Charles H. Brewster, June 11, 1843, New Hampshire Historical Society, Concord, N.H. Charles W. Brewster (1812-68) was the proprietor of the Portsmouth *Journal* for many years and served in the New Hampshire legislature. James G. Wilson and John Fiske, eds., *Appleton's Cyclopaedia of American Biography*, Vol. 1 (New York, 1888), p. 371.

73. *Journals of the Honorable Senate and House of Representatives, June Session, 1835* (Sandbornton, N.H., 1835), 188.

74. See Chapter 11 "The Penitent Murderer" in E. Smith, *Nine Years among the Convicts*, pp. 130-48.

75. *Report of the Warden of the New-Hampshire State Prison* (Concord, N.H., 1865), 29.

76. *Prison Warden's Report (1885)*, 19.

77. See, for example, sermons titled "Slippery Places" and "Opportunities for self gratification [sic]" in Elijah R. Wilkins, "To Spirits in Prison [Vol. 1, 1884-96, Sermons]," MS, [5 and 23], New Hampshire Historical Society, Concord, N.H.

78. Wilkins, "[Sermons Vol. 2, 1899-1905]," MS, [149-50] New Hampshire Historical Society, Concord, N.H.

79. *Report of the Officers of the New Hampshire State Prison...for the Two Years Ending August 31, 1910* (Bristol, N.H., n.d.), 41.

80. *Report of the Officers of the New Hampshire State Prison...for the Two Years Ending Aug. 31, 1914* (Penacook, N.H., n.d.), 31.

81. *Prison Warden's Report (1885)*, 27 and E. Smith, *Nine Years among the Convicts*, p. 58.

82. Peter Haebler, "Nativism, Liquor, and Riots: Manchester Politics, 1858-1859," *Historical New Hampshire*, 46 (1991), 67-91.

83. *Reports of the Warden and Inspectors of the New Hampshire State Prison...June, 1887* (Manchester, N.H., 1887), 9

84. *Statistics Relating to the New Hampshire State Prison...for the Two Years Ending November 30, 1898* (Manchester, N.H., 1898), 21.

85. *Reports of the Warden, Physician and Chaplain of the New Hampshire State Prison* (Concord, N.H., 1847), 16.

86. *Prison Warden's Report (1877)*, 30-31.

87. *Prison Warden's Report (1868)*, 46-48.

88. *Annual Report of the Warden and Inspectors of the New Hampshire State Prison...June Session, 1869* (Manchester, N.H., 1869), 46.

89. *Prison Warden's Report (1880)*, 33.

90. *Statistics Relating to the New Hampshire State Prison...for the Two Years Ending November 30, 1906* (Bristol, N.H., n.d.), 7 and *Report of the Officers of the New Hampshire State Prison...for the Twenty One [sic] Months Ending August 31, 1908* (Penacook, N.H., n.d.), 42.

91. *Prison Warden's Report (1914)*, 33.

92. ALS, Samuel G. Berry, Warden and John Atwood, Chaplain of the New Hampshire State Prison, to Charles W. Brewster, Aug. 1855, New Hampshire Historical Society, Concord, N.H.

93. *Prison Warden's Report (1847)*, 15.

94. *Prison Warden's Report (1853)*, 19.

95. The chaplain made frequent complaints about the damage. See, for example, *Report of the Warden of the N.H. State Prison...June Session, 1856* (Concord, N.H., 1856), 23; *Prison Warden's Report (1857)*, 19; *Report of the*

Warden of the New-Hampshire State Prison...June Session, 1864 (Concord, N.H., 1864), 30-31; *Prison Warden's Report (1865)*, 25; and *Reports of the Warden and Inspectors of the New Hampshire State-Prison...June Session, 1878...* (Manchester, N.H., 1878), 30. In 1866 the chaplain complained of books marked with an "indecent picture or writing, too abusive and obscene to be read or seen by decent people," *Prison Warden's Report (1866)*, 36.

96. *A Catalogue of Books in the Library of the New Hampshrie State Prison, Concord, New Hampshire* (Manchester, N.H., 1881). In Box 1, Secretary of State. State Prison Papers, Div. of Records-Management and Archives, Concord, N.H.

97. *Prison Warden's Report (1912)*, 33.

98. Hosea Quinby, *The Prison Chaplaincy, and Its Experiences* (Concord, N.H., 1873), p. 28 and *Annual Report of the Warden and Inspectors of the New Hampshire State Prison...June Session, 1870* (Manchester, N.H., 1870), 35.

99. *Prison Warden's Report (1862)*, 39.

100. "Minute Book 1812-34," [5].

101. *Ibid.*, [11-12].

102. *Ibid.*, [33-34].

103. *Ibid.*, [58-59].

104. *Prison Warden's Report (1862)*, 10.

105. Every compilation of New Hampshire laws between 1815 and 1901 included the 30-day limit on solitary confinement. See, for example, the original law of June 19, 1812 in *Laws of the State of New Hampshire...* (Exeter, N.H., 1815), p. 147 and William M. Chase and Arthur H. Chase, comp. and ed., *The Public Statutes of the State of New Hampshire and General Laws in Force January 1, 1901* (Concord, N.H., 1900), p. 851. The only exception was the imposition of up to six months of solitary confinement for inmates serving a life sentence who assaulted the warden or guards or who attempted to escape. *The Revised Statutes of the State of New-Hampshire Passed December 23, 1842...* (Concord, N.H., 1843), p. 465.

106. *Prison Warden's Report (1869)*, 13.

107. Joseph L. Shaw, *New-Hampshire State Prison Cruelty Exposed: or, The Sufferings of Joseph L. Shaw, In That Institution in 1837, while John M'Daniel Was Warden* (Exeter, N.H., 1839), p. 16.

108. *Ibid.*, p. 17.

109. *Ibid.*, p. 26.

110. *Ibid.*, pp. 26-29.

111. *Ibid.*, p. 29.

112. *Ibid.*, p. 30.

113. *Journal of the Honorable Senate of the State of New-Hampshire...June 7, 1837* (Concord, N.H., 1837), 192, 207, and 263.

114. *Prison Warden's Report (1870)*, 8.

115. *Prison Warden's Report (1880)*, 7.

116. *Ibid.*, 7 and "Charges Made against Warden John C. Pilsbury by Burnham Wardwell," N.H. Council Chamber, July 21, 1880, MS, 19. Secretary of State. State Prison Papers, Div. of Records-Management and Archives, Concord, N.H.

117. *The People and New Hampshire Patriot*, July 22, 1880, Microfilm (Cambridge, Mass.).

118. See *Ibid.*; Edward D. Rand, *Closing Remarks of Hon. E.D. Rand at the State Prison Investigation: Concord, New Hampshire, Thursday, July 1, 1880* (Concord, N.H., 1880); Henry Robinson, "The New Hampshire State Prison," *Granite Monthly*, 23 (1897), 228-29; and *Concord Daily Monitor*, July 22, 1880, Microfilm (Cambridge, Mass.).

119. *Concord Daily Monitor*, July 22, 1880, Microfilm (Cambridge, Mass.).

120. *Ibid.*, July 1 and 22, 1880.

121. *Ibid.*, July 7 and *The People and New Hampshire Patriot*, July 22 and 29, 1880, Microfilm (Cambridge, Mass.).

122. *Prison Warden's Report (1881)*, 6.

123. *Prison Warden's Report (1882)*, 28-29.

124. *Prison Warden's Report (1886)*, 24.

125. *Prison Warden's Report (1906)*, 8.

126. See prison rules and by-laws of 1812 in "Minute Book 1812-34," [10-11 and 13].

127. ALS, Charles W. Brewster to Lewis N. and Charles H. Brewster, June 11, 1843, New Hampshire Historical Society, Concord, N.H.

128. For example, see E. Smith, *Nine Years among the Convicts*, p. 250 and *Reports of the Warden and Inspectors of the State Prison at Concord...December 1, 1890* (Manchester, N.H., 1891), 6.

129. For example, John D. Cray and Elam Lynds, both prison wardens in early nineteenth-century New York, were both former military officers, W. David Lewis, *From Newgate to Dannemora: The Rise of the Penitentiary in New York, 1796-1848* (Ithaca, N.Y., 1965), pp. 85-87.

130. *Prison Warden's Report (1869)*, 19.

131. *Prison Warden's Report (1879)*, 7.

132. Beverly A. Smith, "Military Training at New York's Elmira Reformatory, 1888-1920," *Federal Probation*, 52 (1988), 34.

133. *Ibid.*, 35.

134. "Minute Book 1812-34," [14].

135. Warden Joseph Mayo also mentioned the fact that Massachusetts and Rhode Island had both abolished parti-colored state prison uniforms. *Prison Warden's Report (1869)*, 15.

136. L.E. Richwagen describes the vivid contrast between the prison life depicted by Henry Robinson in 1897 in the *Granite Monthly* and prison life in 1924 by which time a number of significant reforms had been instituted. See L.E. Richwagen, "The New Hampshire State Prison," *Granite Monthly*, 56 (1924), 571-75.

137. *Prison Warden's Report (1906)*, 7.

138. *Prison Warden's Report (1908)*, 7 and see Ch. 49 "An Act in Relation to the Administration of the State Prison, and to Provide for Necessary Improvements and Repairs" in *Laws of the State of New Hampshire Passed January Session, 1907* (Concord, N.H., 1907), p. 49.

139. *Report of the Officers of the New Hampshire State Prison to the Governor and Council for the Two Years Ending August 31, 1910* (Bristol, N.H., n.d.), 5.

140. See "An Act providing for the regulation and government of the State Prison" (passed June 19, 1812) in *Laws of New Hampshire (1815)*, 147.

141. "Minute Book 1812-34," [21].

142. *Prison Warden's Report (1856)*, 20.

143. *Prison Warden's Report (1869)*, 14.

144. *Statistics Relating to the New Hampshire State Prison...for the Two Years Ending November 30, 1900* (Manchester, N.H., 1901), 21.

145. Alexander W. Pisciotta, "Scientific Reform: The 'New Penology' at Elmira, 1876-1900," *Crime and Delinquency*, 29 (1983), 613 and Rothman, *Conscience and Convenience: The Asylum and Its Alternatives in Progressive America* (Boston, 1980), pp. 33-35.

146. Pisciotta, "Scientific Reform," 619-30 and B. Smith, "Military Training at Elmira," 33-40.

147. Rothman, *Conscience and Convenience*, p. 33.

148. *Prison Warden's Report (1912)*, 30.

149. *Ibid.*, 16.

150. Pisciotta, "Scientific Reform," 619.

151. *Prison Warden's Report (1914)*, 5 and 15.

152. E. Smith, *Nine Years among the Convicts*, p. 50.

153. "Minute Book 1812-34," [12].

154. Eugene D. Genovese, *Roll, Jordan, Roll: The World the Slaves Made* (New York, 1974), pp. 63 and 545-49.

155. "Minute Book 1812-34," [28].

156. *Journal of the Honorable Senate and House of Representatives...June...1832* (Concord, N.H., 1832), 128.

157. *Prison Warden's Report (1847)*, 13.

158. *Prison Warden's Report (1866)*, 15.

159. *Prison Warden's Report (1868)*, 21-22.

160. *Prison Warden's Report (1869)*, 14.

161. *Ibid.*, 14.

162. *Prison Warden's Report (1871)*, 14.

163. Quinby, *Prison Chaplaincy*, p. 86.

164. *Ibid.*, p. 133.

165. See Charge Number 12, 17-20, and 43 in "Charges Made against Warden John C. Pilsbury, July 21, 1880."

166. *Prison Warden's Report (1874)*, 5.

167. *Statistics Relating to the New Hampshire State Prison...for the Two Years Ending November 30, 1902* (Manchester, N.H., 1902), 274.

168. *Prison Warden's Report (1906)*, 8.

169. *Ibid.*, 8.

170. "Minute Book 1812-34," [14-15].

171. Horatio Newhall, MS, Travel Diary, 1819, n.p., Dartmouth College Library cited in William N. Hosley, Jr., "The Founding of the Vermont State Prison in Windsor, 1807-1810," *Vermont History*, 52 (1984), 252.

172. Robinson, "New Hampshire State Prison," 217-18.

173. E. Smith, *Nine Years among the Convicts*, p. 240.

174. Robinson, "New Hampshire State Prison," 217-18 and *Journal of the House of Representatives of the State of New-Hampshire...June 1831* (Concord, N.H., 1831), 176-79.

175. *Prison Warden's Report (1868)*, 8 and *Prison Warden's Report (1869)*, 24.

176. *Prison Warden's Report (1870)*, 6.

177. *Prison Warden's Report (1874)*, 3-4.

178. *Prison Warden's Report (1878)*, 5.

179. *Journals of the Honorable Senate and House of Representatives of the State of New Hampshire, June Session, 1877* (Manchester, N.H., 1877), 556.

180. Robinson, "New Hampshire State Prison," 219 and Garvin, "Concord," 44.

181. *Specification of Materials to Be Provided and Labor Performed in the Erection and Completion of the New State Prison...In Compliance with the provisions [sic] of the Act of the Legislature Approved July 19, 1877* (Concord, N.H., 1878), pp. 30-30a in Box 2, Secretary of State. State Prison Papers, Div. of Records-Management and Archives, Concord, N.H.; and Robinson, "New Hampshire State Prison," 219-20.

182. "Auction Sale of Old New Hampshire State Prison April 12, 1881," Broadside, Box 1, Secretary of State. State Prison Papers, Div. of Records-Management and Archives, Concord, N.H.

183. Henry Robinson, "New Hampshire State Prison," 222. Nahum Robinson was warden of the new prison during the years 1894-96. He was also the father of Henry Robinson.

184. Affidavit of John G. Evans [?], Dec. 11, 1856, MS, Rufus Dow Papers, New Hampshire Historical Society, Concord, N.H.

185. It is not always possible to compare death rates between prison inmates and males age 12 to 79 years or females age 19 to 54 years. The federal census employed inconsistent measures over the years, so we are often left with an insufficiently differentiated population at risk. Nevertheless, it is possible to make some conclusions based on the information supplied by the census. It was not until 1883 that the Secretary of State of New Hampshire and the State Board of Health began compiling systematic records of death. Similar difficulties exist in trying to match up age and sex groups between the prison and the population at risk.

186. The disease, which is of an infectious, inflammatory nature, affects mainly the lungs, although it can affect the rest of the body. It is caused by a bacillus and is transmitted by breathing in infected droplets. The bacillus can survive for months in dried spittle not exposed to sunlight. "Tuberculosis," in Benjamin F. Miller and Claire B. Keane, *Encyclopedia and Dictionary of Medicine, Nursing, and Allied Health*, 3rd. Ed. (Philadelphia, 1983), pp. 1144-45.

187. McKelvey, *American Prisons*, p. 166.

188. *Prison Warden's Report (1852)*. In 1877 Prison Physician A.H. Crosby said the prison's health problems were "due to our wretched, ill-constructed, narrow, and contracted cells, damp in summer, cold in winter, and badly ventilated at all times, as the flues are entirely under the control of the inmates, who try to economize the little warmth they receive at the expense of their lungs." *Prison Warden's Report (1877)*, 34.

189.	"Dysentery" in Miller and Keane, *Encyclopedia and Dictionary of Medicine*, p. 347.

190.	*Prison Warden's Report (1852)*, 15.

191.	*Prison Warden's Report (1908)*, 44.

192.	Howard Kushner, *Self-Destruction in the Promised Land: A Psychocultural Biology of American Suicide* (New Brunswick, N.J., 1989), p. 32.

193.	*Ibid.*, pp. 39, 44, and 48.

194.	*Ibid.*, pp. 52-61.

195.	*Ibid.*, p. 105 and Ronald W. Maris, *Pathways to Suicide: A Survey of Self-Destructive Behaviors* (Baltimore, 1981), pp. 269-70. The methods of self-destruction employed by the 16 "successful suicides" in the sample were as follows: eight hanged themselves in their cells, one swallowed lime and ground glass, two cut their throats, one drowned himself in his night bucket, one jumped off a height, and for three the method is not listed.

196.	*Prison Warden's Report (1855)*, 23.

197.	*Prison Warden's Report (1877)*, 34-35.

198.	*Report of the Warden of the N.H. State Prison...June Session, 1861* (Concord, N.H., 1861), 9 and 28.

199.	*Statistics Relating to the New Hampshire State Prison...for the Two Years Ending November 30, 1904* (Concord, N.H., n.d.), 301.

200.	*Prison Warden's Report (1856)*, 20.

201.	*Prison Warden's Report (1874)*, 21.

202.	John D'Emilio and Estelle B. Freedman, *Intimate Matters: A History of Sexuality in America* (New York, 1988), pp. 68 and 115-16 and Kushner, *Self-Destruction in the Promised Land*, p. 44.

203.	D'Emilio and Freedman, *Intimate Matters*, p. 206.

204.	Hawkins and Alpert, *American Prison Systems*, p. 275.

205.	Anthony M. Scacco, Jr., *Rape in Prison* (Springfield, Ill., 1975), pp. 16-18 and 30-31.

206.	Hawkins and Alpert, *American Prison Systems*, p. 279 and Scacco, *Rape in Prison*, p. 43.

207.	Hawkins and Alpert, *American Prison Systems*, p. 276.

208.	Daniel Lockwood, *Prison Sexual Violence* (New York, 1980), p. 49.

209.	Scacco, *Rape in Prison*, p. 81.

210.	*Ibid.*, pp. 66 and 83 and Lockwood, *Prison Sexual Violence*, pp. 30-31.

211.	Scacco, *Rape in Prison*, p. 66 and Lockwood, *Prison Sexual Violence*, p. 153.

212. Hawkins and Alpert, *American Prison System*, p. 310.

213. *Ibid.*, p. 311.

214. "Minute Book 1812-34," [30].

215. Nicole H. Rafter, *Partial Justice* (Boston, 1985), p. 4.

216. *Prison Warden's Report (1867)*, 9 and *Prison Warden's Report (1869)*, 17.

217. *Prison Warden's Report (1852)*, 9.

218. *Prison Warden's Report (1853)*, 14.

219. Rafter, *Partial Justice*, p. 10.

220. *Prison Warden's Report (1871)*, 8.

221. Ralph Arditi et al., "The Sexual Segregation of American Prisons," *Yale Law Journal*, 82 (1973), 1231. In 1882 the warden lamented the fact that the prison had to hire outside help to do the cooking and washing for the prison officers because there were no female inmates to do the job. *Prison Warden's Report (1882)*, 6.

222. ALS, Rufus Dow to Noah Marston [?], Aug. 17, 1852, Rufus Dow Papers, New Hampshire Historical Society, Concord, N.H.

223. *Prison Warden's Report (1852)*, 10 and *Prison Warden's Report (1853)*, 14.

224. "Charges Made Against John C. Pilsbury, July 21, 1880," 6-8.

225. Rand, *Closing Remarks at State Prison Investigation*, p. 7.

226. There were a record eight female inmates in the prison in 1869. *Prison Warden's Report (1869)*, 17.

227. *Prison Warden's Report (1870)*, 46.

228. *Specification of Materials New Prison*, pp. 54-55.

229. *Prison Warden's Report (1906)*, 11.

230. Estelle B. Freedman, *Their Sisters' Keepers: Women's Prison Reform in America, 1830-1930* (Ann Arbor, Mich., 1981), p.46.

231. *Ibid.*, p. 47.

232. Rafter, *Partial Justice*, p. 23.; Freedman, "Sentiment and Discipline: Women's Prison Experiences in Nineteenth Century America," *Prologue*, 16 (1984), 250; and Rafter, "Hard Times: Custodial Prisons for Women and the Example of the New York State Prison for Women at Auburn, 1893-1933," in Rafter and Elizabeth A. Stanko, *Judge, Lawyer, Victim, Thief: Women, Gender Roles, and Criminal Justice* ([Boston], 1982), p. 247.

233. Rafter, "Hard Times," p. 238.

234. Freedman, *Their Sisters' Keepers*, p. 60.

235. Ayers, *Vengeance and Justice*, p. 200.

236. *Prison Warden's Report (1869)*, 46.

237. ALS, [Warden] Frank S. Dodge to [Governor] Hon. Natt Head, Jan. 3, 1880, Box 1, Secretary of State. State Prison Papers, Div. of Records-Management and Archives, Concord, N.H.
238. Freedman, *Their Sisters' Keepers*, pp. 15-17.
239. Rand, *Closing Remarks at State Prison Investigation*, p. 10.
240. Carleton, *Politics and Punishment*, p. 12.

Chapter VI

Punishment in New Hampshire, 1812-1914:
Criminal Justice Outcomes

At 11 p.m. on the night of December 10, 1819 a 32-year old cooper named William Holland broke into William Jones's store in Portsmouth and stole two gallons of molasses worth $1. For this crime, Holland was sentenced to four years of hard labor in the state prison in February 1820 and served his full term. Holland had previously served a five-year sentence for larceny from 1813 through 1818.[1] On November 2, 1886 a 70-year old Irish immigrant named Daniel Crowley, residing in Portsmouth, poured kerosene on his wife, Mary, and set her on fire. Mary became "sick and distempered in her body...and was grievously injured dangerously wounded and mortally burned." The unfortunate woman "languished" for 18 days and died. Crowley was sentenced for second degree manslaughter and given a year and a half in the state prison which he served.[2]

In this chapter we will attempt to make sense of punishment and see if the above cases were anomalous or typical. We will analyze sentencing disparities and what they mean for criminal justice in New Hampshire 1812-1914. We will analyze sentences passed versus sentences actually served in the context of type of crime committed. This should help us to determine the meaning of punishment. Just as important as sentence and sentence served is the mode of exit from the prison. There were a number of alternatives to simply being discharged from prison at the end of one's sentence. This too will help us understand the meaning of punishment and how it changed over time. We can trace the impact of various reform measures taken in the nineteenth century. Also in this chapter we will discuss recidivism and what the statistics say about the success or failure of punishment in New Hampshire between 1812 and 1914. Was justice enforced more harshly at some times than others? What was the role of capital punishment? We will provide an analysis of outcomes or the legal response to the crimes described in Chapter Three.

The best sources of information on sentences passed and served and method of exit are the prison registers, annual prison warden's reports, and court records. The "Register of Convicts 1812-1883" and its successors, "[New Hampshire State] Prison Records [1874-1915]" and "New Hampshire State Prison: Record of Gain and Loss in Population [1905-36]," are the official record of most prisoners' date of entry and exit from the state prison for the years 1812-1914. The registers usually say whether an inmate was pardoned, paroled, or if the sentence was commuted. Unfortunately, the registers do not always provide this information and we are given no clue as to why a prisoner was given, say, a five-year sentence but served only four years. Occasionally, there is no date of exit listed. Sometimes the published annual prison warden's reports provide the missing information. From the 1850's onward these reports contained a "register of convicts" in abbreviated form. Usually, each inmate's offense, age, birthplace, and sentence was listed. The reports do not tell us how an inmate left the prison. His or her name was simply dropped from the register in the next annual report. It is possible to match up most of the names between the unpublished registers and the register published in the annual reports. In the 1900's the reports began to include helpful separate registers of prisoners paroled, pardoned, etc. Court records supply much valuable information here too. Not only do they describe the offense in some detail, they also usually list the sentence passed on the offender. Thus, court records describe the cause of a person's imprisonment and the legal system's response.

Prison sentences many years long were standard practice in nineteenth-century America. Long sentences satisfied both advocates of retribution and reformers who believed in the possibilities of rehabilitation.[3] Reformers of that era believed that the prison experience would reform the criminal and eventually put an end to crime. Thus, long prison sentences were written into a number of state laws across the country in the early nineteenth century.[4] According to David J. Rothman, over 40% of the inmates at the Auburn, New York penitentiary in 1835 were serving sentences of over five years in length. Most of these sentences were imposed for property crimes rather than crimes of violence.[5] In antebellum Ohio the average sentence for robbery was 7.6 years, for forgery 7 years, and for burglary or larceny 9 years.[6] On the average, sentences imposed on the inmates of the New Hampshire State Prison were shorter by several years for the same crimes compared to those cited by Rothman.

At the broadest level, the length of prison sentences in New Hampshire between 1812 and 1900 was very consistent (see Table 43). The mean overall sentence was 3.8 years. (Mean sentences have not been calculated for the years 1901-14 because indeterminate sentencing went into effect in 1901, making such a calculation impossible).[7] Means have been calculated for sentences passed for every decade between 1812 and 1901 and for type of crime. One should be aware that information on the sentence passed was missing in some cases; these have been left out of the calculations. In addition, eleven life sentences and six death sentences too have been left out

Table 43

New Hampshire State Prison Sentences, 1812-1899 by type of Crime

Decade	Mean Sentence in Years Type of Crime: Property	Violence	Moral	Other
1810's	3.0	3.3		2.0
1820's	3.8	3.0		3.5
1830's	4.4	1.0		
1840's	3.8	5.7		2.0
1850's	4.1	3.8		
1860's	3.2	6.7		2.5
1870's	3.8	4.8	1.3	3.0
1880's	2.9	10.3	2.0	1.1
1890's	2.4	10.0	2.0	1.0
OVERALL MEAN:	3.5	5.4	1.8	2.1

Decade	Mean Sentence in Years Total Mean and (N)
1810's	3.0 (47)
1820's	3.7 (31)
1830's	4.3 (36)
1840's	4.0 (34)

Decade	Mean Sentence in Years Total Mean and (N)
1850's	4.1 (34)
1860's	3.6 (65)
1870's	3.8 (107)
1880's	3.5 (141)
1890's	4.1 (118)
OVERALL MEAN:	3.8 (513)

Note: New Hampshire implemented an indeterminate sentencing law in 1901 which made it impossible to calculate mean sentences for the 1900's and 1910's.

Source: Court Bills and Indictments, 1812-99, Rockingham Cty., MS, Div. of Records-Management and Archives, Concord, N.H.; Court Bills and Indictments, 1870-99, Strafford Cty., MS, Justice and Administration Building, Dover, N.H.; "Register of Convicts 1812-1883" and "[N.H. State] Prison Records [1874-1914]," both MS, Div. of Records-Management and Archives, Concord, N.H.

since they are impossible to fit into calculations of the mean. Sentences have been broken down into broad categories of crime to see how the courts punished different types of crime. The overall steadiness of the length of prison sentences masks some important differences when analyzed in terms of type of crime.

Property and violent crime sentencing patterns diverged. This is contrary to Rothman's findings.[8] Property crime sentences in New Hampshire rose from a mean of 3.0 years in the 1810's to a height of 4.4 years in the 1830's and thereafter gently declined to a mean of 2.4 years by the 1890's (see Table 43). Mean sentences for violent crime started out at 3.3 years in the 1810's but thereafter exhibited a very uneven pattern of increase and decrease. The general direction for punishment of violent crime was longer sentences. The peak came in the 1880's when the mean hit 10.3 years (see Table 43). Thus, property crime was punished fairly consistently while violent crime provoked inconsistent but increasingly severe sanctions.

Property crimes were sometimes punished with severity. The first life sentence imposed on a convict in the sample was for the burglary of $47 worth of clothing from a house in Portsmouth in 1818. However, the burglar was pardoned after serving only two years in prison.[9] The first life sentence for a violent crime was passed in the 1830's.[10] There were far fewer convictions for violent than for property crime so the proportion of life sentences handed down for violent crimes was much higher than for property crimes. Because there were so many convictions for property crime in comparison to violent crime, some of the variability of sentence means was evened out. The volatility of sentences for violent crime was probably exaggerated due to their relatively small number. A smaller number of cases means that the average length of sentence is affected more strongly by a few exceptionally long or short sentences than is the case for property crime where the sheer number of cases tends to even out the mean value.

Longer sentences for violent crime roughly parallel increasing rates of violent crime (see Tables 43-44). Possibly, the perception of increasingly high levels of violent crime provoked feelings of retribution from the Supreme and Superior courts of New Hampshire. In turn, the increasingly tough punishments may have provoked higher levels of violent crime. As far back as the 1760's Cesare Beccaria observed the brutalizing effect of harsh punishments on the general population.[11] From the 1880's through the 1910's sentences of a decade or more for violent crime became increasingly common. Truly long sentences were a post-Civil War phenomenon in New Hampshire.

Moral offenders were given consistently short sentences after the recriminalization of moral transgressions in the post-Civil War era. In the late nineteenth century moral crimes were punished with much greater severity in states other than New Hampshire, for example, in California. In New Hampshire sentences for moral crimes averaged 1.8 years; in California they averaged over 15 years (see Table 43). Friedman and Percival cite a case of sodomy in 1907 where the convicted offender was given a sentence of 25 years in prison.[12] It is ironic that New Hampshire, which had in Puritan times considered sodomy and adultery to be capital crimes, now considered such offenses worthy of only one to three years in prison.[13] Sentences passed for "other" crimes were a little uneven since this category was a miscellaneous grab bag. "Other" crimes were most common in the 1880's when the tramp

Table 44

Seacoast New Hampshire Felony Incarceration Rates, 1812-1914

| Decade | Pop. | Type of Crime (N) and Rate/100,000 Pop. | | |
		Property	Violence	Moral
1810's	50,175	(42) 84	(4) 8	
1820's	55,107	(26) 47	(3) 5	
1830's	44,325	(34) 77	(2) 5	
1840's	45,771	(26) 57	(7) 15	
1850's	49,194	(28) 57	(6) 16	
1860's	50,122	(53) 106	(10) 20	
1870's	77,533	(93) 120	(7) 9	
1880's	84,622	(96) 116	(18) 21	
1890's	88,002	(85) 97	(28) 32	
1900's	90,455	(101) 112	(16) 18	
1910's	91,139	(55) 60	(19) 21	

| Decade | Pop. | Type of Crime (N) and Rate/100,000 Pop. | |
		Other	Total
1810's	50,175	(1) 2	(47) 94
1820's	55,107	(2) 4	(31) 56
1830's	44,325		(36) 81
1840's	45,771	(1) 2	(34) 74

| Decade | Pop. | Type of Crime (N) and Rate/100,000 Pop. | |
		Other	Total
1850's	49,194		(34) 69
1860's	50,122	(2) 4	(65) 130
1870's	77,533	(4) 5	(107) 138
1880's	84,622	(24) 28	(141) 167
1890's	88,002	(2) 2	(118) 134
1900's	90,455	(8) 9	(129) 143
1910's	91,139	(2) 2	(78) 85

Note: Rates before 1870 calculated with Rockingham County population only because Strafford County court records available only for 1870-1914.

Source: Court Bills and Indictments, 1812-1914, Rockingham Cty., MS, Div. of Records-Management and Archives, Concord, N.H.; Court Bills and Indictments, 1870-1914, Strafford Cty., MS, Justice and Administration Building, Dover, N.H.; "Register of Convicts 1812-1883," "[N.H. State] Prison Records [1874-1915]," both MS, Div. of Records-Management and Archives, Concord, N.H.; and *Prison Warden's Reports*, 1813-1914.

law of 1878 was put into practice.[14] The law provided for only a brief sojourn in the state prison, a circumstance accounting for the mean sentence of 1.1 years (see Table 43).

The post-Civil War era witnessed significant changes in sentencing procedures in response to the "new penology" movement. By the 1860's problems with the state prison system in America were too visible to be ignored: prisons were crowded, conditions were poor, inmates were usually not reformed, and crime certainly had not been eliminated. Such were the findings of prison investigations.[15] The new penology movement was promoted by reformers in an effort to introduce professional standards to prison management. The new penology was based upon the idea of conditional release rather than fixed sentences. In other words, release from prison should now depend on evidence of rehabilitation rather than simply serving the allotted time.[16] Sentences grew longer in response to the idea that more time in prison was a prerequisite for successful reformation. Prisons were meant to rehabilitate convicts and if the process took longer than the court originally thought necessary, sentences should be increased to ensure the desired goal.[17]

New Hampshire judges were not alone in passing longer sentences for violent crime in the late nineteenth century. Eric H. Monkkonen discovered three peaks in the 1860's and 1870's when Ohio judges imposed longer sentences on convicts. He traces a generally upward trend in long prison sentences in the 1880's.[18] Friedman and Percival describe sentencing in Alameda County, California between 1870 and 1910 as subject to ebbs and flows. The sample of New Hampshire prison inmates shows little overall increase between 1860 and 1900 except in the area of violent crimes. Excluding the death sentence, which we will discuss later, sentences passed for violent crime increased dramatically in length. They rose from a mean of 3.8 years in the 1850's to 6.7 years in the 1860's, dropped to 4.8 years in the next decade and then soared to 10.3 years in the 1880's and 10.0 years in the 1890's (see Table 43). Why did this happen?

It is likely the heavier sentences passed for violent crime in late nineteenth-century New Hampshire were due to a) increased concern over violent crime and b) judicial response to a perceived dilution of the criminal laws by advocates of the new penology. Although many reformers favored longer sentences for the purposes of rehabilitating criminals, the provision of both a maximum and minimum length could be seen by hardline judges as weakening the certainty of punishment. Also, some of the more onerous aspects of prison life such as striped uniforms and rules of silence were being eliminated in favor of more humane reformatory measures designed to reform rather than merely punish prisoners. As we saw in Chapter Three, the rate of incarceration for violent crime in seacoast New Hampshire shot up to 32 per 100,000 population in the 1890's. This coincides with the longest sentences (see Tables 43-44). No written evidence is available that suggests that New Hampshire judges were more alarmed at violent crime than before but the increase in the number of convictions does coincide neatly with the increased length of sentences for violent crime.[19]

In the post-Civil War era a number of states enacted laws which diluted the fixed sentences given by judges. These measures included probation, commutation, and the indeterminate sentence. New Hampshire passed a commutation law in 1867 which provided for the deduction of a portion of the inmate's sentence in exchange for good behavior.[20] It is possible judges might have reacted against what they perceived to be a dilution of their power by passing longer sentences. In California, judges passed long sentences to counteract the "good time" laws enacted between 1870 and 1910.[21] Even today, the judge passing a sentence on a convicted criminal cannot tell how long the convict will actually stay in prison. Currently, "most convicted criminals do not serve even half of their sentences in confinement" according to John J. DiIulio, Jr.[22] Even murderers average only around seven years.[23]

The ethnic and social background of convicted felons may also have worked against any real shortening of prison sentences passed by the courts. Although most of the New Hampshire State Prison inmates were mostly white native-born males, the presence of immigrants was becoming more noticeable. The largest groups of post-Civil war immigrants were Canadians, Irish, Germans, and Italians (see Table 28). Most inmates came from a lower class background (see Table 32 and Appendix). Rothman blames the continued imposition of long sentences during the era of new penology in part on the fact that the criminal population was increasingly of an immigrant and lower class character.[24] Criminologists have long recognized that attributes such as race, sex, age, and socioeconomic status play an important role in sentencing.[25]

Having a record of prior convictions can also influence a judge's decision to pass a longer sentence. In Alameda County, California a second conviction for petty larceny meant a term in the state prison and a felony record, even though the crime itself was no more serious in effect than before.[26] It is likely this was also the case in New Hampshire since some of the entries in the prison ledgers specifically mention the fact of an inmate's prior incarceration at the same institution or a prison in another state.

Another factor in sentencing was the introduction of indeterminate sentencing laws. The concept of the indeterminate sentence was first put into effect at the reformatory at Elmira, New York in 1877.[27] Under indeterminate sentencing, the judge imposed a sentence that covered a range of time but was not fixed. A convict could be sentenced to, say, two to five years rather than a fixed term of three years. The theory behind indeterminate sentencing was that it was up to the prisoner whether to make the sentence served longer or shorter by exhibiting good behavior and a reformed attitude. This was supposed to help the process of rehabilitation by giving the inmate an incentive to reform. In practice, the indeterminate sentence became a method of keeping inmates longer in prison. The indeterminate sentence became common in the twentieth century as the rehabilitative model of prison justice took over.[28] With indeterminate sentencing, there were more options for release. Prisons began to function under what Rothman calls "medical time" when psychiatrists, social workers, and other professionals began to treat criminal behavior as a curable disease.[29]

Instead of releasing a convict when his or her fixed sentence was up, the indeterminate sentence gave prison professionals the option of keeping a convict in prison until the upper limit of his or her sentence if he or she showed unsatisfactory evidence of rehabilitation.[30] Inmates soon became aware of this fact and learned how to show evidence of rehabilitation to gain an early release.[31] The use of probation and parole in conjunction with the indeterminate sentence was also a source of power exercised by the warden over the inmates. The warden had the power to recommend parole release in most prisons. This gave him great power over unruly inmates who could be threatened by the warden in retaliation for misbehavior.[32]

At no point except for the 1840's during the period 1812-1914 did the mean sentence actually served by the inmates in the sample equal the mean sentence passed by the court (see Tables 43 and 45). On average, inmates served 2.8 years while being sentenced to 3.8 years. It is possible to discern several trends lying behind these numbers.

Whereas the mean sentence passed slowly increased, the mean mean sentence served gradually declined (see Table 45). The length of sentences served rose from the 1810's through 1840's, paralleling the rise in length of sentences passed. After 1849 the patterns diverged. Sentences of approximately the same mean length continued to be passed but convicts in the New Hampshire State Prison began serving less time (see Table 45). Why did this happen? Much of the answer lies in a brief analysis of sentences served by type of crime.

Those inmates convicted of property crimes began serving slightly longer sentences during the years 1812-39 (see Table 45). This pattern resembled the longer sentences imposed on property offenders by the courts. Abruptly, the length of sentence served decreased from a mean of 3.4 years in the 1830's to a mean of 2.3 years in the 1840's (see Table 45). Sentences passed by the court exhibit a milder decline from 4.4 years in the 1830's to 3.8 years in the 1840's (see Table 43). Property crimes made up nearly 80% of the cases, thus the pattern exhibited by property crime sentences is that of the majority of cases in the sample. After a slight increase in the 1850's, sentences served for property crimes stayed more or less even through the 1910's.

Sentences served by those convicted of violent crimes were fully as erratic

Table 45

New Hampshire State Prison Sentences Served, 1812-1914
by Type of Crime

Decade	Mean Sentence Served in Years Type of Crime: Property	Violence	Moral	Other
1810's	2.8	3.3		1.0
1820's	3.2	3.0		3.0
1830's	3.4	4.0		
1840's	2.3	9.0		4.0
1850's	2.8	3.0		
1860's	2.7	3.2		1.5
1870's	2.7	2.0	1.0	2.0
1880's	2.5	5.6	2.0	1.1
1890's	2.3	5.1	2.0	1.0
1900's	2.4	5.1	2.3	1.1
1910's	2.0	2.8	1.0	2.0
OVERALL MEAN:	2.0	2.8	1.0	2.0

Decade	Mean Sentence Served in Years Total Mean and (N)
1810's	2.8 (47)

Decade	Mean Sentence Served in Years Total Mean and (N)
1820's	3.2 (31)
1830's	3.8 (36)
1840's	4.0 (34)
1850's	2.8 (34)
1860's	2.7 (65)
1870's	2.6 (107)
1880's	2.6 (141)
1890's	2.9 (118)
1900's	2.6 (129)
1910's	2.1 (78)
TOTAL OVERALL MEAN:	2.8 (820)

Source: Court Bills and Indictments, 1812-1914, Rockingham Cty., MS, Div. of Records-Management and Archives, Concord, N.H.; Court Bills and Indictments, 1870-1914, Strafford Cty., MS, Justice and Administration Building, Dover, N.H.; and "Register of Convicts 1812-1883," "[N.H. State] Prison Records [1874-1915]," and "N.H. State Prison: Record of Gain and Loss in Population [1905-36]," all MS, Div. of Records-Management and Archives, Concord, N.H.

as the sentences passed by the courts but they followed a different pattern. The terms served in the state prison for violent crimes shot up from a mean of 4.0 years in the 1830's to a mean of 9.0 years in the 1840's (see Table 45). Persons serving sentences for violent crime in the 1840's came closest to the lengthy sentences served by state prison inmates in other states discussed by

Rothman (see Table 45).[33] In the 1850's sentences served for violent crime plunged to 3.0 years and continued to an all-time low of 2.0 years in the 1870's. As will be seen in a discussion of capital punishment, shorter mean sentences served for violent crimes did not necessarily mean that punishment was becoming milder. In the 1880's mean time served for violent crime shot up from 2.0 to 5.6 years, stayed fairly steady through the 1900's and then dropped to 2.8 years in the 1910's (see Table 45).

Mean sentences served for "other" crimes fluctuated between one and three years, which is unsurprising considering the eclectic nature of such crimes. The means of sentence passed and sentence served both converged at 1.1 years during the 1880's. Nearly all of these sentences were for tramps. Perhaps because sentences were already so short, they could not be made much shorter. Some inmates served less than the one-year minimum at various points in the prison's history but nearly all of these short terms were for crimes other than conviction for being a tramp (see Table 45). After all, the tramp law was not passed until 1878.[34] Crimes of morality made up a very small proportion of the sample. Between 1870 and 1914 those serving time for moral offenses served a mean sentence of 1.7 years. The low points were the absolute minimum sentence of 1.0 year in the 1870's and 1910's; the high points ranged between 2.0 and 2.3 years for the decades in between (see Table 45).

The introduction of indeterminate sentencing in New Hampshire in 1901 did not result in longer sentences served - at le.st through 1914. This is contrary to the findings of other historians.[35] However, we have not traced the influence of the indeterminate sentence beyond 1914.[36]

Most inmates did not serve long sentences. Most people sentenced to hard labor at the state prison could expect to get out after serving 2.8 years which was one year less than their original mean sentence. No doubt even a one-year sentence seemed too long considering the poor living conditions, hard and dangerous work, and high death rates which characterized life at the state prison. Few people served very long sentences.

The longest sentences served in the prison between 1812 and 1914 were three convictions for second degree murder. Joseph E. Kelley served 23 years out of 30 years for the April 16, 1897 murder of Joseph A. Stickney in Somersworth, using a policeman's billy club and a razor.[37] Joseph H. Otis too served 23 years out of a 30-year sentence. This was for the murder of Peter F. Duvall in Durham on March 11, 1880 with a blow to the skull from a club.[38] On September 1, 1843 Alfred Hill of Epping choked, beat, and threw eight-year old Ellen Delana down on the ground before smashing her skull with a stick. She lingered in agony for three weeks before dying. This awful crime was compounded by the fact that Hill had also raped the girl. He was convicted of only second degree murder and sentenced to life in prison. Hill was pardoned after serving 21 years.[39] Several other inmates were given life sentences but their actual time in prison was cut short by death or pardon. Very few inmates actually served a sentence of more than nine years. No doubt this helped to maintain the young median age of 26.0 years. Most older inmates were convicted at an advanced age. Only a few men like Hill, Otis, or Kelley grew old in the prison.

There may have been a connection between the mode of exit from the state prison and the fact that a majority of the inmates in the sample did not serve the full sentence handed down by the courts.

The most common method of release was to be discharged from prison upon expiration of one's sentence. Nearly half (45.5% or 373 out of 820 cases) of the sample followed this pattern (see Table 46). This form of release was the most common practice only in certain decades. Even in the first decade of operation, no more than 83.0% of the inmates left the prison by serving a full sentence (see Table 46). Thereafter, the proportion of inmates who were discharged in this manner declined steadily until only 38.2% were so discharged in the 1840's (see Table 46). From the 1850's through the 1890's, convicts discharged upon completion of a full sentence vacillated between 32.3% and 71.6% of the inmate population (see Table 46). The introduction of indeterminate sentencing and parole in 1901 essentially eliminated this mode of exit. The old fixed prison sentence did not fit into the new Progressive scheme of prisoner rehabilitation.

The second-most common mode of exit from the prison was to be pardoned: 18.3% or 150 out of 820 cases were pardoned between 1812 and 1914 (see Table 46). A pardon involved the removal of legal consequences for an offender's actions.[40] Pardons were not a new phenomenon in 1812. At the state level, the governor or governor and council usually had the power to grant pardons to convicted criminals. The use of pardons increased throughout the nineteenth century.[41]

The primary use of pardons in nineteenth-century New Hampshire appears to have been the mitigation of long prison sentences and to ease overcrowding in the prison. The mean sentence length increased steadily from the 1810's through 1840's (see Table 43). It was precisely during this era that pardons jumped from 8.5% of the prison exits to 26.5% (see Table 46).

Kathleen D. Moore suggests a number of reasons for the granting of pardons have been considered throughout the history of crime and

Table 46

New Hampshire State Prison: Methods of Inmate Release, 1812-1914

Decade:	1810's	1820's	1830's	1840's
Method of Release (%)				
Discharge	83.0%	67.7%	61.1%	38.2%
Pardon	8.5%	12.9%	30.6%	26.5%
Commutation				
Parole				
Death*	2.1%	3.2%	5.6%	11.8%
Escape		3.2%	2.8%	
Transfer State Hospital				
Remand	2.1%	9.7%		
Remit				20.6%
Execution				
Unknown	4.3%	3.2%		
TOTAL %:	100%	100%	100%	100%
TOTAL (N):	47	31	36	34

Decade:	1850's	1860's	1870's	1880's
Method of Release (%)				

Decade:	1850's	1860's	1870's	1880's
Method of Release (%)				
Discharge	47.1%	32.3%	42.1%	71.6%
Pardon	44.1%	43.1%	29.9%	14.2%
Commutation	2.9%	12.3%	9.3%	
Parole				
Death*	5.9%	4.6%	8.4%	4.3%
Escape				
Transfer State Hospital				
Remand				
Remit				
Execution		1.5%	1.9%	0.7%
Unknown		6.2%	8.4%	9.2%
TOTAL %:	100%	100%	100%	100%
TOTAL (N):	34	65	107	141

Decade:	1890's	1900's	1910's
Method of Release (%)			
Discharge	67.8%	10.9%	1.3%

Decade:	1890's	1900's	1910's
Method of Release (%)			
Pardon	11.9%	6.2%	6.4%
Commutation		0.8%	
Parole		69.8%	67.9%
Death*	5.1%		1.3%
Escape			
Transfer State Hospital		7.8%	3.8%
Remand		7.8%	
Remit			
Execution			
Unknown	15.3%	4.7%	19.2%
TOTAL %:	100%	100%	100%
TOTAL (N):	118	129	78

*Includes death by suicide, industrial accident,and natural causes but not execution.
Source: "Register of Convicts 1812-1883," "[N.H. State] Prison Records [1874-1915]," and "N.H. State Prison: Record of Gain and Loss in Population [1905-36]," all MS, Div. of Records-Management and Archives, Concord, N.H.; and *Prison Warden's Reports*, 1852-1914.

punishment: pity, sympathy, youth, old age, infirmity, ill health, or imminent death of the offender.[42] Governor Samuel Bell provides insight into the reasons the governor would grant a pardon or remit a prison sentence. He remitted five sentences because three inmates were incurably ill, one suffered from "mental derangement" and another was well-behaved. This last was also supported by petitions for his release by his "aged father and an [sic] helpless family."[43]   Pity, if not guilt on behalf of the state, led Governor Hill to pardon Joseph L. Shaw in 1837 after Shaw lost both legs to frostbite while enduring punishment in solitary confinement.[44] Inmates or their family and friends could start the pardon process by petitioning the governor. Unfortunately, very few documents tell us why a governor chose to pardon the inmates in the sample.

One tactic was to persuade the governor to grant a pardon was to enlist the testimony of other parties on one's own behalf. The case of John Williams alias John Brooks is a good example. On July 4, 1900 Williams, age 29, and two friends apparently went on a shooting spree in Dover. Williams was convicted of second degree murder for the shooting of John McNally with a pistol. He was also convicted of attempted murder when he "grievously wounded" Joseph Gagnon with another pistol shot. Williams was given 50 years in prison for these crimes. His accomplices were not sent to prison.[45] On December 13, 1911 a lawyer wrote to Governor Robert P. Bass that according to his investigations of the past six years, Williams was innocent because his was a case of mistaken identity.[46] Williams's mother wrote to the governor claiming that her son was "wrongfully convicted" of the killing. She played for the governor's sympathy by writing that her son "has become sick and weak in body and mind, and that further confinement at said State Prison will entirely destroy his health."[47] She may well have been right. Also laid before Governor Bass was an affidavit of a witness who claimed that Williams "was not either place and I did not see Williams at ten oclock [sic] with the others." The witness claimed that the police had forced him to testify against Williams.[48] A similar account dated June 10, 1911 was also sent to Governor Bass from the deathbed of another witness.[49] On July 24, 1912 a lawyer wrote to the governor and reported that he had "great reason to feel that there is great merit in behalf of Williams." He also reported that Williams had "a well defined tubercular shoulder."[50] Unfortunately, the prison records do not indicate whether Williams was pardoned. How and when he left the prison is unknown.[51]

It apparently was never too early to try for a reduced prison sentence. A 30-year old shoemaker named John Keating was convicted of breaking and entering into Ira B. Moore's store in Rochester on August 22, 1894 with the intent to steal. Keating was given two years in the state prison.[52] While still in the Dover Jail awaiting removal to the state prison, Keating wrote to the judge asking for a three to six month reduction in his sentence on the grounds that if released then "I will be liberated at a season of the year when the opportunities of procuring honorable employment are more numerous than at the beginning of Autumn."[53] Keating's appeal fell on deaf ears and he served a full two years before release.[54]

Pardons interfered with the role of the prison as a money-making institution. Warden Lawson Cooledge disapproved of the increasingly frequent granting of pardons because it reduced the size of the prison workforce, hence reducing the prison's income yet it was understood that a pardon was "granted more for the purpose of restoring the rights of a citizen, than a reduction of time."[55]

Prison administrators also condemned the use of the pardon because it was bad for morale. The first such objection was registered by Warden Rufus Dow in the 1852 annual report. Dow said, "The free use of the pardoning power is, in my judgment, detrimental to good order and discipline. With such feelings it is hard for them [the inmates] to yield to the rules required in an institution like this."[56] Dow even declared the hope of a pardon to be "one of the principal hindrances to improvement among us." The unpardoned inmate "becomes sad, sour, sullen and when all of his long years have passed over him, he leaves his Prison home uninstructed and uninformed."[57] Warden Joseph Mayo wrestled with this issue repeatedly between 1866 and 1870. On the negative side, Mayo said that too many inmates expected a pardon. The result was poor morale: "so long is he [the inmate] miserably and unfit for anything...impatient, discontented, and unable to set himself to any profitable labor...morose and wretched."[58] Mayo also considered the pardon "so cautiously and judiciously exercised by the Executive has produced happy and salutary effects."[59]

According to Michael S. Hindus, pardons were the main form of early release from prison until the introduction of the indeterminate sentence. Their effect was to give the warden increased control over the inmates since he had control over who was made eligible for pardon although the remarks by the wardens quoted above suggest the opposite.[60] Sometimes pardons were used as a countermeasure to unequal or excessive sentences. The longer the sentence, the greater the chance of a pardon, according to Hindus.[61] This does seem to be true for New Hampshire. Violent offenders had longer sentences but were proportionately granted more pardons than property offenders. For example, in the 1830's 50% of the violent offenders were pardoned versus only 29.4% of the property offenders. In the 1880's 33.3%

of the violent offenders were pardoned versus only 13.5% of the property offenders (see Table 46).

One ironic result of pardoning was that a person sentenced to life in prison not only had a greater chance than other inmates of receiving a pardon, he or she also served on average less time than someone sentenced to 10 years or more. This happened in Massachusetts between 1807 and 1865 according to Hindus.[62]   Samuel Walker ways that those given life sentences in Massachusetts during the period 1828-66 served on average seven and three quarters years before being pardoned.[63]

The use of pardons began to decline precipitously in the 1870's (see Table 46). By the 1900's only 6.2% of the inmates in the sample left the prison via pardon. In the 1850's and 1860's over 40% of the inmates had been pardoned (see Table 46). In 1867 the New Hampshire legislature approved a new form of early release from prison, commutation.[64]

Like commutation, parole in America had its origins in the 1817 New York commutation law.[65]   Parole was linked more closely to reformation by Alexander Maconochie who administered the Norfolk Island prison colony off Australia in 1840. Maconochie created a five-stage plan wherein inmates earned a certain number of "marks" for good behavior and hard work. Each stage brought more responsibility, greater freedom, and better conditions in preparation for the final stage known as the ticket of leave. The ticket permitted the convict to return to normal society. Provided there were no relapses into crime, the convict was granted a conditional pardon and eventually a full pardon.[66] Maconochie's system was adopted in Ireland by Sir Walter Crofton in the 1850's and changed into a three-stage program. Meanwhile in the United States a number of states tried out commutation. Post-Civil War reformers became interested in applying the indeterminate sentence and parole. By 1900 20 states had a parole system and by 1944 all 48 states did.[67]   Parole appealed to the growing ranks of professionals entering the field of prison discipline. Parole also helped provide a safety valve for overcrowded prisons, it was yet another tool employed by wardens to maintain discipline, and it came in after a century of frequent pardoning.[68]

The commutation law of 1867 was the first explicit link made between a prisoner's behavior and his early release from the New Hampshire State Prison. Pardon was dependent on many factors but the evidence of reformation was not necessarily one of them. The more standard discharge upon expiration of sentence had in practice nothing to do with whether an inmate was reformed or not.[69]   Commutation was directly linked to rehabilitation by making the inmate partially responsible for the length of sentence served.

Commutation meant the substitution of a lesser for a more severe sentence.[70] The prison warden was authorized to deduct time off the original sentence for good behavior according to a formula calibrated to different lengths of sentence. Thus, an inmate serving a sentence of two years or less could earn one day off his original sentence in exchange for one month of good behavior. If his original sentence were two or three years in length, he could earn two days off the original sentence for every month of good behavior and so on up to ten days off for every month of good behavior.[71] Commutation was impossible for those serving a life sentence. Inmates could forfeit time earned by reverting to bad behavior.[72] The first commutation law in the United States was passed by the New York legislature in 1817. The law empowered the prison administration to deduct up to a quarter of the original sentence in exchange for good behavior of those inmates serving a sentence of five years or longer. Tennessee adopted commutation in 1833 and Ohio in 1856. By 1869 23 states including New Hampshire had adopted commutation.[73]

At first, commutation seemed to be the ideal form of early release. In exchange for good behavior, the inmate could expect to receive "good time" off his or her original sentence according to a formula set up by state law. Within one year of its introduction in the state prison, the warden declared, "I cannot speak in too high terms of the operation of the Commutation Law, passed at the last session of the Legislature...a most successful agency in promoting good conduct on the part of the men."[74] However, only a small fraction of the inmates actually obtained their release through commutation: 12.3% in the 1860's and 9.3% in the 1870's (see Table 46). For all intents, commutation as a method of early release was dropped after 1879. Pardons also dropped in frequency during the 1880's and 1890's (see Table 46). Perhaps the warden and governor retrenched because by this was a time when convictions for violent crime were on the rise and they didn't want to give the appearance of coddling criminals. Oddly enough, Warden Charles E. Cox gave a ringing endorsement to the concept of commutation in 1900 as if it were something brand new.[75] By this point, however, a much more radical measure was about to become law: parole.

Of all the forms of early release, parole was the most closely related to the goal of inmate reformation. Parole was part of the Progressive reform program that swept over the northeastern and midwestern United States in the early twentieth century. Under the parole system, the judge sets a maximum length sentence. After some time - usually determined by the warden or parole board and varying from one state to another - the inmate is brought before the parole board for a hearing to determine if he or she is eligible for early release. The time of the first parole hearing varies from one state to another.[76] The board then makes a decision on whether or not to release the inmate. Parole is a *conditional* release. The paroled inmate is required to sign a statement agreeing to conditions such as obeying the law, searching for legitimate employment, avoiding criminal behavior, and avoiding criminal associates. A parole officer is assigned to the inmate who must report in person or in writing at specified intervals (commonly once a month). These conditions are to be followed until the expiration of the original sentence.[77]

According to Andrew von Hirsch and Kathleen J. Hanrahan, early release via parole has traditionally been granted on the basis of evidence of inmate rehabilitation and predictions that he or she will not revert to a life of crime. In reality, parole boards also base their decisions on the seriousness of the offense, record of prior convictions, the inmate's disciplinary record, and the local community's attitude toward paroled offenders in their midst. Parole boards have normally not used any specific guidelines in making a decision.[78]

In New Hampshire parole was introduced at the same time as the indeterminate sentence (1901).[79] According to statistics derived from the sample, parole seems to have replaced the pardon between 1901 and 1914. The vast majority of inmates left the New Hampshire State Prison via parole during this period (see Table 46). In New Hampshire, prisoners were eligible for parole after serving the minimum length of their sentence. Early on, the warden realized that "provision must be made for assistance in securing employment in surroundings which are helpful."[80] Such "provision" was essential since one of the three conditions of parole was that the parolee "not lead an idle or dissolute life."[81]

In practice, it was impossible to maintain supervision over all of the paroled inmates. At first New Hampshire relied on an honor system where the inmate was to report to the prison warden in writing once every three months.[82] In 1904 Warden Charles E. Cox complained, "Under the terms of this act there is no power of enforcing the terms of a parole, as I have found by experience."[83] Cox complained further of the fact that in the past two years some inmates had broken parole conditions. A few even committed felonies while out on parole. Cox declared, "This state of affairs [is] a menace to law and order, as well as a cause for regret and chagrin."[84] The state legislature passed an act the following year which provided for the return of parolees to prison to serve out the rest of their sentence if caught violating the terms of their release.[85] At least one convict in the sample committed a crime while on parole and was returned to the prison as a consequence.[86]

The chaplain was made the prison's first parole officer on April 6, 1909.[87] The Reverend Claudius Byrnes was very busy in his new role; he took it upon himself to visit parolees. In one year he traveled 2000 miles by steam and electric car visiting parolees in New Hampshire and northern Massachusetts.[88] Despite Byrnes's activity, the parole system was not functioning properly. According to the Reverend Whitman Bassett (Byrnes's successor) only 66 1/2% of the parolees on average maintained the period contact required by their agreement. He thought the job required a full-time parole officer.[89]

The prison briefly employed two other means of release in the antebellum era: remitting and remanding. Seven inmates had their sentences remitted during the 1840's.[90] An intense search through the New Hampshire session laws and statutes revealed nothing about remitting prison sentences. Most likely, this was just another term for pardoning. All of those with remitted sentences served a sentence shorter than that imposed by the court.[91]

More puzzling is the remanding of a handful of inmates in the 1810's and 1820's. To "remand" is to send back a prisoner in order that further evidence may be obtained.[92]

The New Hampshire criminal justice system did not employ probation during the period 1812-1914 except for juvenile offenders from 1907 on. Probation is a sentence in which the court does not send the offender to prison but imposes a number of conditions such as finding legitimate employment or entering a rehabilitation program and reporting to a probation officer.[93]

The transfer of a few unmanageable prisoners to the New Hampshire Hospital for the Insane can be considered to be an admission of failure to rehabilitate on the part of the prison. The state hospital was established in 1842 during an era of widespread asylum building in America. Just as criminals were deemed reformable via the institutional solution, so too were the insane thought curable. Insanity was no longer considered to be a divine affliction linked to the supernatural but a sickness which could be cured through a regimen of isolation from society and proper treatment.[94]

As early as 1844 the New Hampshire State Hospital for the Insane was taking on a custodial rather than rehabilitative role. The hospital administration consciously decided to accept chronic and incurably insane patients out of humanitarian reasons.[95] Pioneering reformer Dorothea Dix publicized the horrible conditions endured by the insane who had been kept

in almshouses, poor farms, or jails. The state hospital in New Hampshire
offered a regimented and repressive existence to the insane but it was perhaps
marginally better than the available alternatives.[96] It was a dumping ground
for incurably insane persons of poor, lower class, and frequently, immigrant
background.[97]

The prison and state hospital enjoyed close relations from the hospital's
founding. The first prisoner in the sample transferred to the state hospital
was James Reid or Reed in 1849. Reid was an 18-year old youth who,
together with three other teenagers, broke into a store in Portsmouth in
November 1848 and stole $7.75. All except one received five years in prison
for a sentence.[98] Reid was "Removed to Insane Asylum" on November 22,
1849 after serving only nine months in prison.[99] Correspondence between
Andrew McFarland, superintendent of the state hospital, and Warden Rufus
Dow indicates that the institutions enjoyed mutual visiting arrangements: "all
courtesies and attentions which it is in the power of one public institution to
render another."[100]

Despite close ties, it was over 70 years before another such transfer in the
sample occurred. Nearly 8% of the inmates in the sample in the 1900's were
transferred to the state hospital and 3.8% were transferred in the years 1900-
14 (see Table 46).

One possible explanation for the sudden increase in transfers to the state
hospital may be the increasing emphasis on therapeutic criminal justice
discussed by John R. Sutton, David J. Rothman, and others. Unlike previous
prison reform movements, that of the Progressive era emphasized the
classification of inmates and individualized treatment according to what the
reformers saw as scientific principles.[101]

In New Hampshire, however, Chief Justice Charles Doe resisted the use of
psychiatric experts while presiding over the trial of accused murderer Josiah
Pike in 1868 at the Rockingham County Superior Court. Doe thought the
increased reliance on expert testimony undermined the common law powers
of the jury to decide on matters of fact. Judge Doe believed that a jury was
able to decide the fact of a defendant's sanity or insanity at the moment when
an alleged offense was committed.[102] This line of defense was applied most
often to crimes of violence.[103] Doe's objection was discredited by legal
scholars such as Francis Wharton who denied that insanity was solely a
question of fact. The experts were not yet reliable enough for legal theorists
like Wharton. His solution was to use a panel of experts to decide the
issue.[104]

Psychiatric professionals took an increasingly active role in prison affairs.

For example, Charles E. Brigham was convicted of first degree murder for hitting Celia J. Smith on the head with an iron "pinch bar" in 1904. After conviction but before incarceration, Brigham was examined by Doctors Bancroft and Questen who pronounced the 22-year old "to be a man possessing many marks of physical and mental degeneracy. These stigmata are sufficiently pronounced in our minds to lead us to recommend temporary commitment under the law at the New Hampshire State Hospital for further investigation."[105] Brigham was sent to the prison but the records do not indicate how and when he left.[106]

DeForrest A. Robinson and Fred E. Lynde were convicted of arson in 1905. Robinson or his lawyer was evidently planning to enter a plea of not guilty by reason of insanity. The Rockingham County Superior Court ordered an examination to be conducted at the state hospital. Superintendent Charles P. Bancroft examined Robinson and decided, "I think he is congenitally defective and a person of limited intelligence and mental responsibility."[107] Robinson was given five to seven years in the state prison and pardoned after serving only three.[108]

Andrew Charland was a troublemaker who served at least three terms in the state prison. In October 1909 he was convicted of breaking and entering into a house in Londonderry and stealing $10 worth of clothing and other items. Like DeForrest A. Robinson, Charland or his lawyer had entered a plea of not guilty by reason of insanity. Charland was sent to the state hospital for observation. Dr. Bancroft concluded, "Andrew Charland presents no evidence of insanity." Bancroft based his conclusion on the latest criminological theories:

> Bad heredity, bad home environment, entire lack of proper training during childhood, and more or less habitual alcoholic excesses, have produced the usual results, a man of depraved mind...Because of the entire absence of any symptoms of insanity, and his own clear statement of the facts, I am convinced that Charland is sane and responsible, and a good illustration of the habitual criminal.[109]

Charland served a full two-year sentence. He was back in prison for attempted rape in 1913.[110]

Albert M. Glass of Dover was transferred to the state hospital thanks to the plea of not guilty by reason of insanity made on his behalf in 1902. He was convicted of shooting George W. Glass (relationship not described but probably his father) to death. According to the testimony of Dr. George F. Jelly of Boston, Glass was insane. Dr. Jelly had examined Glass 10 years earlier when Glass was under arrest for the murder of his brother George and assaulting his mother. Dr. Jelly blamed Glass's condition on a childhood accident:

> I am clearly of the opinion that he has been somewhat peculiar since he received a severe injury to his head, when six years of age, that he committed the homicide, and assault with which he is charged and which he admits while under the influence of the delusion of conspiracy involving his brother and mother, with marked hallucinations of hearing, and that he was insane and irresponsible, that he is suffering from an organic, degenerative disease of the brain, and that he will never recover.[111]

Dr. Bancroft, superintendent of the state hospital, concurred.[112] Glass spent only five weeks in the state prison before being transferred to the state hospital "until discharged by due course of law."[113]

The insanity defense was used with increasing frequency in nineteenth-century American criminal trials but it was applied inconsistently thanks to shifting meanings of insanity.[114] The insanity defense had its origins in late eighteenth-century French theories which posited that mental disorders affected the emotional and volitional aspects of the mind rather than the reason or intellect.[115] The insanity defense became acceptable in the United States after the M'Naghten case in Great Britain in 1843. The case set the precedent that for the defendant to be legally irresponsible for his or her offense, he or she must have been in such a mental state as to be unable to have known at the time of committing the offense that it was wrong.[116]

The acceptance of the insanity defense was complicated by the fact that psychiatry was a very new discipline in the nineteenth century. The Association of Medical Superintendents of American Institutions for the Insane was established in 1844 in an attempt to differentiate psychiatrists from the general medical establishment.[117] The uncertain status of psychiatry resulted in two points of confusion: the testimony of experts and devising ways of testing the defendant's state of responsibility.[118] The courts increasingly relied upon medical professionals in such cases. Theorists promulgated new definitions of insanity such as "mania transitoria" and the concept of the irresistible impulse.[119]

Psychiatric intervention in criminal justice was an established fact in New Hampshire by the early twentieth century. In 1906, six inmates who "were a constant menace to the safety of the institution," were transferred to the state hospital.[120] In 1914 the warden said that insane inmates should be segregated from the rest. They required "remedial medicinal treatment. This is not the proper function of the prison physician. Such treatment can be given by an alienist only."[121] As far as is known, none of the six had entered pleas of not guilty by reason of insanity. Most of them were transferred after they had already spent some time in the prison. There were other such transfers in the prison's history between 1849 and 1900 but they do not show up in the data for this sample. In 1899 an inmate was examined by both Dr. Bancroft of the state hospital and by Dr. Ralph Gallinger of the state prison. They reported, "We find him in a state of confusional insanity - at times developing into actual maniacal incoherence with outbursts of mild violence...is suffering from an attack of acute insanity." He was transferred.[122]

Capital punishment was reserved for the most serious offenders: first degree murderers. As we saw in Chapter One, New Hampshire had had the death penalty on the books at least as far back as 1641. However, no state prisoner was executed until 1869.

At first, condemned felons were hanged at Portsmouth. There were a total of four hangings between 1738 and 1770. In 1770 executions were made the responsibility of the then-five county governments.[123] Executions were public spectacles. Thanks to pressure from the anti-gallows movement, executions were restricted to within the walls of the county jail in 1837. Finally, in 1867 executions were restricted to within the walls of the state prison.[124] This explains the absence of felons condemned to death in the sample data until 1869. During the period 1770-1869, county governments executed eight felons. Between 1869 and 1893 nine men were executed at the state prison. Three have been hanged since, the latest in 1939.[125] The death penalty was applied most vigorously in New Hampshire history between 1869 and 1879 when six men were put to death.[126]

Ironically, the death penalty was applied most vigorously during a lull in the violent crime rate (see Tables 4 and 46). Other parts of the United States, however, were experiencing a post-war surge in violent crime.[127] The increased use of capital punishment in New Hampshire in the 1870's may have been in part an emulation of other states. It seems paradoxical for the violent crime rate to triple between the 1870's and 1890's in New Hampshire and for the use of the death penalty to decline by two thirds (see Tables 4 and 46). Not all of the condemned prisoners were executed.

Even during the 1870's there were some indications of reluctance to impose the death sentence. Hiram Jones of Newmarket was sentenced to death in October 1870 for murdering his wife Ann by slashing her throat with a razor.[128] His death sentence was "commuted" to life in prison, perhaps because of his age. Jones was 64. He died of natural causes in 1872.[129] In October 1888 James Palmer was sentenced to death for the murder of Henry Whitehouse (discussed in more detail in Chapter Three).[130] Palmer was reprieved on January 10, 1890 just before his scheduled hanging. The court decided to execute him after all but once again Palmer was reprieved on March 7. Finally, on May 1, 1890 Palmer was put to death at 11:04 a.m.[131] Isaac B. Sawtelle was sentenced to death in September 1890 for the murder of his brother in Rochester on February 5. (This case is discussed in Chapter Three). Sawtelle died at age 54 of apoplexy while awaiting execution.[132]

Capital punishment was introduced to the state prison as a solution to the unruly public behavior that had accompanied executions held in county jails. It does seem strange that the most serious form of punishment was left up to county governments for more than 50 years after the state prison's establishment. This may have been because the prison was designed with the goal of reforming convicts. The reforming mission of imprisonment was rendered nearly useless by the death penalty.

At first removal of executions to the state prison did not solve the problem of executions as unruly public events. Josiah Pike's execution was utterly mismanaged. The insanity plea was unsuccessfully invoked during his trial for the murder of Thomas and Elisabeth Brown.[133] Probably because Pike was the state prison's first death-row inmate, the prison administration appears to have greatly relaxed the usual strict discipline applied to inmates. According to Henry Robinson in an article for *Granite Monthly*,

> Pike's last days were redolent of roses, and he was ushered out of life with a surge of sentimental gush that scandalized the state, and aroused the stinging sarcasm of Mark Twain on our effeminacy. Women were allowed to make a fool of Pike. They prayed and sung [sic] with him, and held his hands and patted his cheeks, and entwined his hair with their soft fingers, and fed him on confections, jellies, and other dainties too delicate for home consumption...He seemed to be the especial pride and delight of some ministers' wives and daughters...[134]

Pike certainly seems an inappropriate object of affection. On May 7, 1868, while in a drunken rage, Pike killed Thomas and Elisabeth Brown by striking both in the head with an axe. The Browns were an elderly couple who had employed Pike on their farm in Hampton Falls.[135]

Even the execution was bungled, according to Robinson. Pike was given the opportunity to make a final speech and made to feel as if he were about to suffer martyrdom instead of a well-earned punishment. The hanging rope was too long. Consequently, when Pike dropped from the scaffold he landed on the pavement below with sickening force. The hangman quickly hauled Pike up and finished the job via strangulation.[136] Reverend Hosea Quinby claimed that Pike went to his execution full of penitence and reconciled with God.[137] The Pike execution received widespread negative publicity despite the fact that it was held behind prison walls. The unusually liberal visiting policy can partly be held to blame. This great publicity was also probably due to the fact that Pike's was the first execution on state property rather than county property as had been done previously. None of the subsequent executions appear to have caused as much public agitation.

Paradoxically, the frequency of executions went down just as the rate of incarceration for violent crime went to the top. Perhaps juries were repelled by the excesses of the 1870's and so were reluctant to convict for first degree murder. Executions were extremely rare after 1890. Quentin Blaine suggests this was so for the following reasons: a reduction in the number of capital offenses, state laws transferred the power from the court to the jury to inflict capital punishment and because federal innovations have been created to make sure the jury makes a decision based on reason, not emotion.[138] In 1903, for the first time, the state provided life in prison as an alternative to the death penalty.[139]

Escapes were a problem during the first 50 years of the prison's existence. As early as August 3, 1813 the directors of the state prison began to consider the possible danger of escapes so they hired Nathaniel Walker as an extra watchman for $10 a month plus board.[140] Despite this precaution, 11 prisoners escaped on the night of July 1, 1815. Six were recaptured and put into solitary confinement. One was shot by a guard and "severely wounded."[141] There was another mass escape on February 9, 1818 when seven inmates managed to get over the prison wall. All seven were recaptured.[142] During the 1810's and 1820's there were a number of individual escapes and attempted escapes.

Some of the prison escapes required elaborate planning. This could only be accomplished by circumventing the rule of silence which had been established in part to prevent just such plotting.[143] The 1815 prison break was accomplished in the following manner by "a combination on the part of the prisoners." An inmate named John Phillips sneaked into another cell than his own. Meanwhile, his cellmate placed "an image which had been prepared and placed in the Cell with the back towards the door" to fool the guards. (Apparently, the Auburn system of prison discipline in which inmates worked together in silence during the day but were housed in separate cells at night was already violated in 1815). At midnight Phillips left the cell with "pieces of steel prepared for the purpose" and unlocked several cell doors. The escape was foiled when a servant in the warden's house rose to close a window and spotted the 11 inmates.[144] On the night of February 8, 1818 three inmates drilled a hole in a cell door. "By means of some instruments yet unknown, [they] proceeding in breaking the locks of the other cells, and actually destroyed to the number of twelve." A total of 36 inmates left the 12 cells. Using two levers, the inmates created an opening in the bottom of the "arch" just big enough for one person to crawl through "(tho' with difficulty)." Fourteen convicts crawled through this opening and broke the lock to the prison's outer door. At this point the escapees were discovered by the guards. Seven convicts got over the wall. They were all recaptured a few days later and punished.[145]

Most inmates who escaped from prison were eventually recaptured. Maximillian or Mark Shinburn was recaptured 34 years after making his escape on December 3, 1866. Shinburn was a bank robber and his escape in broad daylight was widely publicized. He ran across the prison yard, broke through a previously-weakened section of the wooden door, and was met by "a fine horse and carriage" in which he fled.[146] In 1900, Shinburn, now aged 58 years, was sent to the New Hampshire State Prison to serve the remaining nine years of his original sentence for breaking and entering and stealing.[147] He was freed seven or eight years later by the commutation of his sentence.[148] This was the last succesful escape in the prison's history through 1914. In 1906 Warden Henry K.W. Scott based part of his opposition to the parti-colored prison uniform on the fact that the uniform's use as a means of identifying an escaped prisoner was pointless since there had been no escape since 1866.[149]

Escapes were foiled after 1866 for two probable reasons: John C. Pilsbury's strict regime throughout the 1870's may well have set a precedent for heightened security and the new prison, completed in 1880, was a much more secure structure than the old one.

Few inmates managed to escape from the New Hampshire State Prison.

Governor John T. Gilman had urged the construction of a state prison in 1804 as a solution to "the frequent escapes of criminals and others from our common prisons."[150] Many tried to escape, especially in the first several decades of the prison's existence. This is not surprising considering the sort of life most inmates led in the institution described in Chapter Five. The available records do not reveal if there were any attempted escapes between 1866 and 1914 but there must have been a few.

The New Hampshire State Prison appears to have had incredibly low rates of recidivism during the period 1812-1914.[151] Two factors probably account for this: the ambiguous definition of recidivism and the information provided by original sources. There is no absolute agreed-upon definition of recidivism. A working definition is habitual antisocial behavior or criminal activity leading to imprisonment.[152] There are problems such as whether to count someone as a recidivist if he or she is reimprisoned for a serious crime or for a less-serious and different sort of offense. Another problem of definitions is raised by the length of time between successive imprisonments.[153]

For our purposes, we have defined a recidivist as a person who was convicted of a felony and served time in a state prison at least twice. As described in Chapter Four, we counted recidivists by checking to see if a convict in the sample was listed two or more times in the prison records. We included as recidivists convicts who had served prior time in state prisons outside of New Hampshire since we are interested in crime at the felony level. We did not count as recidivists those inmates who may have served a term previously in the state prison but who were convicted in a county court other than Rockingham or Strafford, unless this fact was noted in the prison records. It was impractical to check through all of the records.

Recidivism peaked during the 1820's and 1830's. Twenty-two point six percent of the sample in the 1820's had been convicted of a felony before and 19.4% of the sample in the 1830's had been likewise convicted before. Recidivism dropped to a low of 8.8% for the next two decades and rose to 17.8% in the 1870's, dropped rapidly to 6.4% in the 1880's, rose sharply to 17.8% in the 1900's and dropped down to 9.0% in the 1910's (see Table 47). Nearly all of the recidivists had committed property crimes (see Table 35). This is not surprising since most violent crimes are of an impulsive nature. Property crimes usually require more planning. The statistics derived from the sample also indicate that most crime in New Hampshire was property crime (see Chapter Three).

The New Hampshire State Prison c. 1812-1914 was not a "revolving door for criminals" but there was a small group of hardcore recidivists. For example,

Table 47

Known Recidivism among New Hampshire State Prison Inmates, 1812-1914, by Type of Crime

Type of Crime Decade	% and Number (N) of Cases Property		Violence	
	Yes	No	Yes	No
1810's	16.7% (7)	83.3% (35)		100% (4)
1820's	26.9% (7)	73.1% (19)		100% (3)
1830's	17.6% (6)	82.4% (28)	50.0% (1)	50% (1)
1840's	11.5% (3)	88.5% (23)		100% (7)
1850's	10.7% (3)	89.3% (25)		100% (6)
1860's	5.7% (3)	94.3% (50)	40.0% (4)	600% (6)
1870's	18.3% (17)	81.7% (76)		100% (7)
1880's	9.4% (9)	90.6% (87)		100% (18)
1890's	10.6% (9)	89.4% (76)		100% (28)
1900's	18.8% (19)	81.2% (82)	12.5% (2)	875% (14)
1910's	7.3% (4)	92.7% (51)		100% (19)

Type of Crime Decade	% and Number (N) of Cases Moral		Other	
	Yes	No	Yes	No
1810's				100% (1)
1820's				100% (2)

Type of Crime	% and Number (N) of Cases			
	Moral		Other	
Decade	Yes	No	Yes	No
1830's				
1840's				100% (1)
1850's				
1860's				100% (2)
1870's		100% (3)	66.7% (2)	33.3% (1)
1880's		100% (3)		100% (24)
1890's		100% (3)		100% (2)
1900's		100% (4)	12.5% (1)	87.5% (7)
1910's	50.0% (1)	50.0% (1)	100% (2)	

TOTAL NUMBER (N) CASES/DECADE: 1810's: (47); 1820's: (31); 1830's: 36); 1840's: (34); 1850's: (34); 1860's: (65); 1870's: (107); 1880's: (141); 1890's: (118); 1900's: (129); and 1910's: (78).

Source: *Prison Warden's Reports*, 1859-1914; and "Register of Convicts 1812-1883," "[N.H. State] Prison Records [1874-1915]," and "N.H. State Prison: Record of Gain and Loss in Population [1905-36]," all MS, Div. of Records-Management and Archives, Concord, N.H.

James Moore made his first appearance in the prison records in 1825 at the age of 16 when he was convicted of stealing $31.05 from John Harvey's store in Northwood.[154] Eleven years later, Moore was back in prison for breaking and entering. The following information was noted next to his name: "4th. time. Convicted twice here and twice at Charleston [, Mass.]."[155] Luther Austin first went to prison in 1858 at the age of 21 for a burglary committed in Danville. He served a full four-year sentence and was released in 1862.[156] Not in the least reformed by his prison experience, Austin and an accomplice named Ira A. Moody broke into a house owned by two women in Sandown and stole $11.60 worth of clothing, cloth, and butter in 1863. Austin was given a five-year sentence, probably because of his prior conviction, while Moody was given two years.[157] In 1875 Austin was back again in the state prison, serving a seven-year sentence for burglary. He served six years and was either pardoned or his sentence commuted in 1881.[158] Yet again, in 1882, the 45-year old miscreant was convicted of breaking and entering a house for the purpose of stealing. Austin spent the next five years in prison and his trail vanishes after 1886.[159] A few other troubled persons also show up in the prison records as multiple recidivists.[160]

The prison administration first addressed the problem of recidivism in 1852 when Prison Chaplain Eleazer Smith observed, "We have had no difficulty in finding home and employment for such as have been discharged during the year; yet I am sorry to say while some have done well, several have returned to habits of dissipation and idleness, and one has been returned to Prison for crime."[161] From Smith's statement one can see that the prison did make some attempt to follow up in making sure the reforming mission was complete. The 1840's and 1850's were a time of little recidivism in comparison to the 1820's and 1830's (see Table 47) so it is a little puzzling as to why the problem was apparently not addressed until later. In 1855 Smith proudly declared, "There has probably been a less number of cases of relapse into crime than in any year since my acquaintance with the Prison."[162] Less than a decade later Reverend Samuel Cooke was "sometimes saddened by what seems to him a superficial reform; as seen in the fact that many on leaving the Prison return to their former habits, and are soon returned to this or some other prison."[163]

Prison administrators sought an environmental explanation for recidivism. They blamed "demoralizing influences" of society. They also - sympathetically - pointed out some of the disadvantages adhering to a discharged convict. Such a person was "tabooed in the shop and the home, while his weakness of moral principle is easily overcome by the temptations to which he is exposed."[164] Reverend Sullivan Holman graphically explained the situation: "After some years' experience in reformatory efforts," he said, "I find it an unequal warfare with open saloons seven days in a week...they [ex-convicts] are easily enticed into these gateways to ruin, the tares are sown, the efforts of years undone and my hopes of success are blasted."[165] Returning to an environmental explanation Holman said, "We must admit, as an important factor in the problems of reform, that these twigs have been badly bent in early life. Bad seeds early sown produces [sic] a terrible vintage in maturer years."[166]

At least as early as 1852 the New Hampshire State Prison tried to provide some help to discharged convicts in resuming a normal life though it sounds like a one-man effort by the prison chaplain.[167] State law did not provide any assistance of any kind to discharged prisoners until 1842. In that year the warden was directed to furnish inmates with a "cheap suit of clothes, decent and suitable for the season in which he is discharged and a sum of money not exceeding three dollars."[168] Prison administrators soon realized the $3 maximum was inadequate. Reverend Eleazer Smith said that $2-$3 was hardly adequate when a discharged convict faced a journey of up to hundreds of miles before reaching home and many of them left the prison "in feeble health."[169] Even the strict disciplinarian John C. Pilsbury asked in 1879, "What objection can be made to increasing the money grant by a small percentage, upon the value of the prisoner's labor to the State and graduated by his industry and good behavior?"[170]

Informal and private efforts were made to help discharged convicts in the absence of state-sponsored care. In 1869 a person named D.S. Palmer was listed in the warden's annual report as agent for discharged prisoners. Palmer reported that "most" prisoners discharged in the past year had found jobs.[171] By 1881 an organization named the Prisoner's Aid Society had been formed with Oliver Pillsbury as agent and treasurer. The society's main function was to find legitimate employment for discharged prisoners.[172] In 1883 "employment has been obtained for several in this city, some of whom are doing well, and give promise of success: others, alas!"[173] The society was still active in 1898.[174]

The original design of imprisonment in New Hampshire between 1812 and 1914 was subverted by the actual outcomes of criminal justice described here. As we saw in Chapter One, the state prison was constructed with three basic purposes in mind: to reform criminals through a regime of hard labor and moral instruction: to prevent crime, and to be economically self-supporting through the hard labor performed by the inmates.[175] As we have seen, prisoner reformation was subordinated to the overriding concern of keeping the institution profitable via the contract labor system. The prison was extremely unhealthy and discipline could occasionally be brutal. Over time, more efforts were made to educate the inmates. Conditions improved greatly after 1879 and most of the oppressive disciplinary rules were eliminated in the 1900's. However, the experience described in Chapter Five is not the only reason imprisonment largely failed to rehabilitate criminals.

The data analyzed in this chapter reveal discrepancies between the sentences assigned by the courts and the sentences actually served. The factors involved in this include a) the type of crime committed by the offender and b) the mode of exit from prison. In general, violent offenders experienced the greatest discrepancy between sentence passed by the court and sentence actually served (see Tables 43 and 45). In certain decades violent offenders ended up only serving about half of their original sentence. Property crime offenders more nearly served their full sentence. The statutes provided lengthy sentences for violent crimes and justices did not hesitate to hand out long sentences in the 1840's, 1860's, and 1880's through 1910's. The discrepancies were mainly due to legal developments that acted to shorten many a convict's stay in the New Hampshire State Prison.

Pardons were granted most frequently from the 1830's through the 1870's (see Table 46). It is probably more than a coincidence that pardons were used extensively at just the point when longer sentences were being imposed by the courts. Perhaps the use of pardons was to prevent overcrowding in the prison or perhaps as a countermeasure to overly-harsh punishment. Pardons may have actually worked against reformation. They worked to subvert the certainty of punishment which was a cardinal point of Cesare Beccaria's concept of punishment.[176]

Commutation and parole were two methods of release directly connected to the reforming mission of the state prison. Commutation was dangled as an incentive to good behavior. Commutation was less arbitrary than a pardon and followed a definite program. Despite initial enthusiasm, commutation was applied to only 12.3% of the inmates in the 1860's and virtually abandoned after 1879 (see Table 46).

Parole was introduced on a wide scale in 1901 along with the indeterminate sentence: nearly 70% of all inmates imprisoned between 1901 and 1914 were paroled (see Table 46). The use of parole and the indeterminate sentence were part of the Progressive reform campaign to change American prisons. At the same time, some of the harsh disciplinary methods of old were eliminated like the lockstep march, downcast eye, and parti-colored uniform. Parole was a conditional form of release dependent in part on the inmate. Unfortunately, parole boards were not always the best judge of an inmate's progress toward rehabilitation. There was also the problem of inadequate supervision once an inmate was allowed to leave on parole. One third or more of those on parole did not keep to the agreement of periodic contact with the prison authorities.

The State Hospital for the Insane was an institution allied to the New Hampshire State Prison. Unlike the prison, the state hospital quickly recognized the essentially hopeless nature of its mission. As a place of last resort the hospital worked well but it apparently gave up its role of rehabilitating the insane.[177] Late in the period 1812-1914 the state prison began transferring a significant number of unmanageable cases to the hospital. The hospital can be viewed cynically as the final dumping ground of the criminal justice system since reform was probably out of the question.

The state hospital performed another useful service to the criminal justice system in regard to the insanity defense. The hospital provided professional advice in determining if a defendant was insane or not. The increasing transfers to the state hospital in the early twentieth century was also related to the introduction of therapeutic justice by Progressive reformers. In some ways, state hospital personnel functioned as prison psychiatrists might in deciding which inmates were truly insane or which were "defective delinquents" who could never be rehabilitated.[178]

The death penalty was applied most vigorously in the decade following its introduction to the state prison in 1869. It is unclear as to why the rate of executions went down after 1879 since convictions for violent crime shot up in the 1880's and 1890's. A far greater number of inmates died in prison of natural causes than by execution.

Statistics relating to the sample prison death rate confirm the conclusion reached in Chapter Five that the prison was a very unhealthy place. Most inmates dying in prison were afflicted with tuberculosis, the major killer in New Hampshire during this era. In effect, an inmate stood a fairly good chance of serving a life sentence no matter what his crime.

Only the boldest or most desperate inmates took the option of escape. Most escapes ended in failure and recapture. Escape was most possible in the early days of the prison's history. It appears that the prison was not adequately prepared for the possibility of escape. Several mass escapes occured during the 1810's and 1820's. After 1866 there were no reported escapes. Somehow, this option was closed off by increased vigilance and from 1880 on, a new, more secure structure.

At first glance, the statistics on recidivism derived from the sample suggest that the New Hampshire State Prison was a remarkably successful institution. If success (reformation) can be defined as staying out of the state prison, the institution was a great success. Of course, non-reappearance of convicts in the prison is an inadequate measure.

On a purely statistical level it is possible to conclude that punishment in the New Hampshire State Prison was successful. Only 101 out of 820 cases (12.3%) were repeat offenders as far as can be determined. Whether or not the discharged prisoner was really reformed is more debatable. Some, no doubt, profited from at least learning how to read and write. More were probably degraded by the prison experience: a stupefying routine of hard labor, poor living conditions and food, and vile company. A very few may have had a conversion experience where they realized how wrong they were and resolved to lead a better life. Such examples are occasionally cited by the prison chaplain and may well have been induced by him.[179]

Discrepancies between sentences handed out and served are visible in criminal justice as practiced in New Hampshire between 1812 and 1914. They were most pronounced for those convicted of violent crimes. Someone convicted of a property offense was more likely to serve the sentence handed down by the court. Measures were taken from the beginning to reduce the length of time actually served in prison. Samuel Walker describes the law of "criminal justice thermodynamics" in which the local criminal justice system maintains a steady state that can adapt to changes.[180] Perhaps this reduction of time served was criminal justice thermodynamics in action. Pardoning accelerated noticeably in the 1830's and 1840's when sentences grew longer. Commutation was introduced with great enthusiasm in 1867 but was virtually abandoned by 1880. It seems to have had only a marginal effect on sentences. On the other hand, the introduction of parole coincides with a large drop in length off sentences served for violent crime (see Tables 44 and 46). Many New Hampshire prisoners were paroled after the minimum length of their indeterminate had been served. In other words, the criminal justice system was apparently interested in releasing most inmates when they had become eligible for parole. This does seem to go counter to what Rothman and Sullivan say about therapeutic justice and medical time.[181] Perhaps the New Hampshire criminal justice system was more intent on moving bodies through the assembly line rather than in really making sure an inmate was reformed. Some of this may have been the result of inadequate staffing and resources at the prison. Possibly, shorter sentences served may have been a result of the Progressive era liberalization of prison discipline in the New Hampshire State Prison.

Ultimately, punishment in New Hampshire between 1812 and 1914 was unpredictable and inconsistent. Fewer than half of the inmates served their full sentence. There were a variety of reasons why so many inmates did not serve a full sentence. Most of the forms of early release were legally sanctioned. Escapes were not and death was beyond the prison administration's control with the exception of executions or waiting for the expiration of a life sentence. Mean sentences served were shorter than mean sentences passed, and both were short compared to sentences and sentences served in other parts of the country. The cases of William Holland and Daniel Crowley with which we opened this chapter were not so much anomalies as products of an inconsistent criminal justice system.

One reason for the apparent discrepancy was the fact that approved methods of release changed significantly between Holland's incarceration in 1820 and Crowley's in 1886. Pardon, commutation, execution, and even transfer to the state hospital had all been implemented. Oddly enough, the percentage of inmates discharged after serving a full sentence or being pardoned were nearly identical during both Holland's and Crowley's eras (see Table 46). This had not been so from the 1830's through 1870's. A more likely explanation was the fact that Crowley had committed a violent crime. As we have seen, violent crimes were punished far less consistently than were property crimes such as Holland's. Two additional factors which may explain the apparently unfair sentences are: 1) Holland was a recidivist while Crowley was not and 2) Crowley was an old man and a long sentence was thus nearly the equivalent of a life sentence. However, the harm caused by Crowley was far more serious than Holland's burglary and theft of molasses. It is difficult to conclude that the inmates received their just deserts.

312

Notes

1. State v. Holland, No. 723, Rockingham Cty., N.H. (1820) and "Register of Convicts 1812-1883," both MS, Div. of Records-Management and Archives, Concord, N.H. There are no court records extant concerning Holland's 1813 conviction.

2. State v. Crowley, No. [Unlisted], Rockingham Cty., N.H. (1887) and "[N.H. State] Prison Records [1874-1915]," both MS, Div. of Records-Management and Archives, Concord, N.H.

3. David J. Rothman, "Doing Time: Days, Months, and years in the Criminal Justice System" in Hyman Gross and Andrew von Hirsch, eds., *Sentencing* (New York, 1981), p. 377.

4. Alfred Blumstein et al., eds., *Research on Sentencing: The Search for Reform*, Vol. I (Washington, D.C., 1983), p. 58.

5. Rothman, "Doing Time," p. 377.

6. *Ibid.*, p. 377.

7. In 1901 the courts were empowered to pass sentences with both a minimum and maximum cut-off point. Until 1901 sentences were of a definite length. William M. Chase and Arthur H. Chase, comp. and ed., *The Public Statutes of the State of New Hampshire, and General Laws in Force January 1, 1901...* (Concord, N.H., 1900), pp. 801-39 or see Ch. 58 "An Act Relative to Sentences to the State Prison," *Laws of the State of New Hampshire, Passed January Session, 1901* (Manchester, N.H., 1901), pp. 547-48.

8. Rothman says, "The lengthy sentences were as typical for property crimes as for crimes against the person." Rothman, "Doing Time," p. 376.

9. State v. McDaniels, No. 45184, Rockingham Cty., N.H. (1818) and "Register of Convicts 1812-1883," both MS, Div. of Records-Management and Archives, Concord, N.H.

10. Oliver Welch or Welsh was convicted of manslaughter for the killing of Stephen Heath on August 20, 1831 in Chester, using a "waggon stake." Welch/Welsh served seven years before receiving a pardon. State v. Welch, No. 13257, Rockingham Cty., N.H. (1832) and "Register of Convicts 1812-1883," both MS, Div. of Records-Management and Archives, Concord, N.H.

11. William J. Bowers and Glenn L. Pierce, "Deterrence or Brutalization: What Is the Effect of Executions?" *Crime and Delinquency*, 26 (1980), 456.

12. Lawrence M. Friedman and Robert V. Percival, *The Roots of Justice: Crime and Punishment in Alameda County, California 1870-1910* (Chapel Hill, N.C., 1981), p. 207.

13. This tranformation is discussed in Chapter Two. See Ch. 274 "Offenses

Against Chastity" in *The General Laws of the State of New Hampshire...* (Manchester, N.H., 1878), pp. 619-20.

14. Ch. 270 "Punishment of Tramps" in *Ibid.*, pp. 612-13.

15. Blumstein et al., eds., *Research on Sentencing*, Vol. I, p. 59 and Rothman, "Doing Time," p. 378.

16. Samuel Walker, *Popular Justice: A History of American Criminal Justice* (New York, 1980), p. 92.

17. Michael S. Hindus, *Prison and Plantation: Crime, Justice, and Authority in Massachusetts and South Carolina, 1767-1878* (Chapel Hill, N.C., 1980), p. 105.

18. Eric H. Monkkonen, *The Dangerous Class: Crime and Poverty in Columbus, Ohio, 1860-1885* (Cambridge, Mass., 1975), pp. 66-67.

19. Hindus points out that crowded prisons were as much a result of "sentencing waves" as of actual crime waves. Hindus, *Prison and Plantation*, p. 106.

20. *The General Statutes of the State of New-Hampshire...* (Concord, N.H., 1867), p. 541.

21. Friedman and Percival, *Roots of Justice*, pp. 215-16.

22. John J. DiIulio, Jr., *No Escape: The Future of American Corrections* (New York, 1991), p. 63.

23. *Ibid.*, p. 4.

24. David J. Rothman, "Decarcerating Prisoners and Patients," *Civil Liberties Review*, 1 (1973), 10.

25. Blumstein et al., *Research on Sentencing*, Vol. I, p. 70.

26. Friedman and Percival, *Roots of Justice*, p. 210.

27. Walker, *Popular Justice*, p. 27.

28. Blumstein et al., *Research on Sentencing*, Vol. I, p. 60.

29. Rothman, "Doing Time," pp. 379-80.

30. *Ibid.*, p. 380 and Larry E. Sullivan, *The Prison Reform Movement: Forlorn Hope* (Boston, 1990), pp. 27 and 33-34.

31. David J. Rothman, *Conscience and Convenience: The Asylum and its Alternatives in Progressive America* (Boston, 1980), p. 175.

32. Sullivan, *Prison Reform Movement*, p. 32.

33. Rothman, "Doing Time," p. 377.

34. *General Laws of New Hampshire (1878)*, pp. 612-13.

35. Sullivan, *Prison Reform Movement*, pp. 33-34 and Rothman, *Conscience and Convenience*, pp. 193-97.

314

36. We have not traced the influence of the indeterminate sentence beyond 1914. The year 1914 is not very far into the era of rehabilitation when psychiatric and social work professionals began applying a more "therapeutic" form of prison discipline. There is no indication that the New Hampshire State Prison employed such persons until c. 1950 when the warden reported that psychometric testing of inmates had been introduced. *Report of the Officers of the New Hampshire State Prison to the Board of Trustees for the Two Years Ending June 30, 1950* (Concord, N.H., 1951), 14.

37. State v. Kelley, No. 8, Strafford Cty., N.H. (1897), MS, Justice and Administration Building, Dover, N.H. and "[N.H. State] Prison Records [1874-1915]" and "New Hampshire State Prison: Record of Gain and Loss in Population [1905-36]," both MS, Div. of Records-Management and Archives, Concord, N.H.

38. State v. Otis, No. 20, Strafford Cty., N.H. (1880), MS, Justice and Administration Building, Dover, N.H. and "[N.H. State] Prison Records [1874-1915]," MS, Div. of Records-Management and Archives, Concord, N.H.

39. State v. Hill, No. 21484, Rockingham Cty., N.H. (1844) and "Register of Convicts 1812-1883," both MS, Div. of Records-Management and Archives, Concord, N.H.

40. Kathleen D. Moore, *Pardons: Justice, Mercy, and the Public Interest* (New York, 1989), p. 5.

41. *Ibid.*, p. 53.

42. *Ibid.*, p. 54.

43. "Governor's Message to the Senate and House," June 7, 1822, MS, Executive Papers, Div. of Records-Management and Archives, Concord, N.H.

44. See Joseph L. Shaw, *New-Hampshire State Prison Cruelty Exposed: or, The Sufferings of Joseph L. Shaw, In That Institution in 1837, while John M'Daniel Was Warden* (Exeter, N.H., 1839) and "Register of Convicts 1812-1883," MS, Div. of Records-Management and Archives, Concord, N.H.

45. State v. Williams, No. 104, Strafford Cty., N.H. (1901), Justice and Administration Building, Dover, N.H.

46. TLS, Bert Wentworth to Gov. Robert P. Bass, Dec. 13, 1911, Bass Papers, Box 11, Dartmouth College Library, Hanover, N.H.

47. TLS, Eliza M. Berwick to Gov. Robert P. Bass, n.d., Bass Papers, Box 11, Dartmouth College Library, Hanover, N.H. Oddly enough, Berwick gave the names of the murder victim as Thomas Dobbins and the victim of attempted murder as Arthur Russell. The court records say otherwise.

48. TLS, Samuel G. Jackson, Affidavit, Aug. 11, 1911 before Justice of the Peace William S. Pierce, Bass papers, Box 11, Dartmouth College Library, Hanover, N.H.

49. Thomas Barnes, "Facts in the Case of State of New Hampshire v. John Williams," June 10, 1911, Typed MS, 4 pp., Bass Papers, Box 11, Dartmouth College Library, Hanover, N.H.

50. TLS [Illegible] P. Remick to Gov. Robert P. Bass, July 24, 1912, Bass Papers, Box 11, Dartmouth College Library, Hanover, N.H.

51. "[N.H. State] Prison Records [1874-1915]," and "New Hampshire State Prison: Record of Gain and Loss in Population [1905-36]," both MS, Div. of Records-Management and Archives, Concord, N.H.

52. State v. Keating, No. 4, Strafford Cty., N.H. (1894), MS, Justice and Administration Building, Dover, N.H.

53. ALS, John Keating to Judge Smith, Sept. 7, 1894 in *Ibid.*

54. "[N.H. State] Prison Records [1874-1915]," MS, Div. of Records-Management and Archives, Concord, N.H.

55. *Report of the Warden, Physician and Chaplain of the New-Hampshire State Prison, June Session, 1841* (Concord, N.H., 1841), 7 and *Journals of the Senate and House, June Session, 1839* (Concord, N.H., 1839), 375.

56. *Reports of the Warden, Physician and Chaplain of the N.H. State Prison, June Session, 1852* (Concord, N.H., 1852), 11.

57. *Ibid.*, 24.

58. *Annual Report of the Warden and Inspectors of the New-Hampshire State Prison...June Session, 1868* (Manchester, N.H., 1868), 14.

59. *Annual Report of the Warden and Inspectors of the New-Hampshire State Prison...June Session, 1870* (Manchester, N.H., 1870), 12.

60. Hindus, *Prison and Plantation*, p. 112.

61. *Ibid.*, p. 114.

62. *Ibid.*, p. 114.

63. Walker, *Popular Justice*, p. 93.

64. *General Statutes of New Hampshire (1867)*, p. 541.

65. Harry E. Allen et al., *Probation and Parole in America* (New York, 1985), p. 26.

66. *Ibid.*, p. 25.

67. *Ibid.*, p. 27.

68. *Ibid.*, p. 28.

69. David J. Rothman, *The Discovery of the Asylum: Social Order and Disorder in the New Republic* (Boston, 1971), p. 250.

70. Moore, *Pardons*, p. 5.

71. *General Statutes of New Hampshire (1867)*, p. 541.

72. *Ibid.*, p. 541.

73. Walker, *Popular Justice*, p. 94.

74. *Prison Warden's Report (1868)*, 12.

75. *Statistics Relating to the New Hampshire State Prison...for the Two Years Ending November 30, 1900* (Manchester, N.H., 1901), 9.

76. Andrew von Hirsch and Kathleen J. Hanrahan, *The Question of Parole: Retention, Reform, or Abolition?* (Cambridge, Mass., 1979), p. 2.

77. *Ibid.*, p. 3 and State v. Valle, No. 370, Strafford Cty., N.H. (1906), MS, Justice and Administration Building, Dover, N.H.

78. Von Hirsch and Hanrahan, *Question of Parole*, p. 2.

79. See Ch. 58 "An Act Relative to Sentences to the State Prison" in *Laws of the State of New Hampshire, Passed January Session, 1901* (Manchester, N.H., 1901), pp. 547-48.

80. *Statistics Relating to the New Hampshire State Prison...for the Two Years Ending November 30, 1902* (Manchester, N.H., 1902), 262.

81. See parole form in State v. Valle, No. 370, Strafford Cty., N.H. (1906), MS, Justice and Administration Building, Dover, N.H.

82. *Laws of New Hampshire Passsed 1901*, pp. 547-48.

83. *Statistics Relating to the New Hampshire State Prison...for the Two Years Ending November 30, 1904* (Concord, N.H., n.d.), 303.

84. *Ibid.*, 302.

85. *Statistics Relating to the New Hampshire State Prison...for the Two Years Ending November 30, 1906* (Bristol, N.H., n.d.), 10 and *Laws of the State of New Hampshire Passed January Session, 1909* (Concord, N.H., 1909), 461-62.

86. State v. Valle, No. 217, Strafford Cty., N.H. (1903) and State v. Valle, No. 370, Strafford Cty., N.H. (1906), both MS, Justice and Administration Building, Dover, N.H.

87. *Report of the Officers of the New Hampshire State Prison to the Governor and Council for the Two Years Ending August 31, 1910* (Bristol, N.H., n.d.), 44.

88. *Ibid.*, 44-45.

89. *Report of the Officers of the New Hampshire State Prison to the Governor and Council for the Two Years Ending Aug. 31, 1914* (Penacook, N.H., n.d.), 39-40.

90. See entries for Asa Worthen, Benjamin R. Cook, George C. Elliot, Thomas W. Maitland, Nicholas Perno, Frances Chase, and William Thomas

in "Register of Convicts 1812-1883," MS, Div. of Records-Management and Archives, Concord, N.H.

91. *The Oxford English Dictionary* traces the use of the term "remit" in this sense back to sixteenth-century Scotland with "a remitt for the said cryme." "Remit" in J.A. Simpson and E.S.C. Weiner, preparers, *The Oxford English Dictionary*, 2nd. ed., Vol. 13, (Oxford, 1989), p. 592.

92. The four cases which were remanded served the full length of their sentences. All were recidivists, which may be relevant. Unfortunately, no further information is available to determine the significance of remanding. It was not a form of *early* rlease, however. "Remand" in *Ibid.*, p. 580. See entries for Nathaniel Hoyt, Josiah Gordon (twice) and St. Patrick [sic] Purry in "Register of Convicts 1812-1883," MS, Div. of Records- Management and Archives, Concord, N.H.

93. Probation was first tried out by John Augustus of Boston in the 1840's when he took responsibility for the release of petty offenders by paying a recognizance fee and supervising them. Probation was widely implemented during the Progressive era. New Hampshire passed its first probation law in 1907 which was granted to only certain juvenile offenders under the age of 17. Adult probation was not employed in New Hampshire until 1937. Allen at al., *Probation and Parole*, pp. 36 and 41; *Laws of the State of New Hampshire, Passed January Session, 1907* (Concord, N.H., 1907), pp. 120-24 and *Laws of the State of New Hampshire, Passed January Session, 1937* (Concord, N.H., 1937), pp. 260-63.

94. Constance McGovern, *Masters of Madness: Social Origins of the American Psychiatric Profession* (Hanover, N.H., 1985), p. 43.

95. Rothman, *Discovery of the Asylum*, pp. 274-75.

96. *Ibid.*, pp. 151, 275, and 284.

97. *Ibid.*, p. 284.

98. State v. Smith, Reid, and Mills, No. 23911, Rockingham Cty., N.H. (1849), MS, Div. of Records-Management and Archives, Concord, N.H.

99. "Register of Convicts 1812-1883," MS, Div. of Records-Management and Archives, Concord, N.H.

100. ALS, Andrew McFarland, superintendant of the N.H. Hospital for the Insane to Rufus Dow, warden of the N.H. State Prison, Mar. 12, 1852, Dow Papers, New Hampshire Historical Society, Concord, N.H.

101. John R. Sutton, *Stubborn Children: Controlling Delinquency in the United States, 1640-1981* (Berkeley, Calif., 1988), pp. 2 and 95 and Rothman, *Conscience and Convenience*, pp. 123-26. Larry E. Sullivan says that prison reformers began to follow the medical treatment model which entailed the use

of psychiatrists, social workers, and other professionals. Sullivan, *Prison Reform Movement*, p. 27.

102. Janet E. Tighe, "Francis Wharton and the Nineteenth Century Insanity Defense: The Origins of a Reform Tradition," *American Journal of Legal History*, 27 (1983), 224 and Lawrence M. Friedman, *A History of American Law*, 2nd. ed. (New York, 1985), p. 591.

103. Friedman, *History of American Law*, p. 590.

104. Tighe, "Francis Wharton and Insanity Defense," 245 and 247-48.

105. ALS, Dr. Charles R. Bancroft, Superintendant of the N.H. Hospital for the Insane and Dr. Questen to Hon. R.J. Peaslee, Justice of the Superior Court [Rockingham Cty.], Nov. 12, 1904 in State v. Brigham, No. 5248, Rockingham Cty., N.H. (1904), MS, Div. of Records-Management and Archives, Concord, N.H.

106. "[N.H. State] Prison Records [1874-1915]" and "New Hampshire State Prison: Record of Gain and Loss in Population [1905-36]," both MS, Div. of Records-Management and Archives, Concord, N.H.

107. ALS, Dr. Charles R. Bancroft to Hon. R.J. Peaslee, Apr. 10, 1905 in State v. Robinson, No. 5625, Rockingham Cty., N.H. (1905), MS, Div. of Records-Management and Archives, Concord, N.H.

108. "[N.H. State] Prison Records [1874-1915]," MS, Div. of Records-Management and Archives, Concord, N.H.

109. TLS, Dr. Charles Bancroft to Chas. [sic] H. Batchelder, [Rockingham] County Solicitor, Dec. 14, 1909 in State v. Charland, No. 8219, Rockingham Cty., N.H. (1909), MS, Div. of Records-Management and Archives, Concord, N.H.

110. State v. Charland, No. 9845, Rockingham Cty., N.H. (1913) and "New Hampshire State Prison: Record of Gain and Loss in Population [1905-36]," both MS, Div. of Records-Management and Archives, Concord, N.H.

111. ALS, George F. Jelly, M.D. to [Whom It May Concern], Sept. 17, 1902 in State v. Glass, No. 127, Strafford Cty., N.H. (1902), MS, Justice and Administration Building, Dover, N.H.

112. TLS, Dr. Charles R. Bancroft to Hon. John E. Young, Presiding Justice [Strafford County Superior Court], n.d. in *Ibid.*

113. "New Hampshire State Prison: Record of Gain and Loss in Population [1905-36]," MS, Div. of Records-Management and Archives, Concord, N.H.

114. Tighe, "Francis Wharton and Insanity Defense," 228.

115. *Ibid.*, 231.

116. Robert M. Ireland, "Insanity and the Unwritten Law," *American Journal of Legal History*, 32 (1988), 165.

117. McGovern, *Masters of Madness*, p. 87.

118. Tighe, "Francis Wharton and Insanity Defense," 229.

119. Ireland, "Insanity and Unwritten Law," 160-62 and 165.

120. *Prison Warden's Report (1906)*, 53.

121. *Prison Warden's Report (1914)*, 6.

122. ALS, Dr. Charles R. Bancroft and Dr. Ralph E. Gallinger to [Whom It May Concern], Apr. 11, 1899 attached to ALS, Edward N. Pearson, Secretary of State to Charles R. Bancroft, superintendant of the Asylum for the Insane [sic], Apr. 11, 1899 in Box 1, Secretary of State. State Prison Papers, Div. of Records-Management and Archives, Concord, N.H.

123. Quentin Blaine, "Shall Surely Be Put to Death': Capital Punishment in New Hampshire, 1623-1985," *New Hampshire Bar Journal*, 27 (1986), 142.

124. *Ibid.*, 142 and *General Statutes of New Hampshire (1867)*, p. 494.

125. Blaine, "Shall Surely Be Put to Death," 141 and 151-52.

126. *Ibid.*, 151-52.

127. Ted Robert Gurr, "Historical Trends in Violent Crime: Europe and the United States" in Gurr, ed., *Violence in America*, Vol. 1 *The History of Crime* (Newbury Park, Calif., 1989), pp. 35-37.

128. State v. Jones, No. 10765, Rockingham Cty., N.H. (1870), MS, Div. of Records-Management and Archives, Concord, N.H.

129. "Register of Convicts 1812-1883," MS, Div. of Records-Management and Archives, Concord, N.H.

130. State v. Palmer, No. 4649, Rockingham Cty., N.H. (1888), MS, Div. of Records-Management and Archives, Concord, N.H.

131. "[N.H. State] Prison Records [1874-1915]," MS, Div. of Records-Management and Archives, Concord, N.H.

132. *Ibid.*

133. State v. Pike, No. 10261, Rockingham Cty., N.H. (1868), MS, Div. of Records-Management and Archives, Concord, N.H. and Friedman, *History of American Law*, pp. 590-91.

134. Henry Robinson, "The New Hampshire State Prison," *Granite Monthly*, 23 (1897), 223. Mark Twain ends his 1872 essay with the words, "But seriously, is it well to glorify a murderous villain on the scaffold, as Pike was glorified in New Hampshire? Is it well to turn the penalty for a bloody crime into a reward? Is it just to do it? Is it safe?" See "Lionizing Murderers" in Charles Neider, ed., *The Complete and Humorous Sketches and Tales of Mark Twain* (Garden City, N.Y., 1961), pp. 223-26.

135. State v. Pike, No. 10261, Rockingham Cty., N.H. (1868), MS, Div. of Records-Management and Archives, Concord, N.H.

320

136. Robinson, "New Hampshire State Prison," 224.

137. See "Pike, the Hampton Murderer" in Rev. Hosea Quinby, *The Prison Chaplaincy, and Its Experiences: In Two Parts* (Concord, N.H., 1873), pp. 28f.

138. Blaine, "Shall Surely Be Put to Death," 146.

139. William Chase and Arthur Chase, ed. and comp., *Supplement to the Public Statutes of New Hampshire (Chase Edition, 1901)* (Concord, N.H., 1914), p. 529.

140. "Minute Book 1812-1834: Records," [27], Div. of Records-Management and Archives, Concord, N.H.

141. *Ibid.*, [42].

142. *Ibid.*, [57-58].

143. Orlando Lewis, *The Development of American Prisons and Prison Customs, 1776-1845* (Montclair, N.J., 1967 reprint of 1922), pp. 86 and 93.

144. "Minute Book 1812-34," [43], Div. of Records-Management and Archives, Concord, N.H.

145. *Ibid.*, [57-58].

146. Robinson, "New Hampshire State Prison," 235.

147. *Prison Warden's Report (1900)*, 42.

148. *Report of the Officers of the New Hampshire State Prison...for the Twenty One [sic] Months Ending August 31, 1908* (Penacook, N.H., n.d.), 411.

149. *Prison Warden's Report (1906)*, 9.

150. *A Journal of the Proceedings of the House of Representatives of the State of New-Hampshire...June, Anno Domini, 1804* (Portsmouth, N.H., 1804), 24.

151. James Q. Wilson says that 87% of those arrested have been arrested before. Marvin Wolfgang's study of Philadelphia juvenile delinquents born in 1945 shows that once a delinquent had been arrested three times, he stood a 70% chance of being arrested again. "From *Thinking About Crime*" in Hyman Gross and Andrew von Hirsch, eds., *Sentencing* (New York, 1981), p. 213.

152. Jay R. Nash, *Encyclopedia of World Crime*, Vol 5 *Dictionary* (Wilmette, Ill., 1989), p. 307.

153. Richard Hawkins and Geoffrey P. Alpert, *American Prison Systems: Punishment and Justice* (Englewood Cliffs, N.J., 1989), pp. 198-99.

154. State v. Moore, No. 6310, Rockingham Cty., N.H. (1825), MS, Div. of Records-Management and Archives, Concord, N.H.

155. "Register of Convicts 1812-1883," MS, Div. of Records-Management and Archives, Concord, N.H.

156. State v. Austin, No. 5056-58, Rockingham Cty., N.H. (1858), MS, Div. of Records-Management and Archives, Concord, N.H.

157. State v. Austin and Moody, No. 7081, Rockingham Cty., N.H. (1863), MS, Div. of Records-Management and Archives, Concord, N.H.

158. "Register of Convicts 1812-1883," MS, Div. of Records-Management and Archives, Concord, N.H.

159. State v. Austin, No. 1457 and 1482, Rockingham Cty., N.H. (1882), MS, Div. of Records-Management and Archives, Concord, N.H.

160. See, for example, court and prison records for George Johnson, Cleophas Valle, and Andrew Charland: State v. Johnson, No. 16333, Rockingham Cty., N.H. (1879) and his entry which reads "Been in Mass. four times" in "Register of Convicts 1812-1883," both MS, Div. of Records-Management and Archives, Concord, N.H.; State v. Valle, No. 217, No. 370, No. 43, and No. 433, all Strafford Cty., N.H. (1903, 1906, and 1907), MS, Justice and Administration Building, Dover, N.H.; and State v. Charland, No. 4464, No. 8219, and No. 9845, all Rockingham Cty., N.H. (1906, 1909, and 1913), all MS, Div. of Records-Management and Archives, Concord, N.H.

161. Prison Warden's Report (1852), 21.

162. Report of the N.H. State Prison, Accompanied by Reports of the Chaplain and Physician, June Session, 1855 (Concord, N.H., 1855), 35.

163. Report of the Warden of the New-Hampshire State Prison Accompanied by the Reports of the Chaplain and Physician...June Session, 1864 (Concord, N.H., 1864), 31.

164. Reports of the Warden and Inspectors of the New Hampshire State-Prison, Together with the Reports of the Chaplain and Physician, June, 1881 (Manchester, N.H., 1881), 32.

165. Reports of the Warden and Inspectors of the New Hampshire State Prison Together with the Reports of the Chaplain and Physician, June, 1883 (Concord, N.H., 1883), 26-27.

166. Ibid., 27.

167. Prison Warden's Report (1852), 21.

168. Revised Statutes of the State of New Hampshire, Passed December 23, 1842 (Concord, N.H., 1843), p. 466. According to the Standard & Poor's price index, the 1842 dollar equals 344.8 cents in 1967 dollars. A 1986 dollar equals 30.1 cents in 1967 dollars. Standard & Poor's Statistical Service, Basic Statistics (New York, 1988), p. 76 and Chase, ed. and comp., Supplement to Public Statutes (1914), p. 535. According to Standard & Poor's price index, the 1903 dollar equals 334.1 cents in 1967 dollars. A 1986 dollar equals 30.1 cents in 1967 dollars. Standard & Poor's Statistical Service, Basic Statistics, p. 76.

322

169. *Report of the Warden of the N.H. State Prison, Accompanied by the Reports of the Physician and Chaplain, June Session, 1854* (Concord, N.H., 1854), 31.

170. *Reports of the Warden of the New Hampshire State-Prison, Accompanied by Reports of the Chaplain and Physician...June Session, 1879* (Manchester, N.H., 1879), 9.

171. *Annual Report of the Warden and Inspectors of the New Hampshire State Prison Accompanied by Reports of the Chaplain and Physician...June Session, 1869* (Manchester, N.H., 1869), 56.

172. *Prison Warden's Report (1881)*, 34.

173. *Prison Warden's Report (1883)*, 26.

174. *Statistics Relating to the New Hampshire State Prison Together with the Reports of the Chaplain, Physician, and Treasurer for the Two Years Ending November 30, 1898* (Manchester, N.H., 1898), 9.

175. *Journal of the House of Representatives...June, Anno Domini, 1804*, 24.

176. Cesare Beccaria, *On Crimes and Punishments*, trans. by Henry Paolucci, Vol. 7, Library of Liberal Arts (New York, 1963), pp. 58-59.

177. Rothman, *Discovery of the Asylum*, pp. 274-75.

178. The defective delinquent theory was based upon the idea that some offenders were incurably "feeble minded" thanks to bad heredity. This theory became popular with administrators of prisons, reformatories, and insane asylums around 1910 when intelligence testing was introduced. Defective delinquents were the lowest category of inmate in the new classification schemes devised by reformers. New York passed a law in 1920 providing separate institutions for female defective delinquents. See Sullivan, *Prison Reform Movement*, p. 37 and Nicole H. Rafter, *Partial Justice: Women, Prisons, and Social Control*, 2nd. ed. (New Brunswick, N.J., 1990), pp. 54 and 68-74.

179. *Journals of the Honorable Senate and House of Representatives, June Session, 1835* (Sandbornton, N.H., 1835), 188 and Ch. 11 "The Penitent Murderer" in Rev. Eleazer Smith, *Nine Years among the Convicts: or, Prison Reminiscences* (Boston, 1856), pp. 130-48.

180. Samuel Walker, *Sense and Nonsense about Crime: A Policy Guide*, 2nd. ed. (Pacific Grove, Calif., 1989), p. 46.

181. Rothman, "Doing Time," p. 380 and Sullivan, *Prison Reform Movement*, pp. 33-34.

Conclusion: Crime as a Response to Social Change and Hard Labor as Punishment

The increasing crime rate, diverging patterns, and types of crime in nineteenth-century New Hampshire were in part the manifestation of tensions created by the onslaught of economic and social change. Between 1810 and 1890 seacoast New Hampshire was transformed from a mostly rural society to one that was predominently urban. Between the 1810's and 1880's crime rates doubled and then declined through the 1910's. The shift in population was accompanied by a shift in the nature of work. Between 1870 and 1910 the proportion of persons engaged in agricultural work declined by 50% while that employed in manufacturing or trade and transportation rose substantially. The industrialization of New Hampshire created a new economic structure which in turn helped create new opportunities for crime. Demographic changes also caused new pressures and tensions. Native-born population growth remained static or very slow. Much of the population increase was due to foreign immigration. The definition and prosecution of crime changed with the region's economy, settlement patterns, and demography. The most serious offenders against the social order were subjected to a new form of punishment: imprisonment at hard labor.

These economic, social, and demographic changes were reflected in the changing nature of felony convictions during the period 1812-1914. Economic dislocation created new opportunities and incentives for property crime. Larceny and burglary were the most common forms of crime and were mostly a consequence of unstable economic and social conditions. The changing nature of work plus the growing numbers of Canadians, Irish, and other immigrants contributed to economic insecurity. An economy based on manufacturing and trade was more vulnerable than one based on agriculture to the recurring downturns of the business cycle. Burglary may have been encouraged by the increasing number of stores and warehouses built to service the new economy. The growth of an urban proletariat of millworkers, many of them of immigrant origin, was a factor in local crime patterns. Groups such as the Irish and French-Canadians faced social hostility from the Protestant majority in addition to economic insecurity.

Economic status definitely played a role in who was convicted of criminal behavior. The convicts in the sample for whom occupational information exists were virtually all blue collar workers. Most of them can be described as unskilled or low-skilled laborers. Most of the prisoners in the sample were convicted of burglary and larceny; the valuation of property affected was usually quite modest. Money in the form of coins, bills, bank notes, checks, and promissory notes was the most common target of such criminals. Clothing was next most common but lost favor over time, possibly because of its greater availability and cheapness that resulted from the growth of the textile industry. The low median monetary value of property crime suggests that New Hampshire was not a particularly wealthy state. In most cases, criminals and victims alike were of humble origin. Embezzlement was the one property crime in which the perpetrators were usually white collar. Such persons had the business and social connections, the skills, and the opportunities for embezzlement. Unlike most crimes committed by lower-status offenders, white collar embezzlement involved large sums of money.

Violent crime was probably encouraged by certain aspects of lower class life in the nineteenth century. Every violent offender for whom occupation was listed was a manual laborer. None were of white collar origin. Lower class life was crowded, boisterous, and rough. Alcohol consumption was a significant factor in several cases. The temperance movement appealed mainly to middle class Americans. Abstinence from alcohol was not particularly attractive to Irish Catholic laborers for whom heavy drinking was a culturally approved activity. Other cultural factors may have contributed to the participation of certain ethnic groups in violent crime. The Irish had a not-undeserved reputation for brawling and the Italians placed a high value on defending honor. Members of these ethnic groups committed 10.8% of the violent crimes in the sample yet the Irish and Italians made up only approximately 5% of the seacoast's population (see Chapter Five).

Changes in the criminal law were also related to the changing economic, social, and demographic composition of New Hampshire. The criminal statutes were revised periodically and it is possible to trace changing definitions of crime. The variety and complexity of property crimes proliferated in response to the commercialization and industrialization of society. New offenses such as "breaking and entering and stealing" (burglary) were added to the statutes. The issuing of fraudulent stock became a felony in the 1850's. Bribery of municipal and state officials became a felony. Some crimes were specifically related to the appearance of new technology, for example, the placing of obstructions on railroad tracks.

Laws respecting violent crimes reveal a growing disinclination to apply capital punishment. Violent crimes were defined more precisely than before. The law recognized different degrees of murder and manslaughter. Eventually, the death penalty was restricted to first degree murder. By 1903 life imprisonment had become an optional punishment for first degree murder. Abortion was criminalized in 1848 at the same time that male physicians began to displace midwives. The definition of rape was expanded in the late nineteenth century but this was more a result of renewed interest in crimes against morality rather than an attempt to control violence.

Changing moral standards are clearly revealed in the New Hampshire statutes over the period 1812-1914. One can trace the waning Puritan influence up to the early nineteenth century. Moral transgressions had been viewed as serious violations of Biblical commandments but were considered irrelevant or fairly unimportant in New Hampshire's commercial, expanding society of the first half of the nineteenth century. Most of the old prohibitions were recriminalized after the Civil War. New moral offenses were added too. The raising of the age of statutory rape from 10 years to 16 years in the 1890's was part of the legal response to changing moral standards. The renewed punishment of moral offenses was in many ways a result of the growing influence of the middle class. Certainly the recriminalization of moral offenses was related to the changes taking place in social relations. While middle class women were adopting the model of "true womanhood" which valued sexual purity, more lower class women were entering the labor force as factory workers. Reformers campaigned against prostitution and attempted to protect youths from the effects of vice. Lawmakers felt a need to guard against a moral breakdown and so recriminalized old offenses and added new ones to discourage misbehavior.

Changes in the criminal statutes of the late eighteenth and early nineteenth century also show legal reformers attempting to create a distinctly American legal structure. Many American lawmakers adopted an anti-British perspective: they regarded the common law tradition as outmoded elitist, and they regarded capital punishment as a relic of British cruelty. New Hampshire, along with other states, abolished most capital and corporal punishments. Reformers attempted to make the law less repressive. Proponents of codification worried about the power of unelected court officials under the common law system. A true code reduced the law to written form subject to rules of interpretation. Thus, the power of judges was limited under codification while under the common law tradition judicial interpretation played a very important role. New Hampshire continued to operate under a common law structure - New Hampshire laws were never truly codified but instead were consolidations and restatements in which judicial interpretation remained fundamental. However, the struggle to modify the common law tradition was spurred on into the mid-nineteenth century by the influence of Jacksonian ideals.

Traditional anti-lawyer sentiment, Jacksonian ideals, and traditional anti-federalism all contributed to important changes in court structure and trial procedure in New Hampshire. Maxwell Bloomfield and other scholars have contended that American reformers of the time wanted to bring the law under public control. Reformers worried about the possibility of elite control of the judicial apparatus. Anti-federalists were concerned with the power of the central government, which they regarded as a threat to the individual states and citizens of the new country. Consequently, New Hampshire lawmakers introduced various safeguards into the legal system to protect the individual against the power of the central government of his or her own state. For example, in 1791 the New Hampshire legislature passed a law which ensured that a person accused of a capital crime should be given a copy of his or her indictment before the start of the trial. By 1842 a grand jury indictment was required for any imprisonable offense. Other legal safeguards for the accused included provisions for arraignment, bail, and special measures for the protection of juvenile offenders. The common law tradition continues in New Hampshire to this day but the various reforms enacted between the late eighteenth and mid-nineteenth century ensured that accused offenders were given basic protections against state and judicial oppression.

As New Hampshire grew more urban, the state began granting municipalities greater freedom in regard to law enforcement. Demographic changes rendered the old system of village constables and night watchmen less effective. Also, urban life made disruptive behavior such as public drunkenness, brawling, and so forth unacceptable. In 1807 Portsmouth established the first police force in New Hampshire. A number of American cities began employing police officers and detectives in an attempt to control crime and maintain public order. Law enforcement became more professional over the course of the nineteenth century. In 1852 the state made all towns elibible to establish a police court for trying minor crimes. Urbanization contributed to the strengthening of local mechanisms of crime control throughout the course of the nineteenth century.

Crime in New Hampshire was typical of northern states in that most convictions were for property crime and not violent crime. Crime in New Hampshire resembles crime in Massachusetts as described by Michael S. Hindus. This was a contrast to South Carolina, where convictions for violent crime were very common between 1767 and 1878. Edward L. Ayers explains the violence of the nineteenth-century American South by linking it to the high value placed upon honor by white middle and upper class males. A violent response was appropriate for a perceived insult to one's honor. Few, if any, violent felonies in New Hampshire were the product of a cult of honor. Like Massachusetts, crime in New Hampshire mostly involved property.

Felony conviction rates per 100,000 population were lower in nineteenth-century New Hampshire than in most other regions. This was partly a result of the method employed in counting crimes. This study counted felony convictions resulting in incarceration and limited these convictions to Rockingham County between 1812 and 1914 and Strafford County between 1870 and 1914. Other researchers of nineteenth-century crime and punishment have employed alternate methods of counting crime such as counting arrests or counting incarcerations in jails, houses of correction, and reform schools as well as state prisons. However, other more fundamental factors help to account for New Hampshire's relatively low crime rates. Although New Hampshire became more urban over the course of the nineteenth century, it was less urbanized than Massachusetts. No city in New Hampshire at this time rivaled Boston, Philadelphia, New York, or even Columbus, Ohio in size. The urban concentration and sheer numbers characteristic of these locations may have helped to raise their crime rates.

Nevertheless, economic and social changes taking place between 1812 and 1914 made New Hampshire an increasingly violent region. Conviction and incarceration rates for violent crime rose steadily between the 1840's and 1890's except for a momentary dip in the 1870's. Violent crime in New Hampshire peaked around 20 years later than was typical for the rest of the United States. According to Ted Robert Gurr, violent crime in America crested in the 1860's and 1870's, thanks to the aggressive impulses stirred up by the Civil War, the availability of firearms, and relatively light punishments for murder. Oddly, the violent crime rate in New Hampshire dropped in the 1870's before resuming its climb to the top in the 1890's. Possibly, the tensions of adjusting to an urban, industrial, and multicultural society kept escalating until some sort of social equilibrium was reached. By 1890 seacoast New Hampshire was more urban than rural. The violent crime rate subsided over the period 1900-14.

The "typical" convict changed to some extent over this period thanks to increasing mobility and foreign immigration. Convicts were overwhelmingly white and male. The median age was 26 years. The population of Rockingham County and Strafford County was nearly all white and mostly native-born. The proportion of prison inmates born outside New Hampshire increased dramatically over this period. This was probably a consequence of new forms of transportation which made travel much easier than before. Also, changing economic circumstances provided an impetus for population shifts. Foreign immigration was reflected in the changing ethnic composition of the prison population. Young men from immigrant groups were sometimes disproportionately represented in prison in relation to the population at risk (i.e., males age 18-34). This may well have been connected to the difficulties of adjustment to life in a new location. Immigrant groups such as the Irish and Canadians usually started out at the bottom of the economic hierarchy in the United States. Most persons convicted of crime in nineteenth-century New Hampshire were drawn from the lower classes.

The extreme rarity of female convicts probably was a consequence of the restrictions placed on female behavior by gender role prescriptions. Despite significant social and economic changes of the era, very few women were convicted of felonies in New Hampshire between 1812 and 1914. The popularity of the cult of true womanhood which emphasized domesticity and submissiveness did little to encourage women in the pursuit of crime. Today, women in America are freer than ever before and it is interesting to note that their proportion of the American state prison population is presently more than double that of women in the New Hampshire State Prison between 1812 and 1914. However, males are still convicted of felonies far more often than women. This suggests that male criminality is also connected to psychological factors, such as aggressiveness, which are either genetic or encouraged in the socialization process.

The original intentions of the founders of the New Hampshire State Prison were subverted over the course of the nineteenth century. In the first place, the prison experience was almost completely a negative one for the inmates. In this regard, New Hampshire was unexceptional. Life in prison was a punitive experience with very few redeeming features. The reformative component was neglected in favor of hard labor and punishment. Certainly, New Hampshire lawmakers had no intention of coddling criminals but reformation of the convict's character had been one of the basic goals of imprisonment since Governor John T. Gilman's proposal of 1804.

In practice, the primary function of the New Hampshire State Prison between 1812 and 1914 was to earn money for the state. Ostensibly, the prison's goals were to punish convicted criminals, reform them, act as a deterrent to would-be criminals, and to be economically self-supporting. Chapter Six documents that the quest for profitability of prison labor under the contract labor system was absolutely paramount throughout this period. The role of work was very important; it covered the costs of prison administration and created revenue for the state. In theory, work also contributed to the reformation of an inmate's character by instilling discipline and the value of regular, hard labor. Work also functioned as a disciplinary method by supervising the prisoner's time. The more positive aspects of prison labor were neglected in favor of profits. The inmates worked long hours under poor conditions. Working conditions became more dangerous with the advent of mechanization. Dusty, noisy, smokey, and improperly heated workshops contributed to the poor health conditions noted in the prison physician's annual reports. Inmates were literally slaves of the state until 1913 when provision was finally made for paying them for their labor.

The certainty of punishment - a cardinal feature for Beccaria and other early prison reformers - was jeopardized by the application of various forms of early release in the New Hampshire State Prison. The mean prison sentence was 3.8 years while the mean sentence served was 2.8 years. More than half (55%) of the inmates left the prison before the expiration of their original sentence. The most common form of early release was by governor's pardon. Commutation in exchange for good behavior was popular in the 1860's and 1870's while parole was implemented during the period 1901-14. A small number, five percent, of prisoners left early via death, escape, or execution.

The frequent use of pardons, commutation, and later, parole, appears to have been a device for relieving overcrowding more than anything else. The history of the prison between 1812 and 1879 was one in which severe overcrowding was a recurrent phenomenon. Officially, early release was contingent upon evidence of reformation, good behavior, or for reasons such as extreme ill health. Too few original records survive to indicate whether or not the majority of inmates released early were released for legitimate reasons or for more pragmatic reasons such as creating more space. Early release may have been a mechanism for handling the influx of new inmates in the face of inadequate resources.

Early release via parole between 1901 and 1914 suggests that pragmatic rather than idealistic considerations held sway. The indeterminate sentencing law of 1901 provided for a minimum and maximum sentence. The inmate became eligible for consideration for parole once the minimum sentence had been served. In theory, release through parole was based on several criteria, the most important behing evidence of rehabilitation. Every single paroled inmate in the sample was released upon the expiration of his or her minimum sentence. It seems unlikely that all of these convicts were able to convince the parole board that they were indeed rehabilitated. In fact, some inmates were reimprisoned for breaking parole conditions. At least one third of those paroled between 1901 and 1914 violated their parole conditions.

While early release was a boon to prisoners, there were several arguments against this course of action. The sense of fairness was violated by the early release of some but not all inmates even if those released met the official criteria for a pardon, commutation, or parole. Several prison wardens complained of this. Early release demoralized the inmates staying behind. Others became refractory or embittered because they developed anticipations of an early release which never was granted. Advocates of the indeterminate sentence preferred to keep inmates in prison for the maximum sentence to ensure that rehabilitation had really taken place. There is no evidence that such a policy was followed at the New Hampshire State Prison before 1915.

Even if the inmate managed to survive the stultifying and dangerous regime of hard labor, there were further obstacles to the goal of prisoner reformation. Many of the inmates suffered from poor health. Sick and exhausted men were poor subjects for the tentative reform programs tried out at the state prison. The prison was a custodial institution: it indiscriminately mixed young, first offenders with more hardened jailbirds. Juvenile property offenders were housed with murderers, rapists, and moral offenders. The influence of corrupt and potentially violent companions did little to reform first time offenders.

Rehabilitative efforts at the New Hampshire State Prison were ad hoc and inadequately supported. In light of the Martinson study (1975) which analyzed the effectiveness of 231 modern-day prisoner rehabilitation programs, it is not surprising that the New Hampshire State Prison proved to be inadequate to the task. The efforts made at the prison were rather primitive compared to the elaborate therapeutic programs tried out in the twentieth century. Essentially, the prison chaplain was in charge of reforming the inmates through religious instruction. Evangelical Protestantism was a major influence on the reformative efforts made at the state prison. Most of the time, rehabilitation consisted of religious instruction and exhortation to mend one's ways. The one concrete benefit gained by some prison inmates was to attain basic literacy.

Crime in New Hampshire during the period 1812-1914 was mainly the product of a society in transition. Forces of change included a growing urban population, a declining rural population, and major occupational shifts from agricultural to industrial and commercial work. Technological innovations such as railroads, steamships, telegraph and telephone systems, and automobiles contributed greatly to these changes. Foreign immigration increased significantly after the Civil War. All of these forces created pressures and opportunities for criminal behavior.

The pattern of felony convictions in the sample indicates a preoccupation with crimes against property. This is not surprising considering the economic dislocations of the era. The pattern of convictions also reveals that nineteenth-century New Hampshire was becoming a more violent society between the 1840's and 1890's. Admittedly, the overall proportion of violent crime was small (14.6%) but the rate of violent crime quadrupled during this period. The recriminalization of moral offenses in the late nineteenth century was more a reaction against social changes than a conscious revival of Puritanism. The changing relationship between women and work, the imposition of middle class standards of sexual behavior on society, and a concern for protecting young women from prostitution is revealed in the new laws.

The introduction of imprisonment to New Hampshire in 1812 marked the start of a new era in criminal justice. Unfortunately, the prison failed to prevent crime or reform offenders. It did succeed as an economically viable institution most of the time as it usually turned a profit for the state. it was a custodial, not a reformatory, institution. The concern for profits was not unusual although it may have been more pronounced in New Hampshire than in many other states. Imprisonment in New Hampshire began with the same reforming enthusiasm found in other locations during the early nineteenth century. As was true of so many other American prisons, the New Hampshire State Prison ended up as something other than what was originally intended. Punishment in New Hampshire was not particularly harsh compared to other states but it was not much better.

There have been many significant changes in prison administration since 1914: the introduction of therapeutic programs, the abolition of the contract labor system in 1932 and the introduction of the state-use system of prison labor, and the introduction of a wide variety of relevant vocational programs such as computer data processing. Provisions have even been made for religious services in Spanish.[1] The problem of where to house female convicts was solved first in 1941 when the state made provisions for boarding them in Vemont and then Connecticut.[2] Finally, in November 1989 the state began leasing a 100-bed facility for female convicts in Hillsborough County, New Hampshire.[3]

Despite widespread dissatisfaction with prisons in America over the past 30 years, this nineteenth-century form of punishment continues to flourish in New Hampshire and elsewhere. Definitions of crime have changed since 1914 and so has prison administration. Since the 1970's public sentiment has favored a retributive response to crime and American prisons have become grossly overcrowded. The New Hampshire State Prison housed 287 inmates in 1980. There are now over 1500 inmates at the recently-expanded facility.[4]

Notes

1. *Report of the Department of Corrections Including the Report of the Officers of the New Hampshire State Prison...for the Two Years Ending June 30, 1984* (Concord, N.H., 1985), 58.
2. *Laws of the State of New Hampshire Passed January Session, 1941* (Concord, N.H., 1941), pp. 179-80.
3. *New Hampshire Department of Corrections Biennial Report July 1988-June 1990*, i and 50.
4. There were 1247 inmates at the prison as of June, 1990. *Ibid.*, 3. As of December 31, 1991 there were 1533 inmates at the prison. U.S. Bureau of the Census, *Statistical Abstract of the United States: 1993*, 113th. ed. (Washington, D.C., 1993), p. 211.

Bibliography

I. Original Sources

1. Unpublished

Bass, Gov. Robert Perkins. Papers c. 1910-13. Baker Library, Dartmouth College, Hanover, N.H.

Bell, Samuel. Correspondence 1834-38. New Hampshire Historical Society, Concord, N.H.

Brewster, Charles W. Papers C. 1843-44. New Hampshire Historical Society, Concord, N.H.

Council Minutes 1804-33. Division of Records-Management and Archives, Concord, N.H.

Description Register. New Hampshire State Prison [c. 1881-98 and 1899-1906]. Division of Records-Management and Archives, Concord, N.H.

Dow, Rufus. Papers c. 1850-56. New Hampshire Historical Society, Concord, N.H.

Executive Records [Correspondence and Messages] 1801-30. Division of Records-Management and Archives, Concord, N.H.

New Hampshire State Prison: Record of Gain and Loss in Population [1905-36]. Division of Records-Management and Archives, Concord, N.H.

___. Minute Book 1812-34 and 1834-55. Division of Records-Management and Archives, Concord, N.H.

___. Prison Records [1874-1915]. Division of Records-Management and Archives, Concord, N.H.

___. Papers c. 1804-1936. Division of Records-Management and Archives, Concord, N.H.

___. Register of Convicts 1812-1883. Division of Records-Management and Archives, Concord, N.H.

___. [Untitled Register 1887-1907]. Division of Records-Management and Archives, Concord, N.H.

Perry, George W., comp. New Hampshire Prisons 1812-1925. Scrapbook, c. 1960. New Hampshire Historical Society, Concord, N.H.

Rockingham County Superior Court. Bills and Indictments 1812-1914. Division of Records-Management and Archives, Concord, N.H.

Strafford County Superior Court Bills and Indictments 1870-1914. Justice and Administration Building, Dover, N.H.

Thompson, Rev. Franklin C. The New Hampshire State Prison. Typed Transcription of New Hampshire State Prison Records c. 1808-1917. New Hampshire Historical Society, Concord, N.H.

Wardwell, Burnham. Charges against Warden John C. Pilsbury 1880. In New Hampshire State Prison Papers c. 1804-1936. Division of Records-Management and Archives, Concord, N.H.

Wilkins, Rev. Elijah R. [Sermons Given at the New Hampshire State Prison 1884-96 and 1899-1905]. Two Notebooks. New Hampshire Historical Society, Concord, N.H.

2. Published Sources

New Hampshire Session Laws

Laws of the State of New Hampshire Passed January/June Session [Title Varies], 1832-1907, 1937, and 1941.

New Hampshire Statutes

"By the Court: in the Yeares 1641. 1642. Capital Lawes, established within the Jurisdiction of Massachusetts." *Collections of the Massachusetts Historical Society*, vol. IV, 2d Series. Boston: Charles C. Little & James Brown, 1846.

New Hampshire. *The Laws of New Hampshire*, vol. 1 *Province Period [1679-1702]* (John B. Clarke, 1904).

___. *The Laws of New Hampshire*, vol. 2 *Province Period 1702-1745* (Rumford Printing Co., 1913).

___. *The Laws of New Hampshire*, vol. 4 *Revolutionary Period 1776-1784* (1916).

___. *The Laws of the State of New-Hampshire...* (John Melcher, 1792).

___. *The Laws the State of New-Hampshire...* (John Melcher, 1797).

___. *The Laws of New Hampshire*, vol. 7 *Second Constitutional Period 1801-1811* (Evans Printing Co., 1918).

___. *The Constitution and Laws of the State of New-Hampshire...* (Samuel Bragg, Jun., 1805).

___. *The Laws of New Hampshire...*, vol. 8 *Second Constitutional Period 1811-1820* (Evans Printing Co., 1920).

___. *The Laws of the State of New-Hampshire...* (C. Norris & Co., 1815).

___. *The Laws of the State of New-Hampshire Enacted Since June 1, 1815* (Isaac Hill, 1824).

___. *The Laws of the State of New-Hampshire...* (Isaac Long, Jr., 1830).

___. *Revised Statutes of the State of New Hampshire, Passed December 23, 1842...* (Carroll & Baker, 1843).

___. *Compiled Statutes of the State of New Hampshire...* (Butterfield & Hill, 1854).

___. *The General Statutes of the State of New-Hampshire...* (B. W. Sanborn & Co., 1867).

___. *The General Laws of the State of New Hampshire...* (John B. Clarke,

338

1878).

___. *The Public Statutes of the State of New Hampshire...* (John B. Clarke, 1891).

___. *The Public Statutes of the State of New Hampshire and General Laws in Force, January 1, 1901* (Edson C. Eastman, 1900).

___. *Supplement to the Statutes of New Hampshire (Chase Ed., 1901)* (Arthur H. Chase and William D. Chandler, 1914).

___. *Revised Laws of the State of New Hampshire* (Rumford Press, 1942).

Federal Statutes

U.S.A. *The Statutes at Large of the United States of America from December, 1927 to March, 1929*, Vol. 45, Pt. 1 (United States Government Printing Office, 1929).

Other Sources

Bouton, Nathaniel, ed. and comp. *Provincial Papers: Documents and Records Relating to the Province of New-Hampshire from the Earliest Period of Its Settlement: 1623-86.* Concord, N.H.: George E. Jenks, 1867.

___. *Provincial Papers: Documents and Records Relating to the Province of New-Hampshire from 1692 to 1722.* Manchester, N.H.: John B. Clarke, 1869.

A Catalogue of Books in the Library of the New Hampshire State Prison, Concord, New Hampshire. Manchester, N.H.: John B. Clarke, 1881.

Department of Justice. Federal Bureau of Investigation. *Uniform Crime Reports 1992: Crime in the United States*. Washington, D.C.: U.S. Government Printing Office, 1993

New Hampshire House of Representatives. *Journal* [Title Varies]. 1804-39.

New Hampshire Senate. *Journal* [Title Varies]. 1804-39.

New Hampshire State Board of Health. *Annual Report* [Title Varies]. 1883, 1891, and 1902.

New Hampshire State Prison. *Annual Warden's Report* [Title Varies]. 1813-1990. [1813-39 found only in N.H. House and or Senate *Journal*]. Lacking: 1858, 1860, and 1872-73.

New Hampshire Vital Statistics. *Annual Report* [Title Varies]. 1880, 1883, 1893, 1902, and 1988-89.

Old Maps of Carroll County, N.H. in 1892. Fryeburg, Me.: Saco Valley Printing, 1983.

Old Maps of Merrimack County, N.H. in 1892. Fryeburg, Me.: Saco Valley Printing, 1981.

Old Maps of Rockingham County, N.H. in 1892. Fryeburg, Me.: Saco Valley Printing, 1981.

Old Maps of Strafford County, N.H. in 1892. Fryeburg, Me.: Saco Valley Printing, 1982.

Quinby, Rev. Hosea. *The Prison Chaplaincy and Its Experiences: In Two Parts.* Concord, N.H.: D.J. Guernsey, 1873.

Rand, Edward T. *Closing Remarks of Hon. E.D. Rand at the State Prison Investigation, Concord, New Hampshire, Thursday, July 1, 1880.* Concord, N.H.: Evans and Sleeper, 1880.

Shaw, Joseph L. *New-Hampshire State Prison Cruelty Exposed: or, The Sufferings of Joseph L. Shaw, In That Institution in 1837, While John M'Daniel Was Warden.* Exeter, N.H.: Printed for the Author, 1839.

Smith, Rev. Eleazer. *Nine Years among the Convicts: or, Prison Reminiscences.* Boston: J.P. Magee, 1856.

Standard & Poor's Statistical Service. *Basic Statistics: Price Indexes...* New York: Stand & Poor's Corporation, 1988.

U.S. Bureau of the Census. *Mortality Statistics 1910: Eleventh Annual Report*. Washington, D.C.: U.S. Government Printing Office, 1913.

U.S. Bureau of the Census. *Reports* [Title Varies]. 1800-1910. New Haven: Research Publications, Inc. Microfilm:

  Census of Population 1800-1910.

  Census of Vital Statistics [Mortality] 1860-1900.

U.S. Bureau of the Census. *Historical Statistics of the United States: Colonial Times to 1970*. Washington, D.C.: U.S. Government Printing Office, 1975.

U.S. Bureau of the Census. *Statistical Abstract of the United States: 1993*. 113th ed. Washington, D.C.: U.S. Government Printing Office, 1993.

Wines, E.C. and Theodore W. Dwight. *Report on the Prisons and Reformatories of the United States and Canada: Made to the Legislature of New York, January, 1867*. Albany: Van Benthuysen & Sons' Steam Printing House, 1867. Ann Arbor, Mich.: University Microfilms. American Culture Series. Microfilm.

Newspapers

Concord Gazette (Concord, N.H.). 24 Nov. and 1 Dec., 1812.

Dover Enquirer (Dover, N.H.). 21 Feb.; 14 and 21 Mar.; 5 and 12 Sept.; 3 Oct.; and 19 and 26 Dec., 1890.

Exeter News-Letter and Rockingham Advertiser (Exeter, N.H.). 6 and 13 Oct., 1840; 23 Feb. and 2 Mar., 1841

Foster's Weekly Democrat (Dover, N.H.). 3, 10, and 24 Feb.; 24 Mar.; 8 May; 5 June; and 25 Sept., 1899.

New-Hampshire Patriot (Concord, N.H.). 23 June; 11 Aug.; 17 Nov.; and 1 Dec., 1812.

New-Hampshire Statesman (Concord, N.H.). 8 and 14 May, 1853.

People and New Hampshire Patriot (Concord, N.H.). 25 Mar.; 10 June and 22 and 29 July, 1880.

Portsmouth Daily Chronicle (Portsmouth, N.H.). 29-30 May and 1 June, 1888. Cleveland: Micro Photo. Microfilm.

Portsmouth Herald (Portsmouth, N.H.). 18-19 and 29 June and 6 July, 1912. Microfilm.

Public Forum (Manchester, N.H.). Sept. 1871-Jan. 1875.

Rochester Courier (Rochester, N.H.). 31 July and 23 Oct., 1914.

II. Seconday Sources

1. Books

Abbott, Frances M. *Historical Address Prepared for the Duo-Centennial Celebration of the Founding of the City of Concord, New Hampshire July 2-4, 1927.* Concord, N.H.: Rumford Press, 1927.

Adams, John. "Dissertation on Canon and Feudal Law." In *The Works of John Adams: Second President of the United States...*, Vol. 3, by John Adams, Pp. 447-64. Boston: Charles C. Little and James Brown, 1851.

Adams, John P. *Drowned Valley: The Piscataqua River Basin.* Hanover, N.H.: Pub. for University of New Hampshire by University Press of New England, 1976.

Adams, Willi Paul. *The First American Constitutions: Republican Ideology and the Making of the State Constitutions in the Revolutionary Era.* Translated by Rita and Robert Kimber. Chapel Hill: Pub. for Institute of Early American History and Culture by University of North Carolina Press, 1980.

Adshead, Joseph D. *Prisons and Prisoners.* London: Longman, Brown, Green, and Longman, 1845.

Allen, Harry E. and others. *Probation and Parole in America.* New York: Free Press, 1985.

Ayers, Edward L. *Vengeance and Justice: Crime and Punishment in the Nineteenth-Century American South*. New York: Oxford University Press, 1984.

Barnes, Harry E. *The Repression of Crime: Studies in Historical Penology*. George H. Doran Co., 1926; reprint, Montclair, N.J.: Patterson Smith, 1969.

___. *The Story of Punishment: A Record of Man's Inhumanity to Man*, 2d ed. Stratford Co., 1930; reprint, Montclair, N.J.: Patterson Smith, 1972.

Barry, John V. "Alexander Maconochie." In *Pioneers in Criminology*, 2d ed., edited by Hermann Mannheim, 84-106. Montclair, N.J.: Patterson Smith, 1972.

Beccaria, Cesare Bonesana, Marchese di. *An Essay on Crime and Punishments*. Philadelphia: Bell, 1778. Early American Imprints 1639-1800. American Antiquarian Society. Microcard.

___. *On Crimes and Punishments*. Translated by Henry Paolucci. Library of Liberal Arts. New York: Bobbs-Merrill, 1963.

Bender, John. *Imagining the Penitentiary: Fiction and the Architecture of Mind in Eighteenth-Century England*. Chicago: University of Chicago Press, 1987.

Bentham, Jeremy. *The Works of Jeremy Bentham*. Edited by John Bowring. New York: Russell and Russell, Inc., 1962.

Bessmer, Sue. *The Laws of Rape*. New York: Praeger Scientific, 1984.

Black, Henry C. *Black's Law Dictionary*. 5th ed. St. Paul: West Publishing Co., 1979.

Bloomfield, Maxwell. *American Lawyers in a Changing Society, 1776-1876*. Cambridge, Mass.: Harvard University Press, 1976.

Blumstein, Alfred and others. *Research on Sentencing: The Search for Reform*. Washington, D.C.: National Academy Press, 1983.

Bouton, Nathaniel. *A Discourse on the Growth and Development of Concord,*

New Hampshire in the Last Fifty Years: Being the Third Semi-Centennial. Concord, N.H.: Republican Press Assoc., 1875.

___. *The History of Concord from Its First Grant in 1725 to...the Present Period, 1855...* Concord, N.H.: Benning W. Sanborn, 1856.

Brault, Gerard J. *The French-Canadian Heritage in New England.* Hanover, N.H.: University Press of New England, 1986.

Brighton, Raymond A. *They Came to Fish.* Portsmouth, N.H.: Portsmouth 350, Inc., 1973.

Carleton, Mark T. *Politics and Punishment: The History of the Louisiana State Penal System.* Baton Rouge: Louisiana State University Press, 1971.

Cogswell, Elliott C. *History of Nottingham, Deerfield, and Northwood, New Hampshire.* Manchester, N.H.: John B. Clarke, 1878; reprint, Somersworth, N.H.: New Hampshire Publishing Co., 1972.

Cradle of American Shipbuilding: Portsmouth Naval Shipyard, Portsmouth, New Hampshire. Portsmouth, N.H.: Portsmouth Naval Shipyard, 1978.

Davis, David B. *From Homicide to Slavery: Studies in American Culture.* New York: Oxford University Press, 1986.

___. "The Movement to Abolish Capital Punishment in America, 1787-1861." In *Police, Prison, and Punishment*, edited by Kermit L. Hall, 134-57. New York: Garland Publishing, Inc., 1987.

Davis, Michael. "Forced to Tramp: The Perspective of the Labor Press, 1870-1900." In *Walking to Work: Tramps in America*, edited by Eric H. Monkkonen, 141-70. Lincoln, Neb.: University of Nebraska Press, 1984.

de Tocqueville, Alexis and Gustave de Beaumont. *On the Penitentiary System in the United States and Its Application in France.* Translated by Francis Lieber. Philadelphia: Lea & Blanchard, 1833; reprint, Carbondale, Ill.: Southern Illinois University Press, 1964.

Dean, Charles W. and Mary de Bruyn-Kops. *The Crime and Consequences of Rape*. Springfield, Ill.: Charles C. Thomas, Publisher, 1982.

Degler, Carl N. *At Odds: Women and the Family in America from the Revolution to the Present*. New York: Oxford University Press, 1980.

D'Emilio, John D. and Estelle B. Freedman. *Intimate Matters: A History of Sexuality in America*. New York: Harper and Row, Publishers, 1988.

DiIulio, John J., Jr. *No Escape: The Future of American Corrections*. [New York]: Basic Books, 1991.

Dix, Dorothea L. *Remarks on Prisons and Prison Discipline in the United States*. 2d ed. 1845; reprint, Montclair, N.J.: Patterson Smith, 1967.

Dorland's Illustrated Medical Dictionary. 27th ed. Philadelphia: W.B. Saunders Co., 1988.

Douglas, Ann. *The Feminization of American Culture*. New York: Anchor Press-Doubleday, 1988.

Dressner, Richard B. and Glenn C. Altschuler. "Sentiment and Statistics in the Progressive Era: The Debate on Capital Punishment in New York." In *Police, Prison, and Punishment*, edited by Kermit L. Hall, 191-209. New York: Garland Publishing, Inc., 1987.

Dugdale, Richard L. *The Jukes: A Study in Crime, Pauperism, Disease, and Heredity*. 4th ed. New York: G.P. Putnam's Sons, 1910.

Dumm, Thomas L. *Democracy and Punishment: Disciplinary Origins of the United States*. Madison: University of Wisconsin Press, 1987.

Durkheim, Emile. *The Division of Labor in Society*. New York: Free Press, 1984.

___. *The Rules of Sociological Method*. 8th ed. Translated by Solovay and Mueller. Catlin, N.Y.: Free Press, 1966.

___. *Suicide: A Study in Sociology*. Glenco, Ill.: Free Press, 1951.

Ellis, Richard E. *The Jeffersonian Crisis: Courts and Politics in the Young Republic*. New York: Oxford University Press, 1971.

Erikson, Kai T. *Wayward Puritans: A Study in the Sociology of Deviance*. New York: John Wiley & Sons, Inc., 1966.

Eriksson, Torsten. *The Reformers: An Historical Survey of Pioneer Treatments of Criminals*. New York: Elsevier, 1976.

Evans, Robin. *The Fabrication of Virtue: English Prison Architecture, 1750-1840*. New York: Cambridge University Press, 1982.

Federal Writers' Project of the Works Progress Administration for the State of New Hampshire. *New Hampshire: A Guide to the Granite State*. Boston: Houghton Mifflin Co., 1938.

Ferri, Enrico. *Criminal Sociology*. Translated by Walter I. Kelly. Boston: Little, Brown, and Co., 1917.

Foucault, Michel. *Discipline and Punish: The Birth of the Prison*. Translated by Alan Sheridan. New York: Pantheon Books, 1977.

Freedman, Estelle B. *Their Sisters' Keepers: Women's Prison Reform in America, 1830-1930*. Ann Arbor: University of Michigan Press, 1981.

Friedman, Lawrence M. *A History of American Law*. 2d ed. New York: Simon & Schuster, Inc., 1985.

___ and Robert V. Percival. *The Roots of Justice: Crime and Punishment in Alameda County, California 1870-1910*. Chapel Hill: University of North Carolina Press, 1981.

Garofalo, Baron Raffaele. *Criminology*. Translated by Robert W. Millar. Boston: Little, Brown, and Co., 1914; reprint, Montclair, N.J.: Patterson Smith, 1968.

Genovese, Eugene D. *Roll, Jordan, Roll: The World the Slaves Made*. New York: Pantheon Books, 1974.

Gilje, Paul. *The Road to Mobocracy: Popular Disorder in New York City, 1763-1834.* Chapel Hill: Pub. for Institute of Early American History and Culture by University of North Carolina Press, 1987.

Greeley, Andrew M. *Ethnicity in the United States: A Preliminary Reconnaissance.* New York: John Wiley and Sons, 1974.

Greenberg, Douglas. *Crime and Law Enforcement in the Colony of New York 1691-1776.* Ithaca, N.Y.: Cornell University Press, 1976.

Griffin, Clifford S. *Their Brothers' Keepers: Moral Stewardship in the United States, 1800-1865.* New Brunswick, N.J.: Rutgers University Press, 1960.

Gross, Hyman and Andrew von Hirsch, eds. *Sentencing.* New York: Oxford University Press, 1981.

Grunhut, Max. *Penal Reform: A Comparative Study.* Oxford: Clarendon Press, 1948; reprint, Montclair, N.J.: Patterson Smith, 1972.

Gurr, Ted Robert. "Historical Trends in Violent Crime: Europe and the United States." In *Violence in America*, vol. 1, edited by Ted Robert Gurr, 21-54. Newbury Park, Calif.: Sage Publications, 1989.

___., ed. *Violence in America.* Newbury Park, Calif.: Sage Publications, 1989.

Haines, Francis. *Horses in America.* New York: Thomas Y. Crowell Co., 1971.

Hall, Kermit L., ed. *Police, Prison, and Punishment: Major Historical Interpretations.* New York: Garland Publishing, Inc., 1987.

Haller, Mark H. "Historical Roots of Police Behavior." In *Police, Prisons, and Punishment*, edited by Kermit L. Hall, 323-43. New York: Garland Publishing, Inc., 1987.

Hareven, Tamara and Randolph Langenbach. *Amoskeag: Life and Work in an American Factory-City.* New York: Pantheon Books, 1978.

Harring, Sidney L. *Policing a Class Society: The Experiences of American*

Cities, 1865-1915. New Brunswick: Rutgers University Press, 1983.

Hawkins, Richard and Geoffrey P. Alpert. *American Prison Systems: Punishment and Justice.* Englewood Cliffs, N.J.: Prentice Hall, 1989.

Hay, Douglas. "Property, Authority and the Criminal Law." In *Albion's Fatal Tree: Crime and Society in Eighteenth-Century England,* 1st Am. ed., edited by Douglas Hay and others, 17-63. New York: Pantheon Books, 1975.

Hay, Douglas and others, eds. *Albion's Fatal Tree: Crime and society in Eighteenth-Century England,* 1st Am. ed. New York: Pantheon Books, 1975.

Hazlett, Charles A. *History of Rockingham County, New Hampshire and Representative Citizens.* Chicago: Richmond-Arnold Pub. Co., 1915.

Hindus, Michael S. *Prison and Plantation: Crime, Justice, and Authority in Massachusetts and South Carolina, 1767-1878.* Chapel Hill: University of North Carolina Press, 1980.

Hirsch, Adam J. "From Pillory to Penitentiary: The Rise of Criminal Incarceration in Early Massachusetts." In *Police, Prison, and Punishment,* edited by Kermit L. Hall, 344-434. New York: Garland Publishing, Inc., 1987.

Hofstadter, Richard and Michael Wallace, eds. *American Violence: A Documentary History.* New York: Alfred A. Knopf, 1970.

Hollon, W. Eugene. *Frontier Violence: Another Look.* New York: Oxford University Press, 1974.

Hopper, Columbus B. *Sex in Prison: The Mississippi Experiment in Conjugal Visiting.* Baton Rouge: Louisiana State University Press, 1969.

Horwitz, Morton J. *The Transformation of American Law, 1780-1860.* Cambridge, Mass: Harvard University Press, 1977.

Howard, D.L. *John Howard: Prison Reformer.* New York: Anchor House, Inc., 1963.

Hurd, D. Hamilton, ed. *History of Merrimack and Belknap Counties, New*

Hampshire. Philadelphia: J.W. Lewis and Co., 1885.

___. *History of Rockingham and Strafford Counties, New Hampshire with Biographical Sketches of Many of Its [sic] Pioneers and Prominent Men*. Philadelphia: J.W. Lewis and Co., 1882.

Ignatieff, Michael. *A Just Measure of Pain: The Penitentiary in the Industrial Revolution, 1750-1850*. New York: Pantheon Books, 1978.

Inciardi, James A. and Anne E. Pottieger, eds. *Violent Crime: Historical and Contemporary Issues*. Beverly Hills: Sage Publications, 1978.

Ireland, Robert M. *The County Courts in Antebellum Kentucky*. [Lexington, Ky.]: University Press of Kentucky, 1972.

Irwin, John. *The Jail: Managing the Underclass in American Society*. Berkeley: University of California Press, 1985.

Jager, Ronald and Grace. *New Hampshire: An Illustrated History of the Granite State*. Woodland Hills, Calif.: Windsor Publications, Inc., 1983.

Jeffreys-Jones, Rhodri and Bruce Collins. *The Growth of Federal Power in American History*. DeKalb, Ill.: Northern Illinois University Press, 1983.

Jernegan, Marcus W. *Laboring and Dependent Classes in Colonial America: 1607-1783*. New York: Frederick Ungar Publishing Co., 1965.

Johnson, Allen, ed. *Dictionary of American Biography*. New York: Charles Scribner's Sons, 1929. S.v. "Bell, Samuel," by William A. Robinson.

___ and Dumas Malone, eds. *Dictionary of American Biography*. New York: Charles Scribner's Sons, 1931. S.v. "Field, David Dudley," by Frederick C. Hicks.

___, *Dictionary of American Biography*. New York: Charles Scribner's Sons, 1931. S.v. "Gilman, John T.," by William A. Robinson.

Johnson, David R. *Policing the Urban Underworld: The Impact of Crime on the Development of the American Police, 1800-1887*. Philadelphia: Temple

University Press, 1979.

Johnson, Paul E. *Shopkeeper's Millenium: Society and Revivals in Rochester, New York 1815-1837.* New York: Hill & Wang, 1978.

Katz, Michael B. *Poverty and Policy in American History.* New York: Academic Press, 1983.

Kent, Joan R. *The English Village Constable 1580-1642: A Social and Administrative Study.* Oxford: Clarendon Press, 1986.

Kett, Joseph. *The Formation of the American Medical Profession: The Role of Institutions, 1780-1860.* New Haven: Yale University Press, 1968.

___. *Rites of Passage: Adolescence in America 1790 to the Present.* New York: Basic Books, Inc., Publisher, 1977.

Kushner, Howard I. *Self-Destruction in the Promised Land: A Psychocultural Biology of American Suicide.* New Brunswick: Rutgers University Press, 1989.

Lane, Roger. "On the Social Meaning of Homicide Trends in America." In *Violence in America*, vol. 1, edited by Ted Robert Gurr, 55-79. Newbury Park, Calif.: Sage Publications, 1989.

___. *Policing the City: Boston 1822-1885.* Cambridge, Mass.: Harvard University Press, 1967.

___. *Roots of Violence in Black Philadelphia 1860-1900.* Cambridge, Mass.: Harvard University Press, 1986.

Leiby, James. *Charity and Correction in New Jersey: A History of State Welfare Institutions.* New Brunswick: Rutgers University Press, 1967.

Lender, Mark E. and James K. Martin. *Drinking in America: A History.* New York: Free Press, 1982.

Levine, James P., Michael C. Musheno, and Dennis J. Palumbo. *Criminal Justice in America: Law in Action.* New York: John Wiley and Sons, 1986.

Lewis, John D., ed. *Anti-Federalists Versus Federalists: Selected Documents*. San Francisco: Chandler Pub. Co., 1967.

Lewis, Orlando. *The Development of American Prisons and Prison Customs, 1776-1845*. Prison Association of New York, 1922; reprint, Montclair, N.J.: Patterson Smith, 1967.

Lewis, W. David. *From Newgate to Dannemora: The Rise of the Penitentiary in New York, 1796-1848*. Ithaca, N.Y.: Cornell University Press, 1965.

Lockwood, Daniel. *Prison Sexual Violence*. New York: Elsevier, 1980.

Lombroso, Cesare. *Crime: Its Causes and Remedies*. Translated by Henry P. Horton. Boston: Little, Brown, and Co., 1911.

Luker, Kristin. *Abortion and the Politics of Motherhood*. Los Angeles: University of California, 1984.

Lunden, Walter A. "Emile Durkheim." In *Pioneers in Criminology*. 2d ed., edited by Hermann Mannheim, 385-99. Montclair, N.J.: Patterson Smith, 1972.

Lyford, James O., ed. *History of Concord, New Hampshire*. Concord, N.H.: Rumford Press, 1903.

Macdonald, John M. *Bombers and Firesetters*. Springfield, Ill.: Charles C. Thomas, Publisher, 1977.

Maestro, Marcello. *Cesare Beccaria and the Origins of Penal Reform*. Philadelphia: Temple University Press, 1973.

Malone, Dumas, ed. *Dictionary of American Biography*. New York: Charles Scribner's Sons, 1932. S.v. "Hill, Isaac," by William A. Robinson.

___. *Dictionary of American Biography*. New York: Charles Scribner's Sons, 1933. S.v. "Mason, Jeremiah," by Claude M. Fuess.

___. *Dictionary of American Biography*. New York: Charles Scribner's Sons, 1935. S.v. "Plumer, William," by William A. Robinson.

___. *Dictionary of American Biography*. New York: Charles Scribner's Sons, 1936. S.v. "Webster, Daniel," by Arthur C. Cole.

___. *Dictionary of American Biography*. New York: Charles Scribner's Sons, 1936. S.v. "Wines, Enoch C.," by Blake McKelvey.

___. *Dictionary of American Biography*. New York: Charles Scribner's Sons, 1936. S.v. "Wines, Frederick H.," by Blake McKelvey.

Mannheim, Hermann, ed. *Pioneers in Criminology*, 2d ed. Montclair, N.J.: Patterson Smith, 1972.

Maris, Ronald W. *Pathways to Suicide: A Survey of Self-Destructive Behaviors*. Baltimore: Johns Hopkins Press, 1981.

Martinson, Robert, Douglas Lipton, and Judith Wilks. *The Effectiveness of Correctional Treatment: A Survey of Treatment Evaluation Studies*. New York: Praeger Publishers, 1975.

Mason, Alpheus. *The States Rights Debate: Antifederalism and the Constitution*. Englewood Cliffs, N.J.: Prentice-Hall, Inc., 1964.

Masur, Louis P. *Rites of Execution: Capital Punishment and the Transformation of American Culture, 1776-1865*. New York: Oxford University Press, 1989.

McGovern, Constance M. *Masters of Madness: Social Origins of the American Psychiatric Association*. Hanover, N.H.: Pub. for University of Vermont by University Press of New England, 1985.

McKelvey, Blake. *American Prisons: A Study in American Social History Prior to 1915*. Chicago: University of Chicago, 1936; reprint, Montclair, N.J.: Patterson Smith, 1968.

___. "The Prison Labor Problem: 1875-1900." In *Police, Prison, and Punishment*, edited by Kermit L. Hall, 478-94. New York: Garland Publishing, Inc., 1987.

Mennel, Robert. *Thorns and Thistles: Juvenile Delinquents in the United*

352

States 1825-1940. Hanover, N.H.: Pub. for University of New Hampshire by University Press of New England, 1973.

Miller, Benjamin and Claire B. Keane. *Encyclopedia and Dictionary of Medicine, Nursing, and Allied Health*, 3rd ed. Philadelphia: W.B. Saunders Co., 1983.

Miller, Perry. *The Life of the Mind in America: From the Revolution to the Civil War.* New York: Harcourt, Brace and World, Inc., 1965.

___ and Thomas H. Johnson. *The Puritans.* Boston: American Book Co., 1938.

Mohr, James C. *Abortion in America: The Origins and Evolution of National Policy, 1800-1900.* New York: Oxford University Press, 1978.

Monkkonen, Eric H. *America Becomes Urban: The Development of U.S. Cities and Towns 1780-1980.* Berkeley: University of California Press, 1988.

___. *The Dangerous Class: Crime and Poverty in Columbus, Ohio, 1860-1885.* Cambridge, Mass.: Harvard University Press, 1975.

___. "Diverging Homicide Rates: England and the United States, 1850-1875." In *Violence in America*, Vol. 1, edited by Ted Robert Gurr, 80-101. Newbury Park, Calif.: Sage Publications, 1989.

___. *Walking to Work: Tramps in America, 1790-1835.* Lincoln, Neb.: University of Nebraska Press, 1984.

Moore, Kathleen D. *Pardons: Justice, Mercy, and the Public Interest.* New York: Oxford University Press, 1989.

Mullen, Kevin J. *Let Justice Be Done: Crime and Politics in Early San Francisco.* Reno: University of Nevada Press, 1989.

Munyon, Paul G. *A Reassessment of New England Agriculture in the Last Thirty Years of the Nineteenth Century: New Hampshire, A Case Study.* New York: Arno Press, 1978.

353

Nash, Jay R. *Encyclopedia of World Crime*. Wilmette, Ill.: CrimeBooks [sic], Inc., 1989.

Nelson, Charles B. *History of Stratham, New Hampshire 1631-1900*. Somersworth, N.H.: New Hampshire Pub. Co., 1965.

New Enclyclopedia Britannica: Micropedia. Chicago: Encyclopaedia [sic] Britannica, Inc., 1986. S.v. "Coke, Edward," by Gareth H. Jones.

O'Brien, Patricia. *The Promise of Punishment: Prisons in Nineteenth-Century France*. Princeton: Princeton University Press, 1982.

Orland, Leonard. *Prisons: Houses of Darkness*. New York: Free Press, 1975.

Page, Elwin. *Judicial Beginnings in New Hampshire 1640-1700*. Concord, N.H.: New Hampshire Historical Society, 1959.

Pillsbury, Hobart. *New Hampshire: Resources, Attractions, and Its People, A History*. New York: Lewis Historical Publishing Co., Inc., 1927.

Pole, J.R. "Preconditions of American Unity." In *The Growth of Federal Power in American History*, edited by Rhodri Jeffreys-Jones and Bruce Collins, 1-12. DeKalb, Ill.: Northern Illinois University Press, 1983.

Powers, Edwin. *Crime and Punishment in Early Massachusetts 1620-1692: A Documentary History*. Boston: Beacon Press, 1966.

Quetelet, M. Adolphe. *A Treatise on Man and the Development of His Faculties*. Research Source Works Series and Philosophy Monograph Series. Edinburgh: 1842; reprint, New York: Burt Franklin, 1968.

Rafter, Nicole H. "Hard Times: Custodial Prisons for Women and the Example of the New York State Prison for Women at Auburn, 1893-1933." In *Judge, Lawyer, Victim, Thief: Women, Gender Roles, and Criminal Justice*, edited by Nicole H. Rafter and Elizabeth A. Stanko, 237-73. [Boston]: Northeastern University, Press, 1982.

___. *Partial Justice: Women in State Prisons 1800-1935*. Boston:

354

Northeastern University Press, 1985.

___. *Partial Justice: Women, Prisons, and Social Control*, 2d ed. New Brunswick: Transaction Publishers, 1990.

Resch, John P. "The Ohio Penal System, 1850-1900: A Study in the Failure of Institutional Reform." In *Police, Prison, and Punishment*, edited by Kermit L. Hall, 540-67. New York: Garland Publishing, Inc., 1987.

Ringenbach, Paul T. *Tramps and Reformers 1873-1916: The Discovery of Unemployment in New York*. Contributions in American History. Westport, Conn.: Greenwood Press, Inc., 1973.

Rorabaugh, W.J. *The Alcoholic Republic: An American Tradition*. New York: Oxford University Press, 1979.

Rose, Thomas, ed. *Violence in America: A Historical and Contemporary Reader*. New York: Random House, 1969.

Rose, Vicki M. and Susan C. Randall. "Where Have All the Rapists Gone? An Illustration of the Attrition-of-Justice Phenomenon." In *Violent Crime: Historical and Contemporary Issues*. Beverly Hills: Sage Publications, 1978.

Rosen, Ruth. *The Lost Sisterhood: Prostitution in America, 1900-1918*. Baltimore: Johns Hopkins University Press, 1982.

Rothman, David J. *Conscience and Convenience: The Asylum and Its Alternatives in Progressive America*. Boston: Little, Brown, 1980.

___. *The Discovery of the Asylum: Social Order and Disorder in the New Republic*. Boston: Little, Brown, 1971.

___. "Doing Time: Days, Months and Years in the Criminal Justice System." In *Sentencing*, edited by Hyman Gross and Andrew von Hirsch, 374-85. New York: Oxford University Press, 1981.

Russell, Howard S. *A Long, Deep, Furrow: Three Centuries of Farming in New England*. Hanover, N.H.: University Press of New England, 1982.

Saltonstall, William G. *Ports of Piscataqua*. Cambridge, Mass.: Harvard University Press, 1941.

Scacco, Anthony M, Jr. *Rape in Prison*. Springfield, Ill.: Charles C. Thomas, Publisher, 1975.

Scales, John. *History of Strafford County, New Hampshire and Representative Citizens*. Chicago: Richmond-Arnold Co., 1914.

Schlossman, Steven L. *Love and the American Delinquent: The Theory and Practice of "Progressive" Juvenile Justice, 1825-1920*. Chicago: University of Chicago Press, 1977.

Seligman, Edwin R.A., ed. *Encyclopedia of the Social Sciences*. New York: Macmillan Co., 1930. S.v. "Codification," by Charles S. Lobingier.

___. *Encyclopedia of the Social Sciences*. New York: Macmillan Co., 1931. S.v. "Common Law," by Roscoe Pound.

___. *Encyclopedia of the Social Sciences*. New York: Macmillan Co., 1934. S.v. "Penal Institutions," by Thorsten Sellin.

Sellin, Thorsten. "Enrico Ferri." In *Pioneers in Criminology*, 2d ed., edited by Hermann Mannheim, 361-84. Montclair, N.J.: Patterson Smith, 1972.

___. *The Penalty of Death*. Sage Library of Social Research. Beverly Hills: Sage Publications, 1980.

___. *Slavery and the Penal System*. New York: Elsevier, 1976.

Shane-DuBow, Sandra, Alice P. Brown, and Erik Olsen. *Sentencing Reform in the United States: History, Content, and Effect*. Washington, D.C.: U.S. Government Printing Office, 1985.

Sifakis, Carl. *Encyclopedia of American Crime*. New York: Facts on File, 1982. S.v. "Recidivism."

Sills, David L., ed. *International Encyclopedia of the Social Sciences*. [New York]: Macmillan Co. and Free Press, 1968. S.v. "Legal Systems: II.

356

Common Law Systems," by Edward McWhinney.

___. *International Encyclopedia of the Social Sciences.* [New York]: Macmillan Co. and Free Press, 1968. S.V. "Legal Systems: III. Code Law Systems," by Edward McWhinney.

___. *International Encyclopedia of the Social Sciences.* [New York]: Macmillan Co. and Free Press, 1968. S.V. "Penology: The Field," by Daniel Glaser.

Sklar, Kathryn K. *Catharine Beecher: A Study in American Domesticity.* New Haven: Yale University Press, 1973.

Smith, Joan and William Fried. *The Uses of the American Prison: Political Theory and Penal Practice.* Lexington, Mass.: D.C. Heath and Co., 1974.

Spierenburg, Pieter, ed. *The Emergence of Carceral Institutions: Prisons, Galleys, and Lunatic Asylums 1550-1900.* Centrum voor Maatschappijgeschiednies, vol. 12. Rotterdam: Dept. of History, Erasmus University, 1984.

___. "The Sociogenesis of Confinement and Its Development in Early Modern Europe." In *The Emergence of Carceral Institutions: Prisons, Galleys, and Lunatic Asylums 1550-1900.* Centrum voor Maatschappijgeschiednies, vol. 12, edited by Pieter Spierenburg, 9-77. Rotterdam: Dept. of History, Erasmus University, 1984.

Spindel, Donna. *Crime and Society in North Carolina, 1663-1776.* Baton Rouge: Louisiana State University Press, 1989.

Squires, James D. *The Granite State of the United States: A History of New Hampshire from 1623 to the Present.* New York: American Historical Co., Inc., 1956.

___. *The Story of New Hampshire.* Princeton: D. van Nostrand Co., Inc., 1964.

Steinberg, Allen. *The Transformation of Criminal Justice: Philadelphia, 1800-1880.* Chapel Hill: University of North Carolina Press, 1989.

Straus, Murray A., Richard J. Gelles, and Suzanne K. Steinmetz. *Behind Closed Doors: Violence in the American Family*. New York: Anchor Books, 1980.

Sullivan, Larry E. *The Prison Reform Movement: Forlorn Hope*. Boston: Twayne Publishers, 1990.

Sutton, John R. *Stubborn Children: Controlling Delinquency in the United States, 1640-1981*. Berkeley: University of California Press, 1988.

Taxay, Don. *Counterfeit, Mis-Struck, and Unofficial United States Coins*. New York: Arco Publishing Co., 1963.

Teeters, Negley K. *The Cradle of the Penitentiary: The Walnut Street Jail at Philadelphia 1773-1835*. [Philadelphia?]: Pennsylvania Prison Society, 1955.

___ and Jack H. Hedblom. *"...Hang by the Neck...": The Legal Use of Scaffold and Noose, Gibbet, Stake, and Firing Squad from Colonial Times to the Present*. Springfield, Ill.: Charles C. Thomas, Publisher, 1967.

Thelen, David P. *The New Citizenship: Origins of Progressivism in Wisconsin, 1885-1900*. Columbia, Mo.: University of Missouri Press, 1972.

Thernstrom, Stephan, ed. *Harvard Encyclopedia of American Ethnic Groups*. Cambridge, Mass.: Belknap Press of Harvard University Press, 1980.

Twain, Mark. *The Complete Humorous Sketches and Tales of Mark Twain*. Edited by Charles Neider. Garden City, N.Y.: Doubleday & Co., Inc., 1961.

Tyler, Alice F. *Freedom's Ferment: Phases of American Social History ot 1860*. Minneapolis: University of Minnesota Press, 1944.

___. *Freedom's Ferment: Phases of American Social History to 1860*. New York: Books for Libraries Press, 1970.

von Hirsch, Andrew and Kathleen J. Hanrahan. *The Question of Parole: Retention, Reform, or Abolition?* Cambridge, Mass.: Ballinger Pub. Co., 1979.

Walker, Joseph B. "State Prison." In *History of Concord, New Hampshire*, vol. II, edited by James O. Lyford, 1153-61. Concord, N.H.: Rumford Press, 1980.

Walker, Samuel. *Popular Justice: A History of American Criminal Justice.* New York: Oxford University Press, 1980.

___. *Sense and Nonsense about Crime: A Policy Guide*, 2d ed. Pacific Grove, Calif.: Brooks/Cole Publishing Co., 1989.

Ward, David. *Poverty, Ethnicity, and the American City, 1840-1925: Changing Conceptions of the Slum and the Ghetto.* New York: Cambridge University Press, 1989.

Weiner, E.S.C. and J.A. Simpson, preparers. *The Oxford English Dictionary*, 2d ed. Oxford: Clarendon Press, 1989. S.v. "Maim," "Mayhem," "Remand," and "Remit."

Wilson, James G. and John Fiske, eds. *Appleton's Cyclopaedia of American Biography.* New York: D.A. Appleton & Co., 1888. S.v. "Brewster, Charles W."

Wilson, James Q. "From *Thinking about Crime*." In *Sentencing*, edited by Hyman Gross and Andrew von Hirsch, 213-27. New York: Oxford University Press, 1981.

Wines, Frederick H. *Punishment and Reformation: An Historical Sketch of the Rise of the Penitentiary System.* Boston: Thomas Y. Crowell & Co., 1895.

Wolfgang, Marvin E. "Cesare Lombroso." In *Pioneers in Criminology*, 2d ed., edited by Hermann Mannheim, 232-91. Montclair, N.J.: Patterson Smith, 1972.

Wright, Gordon. *Between the Guillotine and Liberty: Two Centuries of the Crime Problem in France.* New York: Oxford University Press, 1983.

Wright, James E. *The Progressive Yankees: Republican Reformers in New Hampshire, 1906-1916.* Hanover, N.H.: Pub. for Dartmouth College by University Press of New England, 1987.

Zalman, Marvin. "The Rise and Fall of the Indeterminate Sentence." In *Police, Prison, and Punishment*, edited by Kermit L. Hall, 670-719. New York: Garland Publishing, Inc., 1987.

Zysberg, Andre. "Galley and Hard Labor Convicts in France (1550-1850): From the Galleys to Hard Labor Camps: Essay on a Long Lasting Penal Institution." In *The Emergence of Carceral Institutions: Prisons, Galleys, and Lunatic Asylums 1550-1900*, vol. 12, Centrum voor Maatschappijgeschiednies, edited by Pieter Spierenburg, 78-124. Rotterdam: Dept. of History, Erasmus University, 1984.

2. Articles

Anton, A.E. "Obstacles to Codification." *Juridical Review* (July 1982): 15-30.

Arditi, Ralph and others. "The Sexual Segregation of American Prisons." *Yale Law Journal* 82 (May 1973): 1229-73.

Bauer, Anne. "The Charlestown State Prison." *Historical Journal of Western Massachusetts* 2 (Fall 1973): 22-29.

Bergel, Jean L. "Principal Features and Methods of Codification." *Louisiana Law Review* 48 (May 1988): 1073-98.

Blaine, Quentin. "Shall Surely Be Put to Death': Capital Punishment in New Hampshire, 1623-1985." *New Hampshire Bar Journal* 27 (Spring 1986): 131-54.

Bodenhamer, David J. "The Democratic Impulse and Legal Change in the Age of Jackson: The Example of Criminal Juries in Antebellum Indiana." *Historian* 45 (Feb. 1983): 206-19.

Bodenheimer, Edgar. "Is Codification an Outmoded From of Legislation?" *American Journal of Comparative Law* 30 *(Supplement 1982: Law in the United States of America for the 1980's)*: 15-29.

Bowers, William J. and Glenn L. Pierce. "Deterrence or Brutalization: What Is the Effect of Executions?" *Crime and Delinquency* 26 (Oct. 1982): 453-84.

Brown, Albert O. "An Outline of the History of Taxation in New Hampshire." *Granite Monthly* 60 (1928): 3-7.

Bruchey, Stuart. "Economy and Society in Earlier America." *Journal of Economic History* 47 (June 1987): 299-319.

Cahn, Mark D. "Punishment, Discretion, and the Codification of Prescribed Penalties in Colonial Massachusetts." *American Journal of Legal History* 33 (Apr. 1989): 107-36.

Clark, Christopher. "The Household Economy, Market Exchange, and the Rise of Capitalism in the Connecticut Valley, 1800-60." *Journal of Social History* 13 (Winter 1979): 169-89.

Conley, John A. "Prisons, Production, and Profit: Reconsidering the Importance of Prison Industries." *Journal of Social History* 14 (Winter 1980): 257-75.

Cromwell, Paul F. "Quaker Reforms in American Criminal Justice: The Penitentiary and Beyond." *Criminal Justice History* 10 (1989): 77-94.

Davis, David B. "Murder in New Hampshire." *New England Quarterly* 28 (June 1955): 147-53.

Dean, Charles W. "The Story of New-Gate." *Federal Probation* 43 (June 1979): 8-14.

Dumm, Thomas L. "Friendly Persuasion: Quakers, Liberal Toleration, and the Birth of the Prison." *Political Theory* 13 (Aug. 1985): 387-407.

Durel, John W. "New Hampshire County Court Records." *Historical New Hampshire* 31 (Spring-Summer 1976): 56-59.

Durham, Alexis M. "Rehabilitation and Correctional Privatization: Observations on the Nineteenth Century Experience and Implications for Modern Corrections." *Federal Probation* 53 (Mar. 1989): 43-52.

Ferdinand, Theodore N. "The Criminal Patterns of Boston Since 1849." *American Journal of Sociology* 73 (July 1967): 84-99.

Flaherty, David H. "Crime and Social Control in Provincial Massachusetts." *Historical Journal* 24 (June 1981): 339-60.

Frank, Benjamin. "The American Prison: The End of an Era." *Federal Probation* 43 (Sept. 1979): 3-9.

Freedman, Estelle B. "Sentiment and Discipline: Women's Prison Experiences in Nineteenth Century America." *Prologue* 16 (Winter 1984): 248-59.

Friedman, Lawrence M. and Robert V. Percival. "The Processing of Felonies in the Superior Court of Alameda County 1880-1097." *Law and History Review* 5 (1987): 413-36.

Garvin, Donna-Belle. "Concord, New Hampshire: A Furniture-Making Capital." *Historical New Hampshire* 45 (Spring 1990): 8-104.

Gaskins, Richard. "Changes in the Criminal Law in Eighteenth-Century Connecticut." *American Journal of Legal History* 25 (Oct. 1981): 309-42.

Graff, Harvey J. "Crime and Punishment in the Nineteenth Century: A New Look at the Criminal." *Journal of Interdisciplinary History* 7 (Winter 1977): 477-91.

Greenawalt, Kent. "A Vice of Its Virtues: The Perils of Precision in Criminal Codification, as Illustrated by Retreat, General Justification, and Dangerous Utterances." *Rutgers Law Journal* 19 (Spring 1988): 929-50.

Greenberg, Douglas. "Crime, Law Enforcement, and Social Control in Colonial America." *American Journal of Legal History* 26 (Oct. 1982): 293-325.

Grob, Gerald N. "Reflections on the History of Social Policy." *Reviews in American History* 7 (Sept. 1979): 293-306.

___. "Welfare and Poverty in American History." *Reviews in American History* 1 (Mar. 1973): 43-52.

Haebler, Peter. "Nativism, Liquor, and Riots: Manchester Politics, 1858-

1859." *Historical New Hampshire* 46 (Summer 1991): 67-91.

Hall, Melinda G. "Constitutional Influence in State Supreme Courts: Conceptual Notes and a Case Study." *Journal of Politics* 49 (Nov. 1987): 1117-24.

Hartog, Hendrik. "The Public Law of a County Court: Judicial Government in Eighteenth Century Massachusetts." *American Journal of Legal History* 20 (Oct. 1976): 282-329.

Hindus, Michael S. "The Contours of Crime and Justice in Massachusetts and South Carolina, 1767-1878." *American Journal of Legal History* 21 (July 1977): 212-37.

Hosley, William N., Jr. "The Founding of the Vermont State Prison in Windsor, 1807-1810." *Vermont History* 52 (Fall 1984): 243-52.

Ireland, Robert M. "Insanity and the Unwritten Law." *American Journal of Legal History* 32 (Apr. 1988): 157-72.

Kealey, Linda. "Patterns of Punishment: Massachusetts in the Eighteenth Century." *American Journal of Legal History* 30 (Apr. 1986): 163-86.

___. "Punishment at Hard Labor: Stephen Burroughs and the Castle Island Prison, 1785-1798." *New England Quarterly* 57 (June 1984): 249-54.

Keller, Morton. "Powers and Rights: Two Centuries of American Constitutionalism." *Journal of American History* 74 (Dec. 1987): 675-94.

Knowlton, Robert E. "Comments Upon the New Jersey Penal Code." *Rutgers Law Review* 32 (May 1979): 1-19.

Kremer, Gary. "Strangers to Domestic Virtues: Nineteenth-Century Women in the Missouri Prison." *Missouri Historical Review* 84 (Apr. 1990): 293-310.

Kulikoff, Allan. "The Transition to Capitalism in Rural America." *William and Mary Quarterly* 3rd Series, 46 (Jan. 1989): 120-44.

Lindemann, Barbara S. "To Ravish and Carnally Know': Rape in Eighteenth-

Century Massachusetts." *Signs* 10 (Autumn 1984): 613-82.

Lindner, Charles and Margaret R. Savarese. "The Evolution of Probation: Early Salaries, Qualifications, and Hiring Practices." *Federal Probation* 48 (Mar. 1984): 3-10.

Masur, Louis P. "The Revision of the Criminal Law in Post-Revolutionary America." *Criminal Justice History* 8 (1987): 21-36.

Meier, Judith A. "A View of the Prison: Nineteenth Century Style." *Bulletin of the Historical Society of Montgomery County [Pa.]* 25 (1987): 262-74.

Melone, Albert P. "The Politics of Criminal Code Revision: Lessons for Reform." *Capital University Law Review* 15 (Winter 1986): 191-204.

Mennel, Robert M. "Attitudes and Policies toward Juvenile Delinquency in the United States: A Historiographical Review." *Crime and Justice: An Annual Review of Research*, edited by Michael Tonry and Norval Morris, 4 (1983): 191-224.

___. "Review of *The Prison Reform Movement* by Larry E. Sullivan." *Journal of American History* 78 (June 1991): 387-88.

Miller, Martin B. "At Hard Labor: Rediscovering the Nineteenth Century Prison." *Issues in Criminology* 9 (Spring 1974): 91-114.

Newman, Graeme and Pietro Marongui. "Penological Reform and the Myth of Beccaria." *Criminology* 28 (May 1990): 325-46.

O'Connor, John E. "Legal Reform in the Early Republic: The New Jersey Experience." *American Journal of Legal History* 22 (Apr. 1978): 95-117.

Odem, Mary. "Single Mothers, Delinquent Daughters, and the Juvenile Court in Early Twentieth Century Los Angeles." *Journal of Social History* 25 (Fall 1991): 27-43.

Pisciotta, Alexander. "Scientific Reform: The 'New Penology' at Elmira, 1976-1900." *Crime and Delinquency* 29 (Oct. 1983): 613-30.

364

___. "Treatment on Trial: The Rhetoric and Reality of the New York House of Refuge, 1857-1935." *American Journal of Legal History* 29 (Apr. 1985): 151-81.

Post, J.B. "Faces of Crime in Later Medieval England." *History Today* 38 (Jan. 1988): 19-24.

Powers, Edwin. "The Legal History of Capital Punishment in Massachusetts." *Federal Probation* 45 (Sept. 1981): 15-20.

Preyer, Kathryn. "Crime, the Criminal Law and Reform in Post-Revolutionary Virginia." *Law and History Review* 1 (1983): 53-85.

___. "Penal Measures in the American Colonies: An Overview." *American Journal of Legal History* 26 (Oct. 1982): 326-53;

Rhine, Edward and others. "Parole: Issues and Prospects for the 1990s [sic]." *Corrections Today* 51 (Dec. 1989): 78-83 and 146-47.

Richwagen, L.E. "The New Hampshire State Prison." *Granite Monthly* 56 (Nov. 1924): 571-75.

Robinson, Henry. "The New Hampshire State Prison." *Granite Monthly* 23 (Oct. 1897): 214-36.

Rothenberg, Winifred B. "The Market and Massachusetts Farms, 1750-1855." *Journal of Economic History* 41 (June 1981): 283-314.

Rothman, David J. "Decarcerating Prisoners and Patients." *Civil Liberties Review* 1 (Fall 1973): 8-30.

___. "Sentencing Reforms in Historical Perspective." *Crime and Delinquency* 29 (Oct. 1983): 631-47.

Ruggles, Steven. "Fallen Women: The Inmates of the Magdalen Society Asylum of Philadelphia, 1836-1908." *Journal of Social History* 16 (Spring 1977): 13-20.

Smith, A.T.H. "Judicial Law Making in the Criminal Law." *Law Quarterly*

Review 100 (Jan. 1984): 46-76.

Smith, Beverly A. "The Female Prisoner in Ireland, 1855-1878." *Federal Probation* 54 (Dec. 1990): 69-81.

___. "Military Training at New York's Elmira Reformatory, 1888-1920." *Federal Probation* 52 (Mar. 1988): 33-40.

Spindel, Donna J. and Stuart W. Thomas. "Crime and Society in North Carolina, 1663-1740." *Journal of Southern History* 49 (May 1983): 223-44.

Stanley, Amy Dru. "Beggars Can't Be Choosers: Compulsion and Contract in Postbellum America." *Journal of American History* 78 (March 1992): 1265-93.

Stern, Barry. "Revising Vermont's Criminal Code." *Vermont Law Review* 12 (Fall 1987): 307-34.

Styles, John. "Crime in Eighteenth-Century England." *History Today* 38 (Mar. 1988): 36-42.

Takagi, Paul. "The Walnut Street Jail: A Penal Reform to Centralize the Powers of the State." *Federal Probation* 39 (Dec. 1975): 18-26.

Tighe, Janet A. "Francis Wharton and the Nineteenth-Century Insanity Defense: The Origins of a Reform Tradition." *American Journal of Legal History* 27 (July 1983): 223-53.

Watson, Alan D. "Review of *Crime and Society in North Carolina, 1663-1776* by Donna Spindel." *William and Mary Quarterly* 3rd Series, 47 (Apr. 1990): 309-11.

Wechsler, Herbert. "Revision and Codification of Penal Law in the United States." *Dalhousie Law Journal* 7 (Apr. 1983): 219-35.

Woodard, Calvin. "Thoughts on the Interplay Between Morality and Law in Modern Legal Thought." *Notre Dame Law Review* 64 (1989): 784-804.

III. Unpublished Secondary Sources

Bergen, Paul F. "Occupation, Household, and Family Among the Irish of Nineteenth Century Dover, New Hampshire." M.A. thesis, University of New Hampshire, 1989.

Devine, Joseph M. "A Legal Study of Colonial New Hampshire, 1640-1692," 1946, TMS. Harvard Law School, New Hampshire Historical Society, Concord, N.H.

Doane, Ashley W., Jr. "The Franco-Americans of New Hampshire: A Case Study of Ethnicity and Social Stratification." M.A. thesis, University of New Hampshire, 1983.

Dodge, Timothy. "Poor Relief in Durham, Lee, and Madbury [, N.H.], 1732-1891." M.A. thesis, University of New Hampshire, 1982.

Appendix

New Hampshire State Prison Inmates, 1812-1914:
Occupational Categories Prior to Conviction

I. White Collar

Bookkeeper
Clerk
Company Agent
"M.D."
Salesman/Commercial Traveler
Savings Treasurer

II. Skilled Manual

Barber
Blacksmith
Brass Worker
Carpenter
Cooper
Currier
Engineer
Fireman
Glass Cutter
"Harness" [Maker?]
Loom Fitter
Machinist
Printer
Ship Fitter
Shoemaker
Tailor
Tinsmith
Weaver
Woolen Weaver

III. Unskilled Manual

Baker

III. Unskilled Manual (Continued)

Bobbin Maker
Brakeman
"Carrage" Painter
"Chair Seating"
Cook
Core Maker
"Cotton Mill" [Worker]
Cordwainer
Farmer
Fisherman
"Hostler"
Husbandman
[Illegible] - Cutter
Knitter
Laborer
Laster
Mariner/Sailor
Painter
Paper Hanger
Sash Maker
"Shoe Vamper"
Spinner
Steam Fitter
"Table Girl"
Teamster
Waiter

Source: Court Bills and Indictments, Rockingham Cty., N.H., 1812-1914, MS, Div. of Records-Management and Archives, Concord, N.H.; Court Bills and Indictments, Strafford Cty., N.H., 1870-1914, MS, Justice and Administration Building, Dover, N.H.; and Description Register 1881-1898] and [1899-1906]," MS, Div. of Records-Management and Archives, Concord, N.H.

Index

Abbott, Joshua
  deeds land for state prison, 60
Abortion, 35, 325
  criminalized, 28-29
Accidents
  New Hampshire mortality rate, 238-43, 247
Adolescence
  concept, 31-32
Adultery
  and socioeconomic status, 188, 192
  capital crime, 10
  frequency, 98, 125
  prison sentences, 277
  punishment reduced, 15, 20-21, 91
  Warren, Charles W., 126
Africa, 215
African-Americans. *See* Blacks
Age (Prison Inmates), 145, 147-55
  age group distribution by decade, 150-151
  and criminality, 200, 209n, 281
  compared to population at risk, 153-55
  distribution by decade, 148
  female inmates, 153-55, 177-78
  male inmates, 153-55
Agriculture
  declining employment, 30, 80, 323
  occupational group, 184-88
  prison inmate occupational change, 183
  transition to industry, 133, 164
Alameda County, Calif.

declining rates of serious crime, 72
  prison sentencing, 280
  property crime, 108
Albany, N.H., 137n
Alcohol
  related to social class and crime, 193-94, 199, 324
  use in prison, 225
Allenstown, N.H., 137n
Alpert, Geoffrey P.
  on prison homosexuality, 249-50
Alton, N.H., 137n
Amputation
  prison industrial accidents, 216-17
  Shaw, Joseph L., legs, 223
Antifederalism
  Jacksonian influence, 55, 325-26
  role in criminal justice system, 54-55
Anti-Gallows movement, 299
Arithmetic
  prison education, 220
Arraignment, 55, 326
Arson, 11
  and occupational status, 189-93
  capital crime, 13, 18
  frequency, 97, 102-03
  motives, 103, 110, 183
  reduced punishment, 21
Ashburnham, Mass., 215
Asians, 156
Assault
  frequency, 98, 110, 119
  punishment, 14
Assault with intent to commit

felony, 110
Assault with intent to steal
  and occupational status, 190-93
  frequency, 98
Association of Medical
  Superintendents of American
  Institutions for the Insane, 298
Atherosclerosis
  mortality rate, 247
Atlanta, Ga.
  federal prison, 196
Attempted murder
  frequency, 97, 110
  legal distinction, 112
  Lee, Edward, 113, 132
Attempted rape
  age of victims, 112-23
  and occupational status, 190-93
  frequency, 98, 110, 119-20
Attempted robbery
  frequency, 97
Attorneys
  anti-lawyer sentiment, 49-50
  prohibited until 1686, 48
Atwood, John (prison chaplain)
  221
Auburn, N.H., 119
Auburn Prison (New York)
  New York State Prison for
  Women at Auburn, 199, 274
  plans compared to N.H. State
  Prison, 60
Augustus, John
  probation, 317n
Austin, Luther
  breaking and entering, 305-06
  burglary, 305-06
  recidivism, 305-06
Austria

inmate birthplace, 164
Automobiles, 330
Axe
  used in crime, 115-18
Axes
  first prison labor products, 214
Ayers, Edward L.
  on blacks and crime in South,
  173, 326
  on violence in South, 70-71

Bail, 55, 326
Baked beans
  prison diet, 228
Baker (prison inmate), 367
Ball and chain, 222
Bancroft, Dr. Charles R.
  Psychiatric examination at N.H.
  State Hospital for the Insane of
  prisoners, 297-99
Bank bills and notes, 95, 105, 324
Bank treasurer (prison inmate),
  183
Banks, Joseph, 102
Barber (prison inmate), 183, 367
Barns
  damaged by arson, 103
Barnstead, N.H., 137n
Barrels
  produced at prison, 214
Barry, Father, (prison chaplain),
  220
Baseball
  at state prison, 226
Bass, Gov. Robert P.
  Progressive prison labor
  legislation, 217, 290, 314n
Bassett, Rev. Whitman (prison
  chaplain), 295

Economic change, 1, 9-20
effect on crime, 29-30, 40-41n,
133-34, 164-65, 174, 201, 323-332
Rockingham County, N.H., 79-85
Strafford County, N.H., 79-85
Economic status. *See also*
Socioeconomic status
relationship to crime, 133-34,
174, 201
Education (in prison), 220-21
religious, 220
secular, 220-21, 254, 310
Effingham, N.H., 137n
Electric Light Company
(Portsmouth, N.H.), 115
Elliot, George C.
sentence remitted, 316n
Elliot, James D.
theft, 101
Elmira, N.Y.
indeterminate sentencing
introduced, 281-82
influence on prison discipline,
226
prisoner grading system, 226
reformatory and military
discipline, 225
sports, 226
Embezzlement
frequency, 97, 103
Mathes, Albert O., 104
punishment, 24
related to socioeconomic status,
183, 189, 324
Emory, Benjamin, Jr., 149
Engineer (prison inmate), 367
England. *See also* Britain.
effects of war on property crime,
149, 164

inmate birthplace, 169-75
Enlightenment
influence on criminal law, 12-13,
57
Enter dwelling as a tramp
frequency, 99
Enteric fever
N.H. mortality rate, 242-43
Enticing child for purposes of
prostitution
frequency, 98, 125
Perry, Constance, 127
Epping, N.H., 113, 123, 285
Epsom, N.H., 137n
Escape, 287-89, 301-03, 309, 310,
329
punished, 26-27
Shinburn, Maximilian, 302
Ethnicity
defined, 205n
comparison of prison population
to population at risk, 166-68,
199-200
prison inmates, 145, 155-75
relationship to crime, 71, 133,
158
relationship to prison sentences,
281
religion of prison inmates, 220
Execution. *See also* Death penalty
hanging, 299
N.H. mortality rate, 241-43
Palmer, James, 300
Pike, Josiah, first state execution,
300-01, 309, 310, 311, 329
population at risk mortality, 239-
40
prison mortality, 236-37, 245-46,
248, 287-89

222-23
McDuffee, Sarah A., 123
McFarland, Andrew
  superintendent of State Hospital
  for the Insane, 296
McFarland, Rev. Asa (prison
  chaplain), 218
McKelvey, Blake
  on tuberculosis in prisons, 235
McKenney, Clyde F.
  false pretences, 103-04
McNally, John, 290
McNeil Island, Wash.
  federal prison, 196
Measles
  N.H. mortality rate, 242-43
Meat
  prison diet, 227
Meat hash
  prison diet, 228
Medical profession
  abortion statute, 28-29
Medical time, 310, 317n
Melancholy
  linked to suicide, 246-47
Mens Rea
  defined in relation to violent
  crime, 112
Meredith, N.H., 137n, 211
Merrimack County, N.H., 137n,
  224
Midwives, 325
Military discipline
  influence on prison discipline,
  224-25, 265n
Milk
  prison diet, 229
Mill worker (prison inmate), 183
Milton, N.H., 104

Mince pie
  Dorsey Dinner, 229
Minors. *See* Juvenile offenders.
"Minute Book 1812-34: Records"
  as primary source, 255
M'Naghten Case
  insanity defense, 298
Molasses
  prison diet, 228, 311
Money
  affected by crime, 92, 95-96, 100,
  105, 324
  counterfeit or forged, 95
Monkkonen, Eric H.
  compares violence in United
  States, 71-72, 111, 128, 134
  on age of criminals, 152-53, 209n
  on crime and poverty in
  Columbus, Ohio, 72, 108, 110
  on Ohio prison sentences, 280
  on "theft by trick", 103
Moody, Ira A.
  breaking and entering, 306
Moore, Ira B., 290
Moore, James
  breaking and entering, 305
  stealing, 305
  recivist, 305
Moore, Kathleen D.
  on pardons, 286, 289
Moral crime
  and ethnicity, 174
  British, 174
  Canadians, 174
  Catholics, 174
  changes in criminal laws, 325,
  330-31
  decriminalized, 20
  defined and punished, 9-10, 15